THE TIMES
ON CINEMA

No one . . . BUT NO ONE . . . not even the readers of THE TIMES . . . will be admitted to the theatre after the start of each performance of 'PSYCHO' *

*

This is to help you enjoy PSYCHO more. By the way, after you see the picture, please don't give away the ending. It's the only one we have.

ALFRED HITCHCOCK'S

PSYCHO

CERT. "X"

STARRING
ANTHONY VERA JOHN
PERKINS·MILES·GAVIN

CO-STARRING MARTIN BALSAM
JOHN McINTIRE

AND JANET LEIGH AS MARION CRANE

Directed by
ALFRED HITCHCOCK

Screenplay by
JOSEPH STEFANO

Based on the Novel by Robert Bloch
A PARAMOUNT RELEASE

SEPARATE
PERFORMANCES
DAILY AT
1.00, 3.30, 6.00, 8.30
SUNDAYS AT
5 and 8 p.m.

All Seats may be booked by post, telephone or at the Theatre Box Office

When booking by post please enclose cheques/postal orders and stamped addressed envelope

SPECIAL SEASON NOW at The PLAZA
PICCADILLY CIRCUS

THE TIMES
ON CINEMA

EDITED BY
BRIAN PENDREIGH

The
History
Press

For Chris, Vin, Chico, Bernardo, Harry,
Britt and (last, but not least) Lee ...
For me, it all began with you guys.

First published 2018

The History Press
The Mill, Brimscombe Port
Stroud, Gloucestershire, GL5 2QG
www.thehistorypress.co.uk

© Brian Pendreigh, 2018

The right of Brian Pendreigh to be identified as the Author
of this work has been asserted in accordance with the
Copyright, Designs and Patents Act 1988.

British Library Cataloguing in Publication Data.
A catalogue record for this book is available from the British Library.

ISBN 978 0 7509 8544 4

Typesetting and origination by The History Press
Printed and bound by CPI Group (UK) Ltd

INTRODUCTION

By Brian Pendreigh, Editor

It's a Wonderful Life: "Not a good film." Unbylined review, April 5 1947
Dr. No: "Perhaps Mr Sean Connery will, with practice, get the 'feel' of the part a little more surely than he does here."
Fight Club: "Starts out like a winner but fades fast."

This is not a cricket book. Obviously.

But the idea began with cricket, and specifically Richard Whitehead's book *The Times on The Ashes*. Richard then suggested I might edit a similar book on cinema. But the Ashes is a self-contained subject; it happens only every few years and Richard could pretty much just work his way through all the cuttings in *The Times* archives. Cinema happens all the time. It sprawls across the arts section, news pages, features and interviews, obituaries, even the sports pages.

19 May 1980. Carrie Fisher with a stormtrooper in London during the release of *Star Wars: The Empire Strikes Back.* (Terry Richards)

Unlike Richard, I could not simply read everything ever written in *The Times* on cinema, going back in time beyond the birth of the talkies in 1927. I had to decide which films, people and subjects I wanted to look at, and then specifically search for those headings. And there are already plenty books on the history of cinema and another stack providing viewers with a comprehensive library of reviews, so this is neither of those, although it does include both cinema history and select film reviews.

So I dipped into the archives, and more than once discovered the cupboard was bare – there is no report on the first Oscars and only a single paragraph on the 1940 event, when *Gone with the Wind* won Best Picture, which is interesting in itself, I hope.

There are some obvious things in here: *Citizen Kane* and *Harry Potter*, Steven Spielberg and Alfred Hitchcock. But there are a lot of less obvious things too. I have included an obituary I wrote for Kay Mander. A little old lady in her mid-nineties when I met her for lunch in a hotel in a quiet corner of Kirkcudbrightshire, there was little in her appearance to suggest she had been a pioneer woman film director, let alone that she had once had a fling with Kirk Douglas.

And then there was John Chambers, who I visited in a care home in California years ago when writing a book on *Planet of the Apes*. He talked about his pioneering prosthetics work with disfigured servicemen and his landmark make-up on *Star Trek* and *Planet of the Apes*. What he did not talk about was the top secret work he had done for the CIA. It later provided the basis for the Oscar-winning film *Argo*, in which he was played by John Goodman.

This is not the history of cinema, but a dip into it, with my own linking material, context and/or commentary. It is not chronological. The selections are subjective and the book is to some extent personal – okay, *Citizen Kane* is there, but so is *Grace of My Heart*; *The Birds* is there, but so is *Frogs*, a similar sort of plot, but with frogs. "It is hard to worry very much even when we leave Ray Milland waiting alone in the last reel, presumably about to be gummed to death," said our review. Personally, I loved it. Cinema is about great art, but it is also about guilty pleasures in darkened rooms.

Although some stories will be familiar, there is hopefully a lot here that will be unfamiliar for even the most dedicated *Times* readers and most devoted film fans – if not David Walliams' take on James Bond and John Lasseter's favourite animated films, then perhaps the story of Nell Shipman, who wrote, directed, produced and starred in her own films in the silent era; or perhaps which part of Britain doubled for the Adriatic in *From Russia with Love*; or the concerns that the addition of sound to movies might distract the audience's attention from the images on the screen. "The special subtlety of acting which is peculiar to the film has been sacrificed, we feel, for a poor imitation of the stage," wrote *The Times* reviewer in assessing *The Jazz Singer*.

Some films stand the test of time and some don't. And, with all due respect to *The Times* critics over the years, some reviews stand the test of time, while there are some that the reviewer, with the benefit of hindsight and the invention of the DVD player, might have wanted to revise. Some readers might take issue with the assessment that *It's a Wonderful Life* is "not a good film" as they sit down to watch it for the fourth Christmas in a row, but contemporary audiences did pretty much agree with the reviewer: the film flopped when it first came out. Until 1967 the reviews were unbylined, but the paper's archivists have worked hard to establish retrospective credits for anonymous reviews and other articles. This particular review, like many others in this volume, was by Dudley Carew, a poet, novelist, cricket aficionado and close friend of Evelyn Waugh, who was the paper's principal film critic from the 1940s to the early 1960s.

In many cases I have been able to juxtapose original reviews with later reassessments, and in the case of *Brief Encounter* I could not resist the temptation of juxtaposing the review of it with that for *Fifty Shades of Grey*. Perhaps it too will be reassessed at some future point – but that's doubtful.

There are also quite a few lists, including a Top 100 from 2008. Second best film of all time? *There Will Be Blood*. Really? It just so happened to come out the previous year. The list is of its time, but no less interesting for that.

Some of the articles have been trimmed slightly for reasons of space. Some of the interviews were subject to slightly more substantial cuts, again because of space, and because this was always intended as a book the reader might dip into, hopefully, again and again.

NEW GALLERY

"IT'S A WONDERFUL LIFE"

The film is turning nowadays to fantasy; heavenly interference in the affairs of mortals is the fashion and the stars leave their courses to influence human behaviour.

It's A Wonderful Life sets out deliberately to glorify the "little man" of the small American town, and Mr. James Stewart is at least infinitely preferable to the horror in the bowler hat whom cartoon has made the English counterpart. George (Mr. Stewart) is the head of a building and loan company which is concerned less with profits than with seeing that the poor get decent houses; opposite him is a Scrooge-like character played with immense malignancy by Mr. Lionel Barrymore. George has always wanted to travel, but marriage and responsibility tie him down and at one time it seems that his sacrifices will be in vain and that Mr. Barrymore will drag him down to ruin and prison. It is at this moment, when George is wishing he had never been born, that the celestial powers intervene and a messenger, in the benign person of Mr. Henry Travers, is sent to earth to show him, by a kind of inverted *Dear Brutus* process, what would have happened had he never existed. The lesson gives point to the title, and all ends with a terrific Christmas scene of emotional good will.

Mr. Frank Capra has exploited the sentimental possibilities of his theme to the full and has reserved subtlety for the incidental touches and humours. It is not a good film, but it is a generous one, and Mr. Stewart, an admirable compound of shyness and confidence, and Miss Donna Reed manage the film's exuberant emotions with tact. It is, however, all very loud and overpowering, and at the end the audience feels as though it had been listening to a large man of boisterous good nature talking at the top of his voice for over two hours.

CINEMA HISTORY

PAH-PAH-PAH-PAH-PAH-PAH, PAH-PAH-PAH

SOUNDTRACK TO A GENERATION OF FILM GOERS

By Bob Stanley,
April 22 2010

There are some pieces of music that just exist, tunes you can't imagine anyone sitting down and writing. The Pearl & Dean theme – or Asteroid to give it its proper name – breathes the same air as Happy Birthday to You and the chimes of Big Ben. It was written by the British arranger Pete Moore in 1968 and has accompanied cinema ads for Westler's hot dogs, Butterkist popcorn, and hundreds of Indian restaurants ever since.

"When I wrote Asteroid," Moore said in 2003, "many people in the profession accused me of writing music for the future, and ahead of its time. With the longevity of this music I thoroughly agree."

You have to assume his tongue was firmly in his cheek, as it bears a rather strong resemblance to that late Sixties time capsule, MacArthur Park. As a teenager, decades before the internet, I remember trying to find out any information I could about the Pearl & Dean music. An unscrupulous record dealer told me it was a snippet of Hugo Montenegro's version of MacArthur Park for which I paid him good pocket money, only to be disappointed.

It turned out I was wasting my time. Asteroid was never released commercially until the Nineties – the only way you could hear it was by sitting in your local Odeon. When it finally surfaced on a compilation called Nice 'n' Easy, to my amazement, it turned out to be all of 20 seconds long. What you hear in the cinema is the alluring Asteroid in its entirely.

Moore's claims to fame since include the theme for David Jacobs's Radio 2 show, while his lounge classic Catwalk has cropped up on Alan Titchmarsh's *How to be a Gardener*. He rerecorded Asteroid for a Pearl & Dean makeover in the Nineties, then in 2006 stretched it into a two-minute jazz odyssey. It took the Brighton ravers Goldbug to put it in the chart when they sampled it, along with the equally momentous Top of the Pops theme, on their 'Whole Lotta Love' hit in 1995. Moore's CV includes sessions with Frank Sinatra, Bing Crosby and Peggy Lee, but Asteroid's bongos and angelic harmonies – the sound of popping corn and frying onions – will be his song for the ages.

Bob Stanley is a member of the pop group Saint Etienne.

CINEMA HISTORY

CINEMA PIONEER HONOURED AT GRAVESIDE

News report by Peter Waymark,
May 6 1971

Family and former colleagues of William Friese-Greene, the cinema pioneer, honoured his memory on the fiftieth anniversary of his death at his grave in Highgate Cemetery, London, yesterday.

A grandson, Mr Anthony Friese-Greene, laid a wreath of roses and carnations at the stone monument designed by Sir Edward Lutyens and bearing the inscription "The Inventor of Kinematography".

A second wreath, in the shape of the Maltese cross – an essential part of the cinema projector from the earliest days – was laid by officers of the Cinema Veterans Association.

The association, for people who have spent more than 40 years in the film industry, was formed shortly after Friese-Greene's death on May 5, 1921. He was taken ill while addressing leading members of the industry in the Connaught Rooms, Holborn.

At the graveside were the widows of Friese-Greene's sons, Graham and Claude, and another grandson, Mr Terry Friese-Greene. Mrs Claude Friese-Greene, aged 81, first met her father-in-law soon after the turn of the century: she remembered him as "a dear old thing, with a strong sense of

humour and absolutely obsessed with his work".

Humour he needed, for in spite of his taking out more than 70 patents connected with cinematography; his work was largely unrecognized during his lifetime and he died with only 1s 10d – then, ironically, the price of a cinema ticket – in his pocket.

The Magic Box

Unbylined review (Dudley Carew),
September 13 1951

To commemorate the Festival (Festival of Britain), the British moving picture industry pooled its resources to make a film commemorating the life of the man who first made pictures move. An admirable idea, since it so happened that Friese-Greene, apart from being an inventor, was an eccentric after the English tradition of the creations of Dickens and H.G. Wells. Everything about his life was extravagant, varied, muddled, and unpredictable.

The cast reads like a programme for a Command performance, Mr Eric Ambler was appointed to write the script, Mr John Boulting to direct, and Mr Ronald Neame to produce. So far, so extremely promising, but the film proceeds at the outset to throw away most of the advantages which, in its inception, it possessed. It was to be expected that the story would be told in a series of flashbacks, moving leisurely and with care for detail over the years of a leisurely age, and so it is told and so it does move, but what was not foreseen was the diffidence with which Mr Robert Donat approaches the part of Friese-Greene himself.

It would have been legitimate to have presented him as an endearing mixture of Uncle Ponderevo and Mr Micawber, but Mr Donat plays him with a muted and diffident shyness which suggests that Friese-Greene was less a "character" and an inventor than some pathetic relation of Mr Chips. As a piece of acting it is sincere and conscientious, a virtue it shares with the film in general, but the man himself seldom breaks and erupts into life.

FLOPS

Editor's note: The *Wizard of Oz* **is now regarded not only as a Hollywood classic, but as a landmark in the history of cinema. Yet it actually lost money on its initial release.** *The Times* **reviewer was not impressed with the film overall and we are left to speculate what he thought specifically of Judy Garland or such songs as 'Over the Rainbow'.**

5 April 1951. Judy Garland aboard the liner *Ile De France* en route to Plymouth from New York, to appear at the London Palladium. (Fitz)

April 1951. Judy Garland with a bouquet of flowers from her daughter Liza, after appearing onstage in London for the first time in thirteen years. (Charles Trusler)

AN AMERICAN FAIRY TALE

The Wizard of Oz

Unbylined review,
January 29 1940

Two of the new films this week are British and characteristic. *The Band Wagon*, with Mr Arthur Askey, which has made itself popular over the wireless, comes to the Leicester Square, and football finds its expression in *The Arsenal Stadium Mystery*, which is to be seen at the New Victoria and Astoria. The third film, *The Wizard of Oz*, at the Empire, is a lavish American fairy-story told, for the most part, in technicolour.

It is presumably to the credit of Hollywood that it can afford to deploy a whole army of dwarfs for the illustration of a single incident in a simple fairy story; this innumerable band of midgets reduces to insignificance the collection of the Gonzagas or, if it comes to that, of Philip IV of Spain. The rest of the spectacle is equally lavish; there are extraordinary vistas of artificial scenery, many amusing tricks and devices of the cinema, witches who fly in a very natural fashion, puffs of scarlet smoke, and a horse which changes its colour from brilliant purple to orange. In fact the ingenuous fairy story from which the film is adapted, the story of a little girl who wanders in a strange country in the company of stranger creatures to look for a wizard who will send her home, is quite overlaid by the fantastic elaboration of the setting. The only drawback to the spectacle is that there is scarcely anything in it to please the eye; although many of the conjuring tricks will certainly arouse one's curiosity, the scenery and dresses are designed with no more taste than is commonly used in the decoration of a night-club. The film is, no doubt, a triumph of technical dexterity and especially of skill in colour photography, but what is the use of making a hollyhock out of cellophane, painting it an ugly colour, and then photographing it with complete accuracy?

AN AMERICAN FAIRY TALE

Two of the new films this week are British and characteristic. *The Band-Wagon*, with Mr. Arthur Askey, which has made itself popular over the wireless, comes to the Leicester Square, and football finds its expression in *The Arsenal Stadium Mystery*, which is to be seen at the New Victoria and Astoria. The third film, *The Wizard of Oz*, at the Empire, is a lavish American fairy-story told, for the most part, in technicolour.

THE EMPIRE

The Wizard of Oz.—It is presumably to the credit of Hollywood that it can afford to deploy a whole army of dwarfs for the illustration of a single incident in a simple fairy story; this innumerable band of midgets reduces to insignificance the collection of the Gonzagas or, if it comes to that, of Philip IV of Spain. The rest of the spectacle is equally lavish; there are extraordinary vistas of artificial scenery, many amusing tricks and devices of the cinema, witches who fly in a very natural fashion, puffs of scarlet smoke, and a horse which changes its colour from brilliant purple to orange. In fact the ingenuous fairy story from which the film is adapted, the story of a little girl who wanders in a strange country in the company of stranger creatures to look for a wizard who will send her home, is quite overlaid by the fantastic elaboration of the setting. The only drawback to the spectacle is that there is scarcely anything in it to please the eye; although many of the conjuring tricks will certainly arouse one's curiosity the scenery and dresses are designed with no more taste than is commonly used in the decoration of a night-club. The film is, no doubt, a triumph of technical dexterity and especially of skill in colour photography, but what is the use of making a hollyhock out of cellophane, painting it an ugly colour, and then photographing it with complete accuracy?

CLASSIC FILM OF THE WEEK

The Wizard of Oz

Review by Kate Muir,
September 12 2014

While most of us have seen *The Wizard of Oz* on television, usually rolling in the background at Christmas, this 3D remastering of the original, on a giant IMAX screen to boot, brings a whole new sense of wonder to Dorothy's yellow-brick road movie.

The initial scenes, shot in sepia, as the twister hits Aunt Em's farmhouse in Kansas, take on a wild energy in 3D and seem all the more effective in these blasé days of CGI. The storm creates stomach-churning lurches and becomes frightening (at least to small children) until a granny flies by the window knitting in her rocking chair. The move to Technicolor, as Dorothy's house lands squarely on the Wicked Witch of the East in Munchkinland, is suitably garish, although a little blurred in the deep background. Directed by Victor Fleming, the film remains in its original 4x3 Academy aspect ratio in IMAX.

You also forget how good a young actress Judy Garland was aged 16 as Dorothy Gale, avoiding artifice for sincerity, even when her eyes seem to be constantly pooling with emotion. Looking at the film again I was particularly impressed by Terry the black Cairn Terrier's natural, unscripted performance as Toto.

And the soundtrack is as catchy as ever. Over the Rainbow won an Oscar for best song, but best picture that year went to *Gone with the Wind*. This *Wizard of Oz* restoration will entertain a modern child far more than the original and provide a perfect serving of nostalgia for adults. Like Dorothy says, we're not in Kansas anymore. We're in 3D IMAX.

PEOPLE

Karl Slover

Diminutive actor who was one of the last survivors of the 124 actors who appeared as the Munchkins in one of Hollywood's greatest success stories, *The Wizard of Oz*

Obituary (Richard Whitehead),
December 24 2011

Karl Slover was one of the last survivors of the 124 actors who appeared as the Munchkins in one of Hollywood's greatest success stories, *The Wizard of Oz*. At 4ft 4in, Slover claimed to be the smallest of the Munchkins and was assigned four roles: lead trumpeter in the band, a soldier, a sleepy head and one of the characters who leads Judy Garland down the Yellow Brick Road. The roles brought him lasting fame but, initially at least, not wealth. "Toto [Garland's dog] got a bigger fee than us," he said. "He had a better agent."

Slover was born Karl Kosiczky in 1918 in Prakendorf, which is now in

Slovakia. As a child he was made to undergo a number of "treatments" for his dwarfism, including being buried in his back garden, immersed in hot oil until his skin blistered and attached to a stretching machine at a hospital. Eventually, frustrated that none of this worked, his father sold him to a travelling show when he was 9.

He toured Europe but moved to the United States in the late 1920s where he appeared in circuses and as part of a touring group known as the Singer Midgets. There were 30 members and they were recruited en masse to play the Munchkins when casting began for *The Wizard of Oz*.

The filming lasted two months and all the actors were subjected to a gruelling schedule. He was paid $50 a week, but when the film came out in 1939 it was an enormous success. [Editor's note: The film actually lost money on initial release.] Initially, he had been assigned the role of second trumpeter but earned promotion when the selected actor was afflicted by stage fright. Slover's various roles gave him little chance to rest. "I had four parts and each time I had to change clothes and do it so fast," he said.

Slover also appeared in a 1938 western, *The Terror of Tiny Town*, billed as "the little guys with big guns", and in the Laurel and Hardy classic *Block-Heads* (1938). He moved to Florida in 1942 where he joined a circus owned by Bert and Ada Slover. He became close to the couple and took their name.

Karl Slover, actor, was born on September 21, 1918. He died on November 15, 2011, aged 93.

JAMES BOND: PART ONE

WHAT'S THE BEST (AND WORST) BOND FILM EVER? EXPERTS RANK THE MOVIES

By Dominic Maxwell,
October 15 2015

Which is the best James Bond film? With less than two weeks to go before Daniel Craig's latest 007 adventure, *Spectre*, opens in British cinemas, we thought the time was right to put all its predecessors in a definitive order. To compile an official, definitive list of all the Bond films released to date, from best (1) to worst (24).

All right, so maybe this little vote of ours isn't strictly official. It is, however, the most comprehensive poll of *James Bond* experts, to our knowledge, anyone has compiled. Steve Cole and Raymond Benson (novelists), Ben Macintyre and Andrew Lycett (Ian Fleming biographers), and David Walliams and Edgar Wright (film industry fans) are just some of the names involved.

We didn't include the abominable spoof *Casino Royale* from 1967 – a film so bad it makes *Die Another Day* look like *The Godfather* – but left on the list the "unofficial" *Thunderball* remake, *Never Say Never Again*, the one film here not made by Bond's (genuinely) official producer, Eon. Then we totted up the votes. There were only a few points between the top four films. The bottom choice, by contrast, was a runaway loser. Sorry, Pierce.

1. *Casino Royale* (2006, Daniel Craig)

Bond begins – belatedly, brutally, brilliantly – as Ian Fleming's first novel finally gets the full Bond-film treatment, 44 years after *Dr. No*. It's a modern action thriller that delivers on the thrills (the parkour chase! That bit at the airport!) but also has room for subtlety, symbolism, psychology and romance. Eva Green's Vesper Lynd is Bond's finest female foil – the label "Bond girl" has never felt so inadequate – the poker sequence is superbly sustained; Craig's final, strategically withheld uttering of the words "the name's Bond … James Bond" sends a shiver up the spine; the naked torture scene (pure Fleming) sends a shiver up a different part of a chap's anatomy. Yeah, you wish that Venetian building at the end wasn't quite so keen to collapse into the canal, but this is Bond as it should be: low on pathetic quips and unlikely gadgets, high on adrenaline and emotion, ambiguity and intrigue.

2. *Goldfinger* (1964, Sean Connery)

Casino Royale edged it out of our poll's top slot – by millimetres – yet this remains the Bond film that other Bond films want to be when they grow up. Sean Connery, the suavest hard man in town, scrubs up a treat in dinner jacket, wetsuit and powder-blue towelling playsuit alike; tosses out the puns as if he actually enjoys them; electrifies as he battles to the death with Oddjob (the henchman's henchman) in Ken Adam's

March 2005. Daniel Craig poses with Eva Green (Bond's leading lady Vesper) while filming *Casino Royale* in the Bahamas. (Paul Rogers)

Fort Knox fantasia design. Then there's Shirley Eaton covered in gold paint; Honor Blackman radiant in her leathers; the funky Aston Martin; the brassiest of theme songs; dynamite dialogue with the larger-than-life baddie. Bond (a laser beam fast approaching his crotch): "Do you expect me to talk?" Goldfinger: "No, Mr Bond, I expect you to die!"

Raymond Benson, author of six Bond novels: "*Goldfinger* is perhaps the most influential film of the 1960s in terms of pop culture. It spawned the big spy boom in other films, television and fashion. It set the gold standard for the action-adventure film."

3. *On Her Majesty's Secret Service* (1969, George Lazenby)

Maligned at the time, now seen as one of the series's most singular successes. Right, so Australian model George Lazenby is stiff; he's also superb in the action scenes, tender when he has to be, and his first-time-actor's unease fits in a story that puts Bond in protracted peril in Blofeld's mountain-top clinic-cum-lair. The camerawork and the skiing are sensational – bolstered by John Barry's best score – and Diana Rigg's Tracy is fine enough to make our lothario vow to forsake all others. OHMSS still divides people; it got the most No 1 placings of any film in the poll, while others reject its early languor, or just Lazenby.

Steve Cole, author of *Young Bond: Shoot to Kill*: "There's an energy and

clout to the action scenes that Bond movies have seldom bettered."

Matthew Parker, Bond author: "Diana Rigg steals it from a plank of wood."

4. *From Russia with Love* (1963, Sean Connery)

The series hits its stride with a taut, glamorous, sometimes self-mocking Cold War thriller that introduces us to the scrupulously hierarchical *Spectre* organisation and its fiendish, faceless, cat-loving leader, Number 1 (later revealed as Ernst Stavro Blofeld). Features some of the best acting and best action of the series in the train face-off between Connery and Robert Shaw, who might yet have bested Bond if he'd only ordered the right kind of wine with his fish supper.

5. *Dr. No* (1962, Sean Connery)

The original and fifth best. An amazing amount of the series's hallmarks are in place from the off – and Ursula Andress emerging from the sea remains one of the most celebrated moments in cinema – but the story itself looks a little stunted these days.

Simon Winder, author of *The Man Who Saved Britain*: "A marvel, of course, and the opening few seconds with the radio interference sounds making a segue to the theme tune could have a claim to be the fanfare marking the start of the 1960s, but it is also regrettably cheap-looking in some ways."

6. *The Spy Who Loved Me* (1977, Roger Moore)

July 1977. Richard Kiel arriving for the premiere of *The Spy Who Loved Me*. (Dempsie)

November 2011. Actors at a photocall in London held to announce production starting for new James Bond film *Skyfall*. From left: Javier Bardem, Bérénice Marlohe, Sam Mendes, Dame Judi Dench, Daniel Craig, Naomie Harris, Barbara Broccoli and Michael G. Wilson. (David Bebber)

The best of the Moores, this is the one with the genuinely jaw-dropping opening title sequence (Bond skiing off a giant cliff before opening a Union Jack parachute); Carly Simon's middle-of-the-road dream of a title tune; Jaws the giant henchman; the submarine-swallowing secret base that the designer Ken Adam secretly got his friend Stanley Kubrick to help him to light. Big fun.

7. *Skyfall* (2012, Daniel Craig)

If you can ignore some logical inconsistencies – and this is James Bond, I'd strongly suggest you try – this is one of the smartest, most stylish entries in the series. It's certainly one of the best looking, thanks to Roger Deakins's photography, and best acted, thanks to Craig, to vengeful peroxide-blonde nutjob Javier Bardem, and to Judi Dench, dying on the job in the only 007 film in which the baddie gets everything he wants. Also the only Bond film to earn $1 billion at the box office and, even adjusting for inflation, the biggest earner in the series (ahead of *Thunderball* and *Goldfinger*).

8. *Thunderball* (1965, Sean Connery)

The last gasps of Peak Connery – maximum insouciance, yet still looks as if he means business – this tropical long-weekend-cum-nuclear-ransom-race-against-time goes on to get waterlogged in the seemingly endless diving sequences. A 20-minute trim away from being one of the best.

9. *You Only Live Twice* (1967, Sean Connery)

In which Bond goes to Japan, Connery eyes the exit, and Donald Pleasence plays the most iconic incarnation of Blofeld, whose fully kitted, hollowed-out volcano remains the acme of supervillain secret bases even today. Top pub fact: Roald Dahl wrote the screenplay. And director Lewis Gilbert liked the plot so much that he repeated it, more or less, in his other two Bonds, *The Spy Who Loved Me* and *Moonraker*.

10. *Live and Let Die* (1973, Roger Moore)

Rog arrives, aged 45, but seizing the Seventies with Bond's LED digital watch and preposterously professional coffee-making gear as M and Moneypenny visit him in his swish Chelsea flat. This is the one with voodoo, the speedboat chase, Jane Seymour, Paul McCartney's theme, Sheriff JW Pepper and the exploding baddie "who always did have an inflated opinion of himself".

Edgar Wright, film director (*Shaun of the Dead*, *The World's End*): "Ridiculously entertaining. Bordering on silliness at times, but frequently weird and wild. Not the best, but perhaps my favourite."

11. *GoldenEye* (1995, Pierce Brosnan)

8 June 1994. Pierce Brosnan at a photocall after being announced as the new James Bond. (Michael Powell)

Brosnan arrives to rescue us from six Bondless years with the best of his four films, directed by Martin Campbell, who would go on to restart the series again with *Casino Royale*. Great opening bungee jump, a tank chase through Moscow, the arrival of Judi Dench's M, Sean Bean acting "posh" as 006, and a sexy assassin who kills her victims between her thighs.

12. *The Living Daylights* (1987, Timothy Dalton)

The first of Dalton's two post-Glasnost, post-AIDS outings is a spy thriller that starts in style in Europe but then, failing to learn the lessons of history, lingers too long in Afghanistan. Was to have been Pierce Brosnan's first Bond film, but at the last minute the producers of his television series, *Remington Steele*, insisted he fulfil his contract and shoot a final season instead.

8 February 1973. Jane Seymour and Roger Moore in *Live and Let Die*.

13. *Diamonds Are Forever* (1971, Sean Connery)

Lazenby resigns, Connery comes back for $1.25 million (which he donates to charity) and a production deal. The result: a scrappy, silly, stylish travelogue that takes a blank-looking Connery from London to Amsterdam to Las Vegas to a drab oil rig (looks as if all the money went on his salary) as the producers try to bring Bond back to his *Goldfinger* heyday. Pub fact: in early drafts the villain wasn't Blofeld (camply played here by Charles Gray) but Goldfinger's vengeful twin brother. A guilty pleasure.

14. *Licence to Kill* (1989, Timothy Dalton)

Bond goes rogue (back before he went rogue every bleeding film) to hunt the Central American drug lord responsible for his CIA buddy Felix Leiter losing a leg to a shark. The second and darker of Dalton's two outings was not a big commercial success, but it hits its vengeful stride in its second half. A third Dalton was being planned before legal issues put the series "on hiatus" for six years.

Raymond Benson: "Totally underrated, in 1989 especially, it presented an accurate tone and feel of Fleming's literary world, in particular the novel of *Live and Let Die.*"

15. *The Man with the Golden Gun* (1974, Roger Moore)

26 March 1974. Roger Moore and Britt Ekland. (Len Blandford)

A hurried effort, with some sorry sexism – Rog locks Britt Ekland in a cupboard while he has sex with Maud Adams – but it's worth relishing Christopher Lee as the three-nippled assassin, Scaramanga, and an outstanding car-jump stunt, spoilt ever so slightly by the composer John Barry's use of a swanee whistle to underline its gravity-defying bravado.

Roger Moore having fun in a photocall to promote the James Bond film *Octopussy*. (Steve Lewis)

16. *For Your Eyes Only* (1981, Roger Moore)

A reaction against the excesses of *Moonraker*, its return to ground-level espionage is hard to get excited by now. And 007 is starting to look less like an experienced older man, more "dad": Rog was 53 when this was released, his love interest Carole Bouquet was 23. In an in-jokey pre-title sequence, Bond dumps an unnamed Blofeld – unavailable for use by the official series because of legal battles with the *Thunderball* producer Kevin McClory – down a chimney at Beckton gasworks in east London.

17. *Octopussy* (1983, Roger Moore)

Bond goes to India, Bond dresses up as a clown to defuse a nuclear bomb, Bond gets to bed a second sexy female criminal with "pussy" in her name. The American actor James Brolin tried out for the lead role before Moore was brought back to help to counter the threat from Connery's return to bondage in *Never Say Never Again* that year.

18. *Tomorrow Never Dies* (1997, Pierce Brosnan)

The one with Jonathan Pryce as a malignant media mogul.

Simon Winder: "It is not really clear what goes so hopelessly wrong with Brosnan's Bond. Brosnan himself has the air of a Moss Bros model worried about ripping his clothing – but it is far more than Brosnan's fault. Scene after scene in this film is simply generic and everything smells of decaying versions of former glories."

19. *Moonraker* (1979, Roger Moore)

Silly? Well, sure, but actually this set-piece-stuffed Moore extravaganza is nicely shot, globetrotting good fun – and that aerial pre-title sequence is amazing – until, uh-oh, it blasts off into orbit for laser battles.

Kevin Maher, *Times* film critic: "Nice to see Jaws again, but that space finale was horrendous in 1979, still sucks today."

20. *A View to a Kill* (1985, Roger Moore)

17 August 1984. Roger Moore, Tanya Roberts and Grace Jones promoting *A View to a Kill*. (Steve Copely)

A Bond too far for our star. On the plus side: Duran Duran's theme, Christopher Walken. On the minus side: the plot is a rubbishy rehash of *Goldfinger*; Bond snowboards to the tune of California Girls; Moore, now 57, is seen baking quiche. Quiche! Has its fans, mind.

Matt Gourley, co-host, James Bonding podcast: "This movie is snowboarding-Beach-Boys-Grace-Jones-Eiffel-Tower-base-jumping bats★★★ crazy and I love it."

21. *Quantum of Solace* (2008, Daniel Craig)

The drabness of the villain's plot – to defraud the people of Bolivia via inflated water rates, mouhahahaha! – is intentional, but the story's satirical stabs at contemporary corporate larceny get lost amid shaky camerawork and rushed storytelling that lacks tension.

Simon Winder: "I was at one of the *Casino Royale* premieres and it ended with everyone cheering. The same event for *Quantum of Solace* ended in an embarrassed silence."

29 October 2008. Daniel Craig and partner Satsuki Mitchell arrive at the Odeon in Leicester Square for the world premiere of the twenty-second Bond film *Quantum of Solace*. (Ally Carmichael)

22. *The World Is Not Enough*
(1999, Pierce Brosnan)

22 November 1999. Pierce Brosnan and partner Keely Shaye Smith arriving in Leicester Square for the European premiere of *The World is Not Enough*. (Paul Rogers)

More not-quite-there Brosnanisms: one villain feels no pain (Robert Carlyle), the big villain is Bond's girlfriend (Sophie Marceau), Desmond Llewelyn says goodbye as Q, yet the only thing that really lingers even vaguely in the memory is a speedboat chase. Oh, and Denise Richards in hot pants as the nuclear scientist Dr Christmas Jones. "I was wrong about you," quips Bond as the pair finally get steamy together. "I thought Christmas only comes once a year." Just call her Dr Goesliketheclappers Jones and be done with it.

23. *Never Say Never Again*
(1983, Sean Connery)

Connery wigs up one last time for this deeply so-so remake of *Thunderball*, which for legal reasons was the only story available to producers in what was the only serious Bond film not to be made by Cubby Broccoli's Eon productions. It doesn't gel at all, even if Klaus Maria Brandauer and Barbara Carrera are nicely bonkers as the baddies.

24. *Die Another Day*
(2002, Pierce Brosnan)

Our voters made this a clear favourite for the bottom slot. Its vulgar excesses prompted a rethink three years later, aka *Casino Royale*. Now that's what I call a comeback.

Tom Sears, co-presenter, James Bond Radio: "Instead of the real Bond we get an invisible car; the worst dialogue in any film ever; the worst, most clichéd Bond girl ever in Halle Berry; the most ridiculous 'stunt' ever when Bond paraglides on a CGI tsunami; and the worst theme song of the entire series, by Madonna. I left the cinema a broken man."

18 November 2002. Halle Berry arrives at the world premiere of *Die Another Day* at the Royal Albert Hall, London. (Alan Weller)

PEOPLE

Guy Hamilton

Urbane British director who shot four *James Bond* films and helped to introduce Roger Moore as 007

Obituary (Wendy Ide),
April 22 2016

Tall, urbane, with a dry wit, distinguished naval career and a penchant for cocktails – and beautiful women – the director Guy Hamilton shared more than a few traits with the character with whom he was most closely associated, Commander James Bond.

As the director of *Goldfinger* (1964), *Diamonds Are Forever* (1971), *Live and Let Die* (1973) and *The Man with the Golden Gun* (1974), Hamilton helped to steward the series from its early popularity into the big, brash cultural phenomenon that it later became.

The son of a diplomat, he inherited some of his father's expert skills of negotiation. Described as "curiously impersonal", dressed often in a striped tie and blazer, and a great raconteur of war stories, he was the sort of man to whom film companies might entrust their millions.

He was also able to sneak the more risqué elements of the Bond films past the eagle eyes of the censors. He recalled showing them without sound effects – a trick used to downplay the violence and heavy petting and thus earn a U certificate. He meticulously fine-tuned the positioning of a cushion to conceal just enough of Shirley Eaton's buttocks in order for the famous gold-painted nude scene from Goldfinger to pass uncut.

The key to his approach was, he said, walking "the line between absolute nonsense and seriousness". He advocated intelligent baddies. "A Bond villain has to be [the] intellectual equal and a worthy opponent of Bond," he said. He also acknowledged the importance of Bond girls – "A lot of 007's appeal, let's face it, stems from his doings with the ladies. So, find the ladies and we've won half the battle." He helped to cast the little-known Swedish actress Maud Adams in *The Man with the Golden Gun* – "She was so elegant and beautiful that it seemed to me she was the perfect Bond girl". He quipped, "One of the rules of the Bond pictures is that you're not allowed to have a leading lady who can act."

However, he was rather more interested in the gadgets, fast cars and aspirational kit. His Bond ethos was: "Don't take a train when you can take a plane, and if you're going to take a plane, take the newest one around. And if you give Bond a car, don't show what's been seen – show what's not out yet."

Guy Hamilton was born in 1922 in Paris where his father was a press attaché to the British Embassy. Instead of bowing to family pressure to follow his father into the diplomatic service, he decided he wanted to make films. "In those days it was like wanting to run a brothel and I got soundly spanked," he said.

At 17, he applied to the Victorine studios in Nice, where he licked wage packets before getting onto the studio floor as a clapper boy. When the Second

World War broke out he fled France with his mother on the same coal boat heading for North Africa as Somerset Maugham. He recalled the author's butler brewing tea in a corned beef tin.

He worked briefly in England for a newsreel company before service in the navy. He was honoured with a DSC for his many missions, and recalled a hair-raising time with the French Resistance during a covert operation to ferry agents into occupied France. "First we stayed with a Breton family, but that got too hot for us," he said. "When the Germans came snooping round they moved us out into this deserted shepherd's hut in the middle of a forest. The Germans knew that we were around somewhere, but we evaded them, and were picked up four weeks later. I had a month's holiday in Brittany."

After the war, he returned to the film industry and, while still in his twenties, became assistant to the director Carol Reed. Hamilton was also assistant director to John Huston on the rough and ready shoot for *The African Queen*. One of his more onerous duties was to be responsible for the upkeep and transport of Katharine Hepburn's personal toilet. "It was in her contract that she had her private lavatory, so there was a little pontoon with a little hut."

He had his directorial debut in 1952 with *The Ringer*, a crisp version of an Edgar Wallace mystery. His first great commercial success was *The Colditz Story* (1954), a study of life in the prisoner-of-war camp which eschewed easy heroics and wry humour. He drew on his own experience: "It has a schoolboy enthusiasm to it. But we did behave a little like that." By then a rising director, he seemed to tread water.

Goldfinger came as a welcome boost. It opened to Shirley Bassey's dramatic theme. "Well, I don't know whether it's going to be a hit or not, Harry," Hamilton told the producer of the Bond films, Harry Saltzman, "but I know dramatically, it works." In 1969 he was then entrusted with *The Battle of Britain*, an expensive prestige project from Saltzman. Despite a cast in which almost every part was taken by a star, and aerial sequences featuring Hurricanes and Spitfires, it was a dull affair which did poorly at the box-office.

He was glad to return to the Bond films, helping to establish Roger Moore as the new 007 in *Live and Let Die*. He shot the carnival funeral scene so that fans "don't even get to think about it". He also persuaded Moore to cut his hair short in order to appear more establishment and encouraged the actor to slim down to 12 stone for stunts. "Nothing Bond does can be simple," said Hamilton. He spent weeks flying over New Orleans in a helicopter surveying swamps and lagoons for locations.

At the start of the 1980s he helmed two Agatha Christie whodunnits produced by Lord Brabourne, *The Mirror Crack'd* and *Evil Under the Sun*. He later admitted that he was no fan of Christie and when first approached by Brabourne had told him he had got the wrong man.

Hamilton retired to his villa on Mallorca, where he had lived since the late Seventies. Built with his fee for *Superman* – from which he had later pulled out – it was a pink modernist complex on a mountainside with a swimming pool and cocktail bar. Here he could be found mixing Camparis with his wife perched on a barstool beside him.

Guy Hamilton, film director, was born on September 16, 1922. He died on April 20, 2016, aged 93.

CINEMA HISTORY

BUZZ LIGHTYEAR'S ONE LINER SHOOTS TO THE TOP AS BRITAIN'S FAVOURITE

Unbylined news report, November 4 2014

"To infinity … and beyond!", the classic line from Buzz Lightyear, hero of *Toy Story*, has been named the best film quote of all time. The space ranger's catchphrase came top of a poll conducted by the *Radio Times* to find the nation's favourite movie one-liner.

Michael Caine's famous phrase from *The Italian Job*, "You're only supposed to blow the bloody doors off!", took second place, followed by "Say hello to my little friend", uttered by Al Pacino in the mob drama *Scarface*.

The top ten also features "He's not the Messiah. He's a very naughty boy!" from Monty Python's *Life of Brian*, in fourth place, and "You're gonna need a bigger boat" from the thriller *Jaws*, which came fifth.

"Frankly, my dear, I don't give a damn!", Clark Gable's famous line from *Gone with the Wind*, took sixth place, ahead of the greatest *Carry On* line of all times, from Kenneth Williams as Julius Caesar in *Carry On Cleo*: "Infamy, infamy, they've all got it in for me!"

Next on the list are lines from *Blade Runner* ("All those moments will be lost in time… like tears in rain") and *Some Like It Hot* ("Nobody's perfect!").

Richard E Grant's classic line from *Withnail and I* rounds out the top ten: "We want the finest wines available to humanity. We want them here, and we want them now!"

But both Sean Connery's "Bond. James Bond" from *Dr. No*, and Humphrey Bogart's "Here's looking at you, kid" from *Casablanca* missed out on the top ten.

CINEMA HISTORY

MARILYN MONROE FOUND DEAD

From Our Own Correspondent in New York, August 5 Published August 6 1962

Miss Marilyn Monroe, the film actress, was found dead in bed in her Los Angeles home, early today. The local coroner said the circumstances indicated a "possible suicide". Miss Monroe, aged 36, had long been suffering from nervous trouble arising from both her professional and her personal life.

The police said Miss Monroe was found by two doctors, who had to break a window to get into her room. She was

16 July 1956. Marilyn Monroe at a press conference in the Savoy Hotel. (Horace Tonge)

15 July 1956. Marilyn Monroe and her husband Arthur Miller receiving photographers in the grounds of Parkside House in Surrey. (Martin)

lying nude in bed with the sheet pulled up to her neck and a telephone in her hand. On the bedside table were bottles of medicines, including an empty bottle of Nembutal, a sleeping pill.

The doctors were called to the house after the housekeeper, noticing that Miss Monroe's room lights remained on for several hours during the night, tried the door and found it locked.

The tragic circumstances of Miss Monroe's life, from her early days as a waif sent from one set of foster-parents to another to her emergence as the "sex symbol" of America, are well known. What is less well known is that as a person she was warm-hearted, friendly and simple. Most people who met and spoke to her outside the glare of publicity (as your Correspondent did) found her a delightful person.

By a coincidence the latest issue of *Life* magazine carried an autobiographical article in which Miss Monroe tells how she felt about everything. She says: "Fame to me is only a temporary and a partial happiness – even for a waif, and I was brought up a waif. But fame is not really for a daily diet, that's not what fulfils you. It warms you a bit, but the warming is temporary …"

"I was never used to being happy, so that wasn't something I ever took for granted. I did sort of think, you know, marriage did that." Her three marriages all ended in divorce.

FIRST FILMS

JOHNNY DEPP

A Nightmare on Elm Street

Review by David Robinson,
August 30 1985

The touching quality in the juvenile audience which is today the economic life-blood of Hollywood is the will to be told the same stories and experience the same thrills over and over again. The most recurrent tale – deriving ultimately from *The Phantom of the Opera* – is about the creature who long ago was in some way abused and disfigured, and comes back to exact revenge by slaying the young offspring of the community that ill-used him (or her).

As writer-director of *A Nightmare on Elm Street*, Wes Craven succeeds in giving new life to the familiar theme. He explores an intriguing supernatural idea, supposing that the killer reaches his victims through their dreams: the spirited heroine alone works out the methods – mainly insomnia – to foil his schemes. An additional attraction of the film is that the youngsters are, for once, real characters, not plasticized dollies. Heather Langenkamp is the ingenious heroine, exasperated by the traditional obtuseness (in this genre of film) of grown-ups in general and cops in particular. Johnny Depp is her comically somnolent friend.

10 January 2008. Johnny Depp arrives in Leicester Square for the European premiere of *Sweeney Todd*. (David Bebber)

BLOCKBUSTERS

YO-HO TO HO-HUM

Pirates of the Caribbean: The Curse of the Black Pearl

Disney's new pirate movie could be a little more shipshape, says Sean Macaulay

Review published July 14 2003

Last week I joked about the trend of original films using colons trying to pass themselves off as sequels, but it is turning into an epidemic this summer. Disney's latest "pre-branded" hit is *Pirates of the Caribbean: The Curse of the Black Pearl*, a title which is cunningly designed to suggest the first of many adventures.

The film plundered an estimated $45 million over the weekend to open at No 1 at the US cinema box office. This may not be enough to warrant a sequel, but it is no small feat considering the curse of the pirate genre. Roman Polanski's comedy *Pirates* was a spectacular misfire in 1985; the most expressive thing in it was Walter Matthau's wooden leg. Renny Harlin's *Cutthroat Island* made an even more spectacular nose-dive in 1995, costing $95 million and grossing $11 million. *Pirates of the Caribbean* re-works the old style without crushing it under ultra-modish editing or overly knowing humour.

Pirates of the Caribbean is drawing on a genre that had lapsed into high spoofery

as early as the 1950s. Burt Lancaster's *The Crimson Pirate* is the era's classic swash-buckler, but it teeters over into action pantomime with its stripy tights and hearty, tooth-some acrobatics.

With nothing fresh left to spoof, *Pirates of the Caribbean* wisely gets on with minting its own fun. One of its pirates has a wooden eyeball. Another is a mute whose parrot does the talking for him. All of them have fabulously rotten teeth. It also draws on another antecedent, being the second film that Disney has based on one of its theme-park attractions. Last year saw *The Care Bears Movie*, based on a singing bear show at Disneyland.

There is some logic in basing a film on a theme-park ride. In the 1980s action adventure films tried to emulate the dips and climbs of the roller-coaster ride. *Pirates of the Caribbean* is duly overstuffed with gratuitous, faintly numbing action set pieces, which adds to a bloated running time of 2 hours 23 minutes.

The real culprit for this, though, is a mammoth first act. It takes 45 minutes for rogue pirate Johnny Depp to set off on his mission to rescue a cursed medallion and kidnapped beauty. Audiences all know this lift-off moment. It is when the plane takes off, the wagons roll, or, finally in this case, when the ship sets sail.

It is sacrosanct in Hollywood that any mission/journey/quest be underway by the 30-minute mark. Cramming more explosions and mass fights into the first act does not create better value. It just dilutes the impact of the fights and set pieces later on.

Nonetheless, the producer Jerry Bruckheimer has shown his dispiritingly consistent mastery in expediently combining the right elements to capture a mass audience. There is the action to lure teenage boys. There is sophisticated humour to appease the adults (Johnny Depp's inspired Mockney accent and tipsy panache is half Keith Richards, half Dudley Moore). There's a veneer of respectability to the scenery chewing with Oscar-winner Geoffrey Rush. And there's the earnest young lovers sub-plot for the teenage date audience, shrewdly cast with new pin-ups Orlando (*The Lord of the Rings*) Bloom and Keira (*Bend It Like Beckham*) Knightley. A producer's victory.

CINEMA HISTORY

◇◇

Editor's note: At the birth of the talkies, *The Times* reviewer goes all existential, while fearing that sound may distract viewers from what is actually happening on screen.

◇◇

The Jazz Singer

Unbylined review (Albert Cookman), September 28 1928

The Jazz Singer, in which Mr Al Jolson may be both seen and heard, is only in part a "talking" film. Most of the story is told with the assistance of "captions", but we hear half-a-dozen of the songs for which Mr Jolson is justly renowned on both sides of the Atlantic, and also one or two fragments of conversation. These appear as interruptions in the flow of visual images, and effectually encompass the ruin of the story, but they are interesting as the most considerable attempt to break the silence of the film drama which has yet been witnessed in this country.

It must be confessed, however, that we are less interested in the dramatic possibilities of the innovation than in its mechanical aspect. Synchronization has been almost perfectly achieved; words are precisely suited to the most trivial action; and our appreciation of a notable mechanical improvement is apt to cause us to overlook the tonelessness of the reproduction of Mr Jolson's voice. In its present stage of development the sounds we hear are a faint parody of the human voice. They seem incapable of the fine shades on which a beautiful style of speaking depends. They would fail us, we feel, in any dramatic crisis which called for quiet intensities. These mechanical defects are no doubt temporary, but it is a more serious consideration that even when we become accustomed to the toneless quality of the sound reproduction we find that the sounds themselves divert our attention from what is passing on the screen. We become strangely aware of the interposition of two mediums between ourselves and the actor; we neither see nor hear him, but he is reproduced for us twice over. And after all the special subtlety of acting which is peculiar to the film has been sacrificed, we feel, for a poor imitation of the stage.

BLOCKBUSTERS

The Lord of the Rings: The Fellowship of the Ring

Review by James Christopher,
December 22 2001

Destined to become one of the seven marvels of the cinematic world, this spellbinding epic charts the story of how one humble Hobbit, Frodo Baggins, saves the world. Entrusted to destroy a magical ring of awesome power, the pint-sized Hobbits brave an army of mind-boggling horrors, too grisly for very young children. The film is a technical wonder. The most striking feature is the seamless join between the rugged New Zealand landscape and the fantastic digital universe that is Tolkien's Middle-Earth. Jackson has created forests that seem to breathe evil. The greatest pleasure is the swamp life that stalks the heroes: rubbery orcs with bloodshot eyes, deathly Ringwraiths, and an awesome stone troll who will have you clutching your pillow in a damp sweat. The trip of the year.

The Lord of the Rings: The Two Towers

Review by James Christopher,
December 21 2002

The most eagerly awaited sequel of the year is a thrilling, bewildering sprawl of battles, pacts and snow-capped vistas. Half a dozen fractured storylines gallop along in tandem. Ian McKellen's Gandalf fights with a demonic fiery demon in the depths of hell. Viggo Mortensen's hunky Aragorn rides to the rescue of King Théoden (Bernard Hill), the last doddery hope for human kind. Orlando Bloom's beautiful, deadly elf and John Rhys-Davies's dwarf are tossed from one bloody fray into another. And a couple of new swashbucklers make their bow: David

10 December 2001. Dominic Monaghan (L), Elijah Wood (C) and Billy Boyd (R) arrive for the world premiere of the film *Lord of the Rings: The Fellowship of the Ring* in London's Leicester Square. (Richard Mills)

consistent tension. Like most trilogies, *The Lord of the Rings* sags in the middle. Peter Jackson's second episode is a vast schematic piece of action with large damp patches of, frankly, wooden acting. The camera seems forever perched on a horizon, gazing across distant plains at humourless armies of yodelling ogres.

Ultimately, the film is stolen by the wonderful Gollum, a slimy marvel who is voiced by and digitally modelled on the British actor Andy Serkis. With his *ET* eyes, lizardy skin and rotten toothpick teeth, this worshipper of the ring entices unexpected sympathy. It's his mysterious love-hate relationship with Frodo that provides the darkest, and most human, chills.

Wenham's Faramir (brother of Sean Bean's Boromir) is the spitting image of Jamie Oliver; Hill's Théoden is handy with a sword when he wakes from a poisonous slumber. Meanwhile, Miranda Otto's Eowyn drools over the strangely asexual Aragorn, and Christopher Lee's Saruman continues to breed super-orcs.

And through it all plods Elijah Wood's exhausted hobbit Frodo, the bearer of the Ring, crawling towards Mordor like a child to the gallows. The battle effects are magnificent, but the grim business of war makes the violence feel far more taxing than the *Dungeons & Dragons* thrills of *The Fellowship*. As ever, it's the monsters that add the most enjoyable spice: Cockney-speaking orcs, sabre-toothed bears and, best of all, giant talking trees called Ents, which plod around forests like amiable wicker men. What we don't get is close and

I'M HOME, MY PRECIOUS

The Lord of the Rings: The Return of the King

Review by James Christopher, December 18 2003

No one can claim that *The Return of the King* is great art, but as a Herculean endeavour it's pure *Boy's Own Viagra*. The plot hinges on Viggo Mortensen's return to Gondor to reclaim his vacant throne but, frankly, who cares? The close-quarter horrors are very much the thrilling point. The Jurassic beasts in the last reel make stone trolls look very plain indeed. Shelob is a stomach-churning arachnophobic nightmare. Even the orcs, impossibly,

look uglier. But it's the parasitic relationship between the Ring, Frodo and
Andy Serkis's scene-stealing Gollum
that gives the spectacle its unexpected
gravity. The way Peter Jackson frames
Gollum's schizophrenia by putting him
in front of a puddle is an inspired touch.
The swashbucklers do their stuff with
the usual wit and flair. The stunts are
marvellous. Orlando Bloom has the best
moment when he slaughters a galloping mammoth without breaking sweat.
It brought spontaneous applause at the
press screening. Ian McKellen milks
Gandalf's secrets like a man who has
had one too many prunes. He's always
dashing offscreen left for no perceptible
reason. And the hobbits are a keystone
joy. At 201 minutes there are distinct
longueurs. One can stomach only so
much heroic dialogue. But these are
light stings. The damn trilogy is a preposterous achievement. It has always
been the scale of Jackson's ambition
that has impressed. If Frodo's crawl
towards the fires of Mordor plucks the
heartstrings, it's the bloodcurdling battle
scenes and close-action photography of
gristle and orc which leaves you weak
at the knees.

CLASSIC CINEMA

MR NOËL COWARD'S NEW FILM

Brief Encounter

Unbylined review (Dudley Carew),
November 22 1945

The title indicates fairly enough the
scope and purpose of the film. A man
and a woman, upper middle-class, early
middle-aged, and married, meet by
chance, fall in love, and, since they have
no hope of happiness together and have
their roots deep in lives that existed
before the encounter took place, agree
to part.

Mr Noël Coward has worked in a
deliberately minor key, and while the
notes are struck with an admirable
clarity and precision, the composition
is lacking in dramatic force and imaginative range. What emotion is distilled
from a clever piece of observation and
reporting is the result of the beautifully
sincere and natural playing of Miss Celia
Johnson as the woman who gets a piece
of coal-dust in her eye while she is waiting on the platform for the train to take
her home from her weekly shopping
expedition, has it removed by a doctor
and is disturbed to find that the trivial
accident assumes a disproportionate
importance. She and the doctor meet
again, they fall desperately in love, and
the whole unhappy, inconclusive affair
is worked out against a background of
railway buffets, cafes, cinemas, and the
gossip and trivialities of provincial life.

There is guilt, humiliation, and a heroic integrity at the centre; the circumference is provided by Mr Stanley Holloway, as a ticket-collector, and Miss Joyce Carey, the refined goddess of the station refreshment room where the encounter has its trivial beginning and its tragic end – comic relief, perhaps, but not over-exaggerated or out of tune with the purpose of the whole. Mr Trevor Howard, as the doctor, matches Miss Johnson in casual charm of manner if he cannot equal her in emotional depth, and Miss Johnson has the difficulties of interpreting with her face close to the camera the audible progression of her secret thoughts – a clumsy device conspicuously out of place in a technically competent film which shows Mr Coward more as a serious psychologist than as a flippant commentator.

mote of soot in the eye at the station and ends in an agony of longing.

Johnson plays the elegant, tweed-suited Laura. She is the epitome of upper middle-class suburban conventionality: a mother of two and, as she claims to be in her cut-glass accent (which takes some getting used to), "hippily merried". But when she meets the helpful doctor Alec, the catchlights in her eyes go on full beam. The two lunch, drive in the country and play truant at the cinema for the afternoon matinee. For a time…

Written by Noël Coward, the subtle and deeply moving drama is seen from Laura's point of view, often in impassioned voiceover as she sits quietly sewing while her dull, pleasant husband does *The Times* crossword.

The opening, and ending, scene in the station tea room is shot twice by the director, David Lean, from reversed angles, with quite different meanings emerging.

CLASSIC FILM OF THE WEEK

Brief Encounter

Review by Kate Muir,
November 6 2015

"You're only middle-aged once," says Trevor Howard as he leads Celia Johnson exquisitely astray in this very English affair of the heart. One of cinema's classic love stories, *Brief Encounter* has been remastered for its 70th anniversary. White steam and inky blacks shroud this extramarital tryst, which begins with a

(NOT) CLASSIC CINEMA

Fifty Shades of Grey

Review by Kate Muir,
February 13 2015

Bondage is probably best when taken seriously, not interspersed with bouts of giggles. But this adaptation of *Fifty Shades of Grey* is a hoot, at least during the first hour of cinematic foreplay before the "hard limits" are reached. Director Sam Taylor-Johnson's dark romance is more glossy magazine shoot than out-and-out spankfest. Think *World of Interiors* meets *The Little Book of Bondage* and you may get the picture, which starts out hilarious, becomes ludicrous and is finally dubious.

E.L. James fans will be delighted with this polished production – I suspect this may be a luxurious five-star experience for them and they will check in more than once. The chemistry between 21-year-old romantic literature student Anastasia Steele (Dakota Johnson) and the world's most eligible billionaire bachelor Christian Grey (Jamie Dornan) works well, particularly in the more horizontal scenes, throbbing to pop ballads and, as the rumpy pumpy escalates, thumping bass. The movie opens with Annie Lennox's cover of 'I Put a Spell on You' and within two minutes Dornan is six-pack topless. Ker-ching.

The 40-minute wait for bedtime is surprisingly entertaining as Kelly Marcel's script and Sam Taylor-Johnson's direction take the gentle mickey out of the source material and ramp up the romance. There's an ironic twist to Dornan's delivery of "Laters, baby" and a top sight gag when Ana sucks a corporate pencil with the word GREY on the side, musing on her future.

The hardware-store scene when Christian arrives asking "Do you stock cable ties?" had the audience at my screening hooting. And when Christian introduces his "playroom", aka the Red Room of Pain, Ana asks: "Is that where you keep your Xbox and stuff?"

Incidentally, the red Moroccan leather and panelling in the playroom is rather Ralph Lauren, while the rest of the glass-walled, marbled penthouse oozes bland hotel glamour, with the addition of works from Taylor-Johnson's artist friends; Ed Ruscha's grey sinking ship looms over an early scene.

But let's get back to the bonking, which is copious, cleverly shot, features beautiful bodies and, as one critical wit put it, "shows much more of Johnson than Dornan's johnson". The initial sensuality and playfulness of the tie-me-up-with-your-tie moment, and an ice-cube scene that brings back *9½ Weeks*, becomes darker as Christian's abusive past and unresolved anger is revealed. The mentions of "anal fisting" and "genital clamps" in the dominant-submissive contract Christian wants Ana to sign, go swiftly from ridiculous to downright creepy.

At this point all the early vim and verve seems to drain out of Ana (perhaps James exercised control in all things here) and she turns into a pink-eyed, constantly tearful mess. Johnson's acting abilities seem to leave her towards the end – after all, things are getting a touch stressful what with the floggers, the canes, and what look like furry badger parts and squirrel scrag ends hanging up on the Red Room fun-racks – and it becomes a one-tone moan. Dornan, who was darkly disturbing as the serial killer in *The Fall* on television, relies here on a pair of frowns, one jealous, one angry.

The performances could be stronger. Young actors need more direction and perhaps, as a former Young British Artist, Taylor-Johnson's abilities as a film-maker tend more towards the visual (although her first feature, the John Lennon biopic *Nowhere Boy*, was accomplished all round). Certainly Marcel has removed some of the more embarrassing clunkers from James's dialogue, keeping "Holy cow!" and "Holy crap!" down to a minimum.

Yet the film suffers from that curse of penny-dreadful erotica, known in some quarters as PWP – porn without plot. Obviously readers can skip from bonk to bonk, propped up by their imaginations, but that's harder for cinemagoers. Still, the production values are high, Seattle looks sleek from Grey's helicopter and affluenza pervades every scene: the latest MacBook Airs, Mercedes and convertibles. Even the signage of Grey's building looks remarkably like that of Vogue House. Mr Grey has a very, very large building.

Grey's official statement, "I don't make love. I f★★★ hard", provides the uneasiness and queasiness that underlies the story. In the book, Ana and her famous "inner goddess" seemed keen on bondage, discipline, sadism and masochism, but the screen version shows serious discomfort, trading whipping for a pathetic whiff of romance.

The film shifts from stomach-churning romantic excitement to stomach-turning brutality. And while Ana temporarily walks out, everyone on Earth knows there are two sequels to come, *Fifty Shades Darker* and *Fifty Shades Freed*, nicely set up in the final shot. Like I said, ker-ching.

◇◇◇◇◇◇◇◇◇◇◇◇◇◇◇◇◇◇◇◇◇◇◇◇◇◇◇◇◇◇◇◇◇◇

Editor's note: The only thing I would add is that I went to a public daytime screening of the film at Vue in Leith, not long after it opened, largely out of curiosity. For a daytime screening, it was unusually busy. There were about 20 people there. And I was the only man.

◇◇◇◇◇◇◇◇◇◇◇◇◇◇◇◇◇◇◇◇◇◇◇◇◇◇◇◇◇◇◇◇◇◇

The Interview: Mel Gibson

By Chrissy Iley, November 6 2016

1999. Mel Gibson at Cannes Film Festival. (Andre Camara)

I first met Mel Gibson 16 years ago at a party on the Sony lot for the movie *The Patriot*. He came up behind me, grabbed me, turned me upside down and carried me around the room. I was hysterical with a mixture of shock, fear and laughter. Meeting Mel was like being on a scary fairground ride – but this was just one of his party tricks. He crackled with charisma. This was Mel the maverick: wild, funny, unpredictable, once voted the sexiest man alive.

Not much appears to have changed in him since then, but of course everything has. At 60, he is still wild in his heart, but he's had to rein it in because of the periods when he was completely out of control. He is also about to become a father again – for the ninth time. While there will be no hoisting me around the room today, he at last feels ready to sit down and talk about himself, his meltdown and what might just be his resurrection.

He arrives flustered at his office in West Hollywood, announcing that he needs a coffee and some food. It's lunchtime, he explains, and he hasn't eaten anything since last night's veal chop and spinach. He's wearing dark jeans, a navy pullover and a giant beard grown for an upcoming movie, *The Professor and the Madman*, with Sean Penn. "Sean and I are going to look like ZZ Top," he says. He likes to twiddle this beard quite a bit.

He combs it and strokes it unconsciously. I wonder if it's nervousness or a new habit. His eyes stare out, not so much at me as all around. Darting, distracted eyes.

Everyone has an opinion about Gibson, especially after his much-reported anti-Semitic drunken rant on the Pacific Coast Highway when he was stopped for driving under the influence of alcohol in 2006, in which he raged, "F★★★★★★ Jews … The Jews are responsible for all the wars in the world." Then, in 2010, there were leaked recordings of searing rows between the actor and his (now ex-) girlfriend, Oksana Grigorieva, a Russian-born model and musician, and the mother of his eighth child, Lucia, now 7, in which he roared racist, misogynistic abuse at Oksana and said she deserved a "bat to the side of the head". The following year Gibson pleaded no contest to a charge of misdemeanour battery, after Grigorieva accused him of punching her at his Malibu home. He admitted he slapped her, but denied that a punch was thrown. He avoided jail, but was put on three years' probation and a year-long domestic abuse counselling programme, which he completed.

How could he come back from all of this – ever? Of course, he said sorry for his drunken rants – he believes he was going through what he calls the "andropause", the male menopause, and has commented, "You get barking mad in your fifties" – but it was going to take more than a namby-pamby apology to achieve redemption. He worked on himself. He had to get the booze issue under control. He did a 12-step programme with all its moral inventory. "I've had to do that stuff, otherwise you don't survive," he has said. "They call it the spiritual path for the psychopath. They say there's only three options: you go insane, you die or you quit."

Both the drink-driving and misdemeanour battery convictions have since been expunged from his record by the California courts – a process open to anyone who successfully completes probation following a misdemeanour under state law. But Hollywood is slow to forgive, and his directing genius remained quiet for a decade. Nevertheless, a gang of Hollywood A-listers stood by him. Jodie Foster cast him in her 2011 movie *The Beaver* in a show of friendship and support. Gary Oldman showed his love in a *Playboy* interview in 2014 ("He got drunk and said a few things," Oldman said, "but we've all said those things. We're all f★★★★★★ hypocrites"), and in 2011 Robert Downey Jr, when

presenting Gibson with an award, asked the audience "to join me in forgiving my friend his trespasses and offering him the same clean slate that you have me ..."

The only real redemption in Hollywood, however, is making a great movie. His new film, *Hacksaw Ridge*, might just be that movie. The Oscar buzz has begun.

Born in upstate New York, Gibson moved to Australia with his family when he was 12. He grew up in Sydney and had a Catholic education. It is tempting to think that his anti-Semitic outburst was somehow linked to his Catholicism, but I believe it was simply born of rage and alcohol and being in a very bad place. His marriage of three decades had broken up, he didn't know how to process pain.

Gibson made his first real impact as an actor in *Mad Max* (1979), an Australian thriller set in a grim future. After that, *Gallipoli* (1981), Peter Weir's unflinching Australian First World War drama, turned him into a star worldwide. For many, Gibson will always be *Braveheart* (1995), the roaring, blue-faced hero of the 13th-century Scottish epic in which Gibson the movie star and Gibson the film-maker collaborated in a perfect reel. The film won him Oscars for best director and best picture.

Hacksaw is the story of Desmond Doss, the first conscientious objector to win the Congressional Medal of Honor for valour in the Second World War. At the Venice Film Festival, where it debuted, it received a 10-minute ovation.

"Nine minutes 52 seconds," Gibson says. How did that make him feel? Happy? Relieved? Back? "Absolutely."

Is he admitting it was hard for him to be a Hollywood outcast and that he feels accepted again? "Well, it's not like I stopped working," he says. "There have been many projects … but this is my first as a director for 10 years."

He points out that it's not unusual for directors to take decade-long breaks between films. "I am discerning and I'm not sure that I want to reach into my own pocket any more because it can pay huge dividends or you can get totally killed."

By this he means he doesn't want to risk financing his own movie, despite one of his largely self-funded projects, *The Passion of the Christ* (2004), being the most successful independent film of all time. "Yes, so that was an excellent bet," he says.

Of Gibson's eight children, seven were with his ex-wife, Robyn Moore. They got together in 1977, when he was virtually unknown and she was a dental nurse. They married in June 1980, and were still together when I first met him; he described her as his rock, more organised than him, a nurturing figure. His drinking led to problems in the marriage; the 2006 drink-driving charge appears to have been the final straw for Robyn. They separated that year, and finally divorced in 2009. Word is he was devastated when Robyn left him, but even when they were at their happiest, he found it difficult to talk about love. Way too girly for him.

In September it was announced that he is expecting another child, with his girlfriend of two years, Rosalind Ross, a 26-year-old former equestrian vaulting champion, now a screenwriter. While much has been made of their 34-year age difference, the relationship seems both steady and steadying. How does he feel about having a ninth child? "Delighted. Things are really good and the last two years have been some of the best."

He says that turning 60 comes with various aches and pains, waking at 5am and crawling across the floor to the bathroom. But it also comes with a profound mellowing – even contentment. He's glad to be over his challenging early fifties and he has said that around 58 or 59 you get an inkling that this is the "third act". He acknowledges that act three has been a long one for his 98-year-old father, Hutton. "I don't know if I want a long third act, but I'd like a full one. I enjoy working. I really love it. I hope my mind stays attuned."

CLASSIC CINEMA

The Terminator

Review by Geoff Brown,
January 11 1985

Los Angeles is visited from the future by a Cyborg – a creature half machine, half man and wholly nasty, who leaves a trail of perforated bodies, bashed heads and smashed cars. The well-equipped Arnold Schwarzenegger, the cyborg sent from the future on a complicated and deadly mission, keeps his words to a minimum, preferring to communicate by driving a car into a police station, decimating a night-club and other tricks. "You've got a serious attitude problem," remarks a burly man after being yanked from his phone booth. The film's own attitude is partly comic: the writer-director James Cameron (an alumnus of Roger Corman's New World company) relishes the plot's absurd details, and even finds amusing things for Paul Winfield's police lieutenant to do with cigarettes, cups of coffee and spectacles. But no amount of flip humour can compensate for the film's mindless crudity.

CLASSIC FILM
OF THE WEEK

The Terminator

Review by Kate Muir,
June 19 2015

As the fifth instalment in the hulking *Terminator* franchise lands next month with the ill-spelt *Terminator Genisys*, the original 1984 movie is being released in cinemas and on DVD.

The Terminator was a box office hit and set Arnold Schwarzenegger on the road to fame, after his debut in *Conan the Barbarian*. Schwarzenegger plays a cyborg assassin, and as the critic Janet Maslin said in *The New York Times* on the film's opening, "Mr Schwarzenegger is about as well suited to movie acting as he would be to ballet, but his presence in *The Terminator* is not a deterrent."

The film still has much appeal: two fighters, one the Terminator android killing machine, the other a war-scarred veteran, Reese (Michael Biehn), are sent back 40 years from the future to alter the past. Their business is battling over a damsel in distress, Sarah Connor, bravely played by Linda Hamilton with a blonde perm and pastel casual wear.

Reese wants Connor to survive because she will be mother to the revolutionary leader John Connor; the Terminator wants her to be toast and arms himself with enough semi-automatic weaponry to equip the entire National Rifle Association. Even naked, as he is beamed to Earth in a flash of blue lightning, the Terminator can rip a man's heart out with a twist of his hand.

Directed by James Cameron, this template for so many back-to-the-future action romps remains pacey and streamlined and has made it into the US National Film Registry as "culturally significant".

SUPERHEROES

20 GREATEST BIG-SCREEN COMIC BOOK HEROES

Comic book heroes dominate the cinema box office, if only because comics look like storyboards busy execs can understand

By Michael Moran,
September 12 2007

With NBC's *Heroes* one of the most talked-about shows on TV, an enthusiasm for super-powered heroes no longer carries the social stigma it once did. 2008 promises yet more comic book characters migrating from the page to the cinema, with big budget debuts for the long-awaited *Watchmen*, *Iron Man*, *The Flash* and half a dozen lesser characters already in production.

We thought it might be timely to review the biggest players in the superhero movie franchise business and assess their future prospects. We've scored them according to a range of substantially arbitrary criteria, focusing on their longevity both in comics and on film, and concocted a box-office score based on an average performance of all movie appearances by the character to date.

Having an iconic costume is a key part of establishing a major superhero brand, so we've added a rather subjective costume category too. This is focused as much on the potential of the outfit to transfer from the printed page to the silver screen as much as it does on sheer elan.

1. *Spider-Man*

After a risible attempt at a big-screen transfer in the 1970s, Spider-Man finally made a successful leap onto celluloid in 2002, with *Evil Dead* director Sam Raimi establishing a kinetic, computer-driven style that connected with comic-book geeks and regular cinemagoers alike. The first movie made over $100 million in its first three days on release and it remains in the top 20 highest-grossing films to this day. There's no doubt that the studio money men will push for a fourth film in the series (there's talk of up to three more films) even if the director and star of the hit films do, as has been predicted, depart now that the record-breaking trilogy is complete. Tobey Maguire is currently planning to at least take a break from playing the misunderstood wall-crawling teenager.

Costume: 10 Coolness: 9 Longevity: 3
Box office: $2,495,718,076

2. *The Incredibles*

Essentially the film that *Fantastic Four* should have been, *The Incredibles* is an excellently crafted story about superheroes that combines knowing nods to the geek fraternity ("Metaman, express elevator! Dynaguy, snagged on take off! Splashdown, sucked into a vortex! No capes!") while still delivering a believable family dynamic and a plot that draws in the casual viewer. And all this with entirely computer-created actors. To his undying credit Brad Bird, the director (and voice of Edna Mode) resisted pressure to create a sequel because, in his own words, he couldn't think of a story that was good enough. If only all film-makers had such integrity.

Costumes: 10 Coolness: 10 Longevity: 1 Box office: $631,442,092

◇◇◇◇◇◇◇◇◇◇◇◇◇◇◇◇◇◇◇◇◇◇◇◇◇◇◇◇◇◇◇◇

Editor's note: A sequel duly appeared in 2018.

◇◇◇◇◇◇◇◇◇◇◇◇◇◇◇◇◇◇◇◇◇◇◇◇◇◇◇◇◇◇◇◇

3. *300*

Not comic book characters in the classic mould, but certainly rooted more strongly in Frank Miller's graphic novel than in any history book, the improbably-toned and barely dressed hoplites were presented in a virtual world which although not entirely novel (*Sin City*, another Frank Miller adaptation, used

broadly similar techniques) showed the way forward for directors seeking to translate the extravagant vistas of the comic book into cinematic reality.

Costume: 2 Coolness: 10 Longevity: 1 Box office: $454,592,590

4. *X-Men*

Marvel's ever-changing line up of mutant heroes have probably the most self-consistent explanation for their super powers of any comic book characters. Indeed, it's worked so well that Marvel have expanded their 'homo superior' backstory to embrace virtually all of their characters. Less successful were some of the costumes, with both Wolverine's brown and yellow coveralls and Storm's revealing negligee being transliterated into speedway riders' leathers for their

12 May 2014. Patrick Stewart, James McAvoy, Ian McKellen and Michael Fassbender attending the *X-Men: Days of Future Past* premiere in Leicester Square, London. (Andrew Sims)

cinematic outings. Although roundly castigated by the fans on release, the third *X-Men* movie has been the best performer at the box office and there is no reason to believe, especially given the rotating cast of characters, that the movie franchise cannot endure almost indefinitely.

Costume: 4 Coolness: 10 Longevity: 3 Box office: $1,163,063,674

5. *Fantastic Four*

One of those films that irritated the fanboys and critics alike, but still did pretty creditable business. The first *Fantastic Four* film is by no means as bad as some people might have you believe, being a fairly faithful rendering of the extended family of heroes as they were depicted in their Silver Age heyday. The *Fantastic Four* movies are one of the few examples of a comic books property being successfully true to the original form, rather than being adulterated with notions of 'dark' or 'adult' themes.

Costume: 6 Coolness: 6 Longevity: 2 Box office: $607,290,873

6. *Batman*

The most-filmed superhero property, not least because his main powers are a good deal of determination and a huge amount of disposable wealth, both of which are comparatively easy to fake on film. The treatments range from the deliberately campy 1966 Adam West effort to Christian Bale's gritty *American Psycho* model which returns the Dark Knight to his gothic roots. The future of the franchise looks safe with another duel with the Joker in *The Dark Knight*

already in production and the constantly bubbling rumours of a World's Finest team up with Superman or even, probably a dream too far, a Justice League of America movie featuring all of DC's major heroes together.

Costume: 9 Coolness: 11 Longevity: 7 Box office: $1,570,772,639

7. *Unbreakable*

The film that took the fashionable 'what if superheroes were real' notions to its extreme, M Night Shyamalan's dark fantasy is a clear antecedent of NBC's current TV hit *Heroes*. Bruce Willis' unwitting superman is pitted against an adversary who lives and breathes comic books and knows how the story is supposed to develop. Rumours of a sequel abound on the Internet, but they seem based more on wishful thinking than insider knowledge.

Costume: 0 Coolness: 7 Longevity: 1 Box office: $248,118,121

8. *The Hulk*

It's difficult to say how it all went wrong for *The Hulk* – although 'wrong' is a relative term when the film is still in IMDb's all-time Top 100 blockbusters. Certainly the trailer, with the jolly green giant playing swingball with tanks, looked like the stuff of movie legend and the world-class director and cast seemed set to deliver a roaring success. Something about the excessive tinkering with the Hulk's origins, with the addition of a superfluous 'genetic engineering' element, weakened the character in a way that the minor modification of his stable-mate Spider-Man's powers did not. A sequel/reboot is currently in the works and it may well be that Marvel can yet add the Hulk to their long list of successful page-to-screen transfers.

Costume: 0 Coolness: 5 Longevity: 1 Box office: $245,360,480

9. *Constantine*

Bearing only the loosest relationship to its source material, a comic called *Hellblazer* from DC's adult-oriented *Vertigo* imprint, *Constantine* is part of a long and noble Hollywood tradition of filleting all of the subversive quirkiness out of an Alan Moore property and turning it into something palatable for popcorn-throwing US preview audiences. Of all of the comics characters most suited to star Keanu Reeves' likeable brand of dim laconic cool, this isn't the one.

Costume: 2 Coolness: 7 Longevity: 1 Box office: $230,884,728

10. *Ghost Rider*

On paper, this looked like being a disaster. A comparatively minor comic book character portrayed by one of the most renowned hams in Hollywood. Where did it all go right? *Ghost Rider* benefited from a well-timed release, and excellent promotional campaign, and an endearingly silly story that anyone could understand. As a bonus, it featured a blazing skeleton in a leather jacket who rode an enormous motorbike. What's not to love?

Costume: 10 Coolness: 6 Longevity: 1 Box office: $228,738,393

11. *Daredevil*

Considered by fans to be a rare dud for Marvel, who have really set the standard for comic-to-movie adaptations: It's hard to see where they lost the public's attention. The character's costume was tinkered with admittedly, but no more than those of Batman or the X-Men. Perhaps, when it comes down to it, if the story isn't up to scratch then no amount of special powers or martial arts skill will win the punters over.

Costume: 7 Coolness: 5 Longevity: 1 Box office: $179,179,718

12. *Superman*

Christopher Reeve's ability to switch between bumbling everyman Clark Kent and saintly Ubermensch Kal-El is what made the first two episodes of 1980s *Superman* franchise the best-loved superhero movies of all time. The character was undone though by his own omnipotence, with expensive affects and a paucity of credible opposition driving the Reeve incarnation into a creative cul-de-sac. The recent Brandon Routh reboot has taken a reverent approach to Reeve's iconic characterisation but the addition of a Super-baby bodes ill for the integration of The Blue Boy Scout into the new pantheon of 'serious' comic book movie stars.

Costume: 8 Coolness: 10 Longevity: 5 Box office: $875,116,559

8 March 2006. Men in Guy Fawkes masks await the arrival of film stars prior to the UK premiere of *V For Vendetta* at the Empire Cinema in Leicester Square. (Clara Molden)

13. *V for Vendetta*

Along with *The League of Extraordinary Gentlemen*, this rather clumsy adaptation of an Alan Moore graphic novel was instrumental in making the Northampton-born comic genius turn his back on the film world. The multi-layered plot of a drably totalitarian Britain was simplified to something a little closer to a standard superhero tale.

Costume: 6 Coolness: 6 Longevity: 1
Box office: $131,411,035

14. *Blade*

One of the advantages, for a screenwriter, of a less well-known comics character is the extent to which artistic liberties can be taken with their personality and capabilities. Certainly Wesley Snipes' Blade is a good deal more taciturn, and more powerful, than the character as originally presented in Marvel Comics.

Costume: 4 Coolness: 6 Longevity: 3
Box office: $338,605,468

15. *Teenage Mutant Ninja Turtles*

One of the most effective comic book-movie-TV-toy synergies ever, the four tortoises named after Renaissance painters began life as a parody of several Marvel Comics characters in a comic published by industry minnows Mirage Studios in 1984. Through a miraculous combination of savvy business dealings and sheer good fortune the characters' creators, Peter Laird and Kevin Eastman, built a merchandising empire peaking with a trilogy of puppet/live-action movies in the early 1990s.

Costume: 3 Coolness: 3 Longevity: 4
Box office: $416,381,410

16. *Hellboy*

Adapted from Mike Mignola's blackly witty books for Dark Horse comics, Hellboy came from apparently nowhere (or, specifically, Hell) to be one of the major genre successes in 2004. Hellboy is a demon adopted by the US military at a young age and employed by them to combat an endless parade of Lovecraftian menaces. Like many of his fans, Hellboy enjoys sugary treats and mild profanity.

Costume: 4 (+6 for the horns) Coolness: 9 Longevity: 1 Box office: $99,318,987

17. *The Punisher*

The Punisher is probably the most plausible of all comics superheroes, being neither 'super' (his only assets being superior marksmanship and hand-to hand fighting skills) nor conventionally 'heroic' (his modus operandi is to summarily execute any criminals he regards as having escaped justice). He is the subject of two feature films – the first a rather generic actioner starring Dolph Lundgren that played like a stylised version of the 'Death Wish' franchise and the second, rather truer to the Marvel canon, where he is portrayed by Thomas Jane. Although neither did stellar box office business it was inevitable that such an easily-evoked character, with such a great costume, will be brought to the screen again and a third beginning to the series will be released in 2008.

Costume: 10 Coolness: 10 Longevity: 2 Box office: $54,700,105

18. *Mystery Men*

Poorly-received on release, but gradually acquiring cult status on DVD, *Mystery Men* is a well-observed but wilfully silly comedy take on superhero archetypes. The team grows through the film from three heroes of marginal competence to a seven-strong squad of limited ability with a script that pokes affectionate fun at a broad range of comic book clichés.

Costume: 5 Coolness: 5 Longevity: 1 Box office: $33,461,000

19. *The Phantom*

Because he was in many ways the original comic book superhero (pioneering the form-fitting costume that has since become the standard) and played on screen by one of Hollywood's most handsome leading men, it's something of a mystery why *The Phantom* was such a disappointment as a movie. Perhaps the period setting, which also weakened audience interest in similarly-themed efforts like *Doc Savage*, *The Shadow*, *The Rocketeer* and *Sky Captain* may be partly to blame: although it must be added that did no harm to the equally pulpy *Indiana Jones* franchise.

Costume: 6 Coolness: 5 Longevity: 1 Box office: $17,300,000

20. *Swamp Thing*

Perhaps the only eco-hero (although of late both Thor and Aquaman have shown leanings in that direction) Swamp Thing is a tragic figure, a scientist forced into a swamp after a chemical explosion, and in some way merged with swamp vegetation to form a hybrid creature with human intelligence, superhuman strength, and really terrible personal grooming. Surely the great groundswell of support for all things green means that time is ripe for a Swamp Thing revival.

Costume: 1 Coolness: 6 Longevity: 2 Box office: $192,816

Iron Man

Armour-plated and bombproof, *Iron Man*, the first comic-book movie hero of the year, leaps off the page

Review by James Christopher, May 1 2008

Iron Man is the first blockbuster movie of the summer, and, despite the topical Taleban atrocities, it's a roaring fairground ride. The director, Jon Favreau, has transformed Stan Lee's 1960s comic strip into a creamy, live-action thriller. The story of a gifted geek who conquers his demons to save the world is a regulation Marvel Inc. fantasy. But the opening scene, showing American soldiers in a battle with Afghan insurgents, is a sour and shocking surprise.

These grim and bloody moments make the film feel older than its 12A years. But the stunts and special effects are a serious joy. The casting of Robert Downey Jr as the playboy hero and inventor of Iron Man is a sublime piece of mischief. Tony Stark is a Molotov cocktail of glamour and scandal, and Downey is all too convincing as the billionaire bachelor. The celebrity arms dealer is as frivolous and mad as Howard Hughes. His ingenious state-of-the-art weapons are the deadly tools that supposedly keep America safe, but he is far more interested in pinching a shapely pair of buttocks.

21 April 2015. Robert Downey Jr attends the European premiere of *Avengers: Age Of Ultron* at the Vue Cinema Westfield, London. (Andrew Sims)

"Are you Leonardo da Vinci, or the Angel of Death?" asks an angry young blonde from *Vanity Fair*. Poor old Gwyneth Paltrow has to sweep these impressionable young journalists out of Tony's water bed the following morning. She is Miss Moneypenny in Tony Stark's empire, and her crush on the hunky charmer has got her nowhere. But despite his flash cars and the pole-dancing stewardesses on his private jet, she knows he has a golden heart.

The film hinges on the fact that Tony is blasted to bits after a weapons demonstration in Afghanistan. He is captured by the Taleban, locked in a cave, and kept alive by an electromagnet (run on a car battery) plugged into his chest that keeps the metal shrapnel from piercing his heart. In his cave he assembles an armoured suit out of old bomb cases. The film's terrific effects kick in when Tony blasts his way to freedom in his bombproof shell suit. He has rockets in his boots, and flame-throwers in his metal wrists. The magical science is the stuff of gadget wonderland. The saving of Tony Stark's soul comes a distant second.

This is where Jeff Bridges's bald and brilliant creep, Obadiah Stane, comes into his own. Stane is Stark's whispering mentor and business partner, who has made a pile out of second-hand neutron bombs. His poisonous and beefy influence is a gripping chill. I enjoyed this film far more than I really meant to. Favreau has done a magnificent job to keep his characters at a cartoon distance, while persuading the audience to believe in them.

Black Panther

This is exactly how you should make the first black superhero movie, says Kevin Maher

February 8 2018

Welcome to Wakanda, tiny fictional east African nation and home to a monarchical ubercivilisation of high-tech tribespeople who use laser-tipped spears, fly anti-gravity spaceships and ride into battle on top of armour-plated rhinoceroses. Oh yes, if you're going to do the first black superhero movie of the modern era, this is how you do it. In for a penny ...

The director Ryan Coogler (*Creed*) and a charismatic cast led by Chadwick Boseman (reprising the role of Black Panther from *Captain America: Civil War*) and Lupita Nyong'o (as secret agent Nakia) turn racial clichés on their head and channel some heavy Shakespearean conflict to create a vivid yarn that's entirely new, frequently startling and, for better and for worse, totally Marvel. The smart move here was to hand over the source material, a 52-year-old comic-book superhero, created by two white guys, Stan Lee and Jack Kirby, to a black director, black writers and a predominantly black cast. They have made a film of serious ideas - third world poverty, social revolution, isolationist foreign policy - and vast cultural scope.

The writers, Coogler and Joe Robert Cole, are as comfortable dropping references to *The Wizard of Oz* as they

8 February 2018. Kevin Coogler (director) and Chadwick Boseman (T'Challa) at the European premiere of *Black Panther*.

are quoting from the 19th-century African-American abolitionist Frederick Douglass (one key character announces that it's better to die a free man than live as a slave). Yet the film nonetheless adheres strictly to the "origins story" template set by its Spandex-clad predecessors Spider-Man, Doctor Strange et al.

Boseman is Wakanda's newly crowned King T'Challa, the catsuited eponymous hero who does regal things by day (flirt with Nyong'o's Nakia, endure ritualistic trials of strength) and has superhero adventures as Black Panther by night. The film establishes its forthright ambitions early, with Black Panther's daring raid on a Nigerian convoy of armed militants who have kidnapped some terrified women and girls (essentially stand-ins for Boko Haram). They are dispatched via Panther's trademark (and only slightly camp) combination of dazzling gymnastics and scratchy claws.

A challenger for the throne appears in the form of angry blood relative Erik Killmonger (Michael B Jordan, stealing the show). Killmonger (what a name!) is introduced to us in London at the, ahem, Museum of Great Britain, where he shoots some security guards, steals an ancient African artefact and lectures a snooty museum guide on the finer points of post-colonial theory (basically, "you stole our stuff, we're taking it back"). Which is important. Because there are several subsequent moments that threaten to creep towards eerie Tarzan kitsch (a tribe of African mountain warriors who mould their appearance, behaviour and vocal patterns on gorillas are especially unsettling). Only the knowledge that this project is, as Killmonger claims, an act of cultural reclamation can stem the sweat of discomfort.

Meanwhile, after a brief tussle with a highly entertaining Andy Serkis, playing a nasty racist from, yup, South Africa (it was either that or Nazi-era Germany), Killmonger makes a violent bid for the throne, setting the stage for a dramatic showdown that will decide the fate of the Black Panther line, Wakanda and, of course, the world.

On the downside, there are some seriously ropey effects. One howler features hundreds of colourful Wakandans gathered dramatically on a cliff face that looks like the opening credit sequence of *The Muppet Show*, and not in a good way, while a midnight "jungle" meet-up appears to have been shot between a couple of potted plants. And, yes, the ending, in the grand tradition of films from *Iron Man* to *Thor: Ragnarok*, is an overlong punch-up between two CGI characters whizzing about in a fully synthetic environment. This is a Marvel movie, after all. Thankfully, it's a good one.

◇◇◇◇◇◇◇◇◇◇◇◇◇◇◇◇◇◇◇◇◇◇◇◇◇◇◇◇◇◇◇◇◇◇◇◇◇

Editor's note: Following the release of *Black Panther*, superheroes occupied four of the top ten slots in the list of all-time highest-grossing films worldwide.

◇◇◇◇◇◇◇◇◇◇◇◇◇◇◇◇◇◇◇◇◇◇◇◇◇◇◇◇◇◇◇◇◇◇◇◇◇

Birdman

Review by Wendy Ide,
January 2 2015

A former action movie star seeking to rejuvenate his stalled career stars as a former action movie star hoping to rejuvenate his stalled career. You can while away long hours trying to work out whether life is imitating art or vice versa in this resounding return to form from Mexican director Alejandro González Iñárritu. But the fact remains that the reason this scalding industry satire works as well as it does is because it has a grounding in some fairly uncomfortable truths about the movie business even as the plot indulges in flights – literally – of fancy.

One wonders if Michael Keaton hesitated when he was offered this role, which has catapulted him back into Hollywood relevance and may even win him an Oscar. It is, after all, a little close for comfort. Keaton, star of *Batman*, *Beetlejuice* and, well, not a lot else of late, plays Riggan, the star of a fictional comic book superhero franchise "Birdman". Job opportunities have withered and fallen off for Riggan, so he is in the process of reinventing himself.

We join him in the run up to the opening night of a self-penned, self-directed Broadway play, in which he also stars. It's a vanity project that is almost as crazy as Riggan himself. The natural monomaniacal self-obsession of the movie star has mutated into something deeper. Riggan imagines himself as a kind of deity, with appropriately destructive powers. He smites his dressing room; fells an overacting co-star. Is it all in his mind? Hard to tell. Suffice to say, the results are real enough. However, so is the voice in his head – the mocking tones of Birdman himself, undermining him at every turn. It's a barnstorming performance from Keaton; he's a toppling dinosaur grappling with the idea of celebrity in the age of social media.

8 February 2015. Michael Keaton attending the EE Baftas at the Royal Opera House in Covent Garden. (Andrew Sims)

ANIMATION: PART ONE

Editor's note: The world was sceptical when Walt Disney announced he was going to make a cartoon that would be as long as a normal, adult, live-action feature film. Cynics scoffed that children would not have the attention span to sit still and follow a single storyline for more than an hour and adults would not want to sit through such a film. They were wrong.

FAIRY TALE AS A FILM

Mr Walt Disney's
Snow White

Grimm Modernized

From Our Own Correspondent,
New York, January 13
Published January 14 1938

The brothers Grimm, who must often deplore the treatment their fairy tales receive in pantomime, would have had their word of praise if they had been present to-day at the Radio City Music Hall, where Mr Walt Disney's first full-length film, *Snow White and the Seven Dwarfs*, made its New York debut.

It is difficult to think of this production as a series of animated cartoons, so skilfully is the spirit of the tale captured and so faithfully is it recorded. Every character is alive and endowed with more character than most actors could possibly convey. *Snow White* is an addition to the ranks of film stars.

Grumpy and Sneezy

Each of the seven dwarfs has his own character and habits, which were described by their names – Doc, Happy, Bashful, Sleepy, Grumpy, Dopey, Sneezy. The Queen combines beauty and wickedness in satisfying fashion, and in disguise makes the best witch imaginable. Of the little animals of the forest, who play an important part throughout the story, need only be said that they are, if anything, more charming than any animals that Mr Disney has devised.

The Grimm tradition has been followed faithfully, with no concessions to modernity – except that a little bird in a fit of exuberance whistles four bars of "Tiger Rag," and the dwarfs impart a somewhat modern tempo to a German folksong. The colour in this film is far more subtle than in Mr Disney's previous productions, and more effective, especially in the backgrounds, which are really impressive. The flight of Snow White through the forest inspires real terror, an emotion which his cartoons hitherto have rarely tried to convey and never succeeded, while the scenes in which the Queen brews the spells for Snow White's destruction are the embodiment of witchcraft, their macabre quality being heightened by small, skilful touches.

Three years to make

The animation throughout is smooth and lifelike, a more remarkable feat when the complexity of some of the scenes with crowds of animals is considered. The synchronization of voices with movement is almost perfect, although some voices already well known to cinema audiences will be heard issuing from the mouths of dwarfs and of the wicked Queen.

Since even fairy tales have a material side nowadays, it may be mentioned that the film cost about $1,500,000 (£300,000) and took three years to make. In all 2,500,000 drawings were made for the film, of which 250,000 were actually used. Some 600 artists, technicians, and others, musicians, and studio workers helped to make the film. For the musical score, which is extremely successful, several special instruments were made, including a kettle-drum which plays four tones higher than any drum formerly in existence.

PERSONAL CHOICE

SPORTS MOVIES, CHOSEN BY MATTHEW SYED

April 2 2016

◇◇◇◇◇◇◇◇◇◇◇◇◇◇◇◇◇◇◇◇◇◇◇◇◇◇◇◇◇◇◇◇

Editor's note: Matthew Syed is a sports journalist and former international table tennis player

◇◇◇◇◇◇◇◇◇◇◇◇◇◇◇◇◇◇◇◇◇◇◇◇◇◇◇◇◇◇◇◇

What makes a great sports movie? The answer is pretty straightforward: one that is not really about sport. If you want great sport, you can see it at the Nou Camp every week and, every now and again, at Old Trafford. You can see it at the All England Club when Rodge or Novak is in town, or at St Andrews when it hosts the Open.

A movie is not, and can never be, sport. The joy of sport is that it is unscripted. We do not know the result when two teams walk onto the pitch, or two players shake hands across the net. With a film, the inverse is true. When we watch a film about Muhammad Ali, we already know the result of each bout before we walk into the theatre.

And that is why in a great movie, sport is merely a prism. It is the vehicle to examine themes that matter most: emotion, love, death, ambition and, in the case of *Jerry Maguire*, money (as in, show me). I love sports films but for different reasons to why I love sport. There is room for both, of course. These movies prove it.

Bend It Like Beckham (2002)

A complete joy, not just because of the struggle of the lead character, Jesminder, to escape the paternalism of her Indian dad, who hates her playing football, but also because of a terrific soundtrack and some wonderful performances.

The Hustler (1961)

Paul Newman plays the youngster who takes on Minnesota Fats in an all-night game of pool, drinks a bottle of bourbon, wins a fortune and then loses it all. The depiction of gambling, exploitation and lost innocence is riveting. The pool is pretty good too.

Raging Bull
(1980)

I once interviewed Jake LaMotta, the homicidal, misogynistic former middle-weight champion, played so searingly by Robert De Niro in this Scorsese masterpiece. The irony is that, at the age of 86, he was even more complex and malevolent in the flesh than in the film.

When We Were Kings
(1996)

It is the combination of reportage, documentary footage and up-to-date interviews with the writer Norman Mailer and the like that make this the definitive portrait of the great icon of 20th-century sport, Muhammad Ali, and the fight, against George Foreman, that will always define him.

Jerry Maguire
(1996)

Tom Cruise is a mesmerising actor, underrated because of his religious views, and this is him at his best as the idealistic agent trying to coax an NFL player (Cuba Gooding Jr) towards authenticity and greatness.

Chariots of Fire
(1981)

A beautiful movie that tells of the rivalry between Eric Liddell and Harold Abrahams as they approach the 1924 Olympics and almost incidentally captures the many ironies in that age of amateurism, chivalry and religious obligation.

BLOCKBUSTERS

Harry Potter and the Philosopher's Stone

Review by Barney Macintyre, aged 6¾

November 5 2001

This is great, the best film I've ever seen, way better than any of the Disney cartoons. The best bit in *Harry Potter* was the Quidditch game, because it was much faster than I imagined it.

I thought Ron Weasley was the funniest kid actor, and I like how he played chess. The best grown-up actor was Hagrid. He was nice and big and funny, a bit like an elephant. The best ghost was Nearly Headless Nick and the way he pulled his head off and it made a squelching noise.

3 November 2001. Kate Muir with her son Barney before a special preview of *Harry Potter and the Philosopher's Stone* at the Odeon, Leicester Square. (Nick Ray)

When Harry went through the wall at Platform 9¾ and suddenly he saw the Hogwarts Express, that was when I got really excited. But there were bits that weren't like how I imagined the book. I thought You-Know-Who would not have a wrinkly face, but a smoother face, and be stern-looking.

Probably this was the scariest movie I've ever seen. The giant chess game was terrifying, and it was frightening when You-Know-Who came out of Quirrell's head. I think this film should only be seen by kids aged 4 and over, but some might still be scared by it. I knew some of the scary bits were coming, like when they went into the library, I knew the horrible head was going to be in that book. I want to see *Harry Potter* again next week, and then I want to see the next film.

4 November 2001. Daniel Radcliffe (Harry Potter) at the world premiere of *Harry Potter and the Philosopher's Stone* at the Odeon, Leicester Square. (Chris Harris)

FIRE UP THE BROOMSTICKS, THIS IS A NEW DIMENSION

Kate Muir sees years of wizardry reach a sensational end

Review by Kate Muir
(Barney's mum), July 8 2011

Harry Potter and the Deathly Hallows: Part 2

★★★★

Hogwarts is falling, its ancient stones raining from a black sky in a storm of orange pyrotechnics. At the same time, the vast edifice of the Potter empire is crashing down too, the end of a story which has held us spellbound for almost 20 hours of wizard cinema. The final instalment, *Deathly Hallows Part 2*, is a bravura duel between good and evil. It's also a cathartic, occasionally clunky nostalgiafest.

Harry, Ron and Hermione, the innocent faces that once munched chocolate frogs on the first Hogwarts Express, are now scarred with the knowledge of darkness. This eighth movie is bloody, and that's not just Ron goofily saying "bloody hell" at regular intervals. Much-loved characters die gruesome deaths, and the sinister atmosphere is aided by shadowy 3D.

Harry and his friends try to avert Armageddon by finding and destroying the enchanted Horcruxes, which empower evil Lord Voldemort. But You-Know-Who is one step ahead, and has possession of one of the Deathly Hallows, the powerful Elder Wand. (You may want to study the book beforehand to keep up.) Even if the magic is a tad perplexing, it is all too clear that Voldemort's armies are gathering like Goth extras from *Braveheart* on the hills above Hogwarts, and doom is imminent.

While Emma Watson has grown into a convincing Hermione, and Daniel Radcliffe is a steadily-improving Harry (except when he makes his squished "Ooh-look-I'm-flying-in-the-wind" face), Rupert Grint as Ron seems to have regressed into some sort of gap-mouthed, doughy yokel. His chemistry with Hermione is non-existent, even when they brave their first damp kiss. Harry's relations with Ginny Weasley are little better. But Harry's real love, as we know, is his mother, who features more prominently than ever in the plot.

The breakout character in this film is the splendidly named Neville Longbottom, who goes from class loser to hero, leading an army against Voldemort and his Death Eaters in the Battle of Hogwarts. His role is proof that ugly hand-knitted jumpers do not maketh the man.

Those child actors grew up in the shadow of the Great Potter Thespians, such as Michael Gambon as Albus Dumbledore, Ralph Fiennes as Voldemort, Alan Rickman as Severus Snape and Maggie Smith as Minerva McGonagall. Even now, the old hands hamming it up for the finale leave Radcliffe and Watson flailing behind. The teenagers are expected to provide naturalism, while the adults are having far too much fun.

Voldemort, with his veined death's head and gills, is weirder than ever, and his deep connection with Harry is shown in increasingly disturbing visions. Small children will be suitably terrified by Voldemort's snake-familiar Nagini, an anaconda with a nasty agenda. The final showdown in the forest between Harry and his nemesis, followed by a heavenly interlude in a whited-out Kings Cross station, and a resurrection, are all more reminiscent of Aslan in Narnia than wicked witches and wizards. J.K. Rowling's magic message is more nuanced than it seems.

It's hard to divorce *Deathly Hallows* from the rest of the Potter canon, but this is a moving, well-crafted end to a British cultural franchise that fired imaginations around the world. Families will race for the multiplex. In the words of many a shrink, we all need closure.

GOODBYE HARRY POTTER, IT'S BEEN MAGIC

Aged 6¾, he reviewed the first film and grew up part of Generation Potter. Ten years on Barney Macintyre explains why the affair had to end

By Barney Macintyre, July 8 2011

My relationship with Harry Potter has lasted more than ten years, and just like a childhood friend I get excited every time he pops up. However, ashamed as I am to say this, I have been neglecting the six-year-old fan in me – and I am sure I am not the only person my age who feels Harry and his world are not as important to me anymore. Is the generation that formed the backbone of the Harry Potter revolution losing interest?

Harry Potter and the Philosopher's Stone was a cornerstone for my reading. If the teacher took down one of the seemingly tome-like novels and handed it to you, that was when you knew you were rolling with the big dogs. From then on I was caught, hook, line and sinker. Soon after book two my obsession also became material. I had to eat the same sweets as Harry, I had to wear a robe and glasses, I had to be the one that played him in computer games. Shampoo potions and broomstick mops haunted our house. Earwax and farm-dirt flavour Bertie Bott's jelly beans and chocolate frogs became a dietary requirement and the cupboard under the stairs my place of residence. Harry Potter became paralleled in many aspects of my life, partly due to the intricately fashioned fantasy world I had read about, and partly just because he was my age.

But my celebration of all things Potter was short-lived. At around 13, after the fourth book, I stopped reading and just started watching. The pubescent Potter was nothing like me, I liked the films for their action and CGI, not the drama and relationships. When the *Twilight* films started coming out in 2008, although not really my kind of thing, I realised they had the potential to usurp the Harry Potter films in the hearts of their teen audience. The themes of sex and death and of course R. Patz himself were more absorbing than the rigmarole of Ron gawping and Harry eventually vanquishing his nemesis, the plastic surgery accident that is He Who Must Not Be Named.

However, it is obvious that J.K. Rowling has tried to adapt. Her writing and ideas have developed and it's all distinctly darker. I respect Rowling's writing for being able to change and develop despite the people worldwide who read her books and perhaps want the same thing again and again. The success of her books and the films are almost certainly due to their universality, even if some of the metaphors are obvious. Everyone wants to be a wizard; everyone understands that the books are an argument for tolerance.

The other day I was idly scrolling down my Facebook homepage when I came across a Facebook group or "like" that I thought exemplified my generation's current love for Harry Potter. It said: "That was some party." – "Dude, you were sitting in my fireplace yelling 'Diagon Alley!'." The joke is, of course, referring to the method of magical transportation known as the Floo network. It showed to me that Generation Potter is still very much spellbound by the books and films we grew up with, even if it's taken with a pinch of irony. As soon as you step into that cinema, you'll watch with all the sincerity, know-how and emotion of a 12-year-old fan. Earlier this year I rented *Deathly Hallows: Part 1* with a friend for a joke – I kid you not that by Dobby's death the floodgates had opened. We both broke down.

Despite my nostalgia, I've grown critical. Once upon a time Harry was just Harry and Ron was Ron, now one is an average actor called Daniel Radcliffe and the other a worse one called Rupert Grint.

Emma Watson is leagues ahead but most of the time it's not her acting I'm concentrating on. Dipping back into the books as well, I now notice the clunky writing and the constant plot twists. The heavy Potter books on my desk look more like building material than literature. Before I would plough through, totally absorbed and unreachable, now I'm ridden with guilt when I think to myself 'Well, I may as well just wait for the film …'

Every year, my anticipation for the film creeps up on me like muscle memory, I can't not get excited. I started listening to the tapes again; the sound of Stephen Fry's voice has an odd effect on me. It just reminds me of the family car, the sweaty car-sick sibling, the service station sandwich which smells so bad you swear it's moving and the surprisingly attentive parents.

Harry Potter has premiered in so many different places in my life. From Leicester Square at the age of 6 and ¾ to my living room sofa at 16, I have watched. I have been on two-hour pilgrimages through the rain to a Welsh fleapit cinema in Builth Wells to watch a fresh-out-the-box Harry Potter film. Nothing beats it. *Prisoner of Azkaban* was always my favourite, both book and film, lots of Quidditch and Hippogriffs.

I came across a signed copy of P of A in my bookshelf yesterday. I plucked it out and opened the first page to find the autographs of Daniel Radcliffe and Emma Watson, from seven years ago. I looked at their infantile writing, the quirky idols of Generation Potter, unlikely dominators of a decade.

Any offers? (I wouldn't sell that book for anything.)

PEOPLE

EMMA WATSON ON HER BOOK CLUB, SEX SCENES AND THE NEW HERMIONE

Will the British actress ever shake off her *Harry Potter* character? She's trying her best

By Kate Muir, July 2 2016

4 November 2001. Emma Watson (Hermione Granger) arrives at the premiere of *Harry Potter and the Philosopher's Stone.* (Gill Allen)

Here in a suite in the Corinthia Hotel in central London is Emma Watson; wearing a black Alexander McQueen dress with a whiff of S&M about the belt, she is here to discuss her latest project, a true-life thriller set in a cult in Chile during the Pinochet dictatorship. It shouts "serious cinema", another step in the carefully curated career of the girl known to the world for ever as Hermione Granger in the *Harry Potter* films.

Watson is now a woman of many parts – a UN goodwill ambassador, a founder of the equality campaign HeForShe and a feminist book club, and a model for Burberry and Lancôme. She has recently been inducted into the Oscar voting academy, and has also been rock-solid in her support for the black actress who is playing the grown-up Hermione on the West End stage in *Harry Potter and the Cursed Child*.

I first spoke to her with Daniel Radcliffe and Rupert Grint at Leavesden studios for *Harry Potter and the Prisoner of Azkaban*. Watson was 14, scruffy, jokey and direct, and talked about how much she liked Crookshanks, her stage cat.

Later I met her at 19 on the set of the final Potter film, when all she wanted to discuss was English literature before she headed off to Brown University in America.

Today the topic is Colonia Dignidad, a closed cult run by a Nazi German evangelist, which helped with the detention and torture of victims of the Chilean dictator Augusto Pinochet. In the film *The Colony*, set in 1973, Watson plays Lena, an air stewardess who goes undercover to join the cult and find her German boyfriend Daniel (Daniel Brühl, star of *Rush* and *Inglourious Basterds*), who has been kidnapped.

Watson's previous post-Potter films, such as *My Week with Marilyn*, *The Perks of Being a Wallflower* and *The Bling Ring*, were decidedly lighter in tone –

31 March 2014. Emma Watson arrives for the premiere of *Noah* in Leicester Square. (David Bebber)

or sillier if we include *Noah* and the comedy-disaster *This is the End.* "We're definitely not in rom-com territory with *The Colony* – not that there's anything wrong with rom-coms," she says. "I hadn't been offered anything like that, so it was nice, and about a piece of history that I knew nothing about and was fascinated by."

Take the trailer for *The Colony*, released a few days before our interview, and made much of online in *The Daily Mail's* "sidebar of shame". "Emma Watson indulges in passionate display with Daniel Brühl as they roll around on the bed in new trailer for dark thriller," was the headline. In fact, Watson gives a powerful, brave performance as an ordinary woman forced to commit extraordinary acts of sacrifice. "Steamy!" continued that paper. "How far she's come since her younger days as she puts on a magnificent display in the teaser." There's a nasty schoolgirl-gets-naked tone to it all.

"Three and half seconds of nude pictures which were not particularly risqué," she says, frowning. "It's deeply irritating." Then she pulls back, perhaps imagining the quote as a headline. "Well. Hang on. Actually no. Let me retract that. I think I used to find it more irritating than I find it now. I used to put a lot more value and a lot more weight on these things but I don't know if it's time or experience or just having been in there long enough, but it does irritate me. Silliness is all it is. You have to accept that there will always be a certain portion of the media who will want to sensationalise and pigeon-hole me in a certain way."

She sighs. "I'm 25 now. I've been in 15 films in total and me kissing somebody else shouldn't be risqué or horrifying, but I think that will continue for a long time. There have been lots of advantages to being part of that franchise, and playing that role for a long time, but inevitably there are obstacles and that's one of them." She pauses. "But you just go, ach, whatever. Ultimately it doesn't seem to be coming in the way of me getting other work."

Unlike many young actors, money is not a worry, with an estimated £24 million paid from *Potter*. (Well, that's the sum Grint is telling the taxman that he earned.) Thus she decided to take a year off from acting in 2016 to concentrate on setting up an online feminist book group – and to enjoy just hanging out in London. The club is called Our Shared Shelf, and her first choice is *My Life on the Road* by Gloria Steinem.

When it comes to women's rights, Watson is a crusader; her Twitter feed is an example to young women, and she recently urged them to sign up and vote in the EU referendum. This year, she interviewed Steinem for 90 minutes on stage, discussing feminism in all its forms. "We should be creating lots of awesome, great alternatives to pornography," said the actress. Watson also discussed a website that uses scientific and academic research to better understand female sexuality, which has the orgasmic title of OMGYES.

Watson's own emotional life is largely kept under wraps. She was born in France to two English lawyers, but returned to Oxford aged five to live with her divorced mother and spent weekends with her father in London. The Oxford link stayed, however; she dated Oxford student Will Adamowicz at university in America, and later Oxford rugby player Matthew Janney. This year she has dated the tech entrepreneur William Mack Knight.

Part of her still likes a touch of childish fantasy and it sounds as though playing a somewhat feminist Belle with Dan Stevens as the Beast, was a delight. "Frankly I couldn't do another thriller after *The Colony* – I'm joking that my nerves were in pieces, but I didn't want to do another edge-of-your-seat thing for a while, so *Beauty* did seem to be a perfect antidote, unapologetically romantic, optimistic and joyful. Singing and dancing teacups was exactly what I needed."

CULT MOVIES

TOP 100 CULT FILMS

By Nick Lezard and Joe Joseph,
published in four parts in
November and October 1995

Cult films do not exist to be seen. They exist to be seen again. The fifth visit is better than the fourth, the fourth better than the third, the first visit being something of an annoying precursor to the thrill of re-experience. The cult film par excellence is the one that brings in crowds for whom the cinema is not their first and only love. It gathers audiences for whom this film answers some deep, troubled need. Cult films are often appreciated by virtue of their defiance of conventional taste. The following subjects, preferably in combination, will almost guarantee cult status: drugs, rock 'n' roll, rebellion, unorthodox sexuality.

100. *West Side Story* (1961)

It's one of those triumphs of Shakespeare's timeless artistry that a play of his – in this case it happens to be *Romeo and Juliet* – can be adapted, shorn of its delicate poetry, crammed full of wham-bam songs, peppered with dance routines, set in an age too distant for Willy to have imagined, acted in an urban New York jungle he could never have envisaged, and portrayed by actors he'd never heard of, and still the original be miles better. But let's not carp. As musicals go, *West Side Story* is a peach. Leonard Bernstein's score shows that melodies in a hit musical need not be ho-hum and syrupy (no names mentioned). And while Sondheim's book may not be his best, his lyrics for 'America', 'Maria' and 'Gee, Officer Krupke' are snappy enough to keep the songs memorable.

99. *Sunset Boulevard* (1950)

Billy Wilder had been a gigolo in Berlin to supplement his income as a youthful journalist. Maybe that's how he came up with William Holden's character as struggling screenwriter Joe Gillis, whom Gloria Swanson – faded star of silent movies – sucks into her fantasy world as her kept lover. Wilder makes his black comedy even blacker by showing us Swanson, as Norma Desmond, watching Erich von Stroheim's *Queen Kelly* – the epic disaster that effectively did for both Swanson's and von Stroheim's careers in real life – and by casting von Stroheim as Norma Desmond's major-domo Max. It is a delicious irony that, in portraying the anguish of her real-life demise as the silent movie queen, Swanson gives the performance of her life. "You bastard!" Louis B Mayer, MGM's boss, yelled at Wilder after seeing the film at a private screening. "You have disgraced the industry that made you and fed you. You should be tarred and feathered and run out of Hollywood."

98. *Edward Scissorhands* (1990)

Rarely does Hollywood produce something so heart-warmingly tender, funny, original, Gothic, romantic, endearing and quietly satirical without stirring eight tablespoons of throat-choking schmaltz into the mixture. Tim Burton brings together the icon of suburban America – in Dianne Wiest's sweet, ding-donging Avon Lady – and creative unconformity in the shape of Johnny Depp's Edward Scissorhands. The denizens of Day-Glo, picket-fence, Fifties Middle America soon learn not to let Edward loose on their Lilos, but the genial boy makes a splash among the locals with his talent for topiary, cutting hair and trimming pet poodles. But conformists can only take so much non-conformity and the scissor-encrusted hands that were once so thrilling soon seem threatening, producing a tragic tale of innocence corrupted.

97. *Dead of Night* (1945)

The apogee of the country-house ghost film, a round robin of mostly excellent spook stories written by, among others, H.G. Wells and EF Benson. The palm goes to Michael Redgrave and his portrayal of a ventriloquist possessed by his dummy – resonant enough to have been subject to a slightly shabby remake, starring Anthony Hopkins, 30-odd years later.

96. *Hellzapoppin'* (1942)

Certainly not a cult film at the time – everyone saw it – but cherished now by people who want to take a trip back in time to the Forties. A skit on the "let's-put-on-the-show-right-here" film-making kit, and, we gently propose, an example of proto-Pythonesque humour, the kind of thing we like to kid ourselves the Americans can't do.

95. *Gilda* (1946)

How to deal with impotence and perversion when the Hays Code is at its strongest? Easy. Well, not easy, but this is a triumph of suggestiveness, the kind of film that gives censors hives because the most lurid and lubricious details are left to our imaginations. This is mostly a matter of shooting everything through blinds, but Rita Hayworth's striptease is one of the medium's tours de force, a languorous and devastatingly erotic scene where everyone gets hot under the collar but all she has removed, it turns out, are her elbow-length gloves. We have to have a cold shower even thinking about it.

94. *Gold Diggers of 1933* (1933)

Busby Berkeley took over the formula started with *Gold Diggers of Broadway* and, so it appears as the years have gone by, went bonkers. Ginger Rogers wearing a monocle, fine, but Ginger singing 'We're in the Money' backwards? Was this meant to be an ironic comment on the fact that, in the depths of the Depression, no one was in the money? We doubt it. It shows instead what the human brain is capable of without LSD.

93. *Once Upon a Time in America* (1984)

Having cut his cinematic teeth as an assistant to various Italian and American film directors who came to work in Italy, and then learnt to chew on strongly sauced spaghetti westerns such as *A Fistful of Dollars, For a Few Dollars More* and *The Good, the Bad and the Ugly*, Sergio Leone sharpened his dentures on *Once Upon a Time in America*, cataloguing half a century in the lives of a fistful of New York gangsters. Squeezing so many years into four hours – and still allowing Robert De Niro plenty of opportunities to go through his Lee Strasberg repertoire of smirks, stares, grimaces, anger, anguish, grins and guffaws – might seem triumph enough. But it was still too long for the Hollywood studio that financed it. The cut version ("butchered" was how Leone saw it) was released in America to audience confusion and tepid critical applause. Fortunately, the full version was screened in Europe.

92. *Vertigo* (1958)

Vertigo is fascinating not just because of plot, suspense, Jimmy Stewart's mesmerising performance and Kim Novak's mesmerising beauty, but because it tells you more about Alfred Hitchcock's fetishistic subconscious than you probably care to know. Trustworthy, kindly Stewart – whose role in *Vertigo*, according to Hitchcock, is that of a man who "wants to go to bed with a woman who's dead; he's indulging in a form of necrophilia" – is the perfect fulcrum for Hitchcock's finest movie as he struggles and blinks his way towards unravelling the murderous trick that his friend has played on him. Novak plays a double role: first the friend's unstable wife with whom Stewart falls in love and who he believes has fallen to her death from a church bell-tower; and later the shop girl that an emotionally confused Stewart recreates in the image of the "dead woman". The climax, when Stewart has sussed how he has been manipulated, is pure Hitchcock.

91. *The Exterminating Angel* (1962)

Age did not wither Bunuel's wonderfully warped way of looking at the world. *The Exterminating Angel* was one of the Spanish director's later films, but the lineage can be traced clearly to his 1930 masterpiece *L'Age d'Or*, where he served notice on anyone in the Church, the Establishment, or in the grip of middle-class morality that, well, he wasn't awfully keen on. Fast-forward to 1962, and to *Exterminating Angel*: here we are, a bunch of rich diners, suddenly and mysteriously unable to leave our host's house. Left for a few weeks to our own devices and morals, we descend into barbarism, bone-chewing, bestiality and even toy with cannibalism. Oh yes, and a bear and a flock of sheep stroll into the scene half-way through the movie.

90. *Fantastic Voyage* (1966)

A team of medics, and Raquel Welch, is miniaturised and sent into a scientist's bloodstream in order to remove a blood clot from his brain. A testament not so much to our capacity to suspend disbelief as to take it into a dark alley and shoot it. A kitsch classic and proof, were it needed, that Hollywood can dumb down even the most off-the-wall ideas, as long as it is given a large enough special-effects budget. Watch out for the attack of the killer antibodies.

89. *Melvin and Howard* (1980)

Jonathan Demme's version of the apocryphal story of an ordinary guy picking up a hitchhiking Howard Hughes is almost too good to make it into this list, but for its relative obscurity. (Had *Something Wild* been seen by virtually no one, that would have qualified instead. As it is, he makes cult films that everyone now goes to see.) A curio, then, but not a trashy one: it cunningly makes us identify with the possibility that something extraordinary can happen to the most mundane of us – and that no one will believe us when it does.

88. *La Belle et la Bête* (1945)

Too clever by far more than half, Cocteau's fluency in hitherto exclusive art forms makes him an object of mixed suspicion and respect: he infuriatingly escapes being the sole property of art, poetry, fiction or cinema. He set out to be his own cult, and it would be churlish here not to acknowledge his success. A charmingly literal, almost matter-of-fact, retelling of the old fable (Greta Garbo, after seeing the film, said: "Give me back my beast"), which, like most of Cocteau's films, brings poetry to the screen; and who among a cult audience does not like to feel like a *poet de temps en temps*.

87. *Fitzcarraldo* (1982)

"Fetch the special-effects computer technicians!" is not a command that slips readily from Werner Herzog's lips. If the script says you've got to haul a steamship over a murderous mountain range, then he reckons you just gotta do it. Herzog likes grandiose themes and likes to execute them grandiosely. But in *Fitzcarraldo* the combination of an obsessive director making a movie about an obsessive Irish adventurer who has got it into his head to bring opera to the Amazon almost proved too grandiose for everyone. Every mishap that could have happened happened. Usually twice. The movie was three years in preparation and another nine months in shooting. They were all lucky to come out of it alive. *Fitzcarraldo* won Herzog the Best Director Award at Cannes and there is no doubt that, given the dispiriting and life-threatening filming conditions, the smooth, lyrical beauty of the finished film is a testament to Herzog's professionalism. Or is it his pottiness?

86. *Nashville* (1975)

Robert Altman's relationship with Hollywood has been like a rumbustious marriage: periods of harmony and bliss are interspersed with long spells when the partners communicate by messages left on the fridge door. *Nashville* marked one of Altman's returns to the marital bed. The swarms who gather in Nashville, Tennessee, for presidential candidate Hal Phillip Walker's country music rally are an expertly crafted mosaic of men and women scarred or tainted by despair, loneliness, greed, arrogance, inarticulacy, ambition and silly, irritating habits. Keith Carradine, as singer Tom Frank, tups the film's female population as methodically as a ram let into a field full of ewes before crooning the hit song 'I'm Easy'. Geraldine Chaplin's cocky BBC reporter is more grating than a Magimix. Lily Tomlin, who plays gospel singer Linnea Reese, is launched into the Hollywood big league. All human life is here, including walk-on parts for such celebrities as Elliott Gould and Julie Christie, guesting in the demanding roles of Elliott Gould and Julie Christie.

85. *Fellini Satyricon* (1969)

Either a masterpiece or a mess, depending on how highly you rate *Fellini*, how strongly you think of *Petronius* – from whom *Fellini* has borrowed a title and a loose frame-work of episodes that don't really build into a coherent narrative – and how much you had to drink before settling down to follow the exploits of Martin Potter. Potter is the pretty young student who steps into a fantastical, freakish and debauched Ancient Rome. He finds that Ancient Romans, lacking a belief in God, were tireless in inventing other pastimes to keep themselves busy on their day of rest – pastimes which, today, would be either illegal or very expensive.

84. *Straw Dogs* (1972)

The gratuitous gore in Sam Peckinpah's movies is only there, says Peckinpah, as an expression of his quest for a better world. *Straw Dogs* certainly puts you off packing up the London house and moving to Cornwall if this is how the neighbours are going to treat you – even if the up-side is spending your life with Susan George. (Obviously, many women might not find the prospect of moving in with Dustin Hoffman adequate compensation for being terrorised by murderous, drunken Cornish hoodlums who have run out of sheep to harass.) Peckinpah's theory is that life is hard, and then you die; so maybe it's best to get in the first shot (or mantrap, depending on what armoury you happen to have handy).

83. *Shirley Valentine* (1989)

Cult audiences do not consist entirely of youngish males who have problems sustaining meaningful relationships. They also consist of people who identify with Pauline Collins and long to have a fling with a Greek waiter who looks like Tom Conti. This is frisky subversiveness for run-down women with a hankering for adventure (Willy Russell, who adapted his own play, knows how to target a socio-economic sector), and the title has entered the collective consciousness.

82. *Planet of the Apes* (1968)

A project at least two removes from H.G. Wells's *The Time Machine*, via Pierre Boulle's novel *Monkey Planet*. We love the idea of implausibly distant futures, where the years reach numbers otherwise only seen on the odometers of Model Ts, and also the idea of Charlton Heston fleeing both lobotomy and castration – fates which, you might think, he has either undergone or deserves. Its numerous sequels and spin-offs are proof that Hollywood could not quite believe its luck in having fluked such a winner.

81. *Jacob's Ladder* (1990)

A film which has had more critical obloquy heaped upon it than any other directed by Adrian Lyne (*Flashdance*, *9½ Weeks*, *Fatal Attraction*, etc.): it is, though, his best, and is kept alive by a hard core of fans who accept the notion that Tim Robbins's memories are not in fact genuine, but the result of some ghastly CIA brain-frying plot, and that his whole post-Vietnam life is, in truth, his death reverie.

80. *Network* (1976)

Maybe it's true that Sidney Lumet doesn't know whether his film is really about middle-age crisis or a satire on the ratings-obsessed broadcasting industry, or a mish-mash of both; but at least now when we poke our heads out of our bedroom windows at night and scream that "we're mad as hell and we're not going to take it any more", our neighbours no longer look on us as loonies, but as sophisticated film buffs, gripped by a midnight desire to share a cultural film reference with the rest of the street.

79. *The Hunger* (1983)

Glib and facile, like nearly everything directed by ex-adman Tony Scott; and, also like the rest of his work, furiously convinced by its own sense of integrity. Its rules are silly (portentous synthesised rock score, tacit confidence in David Bowie's acting ability), but it obeys them. Like many cult films, best appreciated by dope-smokers, who see this updated vampire film as an allegory of undying love. Plus Catherine Deneuve (actually, alas, her body double) and Susan Sarandon in a lesbian sex scene, and David Bowie ageing 50 years in a hospital waiting room.

78. *The Man with the Golden Arm* (1956)

Daring, for its time, portrayal of heroin addiction, and it is its palpable giddiness at tackling a serious subject seriously that edges it over into unwitting camp. Sinatra's best performance ever, though – he was not so good in a better film, *The Manchurian Candidate*, here disqualified by its belated entry into the respectable canon – played with a courage that redounds to his credit. Watch out for that withdrawal scene.

77. *Jubilee* (1978)

Possibly Jarman's silliest film, although one of his most watchable, in which we are invited to take seriously the notion that such an aesthete can maintain a credible posture as a punk (and that Toyah Wilcox qualifies as one, too). *Mise en scène*: Queen Elizabeth I is transported to contemporary Britain by her astrologer and sets up a hysterically gloomy state-of-the-nation address.

76. *How I Won the War* (1967)

Although set in the Second World War, this film exudes so much Sixties atmosphere that you can virtually hear a brand-new Mini parping outside your door. The main reason for this is the presence of John Lennon, playing a baffled Tommy in his NHS specs, under the command of a gung-ho Michael Crawford. Director Richard Lester had worked with Lennon on *A Hard Day's Night* and *Help!*, of course, and if critics decided that his career was on a downward slide, implying that WW2 was a Bad Thing refreshed iconoclasts but made everyone else uneasy. Lennon, not too bad an actor considering, never took his glasses off after this, giving succour to spectacle-wearers around the world and setting a trend that continues to this day.

75. *Double Indemnity* (1944)

Often copied, frequently imitated, Billy Wilder's original has never been bettered: none of its ho-hum successors matched its steaminess, its suspense or Barbara Stanwyck's sly, manipulative sexiness as Phyllis Dietrichson, who plotted her husband's murder to cash in on his life insurance policy. The movie put Wilder on the Hollywood map with his first box-office hit. And it allowed the world to see that Fred MacMurray, who narrates the story as a flashback with the head-shaking anguish of someone who cannot believe he has strolled so blindly into Stanwyck's trap, was a masterful actor before he sank into a comfortable old age of playing sitcom fathers pulling faces at his young sons' pranks and pratfalls.

74. *Celine et Julie Vont en Bateau* (1974)

Watching this film, loosely based on a Henry James story, about two girls who recreate the scene of a murder by sucking on boiled sweets (don't ask; it is a tantalising mixture of the utterly pedestrian and the utterly strange) makes unusual demands on its audience, and to love it is to feel that one has entered the ranks of an elite.

73. *Yellow Submarine* (1968)

Subverting the traditional formula of issuing the soundtrack of a successful movie, *Yellow Submarine* is the film of the songs. Very soon we will all be able to sit at our computers and watch videos, listen to soundtracks, become interactive with our CDi, surf the Internet and talk to chums in Chattanooga. So think of *Yellow Submarine* as a multi-media experience 30 years ahead of its time. Using caricatures of the Fab Four and "groovy" pop-art animation, director George H Dunning weaves – OK, then, Copydexes – together a story that happens, luckily, to offer a home to a variety of Beatles songs. Watching *Yellow Submarine* is the only occasion on which it is still socially acceptable to say, "Oh like, wow, man!"

72. *Dance of the Vampires* (1967)

You have to hand it to Roman Polanski: he has a way with bad taste. Unfortunately, that way often involves making us wonder whether his bad taste is in earnest or offered as a joke. Still, the idea of a Jewish vampire laughing off the crucifix waved in his face remains a great one, and how can we fail to be amused by a film whose alternative title is *The Fearless Vampire Killers, or Pardon Me, But Your Teeth Are In My Neck!*

71. *Mad Max* (1980)

Until *Mad Max* came along, Australian films were all *Picnic at Hanging Rock*, and Mel Gibson had only ever been seen in *Summer City*, a low-budget surf movie in which he played a blue-eyed beach bum out for a good time. Then all of a sudden, Gibson is launched into the Hollywood league with this futuristic action movie, where he plays a blue-eyed ex-cop who sees his wife and children killed, which makes him sort of mad. So mad that he seeks revenge, *Death-Wish*-style, against the psychopathic gangland bikers who now range across a dehumanised landscape of battle-scarred motorways. Gibson is no Rambo and has enough doubts, fears, grief and panic to make Max Rockatansky a complex enough cult character to feed the plots of two sequels.

70. *Cape Fear* (1962)

Had Scorsese not reminded us of this film in an uncharacteristically ill-judged remake, this would have made it into the top 20. What an astonishingly sick film it is, though. Gregory Peck becomes a punch-bag for Robert Mitchum's old lag, seething with a grudge against his ex-lawyer, and as for Mitchum's erotic teasing of Peck's underage daughter...

22 June 1984. Robert Mitchum. (John Voos)

69. *Koyaanisqatsi* (1983)

One of the worst films ever made, it consists entirely of panoramas of urban and rural America, filmed with time-lapse photography, and a soundtrack by Philip Glass. And that's it. It looks impressive for the first three minutes but the amount of marijuana needed to make the rest of this film rewarding is more than can actually be ingested during its course.

68. *One Million Years BC* (1966)

The Surrealists may have given us the fur-covered teacup, but it was Hammer Films that gave us the fur-covered D-Cup. Strangely, the people who watch this movie come away less perplexed by the historical inaccuracy of humans co-existing with dinosaurs than by how prehistoric man found an underwired bra for Raquel Welch a million years before Playtex was even founded. The special effects are as special as they come. It took four script-writers to come up with the screenplay, which consists almost entirely of grunts.

67. *The Night Porter* (1974)

Some found it sick, tawdry or degrading. Some found it *Last Tango in Paris* for sadomasochists. And maybe without the brilliant Dirk Bogarde in the role of the former Nazi concentration camp torturer and Charlotte Rampling as the victim he sexually exploited, Liliana Cavani's film might have been disturbing in a completely different way. As it is, the rekindled sexual relationship that develops between Bogarde, who has found work as a hotel night porter after escaping conviction for war crimes, and Rampling, who runs into him by chance in Vienna a dozen years after the war, is haunting and harrowing. Not many jokes, though.

66. *Invasion of the Body Snatchers*

Which version do you want? 1956 or 1978? Or 1995?

A beautiful original premise, which we surely do not have to re-elaborate here. The first is one of the best sci-fi films ever made, but all versions are culty because they imply that we alone retain our humanity in a world of characterless zombies. Most films with Donald Sutherland are culty to some degree, and in the 1978 remake he gets to make that horrible screechy roar that director Phil Kaufman got the Body Snatchers to make. Whoops! Gave the ending away.

65. *The Damned* (1969)

Made with deadly seriousness by Luchino Visconti, but now something of a camp classic. It's about the rise of the Nazis, you see, so cue: impersonations of Dietrich, announcements such as "in Berlin, the Reichstag is burning", silly green lights playing over people's faces by way of explanation of the evils of National Socialism, the massacre of the Brown Shirts depicted as if it were free-for-all night upstairs at Heaven, and, naturally, a typical portrayal of strangled dignity from Dirk Bogarde.

64. *Superstar: The Karen Carpenter Story* (1987)

The story of the life and death, from anorexia, of the Carpenters' drummer by Todd Haynes, who could be described as something of a maverick. Its two and only stars are Ken and Barbie dolls. Unsurprisingly, the Carpenters' lawyers went nuts and the film was banned, the excuse being unauthorised use of Carpenters songs. So you'll be lucky if you ever see it.

63: *The Evil Dead* (1980)

It had to sit around, guiltily, in a vault somewhere for three years before it was released, and became the film that everyone meant when they used the term "video nasty". This is what has conferred it cult status, and not the plot, which is pretty much the routine story of college students being possessed by evil entities and going berserk with white contact lenses. Someone does get raped by a tree, though, which is pretty imaginative.

62. *Badlands* (1973)

Forget *Natural Born Killers*. Or bear it in mind while watching Martin Sheen and his 15-year-old girlfriend Sissy Spacek (actually 24 when the film was made, but you wouldn't have guessed it) go on a killing spree in South Dakota. Had director Terrence Malick made it less intelligently (even Halliwell gives it three stars, for goodness sake) it would have shot up the list. An astonishing directorial debut, with further cult points being awarded for (a) Malick's subsequent Howard Hughes-like reclusiveness and (b) the fact that he was born in Waco, Texas.

61. *A Touch of Evil* (1958)

A film that draws as much from behind the camera as represents what's in front of it: a blowsy Marlene Dietrich plays a blowsy Marlene Dietrich, delivering the memorably understated line "You're a mess, honey" to a corrupt, piggish

Orson Welles (played by a corrupt, pig-gish Orson Welles). It spins on an axis of self-loathing, and as such has delighted nihilists and cynics ever since.

60. *The Outlaw* (1943)

What we recall is not so much the plot, in which Pat Garrett, Billy the Kid and Doc Holliday fight for the atten-tions of a half-caste beauty, played by Jane Russell with a dab of boot-polish, but the fact that it was co-directed by Howard Hawks and Howard Hughes, the latter using his knowledge of aero-dynamics to design Jane Russell's bra. (We remember that lingering pose of her embonpoint in the barn to this day.) Also one of the first films to portray homosexuality in anything other than a lurid, horrified light; and not too bad a film, either.

59. *The Masque of the Red Death* (1964)

Does it tell us something about our times that Roger Corman, one of the most influential discoverers of new talent (Scorsese, Coppola, Demme, Bogdanovich) was also a churner-out of B-movie hokum made in three weeks for the cost of a package holiday? Yes, but it is great hokum. We select this as representative, the story of Vincent Price as an Italian prince worship-ping the devil while the plague rages outside his castle walls … until Death comes for the pay-off. Cult points for spotting Jane Asher and noticing that the photographer was a 36-year-old Nicolas Roeg.

58. *The Last Wave* (1977)

Eco-guilt has been around for longer than we might think, and this, from Peter Weir, is its advance guard. Here the white man's guilt is the desecra-tion of the Aborigines: this has made us forget what our dreams are ("a dream," explains one Aborigine, "is the shadow of something real"), which means that we are about to drown in a huge flood. So heavy that you wonder how a camera can be robust enough to hold the film, although the water gushing from Richard Chamberlain's car radio is pretty spooky.

57. *Get Carter* (1971)

It is hard to imagine that Michael Caine ever struggled to find film work or that he did not get his big break (in *Zulu*) until he was 30, an age at which modern screen stars have already retired and made a comeback, published a ghost-written autobiography and appeared naked on the cover of *Vanity Fair*. By becoming a success on his own terms – without dropping his cock-ney accent or abandoning his south London roots – Caine opened doors for a new generation of not-so-posh British actors. Many fail to appreciate how hard he works at his fluid perfor-mances. Playing the role of a gangster who wades through a world of por-nography, big-time gambling, drugs and brutal mob violence in his mission to exact revenge for his brother's murder, Caine transforms *Get Carter* from a routine crime action movie into a pacy, high-class thriller.

56. *The Harder They Come* (1973)

The original bad-ass gangsta film, a sort of Jamaican mixture of *A Star is Born* and *Scarface*, with Jimmy Cliff as the reggae singer who makes it to the top by becoming one of Jamaica's Most Wanted. Production values are engagingly primitive – it looks as though it was filmed with a tape recorder – but check out the tunes, the threads, and the ganja.

55. *Harold and Maude* (1971)

The *ne plus ultra* of teen-angst movies. Harold is the rich, pasty-faced teenager who spends all his time trying to kill himself until redeemed by the love of a 79-year-old Ruth Gordon. Yes, and they do It. A relentless parade of bad taste with a soft centre. One 22-year-old said that he'd seen it 138 times.

54. *M* (1931)

Many modern film-makers, who routinely turn already grisly murder scenes into close-up forensic autopsies, might snigger at Fritz Lang's discretion with the camera. But, by leaving us to imagine how the serial child murderer (played by Peter Lorre) might have dispensed with his victims, Lang knows that we will conjure up far more cringing images than his cameras could ever have painted. He also manages to make us feel enough sympathy for Lorre to turn the film into a moving tragedy. But this dark and pessimistic film is also lit by surprising flashes of humour. Lang compared his films to "the loveliest German fairy tales" which, as they progress, take on "an enormous amount of brutality, of cruelty and crime". Lang's first stab at using sound is also a triumph, helping to underscore the film's tension and its atmosphere of fear and menace. Lang's masterwork.

53. *Fritz the Cat* (1972)

A translation of Robert Crumb's feline anti-hero onto the screen and, it has to be admitted, something of a travesty of the original. Still, it gave writer, animator and director Ralph Bakshi the chance to portray more sex and drugs than had been seen legitimately on the screen before. Rarely shown, so even having a ticket for it is a cult experience in itself.

52. *Forbidden Planet* (1956)

Based, as any fule kno, on Shakespeare's *The Tempest*, and still culty despite screenings organised by desperate teachers trying to work up pupils' interest in the Bard. But what the cultist wants is not so much its mixture of Shakespeare and Freud, but their wackily successful grafting on to the sci-fi genre, and, more importantly, the first appearance of Robbie the Robot, the only goldfish bowl with revolving metal ears ever to get his own TV series (*Lost in Space*). Funny to think that director Fred Wilcox started off directing *Lassie* movies.

51. *Mildred Pierce* (1945)

Joan Crawford sacrifices everything to build up a restaurant chain, only to have her daughter, played by the 17-year-old Ann Blyth, ruin everything, bonking the man she was after and letting Mom take the rap for his murder. A big hit at the time, but it re-enters the cult canon by virtue of forming the basis for the Joan Crawford story of *Mommie Dearest* (see later) and inspiring the eponymous song by New York art-punk band Sonic Youth.

50. *Dark Star* (1974)

The funniest intentionally funny film about space ever made, not that there have been that many. John Carpenter, in his first feature, speculates on the fortunes of the crew of a ship sent out to destroy unstable stars; bored and fractious, the only alien life form they've met is a dim orange plastic beach ball with large feet. One of their smart bombs gets a little too smart, quotes Descartes and blows them all up. A deliberate mauling of *2001*.

49. *Cool Hand Luke* (1967)

With outstanding performances from Paul Newman and George Kennedy, a witty script and classy camerawork, *Cool Hand Luke* was something of a period piece until a few months ago: that was when prison authorities in Alabama were struck by a spasm of nostalgia and decided to bring back the reviled chain gang.

48. *Scarface* (1983)

No, not the original – everyone is automatically obliged to see that and like it. But this remake, almost a straight lift, vilified by critics, adored by those who risked contumely in seeing it, has the most over-the-top performance of Al Pacino's career (among some formidable competition), memorable dialogue ("dis town's like one great pussy waiting to get f★★★★★"), the largest pile of cocaine that anyone ever parked their hooter in, and a final shoot-out that is so deranged and bloody it's actually funny. Brian de Palma directed it, then disowned it.

47. *Madchen in Uniform* (1931)

Those who think this film's title has something to do with its inclusion here have a point. But although it might make you think of some sub-pornographic account of the trials of Nazi life, it is in fact a sensitive and well-made portrayal of a soul crushed under the discipline of a Prussian boarding school. One of only two films directed by Leontine Sagan, a woman who must have had some guts to make such a film in Germany at such a time. Yes, there is a lesbian theme, but it's handled intelligently, and sympathetically.

46. *Peeping Tom* (1960)

A young, disturbed cameraman murders his victims with the sharpened leg of his tripod while filming them. They can see themselves being killed in the reflection of a strategically placed mirror. We can see them through the viewfinder, making voyeurs of us all. In his autobiography, Michael Powell filled two pages with some of the critical outrage *Peeping Tom* attracted. "It's a long time since a film disgusted me as much," Caroline Lejeune told readers of *The Observer*. "The sickest and filthiest film I remember seeing," was Isobel Quigley's verdict in *The Spectator*. Powell was rather taken aback: "I was genuinely surprised by the vicious reaction," he said many years later, having spent a couple of lonely decades being shunned by a disgusted British film industry.

45. *Altered States* (1980)

Writer Paddy Chayevsky asked to have his name removed from the credits after seeing this; what, you might wonder, did he expect? You don't make a film with Ken Russell and hope to emerge unscathed. However, Russell, who could be said to be his own worst enemy were there not thousands of others eager to claim that distinction, did not make too bad a job of this, as the premise – that if William Hurt takes loads of drugs and suspends himself in an isolation tank, he turns into a monkey – is so far out that he cannot perform his usual trick of making pedestrian subjects outlandish. It is a good, creepy drug film, and therefore automatically included here.

44. *Solaris* (1972)

The day will come when Tarkovsky's films are prescribed for insomniacs by holistic doctors. At nearly three hours long, this is one of his snappiest little jaunts. A broody sci-fi number with political overtones – it's about a planet which can make one's dreams come true. State-of-the-art special effects, that state being Bulgaria, and long, long pauses, interleaved with stretches where nothing happens. Like *2001* without the flip irresponsibility. Transcendent.

43. *Sweet Smell of Success* (1957)

From Alexander Mackendrick, the man who made the charming, life-affirming *Whisky Galore*, one of the nastiest films ever made. Or at least Burt Lancaster is one of its nastiest pieces of work: as the sinister, power-broking columnist JJ Hunsecker (based, it was said, on Walter Winchell), he makes everyone in New York dance to his tune, especially eager goof Tony Curtis. The only way you'll be able to ask for a light after seeing this film is to say: "Match me, Sidney."

42. *The Killing of Sister George* (1968)

Beryl Reid loses her job – as the star of a television soap – and then she loses her much-put-upon lover, Susannah York. Coral Browne plays the TV executive who takes the wind out of Beryl's sails and puts a little frisky wind up Susannah. Reid sinks so low down the rungs of the showbiz ladder, eventually landing a job as a cartoon voiceover, that we even begin to feel sorry for her. York, meanwhile, turns nastier by the minute. Straddling this emotional see-saw is Coral Browne, brilliantly playing Coral Browne, which she does better than anyone else.

41. *Up in Smoke* (1978)

A film that bravely carried the torch for marijuana at the nadir of its fortunes (the style-setter's drug of choice in those days being cocaine, or amphetamine if that was unaffordable), amassing a hardcore of fans along the way. Starring two dope-heads, Cheech and Chong, as two dope-heads. If you found that last sentence funny you are in the right frame of mind for this film. Great scene when the cop asks a seriously stoned Cheech – or is it Chong – what his name is, and he can't remember!

40. *The Cabinet of Dr Caligari* (1919)

Occupies a central place in the film-buff's pantheon, too, because of its appropriation of Expressionism; but what the cultist admires is the extraordinary, enveloping atmosphere of nightmare: it is, as one critic pointed out, one of the first films to make use of the similarities between dreaming and watching a film. All about madness, murder and sleepwalking, labelled, to cap it all, "degenerate art" by the Nazis.

39. *Enter the Dragon* (1973)

One thinks of this as if retrieved from some Seventies time-capsule, but the smirking fans of that decade should bear in mind that Bruce Lee was a genuine, dedicated fighter, the inventor of Jeet Kune Do, "the intercepting fist", master of the one-inch punch (your fist travels that far; the man on the receiving end of it much farther). He slowed his movements down for the camera, but not enough: the camera had to be speeded up for him.

38. *Apocalypse Now* (1979)

Having taken almost as long to finish as the Vietnam War itself, movie industry wags retitled it *Apocalypse Later*. Joseph Conrad and TS Eliot season the plot. Wagner and The Doors improbably share billing on the soundtrack. And the images – filmed on location in the Philippines – are so spectacular that Coppola makes war look hauntingly beautiful as well as horribly barbaric. "I love the smell of napalm in the morning," purrs Robert Duvall in one of the film's typically hallucinatory moments. *Hearts of Darkness*, the documentary about the making of the film, was almost as gripping as the film itself: everything that could go wrong did. Sets buckled under the lash of tropical storms, Martin Sheen suffered a near-fatal heart attack, Marlon Brando – booked to play a fit and muscular Green Beret – arrived in Manila looking like the Michelin

Man. The budget ballooned even more dramatically than Brando's waistline. "This film is a failure!" Coppola was spotted screaming. "I don't know what I'm doing!" And that may be exactly why it's such a masterpiece.

37. *The Blue Angel* (1930)

"At the time," Marlene Dietrich confessed years later of her role as the nightclub femme fatale who humiliates a bourgeois teacher who becomes infatuated with her, "I thought the film was awful and vulgar and I was shocked by the whole thing. Remember, I was a well-brought-up German girl." Many women have aped the black corset, the suspenders and stockings, the tilted top hat and the mocking stare, but few have bettered Dietrich's feline sexuality.

36. *Shaft* (1971)

Of course Noël Coward had never seen *Shaft* (too thrusting a title for his taste), but he would have recognised the potency of the theme music. That wonder of the wah-wah pedal won an Oscar for Best Song and provided Isaac Hayes with a signature tune for life that chat shows could play to signal his arrival as the next guest. Supporting Hayes's music is a hip thriller which happened to be Hollywood's first big commercial hit with a black private eye.

35. *Repo Man* (1984)

A walk on the wild side of Los Angeles – very, very wild, to be honest – in which Harry Dean Stanton's exquisite perfor-

mance shimmers as blindingly as the decomposing aliens' remains that lurk in the boot of a 1964 Chevy Malibu. We know, as soon as that blinding flash from the Chevy's boot reduces a nosy state trooper to a smoking pair of boots, that English director Alex Cox's film is not so much a thriller as a surreal and satirical movie about the wackiness of Los Angeles and the American dream. *Repo Man* doesn't easily fit traditional movie categories, which may be why Cox has found it tricky to match the energy and wit of his film-making debut.

34. *Reservoir Dogs* (1993)

Blame Quentin Tarantino for making a writing-and-directing debut so stylishly lethal that all film school student's graduate projects now include a mandatory scene in which some poor sucker is getting his ear sliced off in a warehouse while Stealers Wheel's 'Stuck in the Middle with You' is playing in the background. This gangster tale of a botched diamond heist introduced the world to the tricksy Tarantino signature: witty dialogue about inconsequential subjects (such as the true meaning of Madonna's 'Like a Virgin'), casually violent scenes that often make an audience laugh and wince simultaneously, and a spliced plot that weaves forwards and backwards expertly. The movie was a cult before the credits finished rolling.

33. *The Warriors* (1979)

Walter Hill's update, as you doubtless know, of Xenophon's *Anabasis*, in which a New York gang, framed for the murder of a gang overlord, has to cross Manhattan and get back to Coney Island before being beaten to death by all the city's other gangs. Gripping, gaudy, grainy; the close-up of Uma Thurman's mouth in *Pulp Fiction* is a direct homage to one of this film's recurring motifs.

32. *Nosferatu* (1922)

Hollywood may now be able to create the sort of special effects to make even God a little jealous, but it still hasn't managed to produce a scarier, creepier, more grotesque or more intelligent vampire movie than *Nosferatu*, the first (and still the best) film version of Bram Stoker's *Dracula*. Promiscuity, bisexuality, incest, non-procreative sexuality, sexual repression, religious ecstasy – yup, all human life is here and will be recognised by those filmgoers who have been diligently swotting up on their copies of *Teach Yourself Freud*.

31. *The Wizard of Oz* (1939)

It is hard to imagine now that the original first choice to play Dorothy was Shirley Temple. *The Wizard of Oz* is often (justifiably) cited as a triumph of the Hollywood studio system in general – which could blend state-of-the-art cinematography, lavish sets, contract actors, lavish scores, etc. – and of MGM in particular. But remember, this is the same studio system whose executives wanted to cut 'Somewhere Over the Rainbow' from the movie, the one song that won an Oscar.

30. *Zabriskie Point* (1970)

You can't say that Antonioni doesn't like an explosive climax. The shooting of a student by the Los Angeles police became the starting point for this outsider's journey into late-Sixties American culture, although the film is more a stylish pictorial assault on American materialism than an intellectual one. Pink Floyd provide the music to blow up bourgeois refrigerators by.

29. *Johnny Guitar* (1953)

Almost any of the 24 films whose title begins with the name "Johnny" has a claim on our attention here; but let us stick with this one from Nicholas Ray (who was one year away from inflaming teenagers with *Rebel Without a Cause*). A director who could both make money and earn the respect of cinema intellectuals and the devotion of cultists, he made *Johnny Guitar* one of the weirdest of westerns: a Freudian parable with lesbian undertones, and the star of the show is not its eponymous hero, but – once again, we take our hat off to her – Joan Crawford.

28. *And God Created Woman* (1957)

The debut showcase for what were to become two of the most sensational features of the French cinema – Roger Vadim and Brigitte Bardot. Shot lushly on location in St Tropez, *Et Dieu Créa la Femme* told prim 1957 audiences everything they wanted to know and had half-suspected anyway about the French way with sex. What shocked them wasn't so much that a man was willing to offer his new young wife naked on the screen in Cinemascope and Eastman Color, but that on-screen Bardot played an erotic, amoral sex kitten who hops from bed to bed, one of which belongs to her husband's brother.

27. *What Ever Happened to Baby Jane?* (1962)

Bette Davis and Joan Crawford play Jane and the wheelchair-bound Blanche, the sisters from hell. *What Ever Happened to Baby Jane?* was another film in which Hollywood bit the hand that fed it (Robert Aldrich's movie was dubbed the *Sunset Boulevard* of the Sixties). In real life, Hollywood considered Davis and Crawford past their prime and refused to stump up for the film. So Aldrich proved them wrong by filming on a small budget and picking up five Oscar nominations. A film that gains a delicious patina the more we learn about the real lives of Davis and the child-abusing Crawford. "The best time I ever had with Joan Crawford," hissed Davis later, "was when I pushed her down the stairs in *What Ever Happened to Baby Jane?*" As for Crawford, she purred: "Bette likes to scream and yell and I just sit and knit. During *What Ever Happened to Baby Jane?* I knitted a scarf from Hollywood to Malibu."

26. *The Blues Brothers* (1980)

John Belushi, perhaps one of the most arresting natural funny men, decided to die before he got old. Dan Aykroyd has soldiered on, although perhaps he should be cashiered. But in their prime they gave the world *The Blues Brothers*, a story about two white boys crazy about black music that was fashioned in a novel "slapstick-with-soul" genre – so novel, in fact, that initial audiences turned up their noses at it. But moviegoers brought up on *Saturday Night Live*, the satirical TV show on which Belushi and Aykroyd made their names, fell in love with the film on the rebound and *The Blues Brothers* has gone on to become one of the biggest grossing films in the history of Hollywood.

25. *Cat People* (1942)

A masterpiece of restrained horror: Simone Simon plays a woman who fears that at the moment of coitus she turns into a panther. Her shrink (Tom Conway) says pooh, it's all in the mind. Bad move. Directed by Jacques Tourneur (whose *I Walked with a Zombie* could have gone into this list), who was beginning a series of low-budget but effective shockers. That "low-budget" explains the "restrained"; the special effects are little more than hand shadows, but by gum, they work.

24. *Trash* (1970)

Joe Dallesandro has his ups and downs in Andy Warhol's movies. In *Flesh*, which was also directed by Paul Morrissey, the ever-naked Dallesandro has a series of ups as Mr Virile Beautiful Body. In this sister piece, Joe has his downs after being blighted by impotence because of his heroin addiction. With their open, unembarrassed way with nudity, the Warhol/Morrissey/Dallesandro partnership produced the sort of movies that Health & Efficiency's video division might produce if they could only locate a reliable drugs supplier. Moviegoers with a taste for lavish sets and plots might be disappointed.

23. *The Wicker Man* (1973)

Edward Woodward, fated to play clipped-voiced policemen until the crack of doom, plays a clipped-voiced policeman sent to a remote Scottish island to investigate the death of a child. The islanders, largely because they happen all to be practising Satanists, are unhelpful to say the least, and end up stuffing him inside a giant, combustible effigy (authentic pagan practice, actually). Great cult stuff, genuinely scary, also ennobled by the presence of Christopher Lee and with a performance from Britt Ekland that actually trembles on the brink of acting.

22. *Head* (1968)

An extraordinary venture. The Monkees, as you recall, were a group carefully assembled by TV execs to challenge the Beatles' supremacy. This film is about one such group, who begin to resist being moulded in such a way. The film was made by the man who moulded them, Bob Rafelson. Silly, derivative comedy, with laughable psychedelic overtones (although the subject of d-r-u-g-s never comes up; the title is the druggiest thing about it), it has a certain callow charm. And it was co-written by someone called Jack Nicholson.

21. *The Trip* (1967)

Roger Corman, turning into the final bend of his career, directed this corny but effective advertisement for LSD in which a TV ad-man from Los Angeles – played, naturally, by Peter Fonda – takes a tab and, after an extended series of psychedelic visions, becomes reborn. As one critic noticed, he may not look any different to you. Translating inner visions to the screen is almost comically difficult, but Peter Gardiner made a good fist of it under the circumstances. And who was the writer responsible for this piece of classic whimsy? Step forward one Jack Nicholson.

20. *Taxi Driver* (1976)

A confusing work for those tourists to New York who on first seeing *Taxi Driver* assumed it was a well-made documentary rather than a fictional movie. It says a lot about Robert De Niro's performance as the sexually repressed and socially inadequate Vietnam veteran Travis Bickle that even now, in an age when we have grown used to the concepts of road rage, heat rage – even supermarket trolley rage – his portrait of mania is still chilling enough to make you want to take the subway home. Harvey Keitel, as the pimp of child-prostitute Jodie Foster, gets some of the chestful-of-bullets treatment he would later dish out so calmly under Quentin Tarantino's orders, while Martin Scorsese pays homage to John Ford's *The Searchers* by transplanting John Wayne's revengeful Wild West cowboy to Manhattan and turning him into a cabbie. Both Wayne and De Niro are disgusted by the encroach of the barbarians. But, hey, De Niro doesn't fare too badly himself on the barbarian stakes.

19. *Mommie Dearest* (1981)

One of the great cult audience-participation movies of all time, which is odd when you consider that it is based on the harrowing book by Joan Crawford's adopted daughter about life with Mom. What itch, you wonder, are the people who get off on this story of private maternal sadism trying to scratch? Best not to ask, and instead get off on one of the most sublime manifestations of screen nastiness ever accomplished, courtesy of Faye Dunaway, who acts, acts, ACTS all the way like an express train. Unforgettable. Bring a coat-hanger.

18. *Night of the Living Dead* (1968)

"Undoubtedly the best movie ever made in Pittsburgh," chortled Pauline Kael, apologising immediately to say that this is one of the most gruesomely terrifying films ever made. At the time it shocked, then it bombed, and only the dedicated attentions of cultists revived it: it is now justly credited with redefining, and reviving, the horror genre, even unto this day. The premise, of course, is that the dead rise up to eat the living, which is pretty yecchy in itself, but if you are in the right frame of mind, it can be taken to be a powerful statement about consumer culture, or something. Best bit is the zombies aimlessly pushing their trolleys through the shopping mall.

17. *Barbarella* (1968)

"If Homer and Lewis Carroll had read the Marquis de Sade and a little sci-fi, this is what they would have produced," said Roger Vadim, a man who had obviously mastered the Hollywood knack of pitching a story idea in a nutshell. "Homer and Carroll, with a twist of de Sade" is the sort of cocktail you can imagine highbrow studio executives ordering as they loll beside the Beverly Hills Hotel pool. Hey, and Roger, they said, make it a large one. He did. He even helped them swallow this cultural cocktail by delivering Jane Fonda as cinema's first space stripper.

Forget Tom Hanks and Apollo 13 getting lost in space – the 41st century looks a lot more enticing.

16. *Scorpio Rising* (1964)

No list of cult films would be complete without a mention of Kenneth Anger, best known these days as the author of *Hollywood Babylon*, but in his time a notorious art-house director. Let's take *Scorpio Rising* as typical of his work. Soundtrack throughout: contemporary kitsch pop. No dialogue. A young biker tends his machine. He gets dressed. Many shots of his navel. He goes to some gay-biker sex party and we dimly glimpse the odd depraved act. Cut between this, *The Wild One* and ancient film about Jesus. Bikes crash. The End. Half an hour long, hardly even a film, but Todd Haynes owes a lot to him. But is it art, or is it rubbish?

15. *Withnail and I* (1986)

The cover of the published screenplay shows Richard E. Grant (Withnail) and Paul McGann (I, but you find out his name is Marwood) looking like Vladimir and Estragon; and in a way there is this Beckettian quality to the film, the way it squeezes the poetry out of boredom and despair. Tender and generous, but knowing and funny, it is the only British road movie worth the name; and although the decade it depicts is long gone, our identification with its characters is more or less total. And now a new generation of dope-smokers refers to extra-large spliffs as a "Camberwell Carrot".

14. *The Wild One* (1954)

The blueprint for *Rebel Without a Cause*, but perhaps sharper. Based on the true events of what happened when 4,000 bikers "took over" (i.e., stopped for a party at) Hollister, California, in 1947, it made Brando a big star and introduced some pithy catchphrases into the collective teenage unconscious, such as "story of my life" and "What have you got?" (in answer to the question "What are you rebelling against?")

13. *Eraserhead* (1978)

A strange film that revels in its own strangeness, beggaring interpretations: an industrial universe of faulty lifts, hissing radiators and a permanent background throbbing, as if everything takes place inside a giant machine; a black-and-white Joy Division video, without the music. John Nance, hair permanently on end, staggers like Chaplin in a nightmare, as roast chickens wave their legs on the plate ("Just cut 'em up like regular birds!") and he nurtures a hideous foetus.

12. *Rebel Without a Cause* (1955)

If ever a bunch of kids needed a sensible talking to by Claire Rayner, this was it. The evergreen title (adopted by successive generations of restless adolescents), combined with James Dean's sultry good looks and his tragic death, turned a film that could have been called *Day in the Life of an Anguished Youth* into a timeless tale of teenage social rebellion. Of course, it angered the hell out of many parents, who were furious that they were being blamed for their children's delinquency or unhappiness (remember, this was before the days of caring parenting magazines). But Dean, Natalie Wood and Sal Mineo, who plays the orphaned Plato, were saintly towards their older generation compared with modern American youth, who think nothing of suing their parents for raising them badly the minute they fail their university exams or get arrested for staging a bank robbery.

11. *Faster, Pussycat! Kill! Kill!* (1966)

Famous for his top-heavy leading ladies, Russ Meyer was ridiculed by more orthodox Hollywood film-makers who didn't feel as strong a compulsion to cram so much sex, violence, fetishism, lesbianism, rape, sadism and nymphomania into their films. But when his low-budget skin flicks (*Faster, Pussycat! Kill! Kill!* was brought in at just $44,000, having been shot outdoors in the Californian desert with a cast led from the front by king-size breasts) started making big profits, Hollywood began noticing Meyer's genuine talent as a director and editor. It's unclear what bemused Russian audiences made of *Faster, Pussycat! Kill! Kill!* when Meyer's films were screened at the International Moscow Film Festival in 1989 as part of a "Sex in American Cinema" season, but it may well have precipitated the end of communism and the fall of the Berlin Wall.

10. *2001: A Space Odyssey* (1968)

Absurd, intellectually contentious and confused, overlong, trippy and sincere; how could we not put this in the Top Ten? This is one to see again and again (as a child, I forced my bemused grandmother to take me to see it nine times), and the precise visual beauty of every single shot is itself enough to banish tedium.

9. *If...* (1969)

Not the film that Charles and Di were showing young Prince Wills on the night before he headed off to Eton. The sort of people who find *If...* a little fantastical are the sort who dismiss *A Midsummer's Night's Dream* as too far-fetched. There are several nods to Jean Vigo's 1933 *Zero de Conduite* and the theme of rebellion against authority and society's repression of the individual. But that's not what made *If...* one of the most visually mesmerising films of the Sixties. Lindsay Anderson was accused by movie bores of being structurally muddle-headed in his direction, fumbling the shifts between reality and surrealism and between colour and black-and-white. But then how come the film takes such glorious flight? Launched Malcolm McDowell on to a glittering, but still underrated, career.

8. *A Clockwork Orange* (1971)

Culty ever since Stanley Kubrick forbade its showing in the UK after a murder alleged to have been inspired by Alex (Malcolm McDowell) and his Droogs. I have heard another story, whose veracity I suspect but cannot guarantee, that it was a phoned threat to the famously reclusive and ex-directory director that produced this state of affairs. Funny how counter-culturalists flock to the greatest Catholic morality play of the 20th century. The Sixties end here.

Brilliant, intricate mechanism of the Clockwork Orange

A Clockwork Orange
Warner West End

John Russell Taylor

It is a pity that in English the word "confidence" so often brings in its train the word "trick". Confidence is the most extraordinary quality of Stanley Kubrick's new film, but this confidence is no trick. From the first moment, the narrative moves with complete assurance; we meet the principal characters, we are shown the world in which they live, and are caught up in their progress at once, with no pause for explanations, no mess and untidiness. The whole thing works with, yes, the absolute precision of clockwork. Kubrick brooks no argument with his method; indeed, he seems almost not to conceive that argument is possible, and because of that, it isn't.

The temptations to divagate from such single-mindedness must have been immense. Anthony Burgess's novel, on which the film is based, postulates a brave new world not so far hence, not so far different from our own, except that in some respects it has developed, technologically, in others has frayed a little round the edges. Politically we do not know quite what's what, except that we may guess something from the Russianized English argot the younger characters speak. Socially various impulses are channelled through the ready availability of doctored milks which intensify one instinct or another—notably the urge to physical violence, which is what gets our hero into all his trouble. Environmentally the image is of an advanced urban society running out of control: in the brighter modern high-rises the garbage is not collected, the vandalism unchecked.

Kubrick's physical evocation of this future world is stunningly vivid, mainly because it is all strictly functional and never strays into the irrelevant picturesque. Again it is mainly a matter of confidence; nothing is insisted on. There are, I think, no purely atmospheric landscape shots in the film; everything is context for the people, and the colour photography of John Alcott, which would in any other circumstances be dazzling, does not here dazzle because it never calls attention to itself at the cost of the film's overall effect.

And that overall effect is, first and foremost, as a piece of powerfully direct story-telling (which is surprising, perhaps, considering the novel; from which what everyone remembers is the trappings). Kubrick uses a technique which it is tempting to call comic-strip. Episode follows episode brusquely, with no lingering over transitions: the stages of our hero's cumulating misfortune following his indulgence with his three mates, or Droogs, to use Burgess's argot, in a bout of ultra-violence— a therapeutic beating-up of a shambling drunk, an all-out tangle with a rival group, a rape-cum-beating-up of a couple of country-dwelling intellectuals—are economically sketched in, with overwhelming logic. Each episode in the first half when he is up finds its mirror image in the second half, when he is down, drained of his violent and sexual impulses by a new conditioning course of cinematic forced-feeding.

To get through so much so quickly Kubrick has to adopt a bold, caricatural style of playing for his cast. As in *Doctor Strangelove*, many of the characters are played up to and over the edge of outrageous burlesque, and yet always with a certain disturbing resonance. Or almost always: the only exception in *A Clockwork Orange* is the prison officer, played by Michael Bates. As we know, most immediately from *Forget-Me-Not-Lane* Mr Bates can bring complex overtones to a character who could be caricature, but here he seems to be no more than a sort of *Carry On* figure of farce, and the discrepancy, though not a radical flaw, is disturbing. Patrick Magee, on the other hand, who can be the most execrably mannered actor, is beautifully used here by Kubrick: as the intellectual crippled in the first half by the wild bunch, he has a moment of extraordinary grandeur in the second half menacingly inquiring of our hero whether his food and entertainment suit him while continually and clearly in an hysteria of hatred.

As Alex DeLarge, the subject and object of all the action, Malcolm McDowell gives a performance of remarkable variety and controlled power, confirming the promise of *If . . .* that he would be one of the most striking actors of his generation. And the role is taxing, physically and emotionally, calling for considerable athleticism as well as unexpected moments of interior quality, as in the scenes devoted to his seemingly inconsistent passion for Ludwig Van and his Ninth. Incidentally, one cannot help wondering if it was this tissue of musical reference which first drew Kubrick to the book: certainly the music, Beethoven, Rossini, Purcell and all, is used with a virtuosity reminiscent of the soundtrack in *2001*, except again more functionally. There are no passages where we can sit back, listen and admire. The film just hits, and hits hard. It works, as only a master could make it.

7. *The Texas Chainsaw Massacre* (1974)

Enormously influential, not only in terms of its many epigones, but of our nightmares: the image of Leatherface, masked, swinging his chosen instrument of destruction, haunts us still. Director Tobe Hooper was eventually offered real money to make real films (like the Spielberg-produced *Poltergeist*) but he was a good ole boy at heart, and went back to low-budget promotions.

6. *Easy Rider* (1969)

An odyssey through American counter-culture from those days when American counterculture was still a tilt against the Establishment rather than a study of how many pancakes people order when they visit coffee shops in Milwaukee. The film is remembered now for Peter Fonda's pretty face and his even prettier sunglasses; for Dennis Hopper's itchy moodiness; and for catapulting Jack Nicholson into the Hollywood spotlight for his role as George Hanson, the alcoholic lawyer who loses faith in the American Dream and decides to tag along with Fonda and Hopper on their Harley Davidsons. Although it is the epitome of a cult movie, it has worn less well than a fading pair of Levis, partly because a further 25 years of road movies about a couple of rebels who throw it all in for the freedom of the open road – *Thelma & Louise*, for instance – has robbed *Easy Rider* of its novelty. Also Dennis Hopper is now a smooth-shaven 59, and although we are grateful for his marvellous later films,

the fact is he didn't make the ultimate sacrifice James Dean and River Phoenix made, which would have added that extra tang to his early films.

5. *Don't Look Now* (1973)

Obviously not financed by the Venetian Tourism Authority. But that doesn't stop Nicolas Roeg milking the lush palazzo backdrops for all they are worth in this hypnotic chronicle of a death foretold. The tourist-guide beauty of Venice, the discreetly but erotically filmed bedroom scene between Donald Sutherland and Julie Christie, even the spookily gripping trail through the night-time alleyways of Venice in pursuit of the little red coat, don't prepare you for the film's horrific, heart-stopping climax. Unusually for this kind of suspense thriller, the ending gives you an even bigger shock second time around.

4. *Freaks* (1932)

It sounds almost too pat that director Tod Browning ran away as a 16-year-old to join the circus; 17 years after that he joined another one, Hollywood. This extraordinary film harks back to his circus days: a group of midgets, microcephalies, living torsos, etc., gangs up on a trapeze artist who has murdered one of their number. That these freaks are there, real, on the screen, both raises and annihilates questions of bad taste; for whose taste is being shown as "bad"? Our own, possibly? After a San Diego preview, when a woman ran screaming up the aisle, MGM pulled the film and it was banned in the UK for 30 years.

3. *Pink Flamingos* (1972)

There is nothing like a comfortable Catholic childhood to make one want to grow up and make films with titles like *Hag in a Black Leather Jacket* and *Eat Your Makeup*. Or indeed this, made when John Waters really didn't give a damn about anything except upsetting you, and wasn't the licensed jester he is today. Stars Divine as the favourite contestant in a quest to find the sickest person in America: he wins it by eating a freshly laid pile of real dog poo-poo. (Waters said he wanted "a shit-eating smile".) Divine nearly died of food poisoning ("food" doesn't sound right, somehow) but *il faut souffrir pour l'art, hein*?

2. *Performance* (1968)

What bliss it must have been in that dawn to be alive, and to see a collision between East End gangsterism and Notting Hill pop-star sybaritism, as personified by James Fox and Mick Jagger respectively. But that would be too neat, for when Warners saw this film they flipped their corporate wig and sat on it for two years before slipping it out the back door. Perhaps it was too prescient, too ominous a prolepsis of the sour collapse of the decade. It might have spooked Fox as much as the character he played: he quit acting for ten years and joined a religious sect. Something very strange was going on here.

1. *The Rocky Horror Picture Show* (1975)

The obvious choice is often the only one, that cults can be manufactured, and that popularity is still important within a clique. The efforts that audiences go to in order to enhance their enjoyment of this film are remarkable. The film itself has become almost irrelevant in the crush. People arrive dressed up like the characters, i.e. terribly camp transvestites. When it rains on screen, they shoot water-pistols. When Charles Gray proposes "a toast", they throw pieces of toast at the screen. That means that they have, earlier in the day, made toast, and then carried it around with them. What is it about the film that commands them to do this? For there is such a command, subliminal, exclusive; and it is the only possible response to its pumped-up frenetics if you want to stay in your seat for the entire performance. We salute it. But don't make us see it again.

The Rocky Horror Picture Show – the original review

Review by David Robinson,
August 22 1975

Since I never saw the original *Rocky Horror Show* I can at least be neutral about the effectiveness of its translation to the screen, which I would reckon successful to the extent that it does look like a film and not a piece of filmed theatre. Not a very good film, maybe; but the sort of film it set out to be, combining *Top of the Pops* visuals, Sixties camp, and loose parody of the B-picture horror movie tradition.

The parody would obviously have been a great deal more effective if the film-makers had tried harder for the look and style of the originals – the chiaroscuro (which, as Hammer always proved, you cannot get in colour anyway) and the peculiarly electric noise of movie-Gothic thunderstorms – besides simply guying plots and dialogue. The young scientist, in true B-horror style, is driven, with his fiancée, to seek refuge from an infernal storm in the Old Dark House of the strange Frank N Furter, who has just completed his monster.

It's a slick enough first film by *Rocky*'s original stage director, Jim Sharman, who has also scripted the film with the original *Rocky Horror* writer Richard O'Brien, who appears as Riff Raff, the eerie butler; but it needed a lot more purpose and style in conception.

A bit more assurance would have given a lot more piquancy to the notion of a bisexual, transvestite Frankenstein, who makes himself a beautiful beef-cake instead of Boris Karloff; or a Forties hero who gets raped, with evident pleasure, in the night and a virginal heroine who is so turned on that she squeals (in one of the better musical numbers) "Take me, feel me, make me". The flabbiness of camp could have acquired a stiffening of satire.

Tim Curry, who re-creates his stage role as Frank N Furter, must to a great extent have helped *Rocky Horror*'s fluke stage success. He has a certain star authority, and he flaunts the metallic voice and hard eyes of a drag pro. Susan Sarandon and Barry Bostwick have the authentic idiocy of Forties film juveniles; and Charles Gray is nicely self-important as a criminologist narrator of the Edgar Lustgarten school.

PEOPLE

FORGOTTEN PIONEER OF SILENT ERA HONOURED AT CINEMA FESTIVAL

By Mike Wade, December 15 2016

Nell Shipman was the Jodie Foster or Angelina Jolie of the silent age, an actress turned director whose films caused a sensation. *The Grub-Stake* – which she directed, scripted and starred in as an indomitable, valiant heroine – will be shown at HippFest in Bo'ness at Easter, 94 years after it was completed.

Born in 1892, Shipman was a child actress who, by her late teens, had become a vaudeville star. She was bold enough, said Alison Strauss, HippFest's director, to turn down a contract with Samuel Goldwyn, a powerful figure in Hollywood, to pursue her own career.

"Nell didn't like the kinds of heroine cast by Goldwyn, with their hair in pretty ringlets and their pouting lips," Ms Strauss said.

The Grub-Stake opens a five-day festival and will be screened with a newly commissioned score by Jane Gardner performed live. The drama revolves around a determined young woman who flees her husband's treachery but has to survive in the wilderness. Enthusiasts describe it as "a thrilling adventure", with fist-fights, chases, plot twists and a cliff-hanging finale.

Shipman operated outside the studio system. She ran her own production company, devised her own films and performed all her own stunts – action scenes in which brave women rescued men or took on male adversaries.

The Grub-Stake was one of the first films shot on location, in Idaho, where Shipman based herself after quitting Hollywood in 1921. It also reflects her interest in animal rights. Appalled by the treatment of dogs on film sets, Shipman travelled with a menagerie of 70 animals. Some of them feature on screen.

Ms Strauss said: "There is a beautiful mountain scene in which she hides in a cave and is awoken by a bear licking her face. She was an engaging actress and a witty writer. She is never the passive heroine."

Shipman's previous film, *Back to God's Country*, had been a runaway success and caused a sensation, not least because she appeared naked. *The Grub-Stake* was never released because its distributor was bankrupted. Shipman went on to make a further seven films but like many women was forgotten in cinema histories.

PERSONAL CHOICE

FILM SPOOFS

May 5 2012

The best spoofs come from a position of affection, not snideness – taking the piss is easy. Mel Brooks is one of the best exponents of the art: *Young Frankenstein* and *Blazing Saddles* have a reverence that helps to make them work. It's important that you know the subject back to front; it's very easy to be cynically critical of something, particularly if you don't understand it.

Young Frankenstein had a huge effect on me as a comedy writer. It was the first film I saw projected at home, before video. I had dinner with Mel Brooks recently and I was delighted to hear that he'd enjoyed *Shaun of the Dead*, the zombie spoof I co-wrote and starred in (its title is a reference to George A. Romero's *Dawn of the Dead*). I told Brooks that it was indebted to him.

There's huge comedy to be had from playing absurd things straight, which is what we used to do in the TV series *Big Train*. It's also important to have a good story. Contemporary parody films such as *Scary Movie* are just about repetition and making fun; the minute they stop being funny, they really stop being funny because you have no sympathy for them. But in *Airplane!* you're rooting for Ted Striker, so even when you miss a joke, it still works.

The Naked Gun (1988)

So outrageously funny. This is such a tribute to Leslie Nielsen as a serious actor who became a comic actor. Taking the po-faced police procedural drama and turning it into ridiculous comedy – he just did it so well.

Airplane! (1980)

The bit when he looks at the screen and says "what a pisser" made us cry at my 14th birthday. Not just for breaking the fourth wall, but because he said "pisser".

Scream (1996)

This film accepts that we all know the rules of slasher films and replays them with that dramatic irony. It manages to be both a horror film and a comment on horror films. It's odd that *Scary Movie* came about, because *Scream* wasn't taking itself seriously in the first place. There was no victory in *Scary Movie* because it was spoofing a spoof that was cleverer than it was.

Sunset Boulevard (1950)

One of the first truly postmodern pieces of cinema. It has genius moments of self-referentiality, such as the cameos by Cecil B. DeMille and Buster Keaton. It did what *The Artist* did, but back in 1950.

Blazing Saddles (1974)

A loving take, not only on the western, but on film itself, and on racism in film and in society. Sharper than the fart gag that everyone recalls, a relentlessly funny movie that comes entirely from goodwill.

Young Frankenstein (1974)

This showed an extraordinary love and knowledge of Universal horror films; Brooks just pushes it a bit farther into absurdity. Despite references to the "enormous schwanzstucker", it's quite sophisticated.

CLASSIC CINEMA – FIRST IMPRESSIONS

Gone with the Wind

Film version of the novel

Unbylined review
(Alan Clutton-Brock),
published April 18 1940

One could scarcely gather more extensive and miscellaneous information about the past if one spent the whole afternoon at home in the library running through all the old bound volumes of the *Illustrated London News*. For three or more hours curiosities and marvels, panoramas and bibelots are spread before us, and at one moment there is the whole of a battlefield in the American Civil War or a vast monument of Colonial domestic architecture, at another a perfectly authentic bottle of eau-de-cologne of about 1870; the producer has even gone to the expense of having what seems to be a genuine daguerreotype taken of Mr Leslie Howard. Everything is in colour and this added means of verisimilitude is especially valuable when we are shown a really fascinating reconstruction of American interior decoration at its most opulent in the last quarter of the nineteenth century.

But more is added; when the film is over not only have we run through all the old illustrated newspapers but we have also, or so it seems, read the complete works of Mrs Henry Wood and at the same time a lively and melodramatic history of the American Civil War. The history is mostly collected in the ear-

lier half of the film – there is an interval between the two halves – and this is at times really well done, the great house in Georgia, the bombardment of a town, the interior of a military hospital, the destruction of great estates after the war, are all admirable and sometimes even imaginative reconstructions. There are, moreover, several accidents and hairbreadth escapes in the best tradition of the American cinema; no one could quarrel with such luxurious entertainment.

In the second half of the film the story contracts to describe the fortunes of the heroine, the noble self-sacrifices of people who had previously been thoroughly intensely selfish and a whole succession of agonizing death-beds. The chief consolation for this is that the background is still very elaborate and the acting almost always very efficient. Miss Vivien Leigh takes the part of the heroine and acts with genuine gusto and sustained vitality; Mr Clark Gable is one of those dark, dissolute men with a mysterious appeal and looks well in the part; Mr Leslie Howard has too faint and self-effacing a part to give his talent an opportunity, and Miss Hattie McDaniel, as an old Negro servant, almost acts everybody else off the screen when she is allowed to appear in the foreground.

◇◇◇◇◇◇◇◇◇◇◇◇◇◇◇◇◇◇◇◇◇◇◇◇◇◇◇◇◇◇◇◇◇◇◇◇

Editor's note: *Gone with the Wind* **was for many years the highest-grossing film in cinema history. It won ten Oscars, including Best Picture, Best Actress and Best Supporting Actress. Hattie McDaniel was the first black actor or actress to win an Oscar.**

◇◇◇◇◇◇◇◇◇◇◇◇◇◇◇◇◇◇◇◇◇◇◇◇◇◇◇◇◇◇◇◇◇◇◇◇

21 July 2008. Christian Bale arrives for the European premiere of *The Dark Knight* in Leicester Square, London. (Ben Gurr)

21 April 2009. Film Director Ken Loach is interviewed about his new movie *Looking for Eric* in his offices in Soho. (Ben Gurr)

Kate Muir, novelist and film reviewer for *The Times*. (Rii Schroer)

The child stars for *Harry Potter and the Philosopher's Stone*: Daniel Radcliffe (Harry), Rupert Grint (Ron), and Emma Watson (Hermione). (Simon Walker)

19 May 1980. Harrison Ford, David Prowse, Peter Mayhew, Carrie Fisher, Mark Hamill and Kenny Baker in London during the release of *Star Wars: The Empire Strikes Back*. (Terry Richards)

7 March 2005. Filming in the Bahamas for the new James Bond film *Casino Royale*. (Paul Rogers)

22 January 2017. Ewan McGregor (Mark Renton) and Kelly MacDonald (Diane) appear on the red carpet at the *T2:Trainspotting* world premiere in Edinburgh. (James Glossop)

Sean Connery at the Berkeley Hotel, London. (David Bebber)

Actress and comedienne Kathy Burke (Richard Pohle)

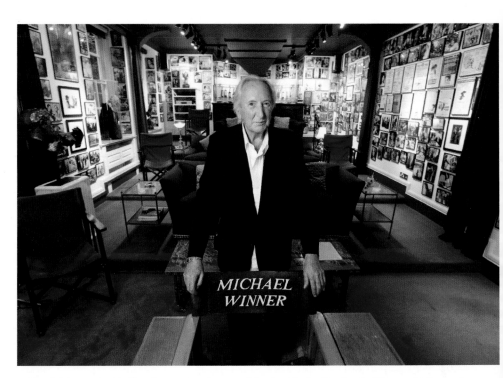

Michael Winner, British film director/producer and food critic for *The Sunday Times*, at his home in Kensington. (Dwayne Senior)

14 October 2009. Bill Murray (Chris McAndrew)

28 July 1986. Director James Cameron with his wife Gale Anne Hurd. (Stuart Nicol)

15 February 2004. Scarlett Johansson at the Bafta Awards in London. (Richard Mills)

24 April 1994. Director Steven Spielberg attending the Baftas. (Robin Mayes)

26 February 1999. Spike Lee with his Inspiration Award at the 1999 Empire Film Awards. (Andre Camara)

16 May 2002. Morgan Freeman at the 55th Cannes Film Festival. (Paul Rogers)

24 February 2002. Dame Judi Dench with the Best Actress Award at the BAFTAs in Leicester Square. (Richard Mills)

A heritage and its history

The Godfather (x)

Paramount, Universal, Empire, ABC1 (Thursday)

John Russell Taylor

It is probably a misfortune that *The Godfather* is now certain to make more money than any other in the history of the cinema (including *Gone With the Wind*). Not, of course, for the makers, who must be justifiably delighted, but for us, or those of us who are only getting to see it now, amid all the dazzling pre-publicity and faced with four major West End cinemas, where it is simultaneously showing, to choose from.

For how could any film quite live up to all that? No, of course it isn't, not by a long way. But it is very good, solid, entertaining—like *Airport*, I was going to say. As a matter of fact it is a lot better than *Airport*, but that should give you a rough idea. It is exactly the kind of holding, not too demanding entertainment you would love to drop into by chance and see at your local. And since there are so few these days it is no wonder that those that do come out make a mint.

It is no secret that the film is about the inner workings of the Mafia in New York. Not that any-one in the film actually uses the dread word, ever. But all the characters are Italian-American, all are involved one way or another in crime, and the word "family" clearly has a far wider connotation than merely brothers and sisters and uncles and aunts. The central drama, though, is literally as well as metaphorically a family affair. The Corleone family are ruled over firmly but reasonably, by Don Vito (Marlon Brando), the father of three sons and one daughter, plus an adopted son who is actually German-Irish. And all of them are connected somehow with the family business, even the youngest, Michael (Al Pacino), who when we first see him is a fresh-faced young soldier who seems likely to make his escape, marry his crisp, WASP-ish girl-friend and perhaps become a respectable academic or some-thing of the sort.

Of course, he doesn't. The film, like Mario Puzo's best-seller on which it is based, stays close enough to the familiar con-ventions of the gangster movie for us to be sure from the start that the mild innocent with vaguely idealistic instincts is bound to end up as the most ruthless of them all. In that respect the plot holds few surprises. But then, the plot is really only a framework for the real matter of the subject, which is a demonstra-tion how the Mafia works. The very opening scene gives some indica-tion, and some indication, too, of the film's ambiguous attitude to its characters and situations. During

Al Pacino and Marlon Brando

his daughter's wedding reception Don Vito receives a petitioner, an undertaker whose daughter has been raped and brutalized, and then has seen the culprits let go free on a suspended sentence (un-likely, surely, in 1945?). He wants justice. And gets it—at the cost of promising a favour in return at some future date.

Already the implication is there that the "family" has its consol-ing aspect, almost a necessary cor-rective to the lapses of the official system. The next job too has this implication. An entertainer in the circle has been denied a role in a film which will put him back on top (no prizes for guessing the fac-tual origins of this incident), and the family leans on the studio head to make sure he gets it. But again, everyone is agreed that he is ideal casting, and it is only personal spite which prevents him from being given the role at once. Again, a wrong is righted, if in a rather brutal fashion. Perhaps the key in-dication of attitude comes in a

scene later on when Michael's girl-friend objects to the line of busi-ness he is in. He replies that really the family functions like the police and politics. She accuses him of being naive; after all, policemen and politicians don't have people killed. He replies, "Now who's being naive?"

Well, who says that gangster films ought to take a critical atti-tude to their subject, anyway? Just on a documentary level *The Godfather* is fascinating—cun-ningly constructed to lead us into the workings of the organization, show us exactly how it is put to-gether. And then, once we have got the idea, comes the action half of the film, vividly illustrating just how the rival families cut one another down, how the business is modified and diversified in answer to the changing conditions of society (should the family dabble in drug distribution, for instance, and if it has to, can it stick to "clean" drugs for consenting adults?).

The film is long—almost three hours—and manages never to be boring. Though for those who loved *You're a Big Boy Now* and *Finian's Rainbow*, it is perhaps a little disappointing and square from director Francis Ford Coppola, it is a stunningly professional piece of work. Some of the 1940s period detail may give one pause—the hair is nearly always wrong, for instance —but otherwise it looks good, is confidently paced and excellently acted. Brando is perhaps a little too obviously giving a performance, but within those limits he is good. And the film is stolen by Al Pacino, who really has the central role (though it only gradually emerges that this is so) and gives a beauti-fully controlled picture of Michael's development from innocent to im-placable "god-father" in place of his own father. It is a film every-one will want to see, and few find disappointing. But try to forget all the ballyhoo before you see it, just in case.

CINEMA HISTORY

The Times did not carry a report of the first Oscars ceremony in 1929, but here is the paper's report of the 1940 event, in full.

AWARDS TO BRITISH FILM ACTORS

FROM OUR OWN CORRESPONDENT
NEW YORK, MARCH 1

Gone With the Wind was chosen last night by the Academy of Motion Picture Arts and Sciences as the best film of 1939. Two English actors received the statuettes known as " Oscars " for the best acting achievements—Mr. Robert Donat for his portrayal of Mr. Chips in *Goodbye, Mr. Chips*, and Miss Vivien Leigh for her characterization of Scarlett O'Hara in *Gone With the Wind*. Altogether nine of the 21 awards given by the Academy went to actors in or producers of *Gone With the Wind*.

CINEMA HISTORY

Editor's note: Throughout the 1970s the British film censors came under sustained pressure from a series of films that challenged the rules and norms on what it was permissible to show on screen, especially in regard to sex, nudity and violence. The films themselves seemed to reflect changing attitudes in society and the censors took an increasingly liberal view about what could be shown to adult audiences. Meanwhile Mary Whitehouse and the self-appointed guardians of traditional values fought a vigorous rearguard action against what they saw as declining social standards. *A Clockwork Orange* not only came under attack in some quarters for its graphic sex and violence, but was also cited as some sort of mitigating circumstance in court cases involving violence and young people. The director Stanley Kubrick reacted by withdrawing the film – effectively banning his own film.

BRILLIANT, INTRICATE MECHANISM OF THE CLOCKWORK ORANGE

A Clockwork Orange

Review by John Russell Taylor, January 11 1972

It is a pity that in English the word "confidence" so often brings in its train the word "trick". Confidence is the most extraordinary quality of Stanley Kubrick's new film, but this confidence is no trick. From the first moment, the narrative moves with complete assurance; we meet the principal characters, we are shown the world in which they live, and are caught up in their progress at once, with no pause for explanations, no mess and untidiness. The whole thing works with, yes, the absolute precision of clockwork. Kubrick brooks no argument with his method; indeed, he seems almost not to conceive that argument is possible, and because of that, it isn't.

The temptations to divagate from such single-mindedness must have been immense. Anthony Burgess's novel, on which the film is based, postulates a brave new world not so far hence, not so far different from our own, except that in some respects it has developed, technologically, in others has frayed a little round the edges. Politically we do not know quite what's what, except that we may guess something from the Russianized English argot the younger characters speak. Socially various impulses are channelled through the ready availability of doctored milks which intensify one instinct or another – notably the urge to physical violence, which is what gets our hero into all his trouble. Environmentally the image is of an advanced urban society running out of control: in the brighter modern high-rises the garbage is not collected, the vandalism unchecked.

Kubrick's physical evocation of this future world is stunningly vivid, mainly because it is all strictly functional and never strays into the irrelevant picturesque. Again it is mainly a matter of confidence; nothing is insisted on. There are, I think, no purely atmospheric landscape shots in the film; everything is context for the people, and the colour photography of John Alcott, which would in any other circumstances be dazzling, does not here dazzle because it never calls attention to itself at the cost of the film's overall effect.

And that overall effect is, first and foremost, as a piece of powerfully direct story-telling (which is surprising, perhaps, considering the novel; from which what everyone remembers is the trappings). Kubrick uses a technique which it is tempting to call comic-strip. Episode follows episode brusquely, with no lingering over transitions: the stages of our hero's

cumulating misfortune following his indulgence with his three mates, or Droogs, to use Burgess's argot, in a bout of ultra-violence – a therapeutic beating-up of a shambling drunk, an all-out tangle with a rival group, a rape-cum-beating-up of a couple of country-dwelling intellectuals – are economically sketched in, with overwhelming logic. Each episode in the first half when he is up finds its mirror image in the second half, when he is down, drained of his violent and sexual impulses by a new conditioning course of cinematic forced-feeding.

To get through so much so quickly Kubrick has to adopt a bold, caricatural style of playing for his cast. As in *Dr Strangelove*, many of the characters are played up to and over the edge of outrageous burlesque, and yet always with a certain disturbing resonance. Or almost always: the only exception in *A Clockwork Orange* is the prison officer, played by Michael Bates. As we know, most immediately from *Forget-Me-Not-Lane* Mr Bates can bring complex overtones to a character who could be caricature, but here he seems to be no more than a sort of *Carry On* figure of farce, and the discrepancy, though not a radical flaw, is disturbing. Patrick Magee, on the other hand, who can be the most execrably mannered actor, is beautifully used here by Kubrick: as the intellectual crippled in the first half by the wild bunch, he has a moment of extraordinary grandeur in the second half menacingly inquiring of our hero whether his food and entertainment suit him while continually and clearly in an hysteria of hatred.

As Alex DeLarge, the subject and object of all the action, Malcolm McDowell gives a performance of remarkable variety and controlled power, confirming the promise of *If...* that he would be one of the most striking actors of his generation. And the role is taxing, physically and emotionally, calling for considerable athleticism as well as unexpected moments of interior quality, as in the scenes devoted to his seemingly inconsistent passion for Ludwig Van and his Ninth. Incidentally, one cannot help wondering if it was this tissue of musical reference which first drew Kubrick to the book: certainly the music, Beethoven, Rossini, Purcell and all, is used with a virtuosity reminiscent of the soundtrack in *2001*, except again more functionally. There are no passages where we can sit back, listen and admire. The film just hits, and hits hard. It works, as only a master could make it.

SERIOUS POCKETS OF VIOLENCE AT LONDON SCHOOL, QC SAYS

Unbylined news report,
March 21 1972

Bullying and violence at Wandsworth Comprehensive School, London, one of the largest in Britain, ended in a fatal playground stabbing, Mr Michael Sherrard, QC, said at the Central Criminal Court yesterday.

He was appearing for the defence of a boy, aged 14, who had pleaded guilty to the manslaughter of Lee Arthur Selmes, also aged 14, of Whitlock Drive,

Wimbledon. The stabbing took place during the morning break at the school, in Sutherland Grove, Southfields. The boy's plea of not guilty of murder was accepted by the court.

Mr Justice Nield made a care order under the Children and Young Persons Act and directed that the boy should be committed to a community home and remain in the care of the local authority until he is 18.

Mr Sherrard told the judge there was a film which had captured the public imagination, called *A Clockwork Orange*, which dealt with teenage violence. This case had a macabre relevance to that situation.

He added: "The real message of this case is that violence begets violence and that in the end those who are most in fear of it resort to violence themselves.

"There were serious pockets of violence at this school. Not only was there bullying to an extent which could be regarded as dangerous and excessive but there was a form of protection racket by which the smaller boys were deprived of their lunch money by the bigger boys."

The defendant became afraid to go to school and when he did attend he was marked as absent because he stayed in the school basement looking after the pets. In February, 1971, the accused returned home from school with deep knife cuts down his jacket. He felt he had to protect himself against the bigger boys.

'CLOCKWORK ORANGE' LINK WITH BOY'S CRIME

Unbylined news report, July 4 1973

LAWYERS REJECT AUTHOR'S ATTACK

By Marcel Berlins, Legal Correspondent, August 7 1973

The violent film, *A Clockwork Orange*, was in the mind of a boy aged 16 who beat an elderly tramp to death, it was alleged at Oxford Crown Court, yesterday. The only money the tramp, Mr David McManus, aged 60, had, 1½p, was missing when his body was searched, Mr John Owen, for the prosecution said the boy, who comes from Bletchley, Buckinghamshire, was sentenced to be detained during Her Majesty's pleasure for murder. He had pleaded guilty.

The boy told the police that his friends had told him about the film "and the beating up of an old boy like this one."

Mr Owen said: "If this was robbery, it was all for 1½p or it may have been carried out for excitement as a result of the film. If so, the makers of the film have much to answer for. It seemed as if momentarily the devil had been planted in this boy's subconscious."

The irresistible conclusion was that it was the influence of the book. Many people had much to answer for, whether they were authors, film directors, television producers or those who allowed those films to be shown. He continued: "It has produced a canker among the impressionable young, which all reasonable people desire to see stamped out at once."

Mr Roger Gray, for the defence, said: "The link between this crime and sensational literature, particularly *A Clockwork Orange*, is established beyond any reasonable doubt."

Immediate reaction in legal circles yesterday to Mr Anthony Burgess's attack on judges who have condemned the film *A Clockwork Orange*, which was based on his book, is that his criticism is aimed at the wrong persons.

Mr Burgess said over the weekend that he was fed up with judges' vague attacks on his book and the film. "These bloody judges and other people are just playing around on the fringes of a very difficult subject," he said. "Let us put the ball in their court and let them tell us what we may or may not write about."

Lawyers point out that it is for Parliament, not judges, to lay down the law. Judges merely interpret the law. They argue, too, that in the cases referred to by Mr Burgess the judges were merely commenting on the film in the context of cases of violence which had appeared before them. They were not trying to lay down what the law should be.

Mr Burgess was reacting to remarks such as that made by Judge Desmond Bailey last week. On sending a boy, aged 16, who was dressed like a character in the film, to borstal for causing grievous bodily harm to a boy, aged 15, the judge said that "this dastardly film" presented an "unassailable argument" for a form of censorship.

Saying that it was the second case within a few weeks in which "a despicable young bully" had attributed his behaviour to having seen the film, he continued: "We must stamp out this horrible trend which has been inspired by this wretched film."

Mr Burgess's attack on the judges raises another important point. Is it one of the judge's functions to make gratuitous comments about something on which he has not heard evidence and that is in no way relevant to whether the accused person was convicted, or to the sentence to be imposed?

Whether the youths in the cases in which *A Clockwork Orange* has been mentioned acted as they did because the film influenced them to do so is something some psychiatrists would question.

KUBRICK'S VILLAINS RAMPAGE AGAIN

By Adam Sherwin, March 11 2000

AFTER nearly 30 years of illicit screenings and bootleg copies, Stanley Kubrick's *A Clockwork Orange* is finally going overground. But as multiplexes prepare to screen the violent satire, has the film lost its power to cause convulsions of disgust?

Kubrick himself withdrew the film in 1973 after receiving death threats. He had been in discussion with Warner Brothers about rescinding his ban after the completion of *Eyes Wide Shut*, his last film. But the director died and *A Clockwork Orange* is being shown again on the first anniversary of his death, with the support of his family. The censors have passed the film uncut and judgement now resides with a new generation of filmgoers.

For many, the story of Alex, the amoral teenage hero who is interested in "rape, ultraviolence and Beethoven", has reached mythical status ... In January 1972 the critics were immediately divided. *The Daily Telegraph* and Communist *Morning Star* were united in condemnation. *Halliwell's Film and Video Guide* called it "a repulsive film". Some local authorities refused to license it. More damagingly, several rapes and murders were linked to the film during its original run.

Kubrick retreated to his Hertfordshire mansion. He quietly withdrew the film when its British run concluded, a decision that came to light only when the National Film Theatre was denied a request for a print in 1979. Julian Senior, a senior vice-president at Warner who worked with Kubrick on *A Clockwork Orange*, said: "It is easy to say on reflection that he overreacted, but he wanted to lay to rest his demons by pulling the film."

Warner respected Kubrick's decision not to screen the film in Britain but it went underground and became a cult classic. Coach parties travelled to the Continent, where the film could be screened. The Scala Cinema Club at Kings Cross in London was sued by Warner for showing a bootleg copy in 1993. But Mary Whitehouse need not be concerned by the film's return, according to the actor Warren Clarke, who received his first break playing Dim, a bowler-hatted droog. "The violence will not have an effect on people's behaviour. It is nothing like *Pulp Fiction*," he said.

ACTORS

20. Morgan Freeman

A latecomer to screen stardom, the Memphis-born Freeman spent five years in the US Air Force before studying acting in the late Sixties. After making his Broadway debut in an all-black version of *Hello Dolly!*, he went on to land two Oscar nominations for *Street Smart* (1987) and *Driving Miss Daisy* (1989). Now 63, Freeman specialises in films with strong anti-racist themes, including his directorial debut *Bopha!* (1993). He received another Academy nomination for *The Shawshank Redemption* in 1994.

Must see: *Seven* (1995)
Avoid: *Chain Reaction* (1996)

19. Cary Grant

As cinema's most debonair romantic leading man, the ever-dashing Archibald Leach hit his stride in charming, sophisticated comedies such as *Bringing Up Baby* (1938) and *The Philadelphia Story* (1940), though his urbane, intelligent bearing and clipped accent lent itself equally well to Hitchcock thrillers, memorably *To Catch a Thief* (1955) and *North by Northwest* (1959). Grant's suave manner belied his troubled early life and his deep personal insecurities.

Must see: *Mr Blandinqs Builds His Dream House* (1948)
Avoid: *Alice in Wonderland* (1933)

18. Dirk Bogarde

Born Derek Jules Gaspard Ulric Niven van den Bogaerde of Dutch descent, this sensitive actor was for many years characterised by good work in bad films and vice versa. It wasn't until the Sixties that his rich, intelligent acting talents were allowed to shine. His vulnerable manner hinted at repressed anguish, lending particular resonance to his roles as a blackmailed homosexual in *Victim* (1961), a decadent valet in *The Servant* and a melancholic dying composer in *Death in Venice* (1971).
Must see: *The Servant* (1963)
Avoid: *Modesty Blaise* (1966)

17. Robert Mitchum

After a period of playing walk-on parts in Hopalong Cassidy films, Mitchum made his mark in a series of RKO B-movies, transforming standard thug roles with his seething masculinity and laconic wit. Mitchum's off-screen hell-raising, which landed him in prison in 1949 on marijuana charges, enhanced his appeal for audiences, who embraced him as the embodiment of evil in the classic suspense stories *Cape Fear* (1962) and *The Night of the Hunter* (1955).
Must see: *The Night of the Hunter* (1955)
Avoid: *She Couldn't Say No* (1954)

16. Harvey Keitel

With his intense, hard-bitten demeanour, the Brooklyn-born Keitel encapsulates the essence of streetwise menace. After making his brooding presence felt in Martin Scorsese's *Mean Streets* (1973), *Alice Doesn't Live Here Anymore* (1974) and *Taxi Driver* (1976), Keitel's career gave way. His return to prominence in the Nineties in *Thelma & Louise* (1991), *Reservoir Dogs* (1992) and *The Piano* (1993) was long overdue and his willingness to bare himself in raw performances is never short of compelling.
Must see: *Bad Lieutenant* (1992)
Avoid: *Monkey Trouble* (1994)

15. John Gielgud

His death in May deprived Britain of one of its best-loved actors, the last member of the acting triumvirate destroyed by the earlier deaths of Olivier and Ralph Richardson. RADA-trained, Gielgud played his first Hamlet in 1930, and though his celluloid Shakespearean roles such as the Duke of Clarence in Olivier's *Richard III* in 1954 won him much acclaim, it was character parts in films such as 1981's comedy *Arthur* and the epic *Chariots of Fire* that brought him to a wider audience.
Must see: *Julius Caesar* (1953)
Avoid: *Arthur II: On the Rocks* (1988)

28 February 1967. Richard Burton and Elizabeth Taylor arriving at the Odeon in Leicester Square, for the Royal Film Performance of their new film *The Taming of the Shrew*.

14. Richard Burton

Born Richard Jenkins near Port Talbot in 1925, cinema's most famous Welshman was a brooding, poetic, charismatic soul who treated his own prodigious talents with boozy contempt. Burton's legendary romance with Elizabeth Taylor catapulted him to international superstardom in his late thirties, and his great roles include *Look Back in Anger* (1959), *The Spy Who Came in from the Cold* (1965) and *Who's Afraid of Virginia Woolf?* alongside Taylor. He died in 1984.

Must see: *Who's Afraid of Virginia Woolf?* (1966)
Avoid: *The Wild Geese* (1978)

13. Jack Lemmon

Lemmon's 1954 debut in *It Should Happen to You* established the persona that has served him well since: a hapless, jittery Everyman fighting a losing battle with fate. He went on to star in two of Billy Wilder's greatest comedies, *Some Like It Hot* and *The Apartment* (1960). Though best known for comedy, Lemmon is also considered to be a great dramatic actor due to his heart-rending portrayals of tragic losers in *Days of Wine and Roses* (1962) and *Glengarry Glen Ross* (1992).

Must see: *Some Like It Hot* (1959)
Avoid: *Luv* (1967)

12. John Hurt

Though he refined his skills in the naturalistic environment of the English stage, Hurt's best-known screen roles employed the trickery of Hollywood. He writhed in space as an extra-terrestrial burst from his chest in *Alien* (1979) and radiated dignity through layers of make-up as John Merrick in *The Elephant Man* (1980). More visually restrained times have seen him excel as the disgraced osteopath Stephen Ward in *Scandal* (1989) and the thought criminal Winston Smith in *Nineteen Eighty-Four* (1984).

Must see: *The Elephant Man* (1980)
Avoid: *King Ralph* (1991)

11. Alec Guinness

10. Humphrey Bogart

"I shrivel up every time someone mentions *Star Wars* to me," Sir Alec once said. Given the obscenely high quality of his output before he played Obi-Wan Kenobi in 1977, it is easy to understand his frustration. From his extraordinary, eight-part performance as the D'Ascoyne family in *Kind Hearts and Coronets* to his Oscar-winning role as Colonel Nicholson in *Bridge on the River Kwai* (1957), he proved himself the finest British character actor of his generation.

Must see: *Kind Hearts and Coronets* (1949)

Avoid: *Raise the Titanic* (1960)

"The trouble with Bogart is that he thinks he's Bogart," said the director John Huston, and whether he's playing Sam Spade (*The Maltese Falcon*, 1941), Phillip Marlowe (*The Big Sleep*, 1946) or Rick of Rick's Bar (*Casablanca*), there are few people who think of him any other way. One of Hollywood's bona fide icons, Bogart remains a formidable force more than 40 years after his death. Yet while his habitual snarl – the result of an injury received while serving in the Navy – might be a gift to impressionists, few have managed to capture his incredible screen presence, and his role in *Casablanca* is the stuff of myth. Though that remains his most famous role, it was his portrayal of the riverboat captain Charlie Allnut in *The African Queen* (1951) that brought him his solitary Oscar. In gentle tribute to the dialogue of 1944's *To Have and Have Not*, his widow Lauren Bacall buried him with a small gold whistle.

Must see: *Casablanca* (1942)

Avoid: *The Return of Dr X* (1936)

9. Jack Nicholson

Few Hollywood actors have enjoyed such an illustrious and remunerative career as the paunchy, sabre-toothed Nicholson, whose journey from a *Little Shop of Horrors* (1960) walk-on part to multi-Oscar winning Hollywood player has spanned four decades. He was raised believing that his teenage mother was his sister and that his grandmother was his mother, a deception that Nicholson discovered only at the height of his fame in a *Time* magazine feature. His first starring role came in the schlock-horror *Cry Baby Kilter* (1958) before parts in a series of cult classics (*Hells Angels on Wheels*, 1967, *Head*, 1968) led to *Easy Rider* (1969), which he co-wrote. Once a fully-fledged superstar, Nicholson picked and mixed roles in classics such as *Chinatown* (1974) with dubious appearances in films such as *Tommy* (1975), and became as famous for his voracious libido as for his acting. In 1997, *As Good as it Gets* won him his third Oscar.
Must see: *One Flew Over the Cuckoo's Nest* (1975)
Avoid: *Man Trouble* (1992)

8. James Stewart

A gangling physique and loquacious manner made this Pennsylvanian one of Hollywood's favourite comedy actors in the Thirties and helped to win him an Oscar for his turn as the chatterbox journalist Macaulay Connor in George Cukor's *The Philadelphia Story* (1940) His All-American image was strengthened by a stint in the US Army Air Corps during the Second World War. Initially refused entry for weighing less than the regulation 148lbs, he ended up flying a string of missions and becoming the highest-ranking movie star in military history (Brigadier General). After returning to Hollywood in 1946, Stewart injected his work with a new depth and gravitas, taking his most beloved role as the small-town hero George Bailey in Frank Capra's *It's a Wonderful Life* (1946) and collaborating with Alfred Hitchcock in such classic thrillers as *Rope* (1948), *Rear Window* (1954) and *Vertigo* (1958).
Must see: *Rear Window* (1954)
Avoid: *The Magic of Lassie* (1978)

7. Gene Hackman

Often cited as one of America's finest screen actors, Hackman almost never reached the big screen. The former Marine studied journalism before turning to drama, by which time he was already 30 years old. Yet Hackman's abundant ability easily transcended film star clichés of youth and beauty, and his third film role, as Clyde Barrow's brother in 1967's *Bonnie and Clyde*, brought him widespread recognition. His experience shone through as he took on such roles as Popeye Doyle, driven by obsession and teetering on a moral precipice in *The French Connection*. Yet he can also play comic figures – as shown by his role as the blind hermit in Mel Brooks's *Young Frankenstein* (1974) – and recent years have seen him assuming a patriarchal presence among younger actors in box-office hits such as the adaptation of John Grisham's *The Firm* (1993).
Must see: *The French Connection* (1972)
Avoid: *Superman II* (1980)

6. Laurence Olivier

"Work is life for me, it is the only point of life, and with it there is almost religious belief that service is everything." Considered by many to be the greatest actor of the 20th century, the future Lord Larry joined Birmingham Rep at 19 and was acting in films by the age of 23. His affair with Vivien Leigh on *Fire Over England* (1936) blossomed into marriage just as *Wuthering Heights* (1939) made the brooding, athletic young star into an international sex symbol. Over a 60-year career Olivier appeared in more than 60 films, balanced working in Hollywood with

launching and running the National Theatre, earned 12 Academy Award nominations and three Oscars, including the Best Actor award for *Hamlet* in 1948, and was made a life peer in 1970. A tireless workaholic, he spent his final years in lucrative but often low-grade film and television work.

Must see: *Rebecca* (1940)
Avoid: *Clash of the Titans* (1981)

01 November 1951. Laurence Olivier and Vivien Leigh attending the first night of *South Pacific* at the Drury Lane Theatre. (Barrett)

5. Orson Welles

"I started at the top and worked my way down" is how Welles summed up his career. The legend of Hollywood's most gifted enfant terrible, whose streak of genius was as inspired and wayward in front of the camera as it was behind it, only seems to grow with the passing years. When Welles was in the frame, his looming presence and wonderfully resonant voice gave his roles an undeniable robustness, best demonstrated in unforgettable turns as Harry Lime in Carol Reed's *The Third Man* (1949), as Falstaff in *Crimes at Midnight* (1965) and, of course, as Charles Foster Kane in his masterpiece, *Citizen Kane*. In 1971 he was awarded an honorary Oscar for superlative artistry and versatility in the creation of motion pictures, but in later years he was content to ham up his increasingly gargantuan persona in forgotten B-movies, voice-overs and sherry commercials.

Must see: *Citizen Kane* (1941)
Avoid: *Hot Money* (1983)

4. Al Pacino

3. Marlon Brando

One of the most popular stage and screen actors of his generation, the diminutive Pacino has given his most rounded performances when playing brooding, intense characters, notably as the honest cop in a corrupt department in *Serpico* (1973), a gay heister in *Dog Day Afternoon* (1975), a Puerto Rican drug baron in Brian De Palma's *Scarface* (1982), and as Michael Corleone in *The Godfather* trilogy. In more recent years, he happily plays to the gallery with high-decibel performances that occasionally border on hammy (*Scent of a Woman*, 1992, for which he received his solitary Oscar, having been nominated on seven other occasions, and *The Devil's Advocate*, 1997). Any criticism on that count would be churlish, however, since he remains an immensely charismatic actor who brings warmth to the characters he portrays and effortlessly conveys unfettered emotional power.
Must see: *Scarface* (19)
Avoid: *Revolution* (1985)

The most famous graduate of the Method school of acting, this Nebraska farm boy could have been a contender for the title of the American Olivier. In the early Fifties, edgy outsider roles in dramas such as *On the Waterfront* (1954) and *A Streetcar Named Desire* made Brando the mumbling spokesman for an entire generation. But he swiftly lost focus and became a has-been, more talked about for his eccentric behaviour than for his increasingly misguided choice of movies. Brando's stature was restored in the Seventies by his weighty depictions of the Mafioso patriarch Don Vito Corleone in *The Godfather* (1972) and a middle-aged sexual predator in *Last Tango in Paris* (1973). He continues to act, and to act up – last year he caused havoc on the set of Frank Oz's latest film *The Score* by arriving for work naked from the waist down.
Must see: *A Streetcar Named Desire* (1951)
Avoid: *The Island of Dr Moreau* (1996)

2. Kevin Spacey

1. Robert De Niro

If this chart were limited to the past five years, Spacey would win hands-down. In 1995 he played *The Usual Suspects'* crippled con-man Verbal Kint and *Seven'*s John Doe, two of the most disturbingly cerebral villains ever seen on the big screen. His piercing intelligence and measured wit were not limited to homicidal roles for long; he was equally at home with parts in slick period thrillers such as the flash detective Jack Vincennes in *LA Confidential* (1997) and megabudget blockbusters such as *The Negotiator* (1998) with Samuel L Jackson. But it was *American Beauty* that saw the famously enigmatic actor from New Jersey reach the peak of his considerable powers. His portrayal of the reborn suburbanite Lester Burnham combined humour, pathos, anger and tenderness, and deservedly won him an Oscar. "This has definitely been the highlight of my day," began his typically disarming acceptance speech.

Must see: *American Beauty* (1999)
Avoid: *Consenting Adults* (1992)

◇◇◇◇◇◇◇◇◇◇◇◇◇◇◇◇◇◇◇◇◇◇◇◇◇◇◇◇◇◇◇◇◇◇◇◇

Editor's note: This was obviously written long before the emergence of various allegations of sexual impropriety, which made the mention of that 1992 film seem somewhat ironic.

◇◇◇◇◇◇◇◇◇◇◇◇◇◇◇◇◇◇◇◇◇◇◇◇◇◇◇◇◇◇◇◇◇◇◇◇

He once said that "the talent is in the choices" and, though *Frankenstein* proves that he doesn't always get it right, De Niro's career has been as broad in scope as it has been rich in quality. His pallid complexion earned him the childhood nickname of Bobby Milk, but his most vaunted roles have been anything but bloodless. After appearing as a hoodlum in *Mean Streets* (1973), the first of eight classic collaborations with Martin Scorsese, he received his first Oscar for playing a young Vito Corleone in *The Godfather Part II* (1974) and his second for his portrayal of the prize-fighter Jake

LaMotta in *Raging Bull* (1980). But his timing, mimicry and energy also made him well suited to comic roles, *Midnight Run* (1988) to *Analyze This* (1999), in which he lampooned the hard-nosed Mafia roles that he had previously made his trademark. He has also shown a willingness to take on small roles (his frazzled ex-con in *Jackie Brown*, 1997) and be overshadowed by more extrovert co-stars (Philip Seymour Hoffman in *Flawless*, 1999). However, he will be remembered best for two traits: a devotion to the Method and a penchant for playing borderline psychos. Both are perfectly illustrated in *Taxi Driver*, for which he drove a cab 12 hours a day for a month as preparation for playing the unhinged Travis Bickle.

Must see: *Taxi Driver* (1976)
Avoid: *Frankenstein* (1994)

PEOPLE

SPACEY DOESN'T DESERVE TO LOSE HIS AWARDS

Many creative geniuses have done appalling things but we must separate the art from the artist

By Melanie Phillips,
November 7 2017

Consternation! The tsunami of sexual allegations that is still gathering force looks like it may wash away the Netflix *House of Cards*, to which I am hopelessly addicted. Its star Kevin Spacey, who plays a monstrously corrupt US president, has been accused of sexually abusing young men working on the show. He is accused of similar behaviour at London's Old Vic theatre where he was artistic director for more than a decade.

Netflix has fired him and suspended filming on the sixth and final season of *House of Cards*. Now there are reports that he could be stripped of the special Olivier award presented to him in 2015 by the Society of London Theatre for his stint at the Old Vic. The International Academy of Television Arts and Sciences has also withdrawn the Emmy it was about to give him.

We know extremes of personality go hand in hand with creativity

Is this really appropriate? These awards are given for great acting and directing. Kevin Spacey remains a great actor and revived the Old Vic.

None of the charges against him has yet been proved. On the assumption, however, that some if not all the claims are true, he'd hardly be the first artist to have gone off the reservation. The list goes back to the Middle Ages when Chaucer was accused of rape and Thomas Malory was jailed more than once for a series of crimes that included extortion, rape and robbery.

Among modern writers, Arthur Koestler, author of the seminal 1940 novel *Darkness at Noon*, was a serial rapist who wrote to his second wife: "Without an element of initial rape there is no delight." The Nobel laureate William Golding, author of the 1954 novel *Lord of the Flies*, admitted in private papers that as a teenager he had tried to rape a 15-year-old girl. Eric Gill, a pioneering sculptor who died in 1940 and whose carvings of Prospero and Ariel adorn Broadcasting House in London, sexually abused his daughters, had incestuous relationships with his sisters and performed sexual acts on his dog. Yuck, ad nauseam.

So can we separate the appalling behaviour of these artists from their genius? Can we enjoy and admire Roman Polanski's film *The Pianist* while knowing he pleaded guilty to having sex with a 13-year-old girl and has been accused of other sexual assaults? Even more troublingly, did such art develop from the personality flaws? Can the creation of what touches us most deeply flow directly from the loathsomeness of the artist?

As Eric Gill's biographer Fiona MacCarthy has written, while his meticulously recorded sexual experiments with his daughters were taking place Gill was using these young women as models for the heartrendingly beautiful images of girlhood in his sculptures and engravings. John Carey's biography of William Golding revealed how, while teaching at a public school, the novelist experimented with setting boys against one another to observe how they behaved. The result of this manipulative abuse of his position was *Lord of the Flies*, the classic depiction of the shocking descent into barbarism and sadism of young boys stranded on a desert island. Spacey specialises in playing complex, twisted, depraved characters. His brother, reflecting on their abusive childhood, has remarked: "Fans love the sinister characters he plays, but what they don't realise is he's not acting; that's really him."

Of course, we cut artists a lot of slack because we know that extremes of personality often go hand in hand with creativity. But doesn't art have a moral as well as an aesthetic purpose? Can an artist express repugnant views and still be considered great? Some of TS Eliot's poems were anti-Semitic. Ezra Pound supported fascism, causing Ernest Hemingway to write that "he deserves punishment and disgrace". Should we listen to the music of Wagner, given its inextricable association with Nazism?

When it comes to miscreant politicians, different rules surely apply again. Living politicians are role models. Dead ones, though, are not only beyond influencing behaviour but lived in an age when people usually didn't know what they were up to. The Liberal politician David Lloyd George, for example, was a promiscuous philanderer; his principal private secretary AJ Sylvester recorded in his diary: "He has lived a life of duplicity. He has got clean away with it." The former defence secretary Sir Michael Fallon has said of the behaviour with women that brought him down: "The culture has changed over the years. What might have been acceptable ten, 15 years ago is clearly not acceptable now."

By what benchmarks then do we make these value judgements? Eric Gill's abuse was little known until MacCarthy's biography revealed it in 1989. Does that knowledge change the intrinsic worth of his art? Do the Gill sculptures suddenly become ugly, or Spacey's performances lose their mesmeric power, just because we become aware of the flaws in the men who have created them? Can the value of a work of art, or the achievement of a lifetime's public service, be assessed independently from the moral worth of the artist or politician?

Knowing about someone's appalling behaviour does make a difference because it makes all of us – audience, voters, colleagues – complicit. If Kevin Spacey and others accused of serious sexual misbehaviour did the things of which they are accused, they must be held to account. While their prospects, though, may have collapsed like a house of cards, their indisputable achievements will endure.

PEOPLE

JACK NICHOLSON INTERVIEW

There are plenty of players, but there's only one Jack. Garth Pearce talks to a man who is among Tinseltown's most lauded and awarded

Published May 18 2003

Jack Nicholson arrives looking as if he has stepped straight from one of the vast billboards advertising his latest film along Sunset Strip. Hair is swept back, devil's eyebrows ride high, a sleek pair of shades hides his eyes and a smile is fixed around a cigar. It would be no surprise if he popped out a full glass of champagne from an inside pocket. The visual statement is clear: he might be old enough for a bus pass, but at 66, this man's still having the time of his life. All, though, is not quite as it appears.

The cigar is crunched out, the sunglasses come off, the smile disappears and a green-check sports jacket is flung carelessly over his chair. Then the words come tumbling forth. He's been in therapy for most of his life, he says. He feels clapped out. His love life has been too uneven. He still can't control his temper.

The usual smoky voice crackles with uncertainty in his choice of meeting place, a small, low-key hotel in the heart of Beverly Hills.

"I am running out of energy," he says, with an audible sigh. "Perhaps I am the only one who dare say it, but I am a quieter man than I was 20 years ago. The girls might be young – but, hell, I've got older. The urge goes. I have always been the wise guy, doing this and that after filming. A good friend of mine said the other day: 'All you seem to do now is work.' I told him: 'It is because I don't have the energy to work and fool around.'"

If he wants to lay bare some home truths other than a whinge about creaking bones, the timing seems odd. He is currently enjoying his biggest box-office success in years, with the comedy *Anger Management*, co-starring Adam Sandler – it has grossed $120m across America in five weeks. He's fresh from his record 12th Oscar nomination for his last film, *About Schmidt* (he lost out this time to Adrien Brody for *The Pianist*), and he knows that, as a three-time winner, nobody is more lauded and awarded.

But he insists: "Being a father to young kids is the best thing in my life at the moment. I know a lot of men would hesitate to have children at my age. My life would not work for most guys. It just works for me. The truth is, whatever you read, I mostly sleep alone these days."

This, of course, is a recent change of circumstances. Nicholson has always been The Man. There were more golden stars of his generation, such as Robert Redford and Paul Newman, but none more dangerous. He would take on roles that they eschewed; and while they would go home to their families at night, he would party, party, party. Warren Beatty tried hard, but could never really keep up. And although the

top Hollywood players now include Harrison Ford, the two Toms, Cruise and Hanks, Al Pacino, Robert De Niro, Mel Gibson and Brad Pitt, there is only one Jack. He's been Jack the lad, Jack of knaves, but mostly just Jack.

He was married for just five years. His divorce from Sandra Knight, in 1968, after fathering daughter Jennifer, ended all wishes ever to be betrothed again. So he took the high road of beautiful women, the best cigars, the most expensive champagne. He also made no promises. The actress Anjelica Huston spent 17 on–off years with him and then complained that he had never grown up. Another actress, Rebecca Broussard, 39, has two more of his children – Lorraine, 13, and Raymond, 11 – but no ring. As his latest squeeze, Lara Flynn Boyle, at 33 half his age, told me last year, marriage has never even been discussed. "Jack is strictly solo," she said, reflecting – correctly – that another break-up would surely be on the way. "Everyone should know the score."

Nobody knows the score better than Nicholson himself. He became a star on the back of the 1969 film *Easy Rider*, won his first Oscar for *One Flew Over the Cuckoo's Nest* in 1976 and has reigned supreme in Hollywood ever since. His edgy choices, such as *Chinatown* (1974), *The Shining* (1980) and *The Postman Always Rings Twice* (1981), and off-screen attitude of hippie-come-party man, established him as a force to be reckoned with.

But such force has apparently needed constant help along the way. "I have been in professional therapy since the 1960s," he reveals. "I was involved in early psychedelic experiments using LSD around the UCLA in Los Angeles, and my wife's therapist at the time was one of the doctors. So I was both a subject for study – and I studied myself. I have stayed in therapy ever since."

He clearly knows he has problems controlling his temper. His famous road-rage case in 1994, in which he swung a golf club and smashed the windscreen of a driver who had offended him, made headlines around the world. It was dealt with out of court. "Shameful behaviour," he now admits, with a shake of his head. "Anger has always been an issue with me."

Nicholson has been here since the age of 17, when he travelled nearly 3,000 miles from his native New Jersey to become an office boy at MGM. He made his film debut in 1958 after training to become an actor. The fact that he has prospered and survived for so long, amid the deal-breakers, star-makers and back-stabbers, indicates considerable powers of negotiation.

He has chosen with care, whether winning an Oscar for best supporting actor in *Terms of Endearment* 20 years ago, cementing his reputation as the devil in *The Witches of Eastwick*, opposite Michelle Pfeiffer, Cher and Susan Sarandon, in 1987, or raking his biggest-ever financial deal, $37m, as the Joker in Tim Burton's *Batman* in 1989.

He has also not been afraid to steal ideas. As he prepares to step back into the California brightness after our talk, he reaches for his familiar trademark sunglasses. How and when, I ask, did he start wearing them?

"It is thanks to Fred Astaire," he says. "I sat next to him at the Oscars in 1960, when he was in *On the Beach*, which had been nominated in two categories. The moment the film lost out, he put on a pair of sunglasses. Nobody knew what he was thinking."

The Jack Nicholson public smile snaps back into place: "I've done the same thing ever since," he says. "My view is that I am here to entertain, not explain."

◇◇◇◇◇◇◇◇◇◇◇◇◇◇◇◇◇◇◇◇◇◇◇◇◇◇◇◇◇◇◇◇◇◇◇◇◇

Editor's note: While the article alludes to a long period of therapy, curiously it does not mention that Nicholson learned in adult life that the person he grew up believing to be his sister was really his mother and his supposed mother was his grandmother, a situation that oddly echoed one of the plotlines of *Chinatown* (1974).

◇◇◇◇◇◇◇◇◇◇◇◇◇◇◇◇◇◇◇◇◇◇◇◇◇◇◇◇◇◇◇◇◇◇◇◇◇

CINEMA HISTORY

Monty Python's Life of Brian

Review by David Robinson, November 16 1979

Editor's note: Sex and violence have been the two staples of cinema controversy over the decades, but some of the fiercest criticism has been prompted by films on religious themes, with major furores breaking out over *Monty Python's Life of Brian* at the end of the 1970s and a decade later over Martin Scorsese's *The Last Temptation of Christ*. The debate over *Life of Brian* included a television face-off between John Cleese and Michael Palin on one side and Malcolm Muggeridge and the Bishop of Southwark on the other that was as funny and surreal as any Python sketch. Many councils rushed to ban the films, often without seeing them. *Life of Brian* remained banned in cinemas in some local authority areas, even after it was eventually shown on television.

You have to respect a film that can make as many enemies as *Monty Python's Life of Brian*. When it opened in the United States, the Lutheran Council spokesman called it "crude and rude mockery, colossal bad taste, profane parody". The Rabbinical Alliance said it was "blasphemous, sacrilegious and an incitement to possible violence". The Catholic Conference was milder in its words, but gave the film a rating as "morally objectionable in toto", and so forbidden to Catholics. The British Board of Film Censors apparently anticipates neither incitement to violence nor actions for blasphemy in this country, for it has awarded the film a double A certificate, which permits accompanied children of any age to see the film. [Editor's note: this

21 November 2013. Monty Python reunite in London. Left to right: Michael Palin, Eric Idle, Terry Jones, Terry Gilliam and John Cleese. (Jack Hill)

is factually incorrect – patrons had to be over 14.]

The BBFC presumably acknowledges that the Monty Python lot were put upon this earth to challenge conventional notions of good taste and bad, and all those other presumptions and institutions of our society – from sexual habits and polite patterns of speech to party politics – that we all take ordinarily too much for granted. In the *Life of Brian* they play let's pretend with a youth who was born just down the lane from the other crib in Bethlehem. The wise men are silly enough to get confused, but there is little real similarity. Brian's mother is a shrill old crone (played by the director, Terry Jones, in drag) who thinks the father may have been a Roman centurion who happened to be billeted on her for a night or two.

Brian grows up in Roman-occupied Palestine, and gets mixed up with in-fighting terrorist groups like the Judaean Liberation Front and its bitter rival, the Judaean Front of Liberation. A local mob perversely decides that he would do as well as anyone for a Messiah, and trails around after him, impertinently demanding miracles and words of inspiration. (The best he can do in this line is "You'll have to work things out for yourselves".) Accidentally caught up in an execution parade, he is crucified with a horde of malefactors. His sacrifice so overjoys his followers that they blithely ignore all his pleas for rescue.

Perhaps even revolutionary groups might take umbrage at one of the funniest gags in the film (borrowed, incidentally, from Woody Allen), when "two rival terrorist groups, meeting on identical missions to kidnap Pilate's wife, noisily beat one another to death under the astonished gaze of Pilate's guards. It is very funny, in the rich and rambling mode of comedy which the Monty Pythons have made their own; and it is, if not actually offensive, at least deliberately assaulting.

LETTER TO THE EDITOR

Published November 21 1979

Sir, The new film, *Life of Brian*, is, from all reports tasteless, probably blasphemous, but most important deeply offensive to the religious susceptibilities of millions of believers. It is no excuse that it is funny, or meant to be funny, or successful in its own genre: this would not serve as an excuse for racialist productions under the existing law, nor for a charge of a breach of public order by using offensive words or behaviour in a public place. The success of this film depends on its capacity to insult and annoy.

Imagine for a moment a similar film of the life of a contemporary of or deutero-Muhammad: the uproar, the stoning of cinemas where the film was showing, would be tremendous. I am sure legal and para-legal means would soon be found to prevent such a showing.

Showing a deeply offensive film to millions in cinemas up and down the land publishes the insult more effectively than a jeering remark at a football match or in the street: the law should extend the definition of "public place". to cover this, and extend the list of interests protected from insult to cover insults to religion as well as colour and race. Yours faithfully,

Antony Allott,
21 Windsor Road, Finchley

in the sky to deal with *Life of Brian* in his own way, however mysterious that may be. I like to think He will take the advice of Mr Charlton Heston.

Penelope Mortimer,
The Old Post Office, Chastleton,
Moreton-in-Marsh, Gloucestershire

LETTER TO THE EDITOR

Published November 24 1979

Sir, I gather from his letter that Mr Allott has not actually seen *Life of Brian*. Neither have I. He implies, however, that "millions … up and down the land" are being forced at spear-point into cinemas to have their religious susceptibilities subjected to the most hideous martyrdom. This is patently absurd.

Nobody has to go and see the film against their will. If a sensitive Christian is offended by it, he can always walk out, or turn the other cheek – the Gospels are full of good advice on how to deal with insults and ridicule. Nowhere, I think, do they suggest uproar, stoning, or the "legal and para-legal means" used by Islam to suppress even the mildest criticism. I have no doubt that fervent Muslims would take great delight in publicly flogging the entire film crew within an inch of their lives. If Mr Allott thinks this is a good thing, then his reading of the New Testament and mine are very different.

The whole concept of "blasphemy" is inconsistent with belief in the omnipotence of God, who is presumably quite capable of looking after His own interests. It is up to that Great Film Critic

IBA BAN ON *LIFE OF BRIAN*

By David Hewson,
Arts Correspondent,
January 3 1985

The Independent Broadcasting Authority has banned Channel Four from showing the Monty Python film the *Life of Brian* because it may cause offence to Christians. The decision on the film, a parody of the life of Christ, 'surprised' Channel Four yesterday.

The IBA said yesterday: "We thought that broadly speaking the whole concept of it would create a degree of discontent among people who felt that it was an unsuitable subject; it would undoubtedly cause offence to a large number of practising Christians and, perhaps, people of other faiths."

SHOW US THE MESSIAH! TOWN LIFTS ITS BAN ON *LIFE OF BRIAN*

By Simon de Bruxelles,
September 25 2008

It regularly tops polls for the funniest film ever made, yet for almost three decades

Monty Python's Life of Brian has remained out of bounds to residents of Torquay.

Organisers of a comedy film festival in the seaside resort next week have been obliged to get special dispensation after discovering that the film was still on the local authority's blacklist, 28 years after its release.

The film, which starred the late Graham Chapman as Brian "He's not the Messiah" Cohen, with John Cleese, Eric Idle, Terry Jones and Michael Palin, was attacked by Christian leaders when it came out for allegedly lampooning Jesus.

Chapman played a character mistaken for the Messiah, whose life curiously paralleled that of Jesus. The Monty Python team insisted that it was a send-up of religious obsession and Hollywood Bible epics of the 1950s, but cinemas that showed the film were picketed and 11 local authorities decided to ban it.

A further 28, including Torquay, gave it an X certificate, which meant that it could be seen only by over-18s. As the film's distributors refused to allow it to be shown with this certificate, *Life of Brian* was effectively banned in those towns as well.

That the ban in Torquay had never been rescinded came to light only when Adrian Sanders, the Liberal Democrat MP for Torbay, was talking to the organisers of the English Riviera International Comedy Film Festival, which was due to show *Life of Brian* as one of its highlights.

Mr Sanders, now 49, had been among the hundreds of young people in Torbay in 1980 who joined the exodus heading

for the nearby town of Newton Abbot, where *Life of Brian* was being screened.

Officials at Torbay Council, which covers the towns of Torquay, Paignton and Brixham, were hurriedly forced to check back through dusty piles of minutes to confirm the ban. They eventually concluded, however, that subsequent legislation meant it no longer applied.

Life of Brian remains banned by a number of authorities. In July, the Mayor of Aberystwyth, Sue Jones-Davies, who played Brian's girlfriend in the film, discovered that it was still banned in her own town. She announced her intention to have the ban lifted but ran into immediate opposition from local church leaders.

Canon Stuart Bell, vicar of St Michael's in Aberystwyth, said: "If someone was going to make fun of my wife in a film then I would oppose that. Making fun of Jesus Christ, whom I love more than my wife, in a film is going to offend me."

The cultural historian Robert Hewison has written a book, *Monty Python: The Case Against*, recording attempts to have *Life of Brian* kept out of the cinemas.

He said: "It had a particularly bad time in the West Country. The Bishop of Bath and Wells and the Roman Catholic Bishop of Clifton together with the Methodists and the United Reformed Church wrote to every council in the West Country urging them to ban it."

Roger Saunders, the manager of the surviving Python's company, Python (Monty) Ltd, which owns the rights to the Python films and television series, said they were ecstatic that *Life of Brian* was no longer banned in Torbay, even though they were not aware that it had been.

9 September 1988. Martin Scorsese (Marc Aspland)

SON OF MAN: MARTIN SCORSESE'S CONTROVERSIAL FILM ABOUT CHRIST IS CLEARLY THE MOST IMPORTANT OF THE WEEK'S RELEASES

The Last Temptation of Christ

Review by David Robinson, September 8 1988

As ever, *Variety* found a succinct headline for the clamour against Martin Scorsese's *The Last Temptation of Christ*: "CLERGY NAIL 'CHRIST' AND UNIVERSAL". When the film opened in New York the Odeon Ziegfeld had a 100-man police guard as protection against the Christians, in response to nation-wide threats of bombs and screen-slashing, in addition to the boycotts.

The fiercest enemies of the film, should they actually steel themselves to see it, could hardly question the sincerity of its thesis, which centres on the issue of Christ as the Son of God become Man. Unless we take this concept literally, His ministry loses its significance. If we suppose that Christ retained His divinity, remaining super-human and omniscient; the passion and the crucifixion lose their meaning. Only if we believe that He assumed human form and feelings, with all the frailties and doubts and difficulties and vulnerability to pain, can the suffering and sacrifice be comprehended.

This, at least, is what *The Last Temptation of Christ* sets out to examine.

It begins by showing Christ in the virtually unrecorded first 30 years of His life, subject to the same weakness and self-doubt as other men, doing humiliating work as a carpenter supplying crosses for the Romans to crucify Jews. To take up His ministry requires an effort, almost superhuman, to overcome fear and failings.

On the cross, the Gospel words about taking away the cup of suffering are interpreted as a delirious dream of escaping His divine destiny, of being rescued from the cross by Satan, in the guise of a pre-Raphaelite angel, and allowed to live and die as an ordinary, fleshly man, enjoying sexuality, love, wives and children. Christ perceives this in a vision, rejects the ultimate temptation and returns of His human free will to the cross.

It is of course this passage of the film that has given most alarm to the film's opponents, along with the very idea of Christ as a man who has to conquer cowardice and temptation to make Himself worthy of the mission entrusted Him by God. Seeing the film rationally and as a whole, it appears quite without blasphemy or disrespect. It does, however, invite its audience to think; and for fundamentalists of all persuasions, thought and faith have often seemed inimical.

The irony is of course that *The Last Temptation of Christ* – a serious, thoughtful, intelligent, reverential and somewhat over-long religious inquest – is the kind of film which, without the furore of protest, would attract very limited audiences. It makes no concession to drama or entertainment in the conventional sense.

CHRIST FILM CLEARED

Unbylined news item, published September 2 1988

The Director of Public Prosecutions has decided not to launch a prosecution for blasphemous libel against *The Last Temptation of Christ*, which is to be released in Britain next week on an 18 certificate. Mr Allan Green, QC, the DPP, said yesterday that he had now seen the Martin Scorsese film and concluded that showing it to people aged 18 and over would not be against the criminal law. Mrs Mary Whitehouse is to step up her campaign for people to lobby local authorities to refuse to grant local licences.

CLASSIC CINEMA – FIRST IMPRESSIONS

THE BRUISE BROTHERS LOSE ON POINTS

Fight Club starts out like a winner but fades fast, says a defeated Adam Mars-Jones

Review, November 11 1999

If the whole of *Fight Club* was as good as the first half hour, the film would have everything going for it. The drive and crispness of the screenplay (by Jim Uhls from Chuck Palahniuk's novel), the dynamism of David Fincher's direction, and the persuasiveness of Edward Norton as the narrator, combine to produce something more than promising in tone and texture, visually and even intellectually arresting.

The narrator's alienation and insomnia send him on a darkly funny odyssey through the secret life of the city, finding comfort in the last place he would have looked for it, in the arms of another man, a sobbing man (played by Meat Loaf) at a support group who wants him to cry too, to let it all out at last. He cries so much he leaves wet marks on the stranger's vast T-shirt.

Then unfortunately the film starts to live up to its title, and runs almost immediately into the buffers. The idea is that people (well men, actually) are estranged from their bodies. They have no idea of their strengths and weaknesses, their ability to achieve or endure, so when the narrator and his strange new friend Tyler Durden (Brad Pitt) start fighting almost by accident, with total commitment and no malice, they start a trend.

Everybody wants to measure himself in the extreme but paradoxically supportive experience of fighting a stranger one-on-one. It isn't about winning, somehow. Even if you lose, you keep your dignity, and a few lost teeth or a broken finger is a small price to pay for that sort of affirmation.

The director stages the fights uncompromisingly but without gloating – yet these are still recognisably Hollywood encounters. The sound of combat is the familiar smack of a fist against a side of beef. It's fantasy fighting with state-of-the-art bruise make-up, that's all. In one of the rants that soon swamp the film, Durden inveighs against the purely cosmetic virility of a gym-toned physique, and the bouts in their clandestine location are attended by some suitably rough-looking types, but all the same the director takes care that no one takes his shirt off who doesn't have the right stuff to show off.

From the amount of screen time they're given, it's clear that the filmmakers are pretty impressed by Durden's anti-materialistic tirades ("the things you own, end up owning you" and so on). They obviously weren't around in the Sixties, when at least those messages didn't come so relentlessly packaged, as if this was all one big promotion for a Calvin Klein fragrance. And it's funny, David Fincher didn't seem so hostile to materialism when he was doing campaigns for Nike, Levi's, Coca-Cola and Budweiser.

The pity is that the film had found a perfectly juicy subject before the fighting started, when the narrator was attending a different support group every night, and claiming to have every disease under the sun. Sure, he was a fake, but he'd found something real to tap into, and everything was working fine until he ran into another trauma tourist, the appalling Maria, chain-smoking even at the TB support group. Helena Bonham Carter is surprisingly effective in the role – being cast as an American, as she showed in Woody Allen's *Mighty Aphrodite*, enables her to shed a ton of mannerisms and start from scratch.

In one of his first lines in the film, Pitt's character asks Norton's: "How's it working out for you, being clever?" There's no smug answer to that, but it's something the film-makers should have asked themselves. The edges of the film are so sophisticated, its core of cults and crypto-fascists so silly – and that's even before an anti-clockwise plot twist that puts *Fight Club* almost in the league of *The Sixth Sense*.

PEOPLE

Editor's note: Alan Sharp was one of the most fascinating and charismatic characters I ever met in my professional life as a journalist. I first met him in 1992 when he was staying in an ex-wife's London home, though he forgot I was coming and was watching the Olympics in his dressing gown when I arrived in the middle of the day. Like his ex-wife Beryl Bainbridge, I used him in one of my fiction stories. He was the inspiration for the novelist, who goes off to Hollywood then turns his back on the world, in *Sometimes She'll Dance*. I was also the writer of this *Times* obituary.

Alan Sharp

Novelist and scriptwriter who for a time was the toast of Hollywood with a series of film screenplays

Obituary (Brian Pendreigh),
February 16 2013

Alan Sharp came out of the Clydeside shipyards and electrified critics with his debut novel *A Green Tree in Gedde* in 1965. It prompted comparisons with James Joyce, he was the darling of the literary scene and he and Beryl Bainbridge were a couple. Sharp seemed set to become one of the greatest British novelists of the 20th century.

But he turned his back on it all and headed off to America to pursue the

Hollywood dream. As a boy, growing up in Greenock, he loved the movies. He wrote five scripts on spec. Every one went into production, with big studios, and with major stars. But those films – including the western *Ulzana's Raid* (1972), with Burt Lancaster, and the thriller *Night Moves* (1975), with Gene Hackman and a very young Melanie Griffith – were just a little too dark and a little too complex to be big commercial hits.

Sharp seemed to shun the limelight. He dropped out of sight again and again. He worked in American television; he made it clear that he did it for the money. He was moderately wealthy. He lived some of the time in California, some of the time in London, some of the time on a small island in New Zealand.

New Zealand was hardly even a cinema backwater then. This was long before Peter Jackson came along. The producer Peter Broughan tracked him down and undertook a 48-hour trip from Scotland to Kawau in the north to try to persuade him to write a film about Rob Roy in the early 1990s. Broughan arrived jet-lagged, only for Sharp to suggest it would be a good idea for them to talk while going for a sail in his boat, which once in the open ocean promptly capsized.

Rob Roy came out in 1995, with Liam Neeson as the Scottish outlaw, and went head to head with Mel Gibson's *Braveheart*, which grossed a lot more and won the Best Picture Oscar. But many felt *Rob Roy* was the better movie, noting that Sharp's script effectively turned a chapter of Scottish history into a Scottish western. And then Sharp more or less disappeared again.

He never quite became a household name. He had a life and a lifestyle he enjoyed and that seemed to be enough. He had a huge talent, but sometimes seemed to lack ambition, or was reluctant to commit himself or seemed afflicted with doubt about his own abilities, dismissing his work as "pastiche".

Alan Sharp was born in 1934 in Alyth, near Dundee. He was illegitimate and was adopted by a Greenock shipyard worker and his wife when just a few weeks old. He did not particularly excel at school, but made up stories to amuse friends and pretended they were the plots of books he had read, to give them more credibility, and they believed him.

He left school at 14 and worked in the shipyards, but an advertisement for a private detective's assistant seemed to offer romance, adventure and escape. His first assignment was to meet a mysterious stranger off a train. "He's got something for me," his boss said, and Sharp's imagination ran riot at the possibilities. The mystery consignment turned out to be a gas cooker and Sharp was left with the problem of getting it across town.

His employer was basically a debt collector, who spent most of his time in the pub, and did divorce work on the side. After National Service, Sharp returned to the yards, marriage and children. His future seemed set, but he got a grant to go to college in the hope of becoming a teacher. He gave his wife the money and disappeared off to Germany instead.

He felt he would not be welcome back in Greenock and decided to go to London and become a writer. *A Green Tree in Gedde* appeared in 1965 to tremendous acclaim. It follows the fortunes of four young people, including an incestuous brother and sister, which got it banned from some libraries. It was meant to be the first part of a trilogy. *The Wind Shifts* came out in 1967, but there was no third book to complete the story.

By that time Sharp was in Hollywood. His first five scripts were filmed in quick succession. There were three westerns – *The Hired Hand* (1971), with Peter Fonda, which was rereleased in the UK and the US in the 2000s; *Ulzana's Raid* (1972), which many aficionados regard as one of the best westerns of all time, with Burt Lancaster as a grizzled scout and a degree of violence and respect for the Apache raiding party that some found unsettling; and *Billy Two Hats* (1974), with Gregory Peck.

There were two dark thrillers, *The Last Run* (1971), with George C Scott; and *Night Moves* (1975), directed by Arthur Penn and starring Gene Hackman as a small-time private detective. His films were always literate, but they also showed a deep understanding of film genre conventions – and how to subvert them. There is a wonderful final scene in *Night Moves* of a boat going round in circles, going nowhere. The boat is called *Point of View*. America was reeling from Watergate at the time.

In 1975 Sharp also served as the model for the title character in Bainbridge's novel *Sweet William*. In a 1980 film version Sam Waterston played the main role of the brilliant, charming, warm-hearted, but unreliable and unfaithful writer, who declares he will always love the main female protagonist, just as she is giving birth to their child, and then leaves forever. Sharp and Bainbridge had had a daughter together, the actress Rudi Davies.

After Sharp's incredible opening burst in Hollywood, he did uncredited rewrites, including work on *The Year of Living Dangerously* (1982), he scripted Sam Peckinpah's final film *The Osterman Weekend* (1983), and he did a lot of television, before Peter Broughan turned up on his doorstep.

In 1996 Broughan announced that he and Sharp would be making two further feature films together – *Vain Glory*, a period thriller about the murder of the Elizabethan playwright Christopher Marlowe, and an adaptation of *Confessions of a Justified Sinner*, James Hogg's prototype psycho-thriller and one of the great classics of Scottish literature. But they fell out and the films never happened.

The director Vadim Jean worked with Sharp on developing a film about Robert Burns, focusing on the sudden celebrity and the sexual chaos in his life, with which Sharp identified. But the film was never made. Sharp continued to mine a lucrative vein writing films for American television.

His final film, *Dean Spanley* (2008), was a low-budget production, set in Edwardian times, about a man who was a dog in a previous life, maybe. Sharp had written the original screenplay many years earlier and once more it involved a producer, Matthew Metcalfe, tracking Sharp down in New Zealand and persuading him to pursue it.

Peter O'Toole was so impressed with the script he agreed to play the lead. With very little promotion *Dean Spanley* was in contention for the Baftas that year. GQ magazine called it "the film of the year". Sharp subsequently worked on an American TV mini-series of *Ben-Hur* (2010).

He is survived by his wife, Harriet, and his six children.

Alan Sharp, writer, was born on January 12, 1934. He died of cancer on February 8, 2013, aged 79.

PERSONAL CHOICE

FOODIE FILMS, CHOSEN BY AUTHOR JOANNE HARRIS

December 15 2012

◇◇◇◇◇◇◇◇◇◇◇◇◇◇◇◇◇◇◇◇◇◇◇◇◇◇◇◇◇◇◇

Editor's note: Joanne Harris is the author of the novel *Chocolat*, which was turned into a film starring Johnny Depp.

◇◇◇◇◇◇◇◇◇◇◇◇◇◇◇◇◇◇◇◇◇◇◇◇◇◇◇◇◇◇◇

Food is under-used as a metaphor in film, perhaps because of the difficulty in conveying its multisensory appeal. Food that photographs beautifully is often less than engaging and few actors carry off the trick of eating elegantly on screen.

However, some of the most memorable scenes in film focus on food; its dramatic appeal and emotional resonance. Food can mean humour, passion, disgust, tenderness or cruelty. Who can forget Charlie Chaplin in *The Gold Rush*, eating his boots with a knife and fork? Or Mel Gibson in *Mad Max 2*, eating dog food out of a can.

Who doesn't feel a visceral reaction when Hannibal Lecter fondly recalls consuming his victim with fava beans and a nice chianti? And who could fail to respond to the mouth-watering seductions of *Babette's Feast*?

Food is universal, a language that speaks to everyone. It brings us together; allows us to express ourselves; redeems the unredeemable. Revelations, outbursts, declarations of love – all happen at the dinner table.

People are often more vulnerable over food; more in touch with their senses and emotions. A good scene is one in which we can empathise with the characters; feel what they feel; taste what they taste. Film, like good food, ought to be a deeply immersive experience.

Tampopo

Perhaps the most beautiful and multilayered of all, it is a Japanese tapestry of stories, all based around different aspects of food, bound together by a central narrative in which a lorry driver who is passing through town helps a young woman struggling to keep her noodle bar open to discover the secret to making perfect ramen. A spaghetti western with noodles, and much more.

Babette's Feast

Beautifully contrasting the repressive, austere atmosphere of 19th-century Jutland with increasingly vivid depictions of cooking, this story of redemption through food, quiet patience and love breaks down all the barriers.

Eat Drink Man Woman

Ang Lee's fabulous story of a dysfunctional Chinese family and the conflicts within it, features a chef who has lost his sense of taste trying to connect with his three difficult daughters over the dinner table.

Delicatessen

Jeunet and Caro's dark and surreal post-apocalyptic comedy, set in a world in which food is so scarce that it is used as currency. *Soylent Green* meets Cirque du Soleil. Fantastic.

Waitress

A waitress trapped in a humdrum life and a loveless marriage sublimates her emotions through baking. The names she gives to her pies (such as the I Don't Want Earl's Baby pie or the Fallin' in Love Chocolate Mousse pie) reflect her inner dialogue.

Pan's Labyrinth

Contains one of the most unsettling food scenes in film fiction, in which the young heroine must tiptoe past a beautifully laden table without touching a morsel, or waking its sinister guardian. The food here has a special impact when seen in the context of wartime austerity. Its magical, fairy-tale qualities are pure Brothers Grimm.

FLOPS

◇◇◇◇◇◇◇◇◇◇◇◇◇◇◇◇◇◇◇◇◇◇◇◇◇◇◇◇◇◇◇◇◇

Editor's note: It is now established as one of the great Christmas classics, but *It's a Wonderful Life* lost money on its original release. It was only in the 1980s that its popularity really took off, after the copyright holders failed to renew the rights – television stations could show it and video companies bring out cassettes without having to pay anyone. "It's the damnedest thing I've ever seen," said director Frank Capra. "The film has a life of its own."

◇◇◇◇◇◇◇◇◇◇◇◇◇◇◇◇◇◇◇◇◇◇◇◇◇◇◇◇◇◇◇◇◇

It's a Wonderful Life

Unbylined review (Dudley Carew),
April 5 1947

The film is turning nowadays to fantasy; heavenly interference in the affairs of mortals is the fashion and the stars leave their courses to influence human behaviour.

It's a Wonderful Life sets out deliberately to glorify the "little man" of the small American town, and Mr James Stewart is at least infinitely preferable to the horror in the bowler hat whom cartoon has made the English counterpart. George (Mr Stewart) is the head of a building and loan company which is concerned less with profits than with seeing that the poor get decent houses; opposite him is a Scrooge-like character played with immense malignancy by Mr Lionel Barrymore. George has always wanted to travel, but marriage and responsibility tie him down and at one time it seems that his sacrifices will be in vain and that Mr Barrymore will drag him down to ruin and prison. It is at this moment, when George is wishing he had never been born, that the celestial powers intervene and a messenger, in the benign person of Mr Henry Travers, is sent to earth to show him, by a kind of inverted *Dear Brutus* process, what would have happened had he never existed. The lesson gives point to the title, and all ends with a terrific Christmas scene of emotional good will.

Mr Frank Capra has exploited the sentimental possibilities of his theme to the full and has reserved subtlety for the incidental touches and humours. It is not a good film, but it is a generous one, and Mr Stewart, an admirable compound of shyness and confidence, and Miss Donna Reed manage the film's exuberant emotions with tact. It is, however, all very loud and overpowering, and at the end the audience feels as though it had been listening to a large man of boisterous good nature talking at the top of his voice for over two hours.

WESTERNS: PART ONE

WATCHING BRIEF ... MODERN WESTERNS

By Ian Johns, December 13 2001

Doom merchants have been pronouncing the death of the western for years. If it wasn't Sam Peckinpah splattering its entrails in slow motion in *The Wild Bunch* (1969), it was Robert Altman covering it in mud in *McCabe and Mrs Miller* (1971), or Michael Cimino making it too costly with *Heaven's Gate* (1980). But it wasn't any one film which threatened to kill off the genre so much as a self-consciousness that crept into Hollywood's Wild West.

Pastiches such as *Silverado* (1985) and *Young Guns* (1988) starred townie actors indulging in gunplay who wouldn't have lasted two minutes with John Wayne on the Chisholm Trail. The new film *American Outlaws* casts the Jesse James gang as latter-day Robin Hoods who derail the fatcat railroad. A few bank robberies later they are celebrities. By the end, Jesse is seen reading about himself in a dime novel.

But self-awareness shouldn't make the western redundant. Clint Eastwood used it to great effect in *Unforgiven* (1992), in which the white-hatted hero and black-hearted villain became intermingled.

It's the town's prostitutes who demand justice from local sheriff Gene Hackman whose brutal methods have nonetheless kept the peace. The film's most obvious villain is a writer who's preparing to turn the bloodletting into myth.

Eastwood's movie is a fine example of how the Hollywood western has adapted to changing times. After the Second World War, the western's moral landscape became bleaker, the heroes darker and more tortured. Many of Anthony Mann's 1950s saddle sagas (*The Naked Spur, The Man from Laramie*) were nihilistic revenge tales. As a stunned America watched nightly news footage from Vietnam, the celluloid frontier grew more violent. The ageing outlaws in *The Wild Bunch* are the grunge answer to Newman and Redford's Butch and Sundance. The film is a bloody meditation on social collapse, human inadequacies and a longing for a lost past.

Downbeat westerns followed in the 1970s (*Soldier Blue, Bad Company*) and with it a feeling that the heart of America had shifted from the country to the big city. We now had westerners such as Eastwood in *Coogan's Bluff* and Jon Voight in *Midnight Cowboy* looking ridiculous in a New York of flower children, drug users and fast-talking hucksters.

Today's big-screen westerns combine a 1970s cynicism with a nostalgia for a mythic past. *All the Pretty Horses* is set in 1949 but shot as if it were the Old West. "To hell with jobs, cars and aeroplanes and payrolls and everything else except a good horse," says Woody Harrelson in 1930s Mexico in *The Hi-Lo Country*. He's the perfect hero for an age that is cynical about heroism, yet nostalgic for heroes. But in our current unsettling times, audiences may once again crave the archetypal western in which good triumphs over evil. Law and order prevail over chaos. The lone warrior defeats the evil empire. Wait a minute – that sounds like *Star Wars*.

HITCHCOCK

MR ALFRED HITCHCOCK'S ZEST FOR THE CINEMA

From Our Special Correspondent, June 24 1964

"Really, I'm not very interested in subjects and characters: only in making films. It's like asking a still-life painter if he's interested in apples: the only answer is 'Not particularly, but you've got to paint something'. Well, it's the same with me: I've got to make films about something, but I don't really attach all that importance to what it is." The director who said all that recently on a flying visit to London was not, as you might imagine, some wild young man who had just fallen in love with that wonderful box of tricks that is the cinema, but Alfred Hitchcock, veteran of over 40 years in the cinema and happily about to embark on his fiftieth feature film, which will probably be a return to Buchan with *The Three Hostages*.

As one would gather from what he says, and even more from what he does in the cinema, Mr Hitchcock has never lost his sheer zest for the medium; his habit of setting himself technical problems, like making a whole film without a cut (*Rope*), or from one limited point of view (*Rear Window*), or with twice as many trick-shots as any previous film (*The Birds*), for the pleasure of working them out is proverbial; and moreover for the past ten years in addition to his film-making for the cinema he has personally supervised several television series under the title *Alfred Hitchcock Presents* and filled in any spare time he may happen to have by directing half hour and hour episodes for them. In spite of his evident mastery of the techniques of the modern cinema – commercial as well as artistic – he has some harsh things to say about the way it is run, particularly in Britain and Hollywood.

Getting an idea

"There was nothing wrong with the silent cinema except that people opened their mouths and nothing came out. If only sound pictures could have contented themselves with remedying this slight defect! But because of the greed and meanness of the producers they soon started buying up successful stage plays and films became just nice pictures of people talking. I have always fought against that, tried to tell the story in cinematic terms, not in endless talk. In the old days it was not too difficult: I'd get an idea for a film, and then I and some capable journalist – not a distinguished literary figure, you know, but a practical journeyman writer – would talk out and then write down an outline. Once that was there the film was there; then someone literary would be brought in to fill in the gaps where dialogue was really needed with something which would round out the characters sufficiently: first you decide what the characters are going to do, and then you provide them with enough characteristics to make it seem plausible that they should do it.

"Now, of course, with all the rules and regulations controlling the employment of writers and the allotment of credits, I can't do it this way; but I like to come as near as I can. I decide on a subject, hire a writer and just talk to him about it for several weeks until I think he knows what I want. Then I send him off to write a draft script, and when he comes back I start pulling to pieces and rearranging, always with the writer standing by, then I myself redictate the whole final script from beginning to end. At that stage I have virtually the whole film in my head, and change and improvise very little on the set though I had to more than usual with *The Birds* because it was difficult to calculate the reactions of the characters until we had something for them actually to react to."

How far did Mr Hitchcock find that audience reactions to his fashion of story-telling on the screen had changed over the years? "Well, I have more trouble now than I used to have in the 1 930s with satisfying the dictates of what I call idiot logic. When I made the second version of *The Man Who Knew Too Much*

(which was perhaps not a good idea anyway, but I wanted a vehicle for James Stewart quickly, and it was just lying to hand) I found that most of the trouble was filling gaps in the story which no one in his right mind would want filled anyway, except that people would complain, if all these inessentials were not spelt out. I think I've sometimes given in too far about this. In *The Birds*, for example, I believe I really devoted too much time to spelling out the ordinariness of the characters' lives before the catastrophe, so that the beginning is rather boring; it would be better if you could take more of that on trust, like in Wells's books – *The War of the Worlds* and so on – which were what I had at the back of my mind. Again, when I first thought of *North by Northwest* it was much more abrupt and disjointed. I saw it like an early Nevinson painting, you know, all jagged, angular shapes. But I had to fill in the gaps, to make it smoother-flowing so that the modern public shouldn't be too puzzled, and I think that was a pity."

Mr Hitchcock seemed, I said, more than any other director to have mastered the star system, so that stars were in his films a positive asset rather than a liability. This amused him, "Oh, stars are always a liability. The only advantage they have is that they raise the intensity of an audience's involvement; they're that much more involved if it's Cary Grant up there hanging off a cliff edge than if it's a nobody, however good an actor he may be. But anyway acting's for the stage; all you want on screen is for actors to be themselves, not to create characters – even Olivier can't bring that off." How did *The Birds* fit into this; it had no important stars in it? "It doesn't, really. The trouble there was a matter of balance between the people and the birds. If you are too interested in the people, if they're Cary Grant and Audrey Hepburn, then the birds will be an irritating irrelevance; on the other hand I admit that if you're not interested in them at all then the period before the birds come will be very boring indeed. That was a real problem, and I don't think I solved it."

Mr Hitchcock is relatively reticent about his latest film *Marnie*, due soon in the West End ("Well, that's another direction") but talks happily about his projects, *The Three Hostages*, and, of all things, a version of *Mary Rose, The Island that Likes to be Visited* ("I see it essentially as a horror story"). To hear him describing effects he has in mind for the latter, like having the semi-phantom Mary Rose lit from inside, so that she casts a ghostly glow instead of a shadow on the walls, and in the death scene letting her husband feel her brow when she goes into a trance and find his hand covered in blue powder ("I don't know exactly what it signifies, but I like the idea"), one is left in no doubt that he starts his films very much from the visual end of things. But from there on nothing is left to chance, nothing wasted; a great director at the very height of his powers – what better films has he made than *Psycho*, or *Vertigo*, or *The Trouble with Harry*? – he seems to have no limits before him. There is no knowing what he may do next, but one can be certain that whatever it is it will be well worth waiting for.

Editor's note: Hitchcock abandoned his plans to film *The Three Hostages*, because of difficulties over the rights and also the plot, and also for a film of JM Barrie's *Mary Rose*, seemingly because of resistance at Universal Studios. His 50th film was *Torn Curtain*, a Cold War spy thriller with Paul Newman and Julie Andrews.

MR HITCHCOCK AND HORROR

Flair for startling seen in *Psycho*

Unbylined review (Dudley Carew), August 5 1960

We, the people who go to the cinema that is, have much cause to be grateful to Mr Alfred Hitchcock. Sometimes he has depended too much on tricks, on visual surprises and shocks, and sometimes, in later years, as in *Rope*, *Lifeboat*, and *Rear Window*, he has appeared to be interested mainly in setting himself difficult technical problems and then using his ingenuity to overcome them – a kind of game he personally seemed to find absorbing. Still, in the words of an acute American critic, "Mr Hitchcock continues to be one of the most interesting and accomplished of America's star directors. Few move their cameras so daringly, frame their action so expertly, or know so well the precise moment to cut from action to reaction. Few have his flair for staging a scene to give it the rare quality of reality caught by chance …"

All that is true, yet Mr Hitchcock has not always been happy in his choice of scripts, and *Psycho*, now to be seen at the Plaza Cinema, which has a script by Mr Joseph Stefano and is based on a novel by Mr Robert Bloch, is no exception to the rule. There has been a vast amount of publicity pointing to the fact that here was a story so different that no one could be admitted to the auditorium once the film had begun, but actually *Psycho* is conventional enough in outline and only at the end does Mr Hitchcock's flair for the startling – not to say the shocking – give some justification to all the fuss.

A nice girl, Marion (Miss Janet Leigh), gives way to sudden temptation, steals 40,000 dollars, and finishes up at a desolate "motel" run by Norman (Mr Anthony Perkins), an apparently nice young man. Norman appears (the story is, after all, sufficiently subtle in its implications to demand such equivocal verbs) to have a domineering old mother, who lives in a kind of Charles Addams residence, and, when first Marion and then a private detective (Mr Martin Balssam) are murdered, it seems that the old mother is involved. And so in a way, a psychological way, she is, for the title of this film is, after all, *Psycho* and so a split personality cannot be far away. *Psycho* is neither so horrifying nor so surprising as might have been expected, and, there are scenes and lines of dialogue which inspire the wrong kind of laughter.

PSYCHO SHOWER SCENE VOTED MOST SHOCKING

By Robin Young, October 28 2004

The spine-chilling motel shower murder in Alfred Hitchcock's 1960 film *Psycho* has been voted the most terrifying moment in cinematic history. Jack Nicholson's demonic shriek as he axes down a door in *The Shining* was runner-up in the poll of 4,500 film fans by the entertainment conglomerate Blockbuster. The stomach-churning moment in *The Exorcist* when a possessed girl's head spins round a gruesome 360 degrees took third place.

Steve Foulser, commercial vice-president for Blockbuster UK, who commissioned the survey, said: "These spine-chilling movie moments really stick in your head. Even people who haven't seen the films will probably know the particular scenes in this poll. Hitchcock definitely set the pace with his style of direction. For this genre of film, he hasn't been eclipsed and probably never will be. He was the master of his art and this poll is testament to that fact."

Samara's ghoulish appearance as she emerges from the TV screen in *The Ring* came fourth, while the ankle-breaking scene of the psychotic monster Kathy Bates, from the 1990 hit film *Misery*, completes the top five.

VERTIGO: MR ALFRED HITCHCOCK AND THE SIMENON TOUCH

Review, From Our Film Critic
(Dudley Carew), August 11 1958

Suspense is, of course, the first quality to be looked for in the films Mr Alfred Hitchcock directs. The word attaches itself to him automatically, as "pessimism" does to Hardy, yet suspense is not the beginning and the end of Hitchcock. He is a cunning director who sets his scene with a precision and economy that recall Simenon. He plays as fair (or nearly) with his audience as that writer does with his readers, and he requires, in his turn, concentration from it – at one point in *Vertigo* a split second of inattention would lead to complete confusion as to what was going on in the last third of the film. *Vertigo* is not an important film or even major Hitchcock, but it entertains and is admirably photographed.

For the ingenuity of the story, the authors of the novel *D'Entre les Morts*, on which the film is based, must have a considerable share of the credit; and ingenious, over-ingenious, as some may think, *Vertigo* certainly is. "Scottie" Ferguson (Mr James Stewart) resigns from the police force in San Francisco because he cannot trust himself to chase malefactors over roof tops – he is, in other words, a victim of vertigo. He is engaged by Gavin (Mr Tom Helmore), who is an old friend of his and who has married the rich Madeleine (Miss Kim Novak), to follow her, not for the purposes of procuring evidence for divorce but because she seems to be living in the past rather than the present. She appears to be obsessed by the personality of her Spanish great-grandmother, a woman who had a tragic and eventful life culminating in suicide.

In the course of carrying out his duties Scottie falls in love with Madeleine, but is not able to save her from throwing herself off a church tower that haunts her dreams. At least that is how it looks at the time. "Scottie" then has a nervous breakdown and afterwards meets Judy, a working girl who wonderfully resembles Madeleine, which is not surprising since she, too, is played by Miss Novak. The pattern begins to repeat itself, and the top of

Mr. Alfred Hitchcock and the Simenon Touch

FROM OUR FILM CRITIC

Suspense is, of course, the first quality to be looked for in the films Mr. Alfred Hitchcock directs. The word attaches itself to him automatically, as "pessimism" does to Hardy, yet suspense is not the beginning and the end of Hitchcock. He is a cunning director who sets his scene with a precision and economy that recall Simenon. He plays as fair (or nearly) with his audience as that writer does with his readers, and he requires, in his turn, concentration from it—at one point in *Vertigo* a split second of inattention would lead to complete confusion as to what was going on in the last third of the film. *Vertigo*, which is now at the Odeon Cinema, Leicester Square, is not an important film or even major Hitchcock, but it entertains and is admirably photographed.

For the ingenuity of the story, the authors of the novel *D'Entre les Morts*, on which the film is based, must have a considerable share of the credit; and ingenious, over-ingenious, as some may think, *Vertigo* certainly is. "Scottie" Ferguson (Mr. James Stewart) resigns from the police force in San Francisco because he cannot trust himself to chase malefactors over roof tops—he is, in other words, a victim of vertigo. He is engaged by Gavin (Mr. Tom Helmore), who is an old friend of his and who has married the rich Madeleine (Miss Kim Novak), to follow her, not for the purposes of procuring evidence for divorce but because she seems to be living in the past rather than the present. She appears to be obsessed by the personality of her Spanish great-grandmother, a woman who had a tragic and eventful life culminating in suicide.

In the course of carrying out his duties, "Scottie" falls in love with Madeleine, but is not able to save her from throwing herself off a church tower that haunts her dreams. At least that is how it looks at the time. "Scottie" then has a nervous breakdown and afterwards meets Judy, a working girl who wonderfully resembles Madeleine, which is not surprising since she, too, is played by Miss Novak. The pattern begins to repeat itself, and the top of that church tower once more into the picture.

It would not be fair to say more, but the glimpse and feel of the supernatural are resolved at the end into the mechanics of crime, far-fetched though these may be. Mr. Stewart is at his best in his light, off-hand moments with the commercial artist Midge (Miss Barbara Bel Geddes), who, with humorous resignation, dotes on him—nervous breakdowns and long, passionate kisses do not suit his casual style. Mr. Hitchcock tries hard to make Miss Novak act and, at moments, succeeds.

A CRY FROM THE STREETS

British comedians who have proved themselves on the stage or over the air are sometimes made to run, as Mr. Norman Wisdom can testify, a kind of non-stop farcical obstacle race when they find themselves on the screen. Mr. Lewis Gilbert, who directs *A Cry From the Streets*, now to be seen at the Plaza, is wiser—he has realized that Mr. Max Bygraves is a relaxed kind of actor and allows him to act in a relaxed kind of way. The setting (King's Cross and district) of Miss Elizabeth Coxhead's novel *The Friend in Need* and the rather too self-assured character of Ann, the heroine, a children's welfare officer, are kept intact—her efforts to look after the youthful flotsam and jetsam of the slum streets, the unwanted children, form the core of the story.

Sentiment, of course, there is, and sometimes sentimentality, but the film by no means always chooses the easiest, most obvious, cliché, while Mr. Bygraves, as an electrical engineer who becomes interested both in Ann and her work, shows himself the possessor of a delightful personality. He is here not so much a professional funny man as a pleasant person who could obviously be funny if he wanted to be. Miss Barbara Murray is a little too smooth as Ann, but then she has some formidable competition from a bevy of child actors including Colin Petersen, who played "Smiley," David Bushell, and Dana Wilson whose surname should have been Weller—with a "we."

NOR THE MOON BY NIGHT

"Rusty" Miller (Mr. Michael Craig), a game-warden like his elder brother, Andrew (Mr. Patrick McGoohan), says somewhere in this film that his ex-wife had a peculiar idea of Africa—and so, if it takes *Nor the Moon By Night* (at the Odeon, Marble Arch) literally, will the audience. At least there is, for the principals at any rate, never a dull moment. If there is not a rogue elephant to be shot, there is a lion to be knifed, a bush fire to be put out, the victim of a murderous native attack to be succoured, a white poacher to be caught, a local chief to be disciplined. The director, Mr. Ken Annakin, strives to make all these breathless goings-on plausible each one, considered separately, might well pass muster—but it is tough going, and Miss Belinda Lee, as an ex-nurse, who arrives from England to marry one brother and falls in love with the other, is not of much help. If any suffering was caused to animals, this is a difficult film to forgive.

that church tower comes once more into the picture.

It would not be fair to say more, but the glimpse and feel of the supernatural are resolved at the end into the mechanics of crime, far-fetched though these may be. Mr Stewart is at his best in his light, off-hand moments with the commercial artist Midge (Miss Barbara Bel Geddes), who, with humorous resignation, dotes on him – nervous breakdowns and long, passionate kisses do not suit his casual style. Mr Hitchcock tries hard to make Miss Novak act and, at moments, succeeds.

26 July 1971. Alfred Hitchcock produces and directs the film *Frenzy* on location in Covent Garden, London. (Harry Kerr)

VERTIGO SCALES THE DIZZY HEIGHTS TO BE NAMED BEST FILM AFTER HALF-CENTURY

By Ben Hoyle, Arts Correspondent, August 2 2012

When *Vertigo* came out in 1958, *The Times* film critic said that it was "not an important film or even major Hitchcock, but it entertains and is admirably photographed".

It was a typical reaction to a film that flopped at the box office and was later withdrawn from circulation by Alfred Hitchcock, its British director.

More than half a century later, however, this complex, romantic, dreamlike, anxiety-drenched thriller is rather better regarded: today, in the most authoritative poll yet taken of the world's film critics, *Vertigo* is declared the greatest film ever to have been made.

The cineaste magazine *Sight & Sound* has been surveying film critics' preferences every ten years since 1952. The first poll was topped by Vittorio De Sica's *Bicycle Thieves*. In every poll since then the winner has been *Citizen Kane*. Now Orson Welles's monumental epic has finally been toppled, by an unexpectedly large margin, and by a film that did not enter the *Sight & Sound* chart until the 1980s.

Vertigo stars James Stewart as a private eye who becomes infatuated with a woman he believes to be his friend's straying wife, played by Kim Novak.

It was the first in a trio of very different films that Hitchcock made at the height of his fame in the late 1950s, followed a year later by the comedy-thriller *North by Northwest* and in 1960 by the innovative horror film *Psycho*. They feature at 53 and 35 respectively in *Sight & Sound*'s list. *Vertigo* has been steadily climbing the chart from seventh in 1982 to second ten years ago.

The 80-year-old magazine, published by the BFI, asked more than 1,000 critics for their ten "greatest films" in no particular order. The magazine received 846 replies, representing film critics all over the world. *Vertigo* came top by 34 votes, with *Citizen Kane* a further 50 votes clear of Yasujiro Ozu's *Tokyo Story* in third.

More than half of the top ten are black-and-white films, and seven figured in the same list ten years ago. The most recent is Stanley Kubrick's *2001: A Space Odyssey* from 1968. The highest-placed 21st century film in the Top 100 is *In the Mood for Love* by the Chinese director Wong Kar-wai at 24.

A parallel survey of 358 film directors, including Martin Scorsese, Francis Ford Coppola, Woody Allen and Quentin Tarantino, has a slightly more current look about it with *Taxi Driver*, *Apocalypse Now* and *The Godfather* in the top ten. It was the second time that this poll had been run and *Citizen Kane* was again deposed, this time by *Tokyo Story*.

Nick James, the editor of *Sight & Sound*, said: "In a way *Kane* is now seen as a more dated film. In a lot of ways *Vertigo* has survived as a modern film. It's about two people in the city who have lost their sense of themselves and [in places] it feels very much like a reality TV game."

CRITICS' CHOICE: THE TOP 25

1 *Vertigo* (Alfred Hitchcock, 1958)
2 *Citizen Kane* (Orson Welles, 1941)
3 *Tokyo Story* (Yasujiro Ozu, 1953)
4 *La Règle du Jeu* (Jean Renoir, 1939)
5 *Sunrise: A Song of Two Humans* (F. W. Murnau, 1927)
6 *2001: A Space Odyssey* (Stanley Kubrick, 1968)
7 *The Searchers* (John Ford, 1956)
8 *Man with a Movie Camera* (Dziga Vertov, 1929)
9 *The Passion of Joan of Arc* (Carl Theodor Dreyer, 1928)
10 *8½* (Federico Fellini, 1963)
11 *Battleship Potemkin* (Sergei Eisenstein, 1925)
12 *L'Atalante* (Jean Vigo, 1934)
13 *Breathless* (Jean-Luc Godard, 1960)
14 *Apocalypse Now* (Francis Ford Coppola, 1979)
15 *Late Spring* (Yasujiro Ozu, 1949)
16 *Au Hasard Balthazar* (Robert Bresson, 1966)
17 *Seven Samurai* (Akira Kurosawa, 1954)
= *Persona* (Ingmar Bergman, 1966)
19 *Mirror* (Andrei Tarkovsky, 1974)
20 *Singin' in the Rain* (Stanley Donen, Gene Kelly, 1952)
21 *L'avventura* (Michelangelo Antonioni, 1960)
= *Le Mépris* (Jean-Luc Godard, 1963)
= *The Godfather* (Francis Ford Coppola, 1972)
24 *Ordet* (Carl Theodor Dreyer, 1955)
= *In the Mood for Love* (Wong Kar-wai, 2000)

ACTRESSES

Taken from 'Top 100 Actresses', unbylined, published December 23 2000

20. Kathy Burke

While characters such as the pizza-scoffing, chain-smoking Waynetta Slob in *Harry Enfield and Chums* made Burke's name as Britain's funniest female, her CV also boasts some impressive acting credentials. Early celluloid outings include Alex Cox's *Sid and Nancy* (1986) and *Straight to Hell* (1987), while her portrayal of a battered wife in *Nil by Mouth* saw her beat off Kim Basinger and Sigourney Weaver for the Best Actress Award at the 1998 Cannes Film Festival.

Must see: *Nil by Mouth* (1997)
Avoid: *Kevin and Perry Go Large* (2000)

19. Christina Ricci

To be considered one of the greatest actresses of all time before your 21st birthday is no mean feat. But then none of her contemporaries can touch Ricci for piercing intelligence and quirky charisma. She first hit the screen at the age of ten in *Mermaids* (1990), but really announced her talents to the world the following year as the caustic Wednesday in *The Addams Family*. Recent leftfield roles in films such as *Buffalo 66* and *The Opposite of Sex* (both 1998) have kept her credibility enviably high.

Must see: *The Ice Storm* (1997)
Avoid: *Now and Then* (1995)

18. Dame Peggy Ashcroft

17. Frances McDormand

In 1988 McDormand received a Best Supporting Actress Oscar nomination for *Mississippi Burning*. When she lost out to Geena Davis for *The Accidental Tourist*, many felt that McDormand had been robbed. The Academy rectified the oversight in 1996 by awarding her the Best Actress statuette for her role in *Fargo*, co-directed by her husband Joel Coen. Ironically, she nearly rejected the role of the pregnant sheriff, afraid of looking like "a big brown turd in a white field".

Must see: *Fargo* (1996)
Avoid: *Passed Away* (1992)

16. Greta Garbo

"Garbo Talks!" proclaimed the posters for *Anna Christie* (1930), and the world held its breath to find out if the Swedish silent movie goddess sounded as good as she looked. She did. Despite four nominations in the Thirties, Garbo had to wait until 1954 for an "honorary" Oscar. True to the spirit of her own immortal maxim "I want to be alone", the queen of costume drama refused to emerge from the self-imposed retirement she had maintained from the age of 36 to collect the statuette.

Must see: *Camille* (1936)
Avoid: *Two-Faced Woman* (1941)

A far more prolific stage actress than screen star, her rare film roles were decades apart, but they were always of the highest calibre. In later years she often became a fixture of quality television drama, from *The Jewel in the Crown* to John Le Carre's *A Perfect Spy*. She gained global acclaim as one of the oldest first-time Oscar winners for her role in *A Passage to India* in 1984. Her radical credentials were enhanced by an affair with Paul Robeson.

Must see: *A Passage to India* (1984)
Avoid: *Joseph Andrews* (1977)

15. Joan Crawford

To F Scott Fitzgerald she symbolised "the apex of sophistication", but Joan Crawford's life was tough right from the start. Her parents separated before she was born and by the age of 11 she was working in a laundry to pay her own school fees. Still, that didn't stop her from becoming one of the top stars at MGM during the Thirties, so much so that her rival Bette Davis once carped bitterly: "She's slept with every male star at MGM except Lassie". It's tough at the top.

Must see: *Possessed* (1947)
Avoid: *Trog* (1970)

14. Sigourney Weaver

"I think I get sent the roles Meryl's not doing," she has famously declared. Both blessed and cursed by becoming a pop culture icon with her debut starring role, Ridley Scott's 1979 sci-fi thriller *Alien* made this self-styled "late bloomer" an international star. Weaver branched out successfully into comedy with *Ghostbusters* (1984) and social satire in Ang Lee's *The Ice Storm* (1997), but the *Alien* franchise remains her pension scheme, with four instalments and counting.

Must see: *Aliens* (1986)
Avoid: *Half Moon Street* (1986)

13. Meryl Streep

Only matched by Katharine Hepburn in Oscar nominations, with a dozen each, Mary Louise Streep's commitment to the craft of acting is legendary. Her first Academy nomination for Michael Cimino's *The Deer Hunter* in 1978 was followed by hit after hit over the next decade, including Oscar-winning turns in *Kramer Vs Kramer* (1979) and *Sophie's Choice* (1982), plus nominations for *The French Lieutenant's Woman* (1981), *Silkwood* (1983), *Out of Africa* (1985), *Ironweed* (1987) and more.

Must see: *Sophie's Choice* (1982)
Avoid: *She Devil* (1989)

Maggie Smith in her dressing room at the Elizabeth Theatre. (Culley)

12. Maggie Smith

Quite literally one of British theatre's grand dames, Maggie Smith's career is set to make another stellar leap when she plays Professor Minerva McGonagall in the forthcoming *Harry Potter* film. Her glorious array of cut-glass British eccentrics has made her worthy of the epithet "well-loved" and yet, as her Oscar-winning performance in *The Prime of Miss Jean Brodie* proved so clearly, she never sinks to caricature.

Must see: *The Prime of Miss Jean Brodie* (1969)

Avoid: *Sister Act II: Back in the Habit* (1992)

11. Audrey Hepburn

"God kissed the face of Audrey Hepburn and there she was," said Billy Wilder, and for many the director's explanation remains convincing. Yet while this unlikely member of The Lavender Hill Mob soon became a byword for style and elegance, the guise of alluring gamine never prevented her carrying a film and creating priceless screen chemistry with many of Hollywood's leading men including Cary Grant and Gregory Peck. She remains one of Hollywood's most enchanting presences.

Must see: *Breakfast at Tiffany's* (1961)
Avoid: *My Fair Lady* (1964)

18 August 1965. Catherine Deneuve on the day of her wedding to photographer David Bailey at St Pancras registry office. (Tom Dixon)

27 April 1951. Audrey Hepburn on set at Ealing Studios.

10. Catherine Deneuve

"Why would I talk about the men in my life? For me, life is not about men." An international icon not just of Frenchness but of ageless, androgyne sexuality, Paris-born Catherine Dorléac borrowed her mother's maiden name for her teenage screen debut. After the director Roger Vadim ditched Brigitte Bardot for the 16-year-old Deneuve, she built a career on such controversial roles as the housewife prostitute in Luis Bunuel's *Belle de Jour* (1967). Though briefly married to the photographer David Bailey she later declared marriage "obsolete and a trap". She had children with both Vadim and the Italian screen idol Marcello Mastroianni but refused to marry either. Deneuve continues to work with the cream of European directors, most recently in Lars Von Trier's *Dancer in the Dark* (2000). As Gerard Depardieu once said of Deneuve: "She is the man I would have liked to be."
Must see: *Repulsion* (1965)
Avoid: *The Hunger* (1983)

9. Lauren Bacall

At the age of 19 Bacall became an overnight star with her sizzling delivery of the following instruction to Humphrey Bogart in *To Have and Have Not*: "You know how to whistle don't you, Steve? You just put your lips together and blow." Despite being 25 years her senior, Bogie became Bacall's first husband. They made a formidable team, both on and off screen, until Bogart's death by cancer in 1957. Though Warners vigorously promoted Bacall's career, calling her "The Look", she refused to toe the strict studio line and proved just as feisty in real life as she appeared on the screen. The studio suspended her 12 times for refusing parts that she didn't want to play. In 1966, with the glory days of *The Big Sleep* (1946) and *Key Largo* (1948) long gone, Bacall temporarily retired from the screen. Eight years later she was coaxed back for *Murder on the Orient Express* and has continued to work ever since.
Must see: *To Have and Have Not* (1944)
Avoid: *All I Want for Christmas* (1991)

8. Susan Sarandon

There are few actresses who have managed to buck the dominant Hollywood ethos as efficiently as Susan Sarandon. While ever-older men are paired with ever-younger women, Sarandon has developed a vocation for depicting mature, truthful sexuality in a way that makes the screen smoulder. Her performances in *Thelma & Louise* (1991), *Bull Durham* (1988) and *White Palace* (1990) all convey a resilient toughness cut with vulnerability, a combination that makes her a particularly modern star. Sarandon and her husband Tim Robbins are two of Hollywood's most vocal political activists, hence her part in campaigning films such as *Lorenzo's Oil* (1992) and *Dead Man Walking* (1995). It's a long way from her role as Janet in *The Rocky Horror Picture Show* (1975), but even that showed an actress who would grow along with her audience, real-life wit and wisdom slowly conquering disposable culture.

Must see: *Bull Durham* (1988)
Avoid: *Stepmom* (1998)

7. Judi Dench

Though her stage performances have been winning her ecstatic curtain calls for decades, it is only relatively recently that Britain's best-loved contemporary actress has come to global prominence in films. Dame Judi caught the eye for her memorable performance as the eccentric author Eleanor Lavish in *A Room with a View* (1986), and won a Bafta for her part in *A Handful of Dust* (1988). But it was the inspired combination of stubborn authority and vulnerability that she brought to the role of Queen Victoria opposite an intractable Billy Connolly in *Mrs Brown* (1997) that really made her name in Hollywood. She went on to win an Oscar for a triumphant eight-minute cameo as another formidable monarch, Elizabeth I, in *Shakespeare in Love* (1998) and has recently cemented her status as a national institution by taking on the role of M, 007's stern boss, in the last three *James Bond* films.

Must see: *Mrs Brown* (1997)
Avoid: *Jack and Sarah* (1995)

6. Jessica Lange

Her debut as the heroine in the dire remake of *King Kong* almost stalled Lange's film career before it had begun. By the early Eighties, however, she had demonstrated that she was much more than decorative eye-candy. While her fair features can suggest a fragile vulnerability, her performances are invariably gutsy and wonderfully intuitive. Her sensual turn in *The Postman Always Rings Twice* (1981) preceded a powerhouse performance as the mentally unstable actress Frances Farmer in the 1982 biopic. Her film career since has been defined by faultless performances often portraying complex women given a raw deal in such films as *Sweet Dreams* (1985), *Music Box* (1990) and *Blue Sky* (1994). Not limited to the silver screen, she is currently providing further evidence of her versatility on the stage, wowing London theatre audiences in Eugene O'Neill's *Long Day's Journey into Night*.

Must see: *Frances* (1982)
Avoid: *King Kong* (1976)

5. Elizabeth Taylor

"What is the victory of a cat on a hot tin roof?" muses Paul Newman in the 1958 film of Tennessee Williams's play. "Just staying on it, I guess, as long as she can," Taylor purrs in response, an observation that could apply to her own remarkable tenacity in the public eye. With *Father of the Bride* (1950), Taylor leapt from being the child star sidekick of lively pets in *Lassie Come Home* (1943) and *National Velvet* (1944) to become one of the brightest stars in the firmament. Nominated several times, Taylor finally won the Best Actress Oscar in 1960 for her portrayal of "the slut of all time" in *Butterfield 8*. The honour came her way again in 1966 for her unforgettable performance opposite her husband Richard Burton in *Who's Afraid of Virginia Woolf?* A string of health problems, a tabloid-friendly sideline as a serial bride and her reinvention as an AIDS activist have only enhanced Taylor's status as an international treasure.

Must see: *Cat on a Hot Tin Roof* (1958)
Avoid: *Boom!* (1968)

4. Jodie Foster

She started acting at the age of two and by 13 her inspired Oscar-nominated performance as a teenage prostitute opposite Robert De Niro in Scorsese's *Taxi Driver* (1976) had made her a worldwide star and inspired John Warnock Hinkley Jr's assassination attempt on Ronald Reagan in 1981. Since then, cinema's favourite overachiever has managed to squeeze in an English Literature degree at Yale, more than 30 screen roles and three films in the director's chair, as well as doing her own voiceovers in the French-dubbed versions of her films. A chillingly believable performance as a rape victim in *The Accused* (1988) and her most famous role as the tenacious FBI agent Clarice Starling in *The Silence of the Lambs* (1991) made her the first actress to win two Oscars before the age of 30. Though her recent output has been more erratic, her place in the Hollywood pantheon is assured.
Must see: *The Accused* (1988)
Avoid: *Catch Fire* (1989)

3. Ingrid Bergman

Radiating an unaffected composure along with a serene beauty, this Swedish legend was born to play haunted, often tragic, heroines. In the Thirties and Forties she gained the admiration of audiences with the fresh naturalism of Hitchcock's *Notorious* (1946), an Oscar-winning performance in *Gaslight* (1944) and her unrivalled portrayals of composed vulnerability in *For Whom the Bell Tolls* (1943) and *Casablanca*. After her scandalous affair with the director Roberto Rossellini and, having been branded "Hollywood's apostle of degradation" in the US Senate, she spent six years in Europe showing her versatility as an actress in progressive arthouse films such as *Voyage in Italy* (1953). However, her Hollywood comeback in *Anastasia* (1956) won her a second Oscar, re-establishing her iconic status.
Must see: *Casablanca* (1942)
Avoid: *Stromboli* (1949)

24 November 1958. Ingrid Bergman and fiancé Lars Schmidt attending the premiere of the film *The Inn of the Sixth Happiness* at the Odeon in Leicester Square. (A. Harris)

2. Bette Davis

"Until you are known in my profession as a monster, you're not a star," Hollywood's most formidable leading lady once purred. From her poison-tongued feud with Joan Crawford to a tempestuous love life, which included four marriages and numerous affairs, Davis's abrasive demeanour was the stuff of legend. Her vast emotional range and unconventional but exqui-

site looks led to Oscars for *Dangerous* (1935) and *Jezebel* (1938). Throughout the Thirties and Forties she rarely made fewer than three movies a year. Just as her star was threatening to fade she returned with a vengeance as the ageing Broadway star Margo Channing in Joseph L Mankiewicz's *All About Eve* (1950), then remade herself as a vamp in *What Ever Happened to Baby Jane?* (1962). The stuff screen legends are made of. "She did it the hard way," reads her aptly worded tombstone.

Must see: *All About Eve* (1950)
Avoid: *Beyond the Forest* (1949)

1. Katharine Hepburn

In terms of ability, longevity and sheer bloody-minded charisma, Hepburn was equally capable of dominating the screen in sweeping epics (*The African Queen*, 1951), harrowing dramas (*Long Day's Journey into Night*, 1962) and sparkling comedies (*The Philadelphia Story*, 1940). No actor or actress has been held in such esteem by the Academy; she has received an unprecedented 12 Oscar nominations, winning her first statuette for *Morning Glory* (1933) and claiming her fourth and final almost five decades later for *On Golden Pond* (1981). But her charm and durability went far beyond awards. She refused to play to Hollywood's rules, enduring a lean critical spell in the Thirties and slouching around on sets in slacks and no make-up. Though they never married, the love of her life was Spencer Tracey, with whom she starred in nine films, beginning with *Woman of the Year* (1942). The sequence finished with the sublime *Guess Who's Coming to Dinner* (1967), a film she refused to watch because it was Tracey's last before dying of a heart attack in the same year. "I'm a personality as well as an actress," she once stated with characteristic bluntness. "Show me an actress who isn't a personality, and you'll show me a woman who isn't a star."

Must see: *The Philadelphia Story* (1940)
Avoid: *Sylvia Scarlett* (1936)

Editor's note: Meryl Streep broke Hepburn's Oscar record, clocking up an amazing 21st nomination in 2018 for *The Post*. She won three.

16 April 1952. Katherine Hepburn at rehearsals for *The Millionairess* by George Bernard Shaw, which was being directed by Michael Benthall. (Gough)

CLASSIC CINEMA

Bicycle Thieves

Unbylined review (Dudley Carew),
December 22 1949

Bicycle Thieves has not stolen upon the country unawares. For a long time those whose business is with the cinema have been agitated by rumours of an Italian film which would rival the masterpieces of the old silent days, of a technique which would set the screen telling its story by the proper method of composition, movement, and image, of acting which, amateur in status, would put the deliberated methods of the professionals to shame.

The film has now been seen in London, and rumour can be acquitted of all charges except, perhaps, the minor one of pitching its story a little too high. "Masterpiece" is a dangerous, a difficult, word to define, especially where the cinema is concerned, but, if it is left aside, then *Bicycle Thieves* is all that it is reported to have been. It can, in the first place, easily be understood without the help of sub-titles or any knowledge of the Italian language, and the director, Vittorio De Sica, is never to be put off his concentrated work of conveying to his audience the emotion, as well as the outline, of the simple content of his material. An unemployed Italian, Antonio (Lamberto Maggiorani), gets an offer of work as a bill-poster if he has a bicycle. He has a bicycle, but it is in pawn. His wife (Lianella Carell) sells the sheets to get the bicycle out of pawn, and Antonio starts out on his job. Within a few hours his bicycle is stolen, and the rest of the film resolves itself into a heart-breaking effort on the part of Antonio to recover what he has lost. He has to help him his small son, a child with a head rather too big for his body, a pair of sardonic eyebrows, a sense of values too acute and understanding for his age, and, as he is played by Enzo Staiola, an enormous capacity for suffering, although the hands thrust forward belligerently into shabby knickerbocker pockets would deny it. De Sica conducts their search through Rome, through its back streets and black markets, its brothels and churches, its humours, dramas and sports with an eye that is at once satirical – a little too easily satirical in its church scene? – and observant, and always the screen is formed into a deliberate pattern of mass and of movement, of light and of shade. The need for a bicycle drives Antonio into stealing one for himself, and De Sica's greatest triumph consists in his success in making that mad, desperate need comparable to that of Richard Plantagenet for a horse when Bosworth Field was in the balance.

CLASSIC FILM OF THE WEEK

Bicycle Thieves

Review by Kate Muir,
August 14 2015

★★★★★

Often in critics' all-time top tens, the Italian director Vittorio De Sica's *Bicycle Thieves* is tender and immediate, a simple tale of a man whose bike is stolen when his job and life depends upon it. The proverb "all for the want of a horseshoe nail …" underpins the tense, compelling scenario, and the amateur actors – a man and a boy played by Lamberto Maggiorani and Enzo Staiola – give utterly involving performances.

In postwar Rome, poverty abounds and the unspoken detail is caught by De Sica's camera: new concrete flats with no water; the middle classes in pearls running soup kitchens for the poor, who doff their caps; a pawn shop with endless shelves to the sky. Carlo Montuori's cinematography leaches any glamour from the black-and-white city, which in one scene is almost exquisitely smeared by rain.

There's always a sense of documentary-like movement in the background: citizens and bikes rushing and stadiums emptying into the streets, while the moral scales weigh the fate of the man, Antonio Ricci, and his son Bruno, whose size belies a smart survival instinct.

"I feel like a man in chains," says Ricci, unable to take a job pasting up street posters without a bike. The sheer precariousness of his life leaves the viewer desperately rooting for him.

FIRST FILMS

LAUREN BACALL

To Have and Have Not

Unbylined review (Dudley Carew),
June 15 1945

The film is freely adapted from a novel by Mr Ernest Hemingway and reflects something of the tough style, the clipped sentences, and monosyllabic dialogue of that writer, although his more serious intentions would seem to pass it by.

The setting is Martinique in 1940 after the fall of France, and, although with the supporters of Vichy and the Free French elements, the situation is dangerous and involved, Mr Humphrey Bogart is the master of it from the beginning. As the American captain of a fishing boat he is able to help the patriots, and the story of his adventures on the high seas and with the Vichy police, represented by a man of impressive size and unpleasantness, are told with a feeling for menace, for the danger in the swing of a latticed door, the flare from a lamp, the crash of chords on a cafe piano. Mr Bogart never hurries and never raises his voice, and both the director and Miss Lauren Bacall, as the mysterious young heroine, take their cue from him. So intent, indeed, are they on avoiding the clichés of dramatic situation and acting that lines are thrown away and Miss Bacall, who has a sense of humour tucked away behind the slinky-cynical decorations of her part, is at moments almost inaudible. *To Have and Have Not* is a rather more successful film than *Casablanca*, which, in form and spirit, it closely resembles.

CULT MOVIES

◇◇◇◇◇◇◇◇◇◇◇◇◇◇◇◇◇◇◇◇◇◇◇◇◇◇◇◇◇◇◇◇

Editor's note: *Blade Runner* and *The Wicker Man* may be acknowledged as classics now, but that was not always the case. *Blade Runner* was part of a spate of movies in the early to mid-1980s which mixed different genres together. The critics were not overly excited by such innovations and the films often did poorly at the box office, but several were later acknowledged as classics or found an enthusiastic audience via video and DVD, whereas in a previous age they might have been forgotten. *Blade Runner*, film noir in a sci-fi setting, lost money on it is initial release, but over the years its reputation and audience just grew and grew. For many it was not just a single night's entertainment, but an intriguing mystery, an obsession. There were at least seven different versions, including a director's cut – which the director himself disowned. And it is now pretty much agreed *Blade Runner* is a masterpiece ... Personally I still like the original version best, complete with voice-over. A few years later *Highlander* mixed sci-fi with historical action and *Predator*

was a hybrid of military and monster movies, though it at least was a hit with the public from the outset. *The Wicker Man*, which came out a decade earlier, was a unique mix of thriller, horror, black comedy and folk musical. Now recognised as one of the most original films ever made in Britain and justly celebrated as the ultimate cult movie, it did not even merit a review in *The Times* when it first appeared, quickly consigned to the bottom half of a double bill with *Don't Look Now*.

◇◇◇◇◇◇◇◇◇◇◇◇◇◇◇◇◇◇◇◇◇◇◇◇◇◇◇◇◇◇◇◇

Blade Runner

Review by David Robinson,
September 10 1982

Blade Runner is a peculiar piece of hybridization, a 1980's future-world style (technological mystification and special effects) crossed with 1940's film noir – with 21st century private eye, first-person voice-over narrative, femme fatale with Mary Astor hair-styling, and even neon lighting, filtered through Venetian blinds. The story also pulls in elements of *Frankenstein*, *Metropolis*, *Caligari*, *Swan Lake*, *Doctor Mabuse*, *Coppelia* and indeed practically any popular myth that comes to mind. As an adaptation of its own acknowledged original, Philip K Dick's *Do Androids Dream of Electric Sheep?*, however, it is very bitty, full of loose ends and unexplained references which make a simple tale (private-eye hero assigned to exterminate six humanoid robots who have revolted and turned terrorist) hard to follow.

The director Ridley Scott is clearly much less concerned with story than with visual effects and these certainly offer variety and colour. Even if you question a future (AD 2019) where people still wear lounge suits with revers, read newspapers at lunch counters and have no more sense than to make robots in forms indistinguishable from themselves, the concept is striking. Los Angeles has become a vast Chinatown. The skies are murky and a perpetual rain beats down. Sophisticated jet-propelled aerial automobiles streak above streets which have been taken over by garbage and marauding gangs. Scene and story alike predict a gloomy future, envisioned out of the most ugly and violent aspects of city streets in our own times.

The best thing by far about *Blade Runner* is that it is accompanied by Clare Peploe's half-hour short *Couples and Robbers*, which considerably dispels the gloom. It is an unassuming, witty anecdote, nicely played by Frances Low, Rik Mayall, Peter Eyre and Frank Grimes. Set in familiar, London social milieu, it concerns (and it would be a shame to spill more of the beans) a newly-wed couple's ruses to achieve Sunday supplement happiness.

Blade Runner: Director's Cut

Review by Geoff Brown,
November 26 1992

Blade Runner has already earned its niche in history. For better or worse –

to my mind the latter – Ridley Scott's 1982 epic set in motion fantasy cinema's current obsession with chokingly dense visual effects, scanty or bewildering plots, marauding mutants and all-pervasive black.

Ten years on, in this new "director's cut", the work of Scott's design team remains impressive. No science-fiction city since Metropolis has looked so awesome as this Los Angeles of 2019, with its encrusted pyramids of industrial might, towers belching acrid fire, huge video screens and neon adverts looming through foul brown air and rain-swept streets. But we pay a high price for the film's design fetish. Despite the wicked grin of Rutger Hauer's rebel android, far more fetching than the weary hero in pursuit, this is a monotonous tale, its dramatic life choked by visual artifice.

When first released after nervous studio tinkering, two points grated with critics and public. Harrison Ford's hard-boiled narration jarred; while the film collapsed in the home stretch with a contrived happy ending for Ford, the android hunter, and Sean Young, the sinuous android dressed in Forties' high style. The present version, based on Scott's original cut, removes both blights. The thriller plot now chugs along unimpeded, and the end is bleaker. Along the way some scenes get tightened, others, particularly those with Ford and Young, lengthened.

Blade Runner Mark Two is undoubtedly a better film, one no science-fiction devotee should miss. But it still seems a dangerous classic: arid, monumental, a doleful signpost to a decade of films drenched in black, smoke and rain, of cartwheeling mutants and cyberpunk gadgetry, a decade when high technology won and the human heart lost.

AT LAST, A BLADE TO RUN WITH

Blade Runner: The Final Cut

Review by James Christopher, September 6 2007

Ridley Scott is happy with *Blade Runner: The Final Cut*. So is our chief film critic.

The desire of directors to have the last word on their masterpieces has been with us as long as the home video. But few directors have had such an obsessive relationship with a single film as Ridley Scott has. It has taken 25 years, five working prints and three quite different cinema releases to arrive at the definitive version of his sci-fi thriller, *Blade Runner: The Final Cut*. Last Saturday in Venice he declared himself more than happy to have finally come up with a version that won't "irritate" him.

But what about us? Despite being only a minute longer, *The Final Cut* is radically different from the 1982 original, but not that dissimilar to the *Director's Cut* of 1992. A third edit is a profound nuisance for fans of *Blade* versions 1 or 2.

Has it been worth the wait? Until I saw the final article on a huge screen in the Sala Grande last week I would have said no. But there is something utterly awe-inspiring about this remastered vision of Los Angeles in 2019. The dystopia seems more prophetic and bitter. The differences between Harrison Ford and the six genetically engineered "replicants" he is hired to terminate are less easy to define. And the Fritz Langian metropolis where it always seems to rain is polished to gloomy perfection.

The Final Cut is a far greater adult pleasure than *Blade Runner*, and it is the film Scott would have released if he had his way all those years ago. There is no rambling voiceover by Ford which Warner Brothers insisted on dubbing over the original release. According to one of Scott's producers, Charles de Lauzirika, "audiences didn't get the movie in test screenings. It was too dark, too downbeat, and the hero was ultimately too different from Harrison Ford's *Star Wars* screen persona for comfort."

The trouble started during postproduction. The terms of the completion bond locked Scott out of the editing suite. The studio released its own version of the film, with the voiceover and a happy ending stapled to the credits. Instead of the bleak and uncertain ending that Scott has now restored to the film, the hero Deckard (Ford) and the beautiful, melancholic replicant (Sean Young) he has fallen in love with are seen driving north through forests towards a romantic future.

Scott didn't have the chance to change a single frame of *Blade Runner* until 1991, when Warners sent an early "work print" version of the film to a repertory cinema by mistake. The screening of this cut became a word-of-mouth sensation, prompting Warners to invite Scott to re-edit the film. But the director was too busy shooting *Thelma & Louise* and preparing the Christopher Columbus epic *1492* to take part. He agreed to let Warners assemble a new version that chimed with his original ideas. Thus *Blade Runner: The Director's Cut* is not the director's cut after all, but an approximation of what Scott wanted. Ford's voiceover was stripped out, the happy ending was axed and a controversial black and white dream sequence was included which worryingly suggests that Deckard might be a replicant himself.

But according to de Lauzirika, the 1992 rerelease never got the Ridley seal of approval. In 2000 the producer had a meeting with Warners and the film's co-executive producers, Bud Yorkin and Jerry Perenchio, to get their blessing, and then persuaded Scott to personally re-edit his masterpiece.

From a distance it looked like a grotesque act of vanity. Up close the project assumed near-mythic status. All 977 boxes of negatives were re-examined, frame by frame. A day of reshoots involving Joanna Cassidy's half-naked snake dancer and Harrison Ford's grown-up son Ben were scheduled to synchronise a previously baffling scene at Abdul Al-Assan's seedy serpent shop. Links in the plot have been subtly strengthened. The sharp new ending gives Deckard an existential exit line, and the sense that the chaos is far from over.

Even the music by Vangelis feels organic: an irony considering that the entire movie is consumed by the question of what it is to be human. Whether Harrison Ford dreams of electric sheep or not is actually beside the point. What's significant about *The Final Cut* is that one of the great visual touchstones of modern cinema has been restored as truly intended.

Highlander

Review by David Robinson,
August 22 1986

The hard fact that today's commercial cinema has to face is that the great power of patronage lies with the young teenage audience, and that they call the tune. *Highlander* is symptomatic of this economic reality, one of a growing group of films in which huge resources of money, technology and craftsmanship are lavished on scenarios more suited to strip cartoons.

Highlander is a mishmash of synthetic mythology, about a group of immortal beings, variously representative of good and evil, who can only be destroyed by beheading. They meet from time to time through the ages, to fight for the prize of universal intelligence; which must never pass to Kurgan the Evil, whose neck is held together with safety-pins after repeated attempts on his immortality ("Who wontster live frevva?" asks a pertinent Queen song on the sound-track).

The sword-fighting shifts from 16th-century Scotland to 1986 New York, with little rhyme or reason: but – to

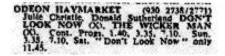

show that we can do this sort of thing as well as the Americans – the photography (Gerry Fisher) is spectacular and the special effects (the credit titles list an army of wizards) are astonishing and faultless. The film is calculated for an audience which demands only an unrelenting succession of visual effects, backed by an overpowering soundtrack. The director, Russell Mulcahy, comes appropriately from the world of pop video.

The most baffling special effect of all is how the Neanderthal face of Christopher Lambert, who plays the *Highlander* hero, is maintained in a constant state of three days' beard-growth. Presumably this is where the skill of the credited "prosthetic make-up artist" comes in.

THE COMIC STRIP KILLERS

Predator

Review by David Robinson, December 24 1987

A large part of today's Hollywood is given over to the manufacture of live-action comic strips. The special effects teams who are the new elite of the industry have realized, in three-dimensional motion, the space machines and monsters that once existed only in the lurid colours of comic books.

Exploding guns or bombs or people have the same style of visualization as the jagged-edged patches that exclaimed "Pow!!" and "Wham!!!" in the comics.

The aesthetic is adopted in more radical ways: in *Predator*, for instance, the camera set-ups constantly imitate the angular viewpoints and dramatic foreground close-ups favoured by cartoonists.

Film actors in this genre themselves seem to be drawn in the hard lines of cartoon figures. Their dialogue also tends to the basic, repetitive simplicity of block letters in picture balloons.

Predator opportunistically combines jungle war and supernatural horror. Schwarzenegger is a mercenary sent to support a CIA operation in one of those untrustworthy Central American countries. When the Commie guerrillas have all been blasted, he finds himself up against the most amorphous monster the comic strip screen has yet devised. Sometimes it appears like a levitating samurai; sometimes it has tree-branch limbs and computer entrails.

By the time of the final show-down with the indomitable hero, it has the body of an athlete, laser vision and a face as hideously deformed as special effects can devise. Its final metamorphosis is into a mushroom cloud. Whatever its shape, however, its habits remain as nasty: skinning and disembowelling Schwarzenegger's buddies and thereby further testing the ingenuity of the special effects men.

These horror comics are rarely innocent of political intent: this one belongs to the Cold War rear-guard, with its message that there are always sinister Soviets behind the murderous Latin lefties.

The comic strip killers

FILMS

Predator (18)
Leicester Square
Theatre, Odeon Marble
Arch

**Masters of the
Universe (PG)**
Cannon Haymarket,
Oxford Street

**The Adventures of
Mark Twain (U)**
ICA

Sarraounia
ICA

Trained killers: Carl Weathers and the gun-toting Arnold Schwarzenegger take a break from blasting baddies out of the jungle in *Predator*

A large part of today's Hollywood is given over to the manufacture of live-action comic strips. The special effects teams who are the new elite of the industry have realized, in three-dimensional motion, the space machines and monsters that once existed only in the lurid colours of comic books.

Exploding guns or bombs or people have the same style of visualization as the jagged-edged patches that exclaimed "Pow!!" and "Wham!!!" in the comics. The aesthetic is adopted in more radical ways: in *Predator*, for instance, the camera set-ups constantly imitate the angular viewpoints and dramatic foreground close-ups favoured by cartoonists.

Film actors in this genre themselves seem to be drawn in the hard lines of cartoon figures. Their dialogue also tends to the basic, repetitive simplicity of block letters in picture balloons.

Predator opportunistically combines jungle war and supernatural horror. Schwarzenegger is a mercenary sent to support a CIA operation in one of those untrustworthy Central American countries. When the Commie guerillas have all been blasted, he finds himself up against the most amorphous monster the comic strip screen has yet devised. Sometimes it appears like a levitating samurai; sometimes it has tree-branch limbs and computer entrails.

By the time of the final showdown with the indomitable hero, it has the body of an athlete, laser vision and a face as hideously

deformed as special effects can devise. Its final metamorphosis is into a mushroom cloud. Whatever its shape, however, its habits remain as nasty: skinning and disembowelling Schwarzenegger's buddies and thereby further testing the ingenuity of the special effects men.

These horror comics are rarely innocent of political intent: this one belongs to the Cold War rearguard, with its message that there are always sinister Soviets behind the murderous Latin lefties.

S ome new ground, at least, is trodden in *Masters of the Universe*, in that it is created from a best-selling line of toys of the same name introduced by Mattel five years ago and which have already inspired a television series.

Script, story and characters would do fine for plastic dolls, though the film has live actors and shameless borrowings from *Star Wars*. Skeletor (Frank Langella), the embodiment of evil, and his army

of Darth Vader lookalikes plot to get the key which will make them masters of the universe. He-Man (Dolph Lundgren) and his chums are out to save the world for Good.

This cosmic conflict rapidly moves to a record store in Hollywood — why not? — where a high school couple and an idiot detective get involved, and the whole thing gets progressively sillier and more tedious. It may be very rewarding if your toy box is full of Mattel products.

For those without toy boxes, the single compensation could be Billy Barty as a bearded dwarf computer wizard. Barty is a skilled, two-feet-tall comedian, who goes back a long way in films: in Warner musicals of the early Thirties he always played the lecherous baby. Here he is mischievous and engaging, even if he does not have much in the way of funny lines.

Alongside these aggressive and ugly shows, The Adventures of Mark Twain is refreshingly civi-

lized, and the only remotely Christmassy entertainment the London cinema offers this year. Produced and directed by Will Vinson, it uses a technique called "Claymation" in which figures modelled in Plasticine are animated by stop-action. The movement and facial expression are amazingly life-like; and the voicing of the characters (notably James Whitmore as Twain himself) is excellent.

T he film would have benefited from a firmer story-line. Susan Shadburn's script has Twain setting off on a final journey in an aerial machine which is part balloon and part Mississippi paddle-boat, with Tom, Huck and Becky Thatcher as stowaways.

His aim, it seems, is to fulfil a particular (and real-life) destiny: he came into the world with Halley's Comet in 1835, and was determined to make his exit with its 1910 manifestation.

In the other half of the world, film

is used more purposefully, to tell people about their history and heritage.

Med Hondo's *Sarraounia*, made in Burkina Faso (formerly Upper Volta), is the most ambitious African production to date, a historical epic set in colonial days at the end of the last century.

Sarraounia was Queen of the Aznas, trained in the arts of warfare and magic, and one of the few chiefs to oppose the colonial invaders. Sarraounia's story, which takes up the early part of the film, is told with more authority than the central section, which deals with the depredations of Captain Voulet, a maverick French officer (also a historical figure) who eventually turns upon his own comrades. The film is shot with great assurance and acute feeling for landscape, for crowds and armies, and for the contrasting colours of Africa and the uniforms of the alien armies.

David Robinson

PEOPLE

Robin Hardy

Much-married film director who collaborated with Anthony Shaffer on the eerie tale of *The Wicker Man*

Obituary (Brian Pendreigh),
July 7 2016

Many actors are associated with a single role, and many authors known for one great novel only, but few directors are as singularly linked to a film as Robin Hardy, who built an entire career around the belated success of the original 1973 version of *The Wicker Man*.

The eerie film, which horrified its audiences without showing a drop of blood, was deemed so uncommercial when it was first released that it was heavily cut by the studio. It might easily have been forgotten, despite its imaginative premise of a pagan society thriving on a Scottish island and the disturbing final scene in which Edward Woodward, playing Sergeant Neil Howie, is burnt alive in the giant wicker construction of the title. Over time, however, it became a genuine cult classic, with one magazine hailing it as "the *Citizen Kane* of horror". Its dedicated fans were dubbed "Wicker-heads".

Hardy wrote a novelisation after the film's initial release and worked on other screenplays with a similar theme – one, *The Wicker Tree*, went into production in 2009. At the time of his death he was raising funds for the third part of his "trilogy", *The Wrath of the Gods*.

While *The Wicker Man* was a heady mix of sex, violence, horror and pagan ritual, its director was well-spoken, urbane and debonair: Hardy would not have looked out of place in the bar of one of England's most exclusive golf clubs. He dressed conservatively in suit and tie, with a handkerchief neatly poking out from his breast pocket, or would sometimes wear a blazer and cravat. Intelligent, charming and well-travelled, he exuded old-school charisma.

Born in Wimbledon in 1929, Robin St Clair Hardy left school at 16 and went to study art in Paris, before crossing the Atlantic to take a job with the National Film Board of Canada and working in television in America.

Returning to London, he struck up a partnership with Anthony Shaffer, the twin brother of the playwright Peter Shaffer. They established their own company, making television commercials, and worked together through much of the 1960s, with Shaffer as writer and Hardy as director. The rapport between them was defined in part by a mutual love of practical jokes, with each constantly trying to outdo the other. "Sometimes I was furious at what he had done, and he was furious at what I'd done, but it kept us amused," Hardy once said with a wry smile.

26 April 2006. Robin Hardy, director of *The Wicker Man*. (Adrian Sherratt)

Top film awards go to Britain

Paris, April 16.—The Grand Prix of the third International Festival of Fantasy and Science Fiction Films was awarded today to the British film *The Wicker Man*, directed by Robin Hardy. The film deals with "paganism" in an isolated part of Scotland.

The Amazing Mr Blunden (Britain), directed by Lionel Jeffries, was judged best screen play, and Vincent Price best actor for his role in the American film *The Return of the Abominable Dr Phibes*.—Reuter.

Encouraged by his brother Peter's success with plays such as *The Royal Hunt of the Sun*, Anthony eventually quit the commercials business to concentrate on plays and films, writing *Sleuth* in 1970 – which was adapted for the big screen with Laurence Olivier and Michael Caine. He joined forces again with Hardy on *The Wicker Man*.

"Tony and I were great horror film buffs and used to see lots of the original Hammers," Hardy said. "We wondered why it was that they always centred on pentacles, garlic, stakes in hearts and all those other things to do with black magic. We thought it would be fun to go back to the religion on which all this hokey witchcraft stuff was based – the old religion – and re-create a contemporary society that was pre-Christian."

Hardy claimed that they had "a long series of conversations over a number of years" about creating *The Wicker Man* but that he wrote the initial story, which Shaffer turned into a screenplay. His comments were made long after the film's original release, at a time when it was attracting serious attention and acclaim. Shaffer dismissed the remarks as "unmitigated crap", maintaining that the idea was his. He said that he recruited Hardy as director because of their previous work together, and Shaffer received sole credit as writer on the film. The subsequent novelisation was credited to both men. "We are no longer friends," Shaffer would later tell one interviewer.

The film was shot on location in the west of Scotland, with Woodward as a stuffy, religious policeman who flies to a remote island to investigate the disappearance of a young girl. He finds a strange pagan community and is shocked by their loose moral and sexual standards. Christopher Lee played the local laird, Lord Summerisle. An unnerving combination of horror, thriller and musical, it ends with the locals singing folk songs as Woodward goes up in flames. Dilys Powell wrote in *The Sunday Times* that "the story turns into a barbarous joke, too horrible for pleasure".

In the years that followed Hardy wrote several novels, including *The Education of Don Juan*. He wrote and directed the thriller *The Fantasist* and produced *Forbidden Sun*, a film that mixed gymnastics, rape and Cretan legend. He also worked on *Winnie*, a stage musical about Winston Churchill, though this lasted only a few weeks in London's West End in 1988.

The Wicker Man's critical reassessment gathered momentum that same year after the BBC showed it in Alex Cox's *Moviedrome* series of cult films.

It was claimed that the original negative had been buried under the M4 motorway. An alternative theory was that Rod Stewart had wanted to buy and destroy it to stop people seeing the "bare bottom" of his girlfriend Britt Ekland, who played Willow, the daughter of Lord Summerisle. Ekland had in fact been provided with a bottom double after complaining that she had "an arse like a ski slope". "I think you'll find very few women who elect to be shot from the back if they can avoid it," said Hardy, who thought the story about Stewart was likely the invention of a press agent.

Latterly he and his fifth wife, Victoria Webster, whom he married in 2000, split their time between homes in London, Somerset, Corsica and Quebec. She survives him, along with his eight children from previous relationships. Though enigmatic about his private life, Hardy was a devoted father who loved to tell tales to his children and take them to historical sites. The past was a constant source of fascination for him – he became involved in the historical theme park business, setting up a company, Euro Centre Time Traveller Parks, and putting forward a number of proposals in Scotland, Italy and the US, though none of these materialised.

A 2006 remake of *The Wicker Man* starring Nicolas Cage made significant changes to the story, relocating it to Washington. Hardy had no direct involvement and asked for his name to be taken off promotional material. "It was a disaster. Poor Nicolas Cage … stumbled about dressed up in a bear suit and made himself look ridiculous. It was an entirely different film."

Robin Hardy, film director, was born on October 2, 1929. He died on July 1, 2016, aged 86.

JAMES BOND: PART TWO

Editor's note: *Dr. No* premiered on October 5 1962, the same day the first Beatles single was released. In retrospect, you might argue that the 1960s began that day, not that anyone argued that at the time. *The Times* considered *Dr. No* the least important of that week's new releases and its review was tucked away underneath a crit for a film version of the play *The Quare Fellow* by Brendan Behan and another for a Sandra Dee comedy called *If a Man Answers*. *The Times* did not write *Dr. No* off completely – the anonymous reviewer suggested that "perhaps Mr Sean Connery will, with practice, get the 'feel' of the part". By the time of the second film, *From Russia with Love*, it was obvious there was an audience for Bond, but even then no one knew just how big or long-lasting the series would be. Half a century later I was involved in tracking down exact locations for *From Russia with Love* and basically recreating a helicopter chase … which was fun. Guy Hamilton, who directed four of the early Bond movies, was one of the most fascinating men with whom I ever had dinner. The stories in his obituary about action behind enemy lines are probably true, though the claim that he somehow managed to secure a U certificate for his Bond movies is pure fantasy.

Dr. No

Review by Our Film Critic (Dudley Carew), October 5 1962

At last Mr Ian Fleming's James Bond makes his bow on the screen, and it is doubtful whether either his admirers or his detractors will recognize him. True, this Bond is mighty handy when it comes to in-fighting, but then clever cutting is responsible for the breathless speed with which he goes into action and there is that about him, a faint Irish–American look and sound, which somehow spoils the image. Sherlock Holmes – not that he is Bond's spiritual ancestor – has seldom looked right on the screen, but perhaps Mr Sean Connery will, with practice, get the "feel" of the part a little more surely than he does here.

For the rest, *Dr. No* is a carefully, expertly made ("manufactured" would perhaps be the better word) exercise in violence and sadism so shaped that the audience is conditioned into believing that it is witnessing the last word in sophisticated thrills decked out with even more sophisticated trimmings of sex. True the tarantula put into Bond's bed strikes a regrettably old-fashioned note, but for most of the time Bond is operating in Jamaica events and circumstances form an expensive, up-to-date pattern. The villain, Dr. No (Mr Joseph Wiseman), one of those suave, sinister master-criminals who dream of world domination, has built a formidable atomic station on Crab Key, which enables him to play disconcerting tricks with American rockets launched from Cape Canaveral. Bond and the girl Honey (Miss Ursula Andress) have some nasty, in every sense of the word, experiences before the end: the director, Mr Terence Young, is, as it were, up to every trick in this particular type of book.

From Russia with Love

Review by Our Film Critic (John Russell Taylor), October 10 1963

Having hit on a winning formula in *Doctor No* [sic], the producers, lucky enough to have acquired the film rights of Ian Fleming's *James Bond* books, are not being slow to cash in on their investment: already Sean Connery has fought his way through the second instalment and the fadeout promises us a third, *Goldfinger*, in the near future.

What more is there to say about James Bond? He is, of course, the secret ideal of the congenital square, conventional in every particular (in the present case, for instance, he is vastly shocked by a villain who orders red wine with fish) except in morality, where he has the courage – and the physical equipment to do without thinking what most of us feel we might be doing, if only we were not strait-jacketed by the ordinary necessities of life, if we were twice as handsome, and if we had no particular scruples and inhibitions to put aside. He is tough, resourceful, sexually irresistible, impeccably well-dressed in a smoothly conformist fashion, and acts out all our less reputable fantasies without ever going too far – he is violent without being sadistic, a Casanova who on the whole treats his women well (though he may slap them about a bit if his patriotic duty requires it). In fact really he is the Four Just Men, 1960s model, all rolled into one.

This means that one can take him or leave him, according to taste, but for those who do not demand something a little more picturesque and exotic from their tough guys (early Bogart, say, or James Mason in his whip-cracking 1940s heyday) he does well enough. Possibly the films drawn from the adventures coarsen him slightly – Mr Connery is not everyone's idea of Bond, but certainly he looks handsome and tough enough to live up to the basic requirements. And at least the scriptwriter, Richard Maibaum, and the director, Terence Young, keep the action moving along briskly (though in the few moments when nothing much is happening a lack of positive distinction is plainly visible) and the production values – interesting locations in Istanbul which set one wondering inevitably if this is what was really happening to the enigmatic heroine of *L'Immortelle*; unusually convincing disasters to a helicopter and some motor boats are all excellent. This time there is really only one girl to speak of, sufficiently embodied by Daniela Bianchi, but in recompense we are given a memorably bizarre villainess in the shape of Lotte Lenya's formidable Colonel Klebb, a recent graduate to Spectre from Smersh. In fact the nonsense is all very amiable and tongue-in-cheek, and will no doubt make a fortune for its devisers.

21 September 2012. Eunice Grayson – the very first Bond Girl. (Jon Bond)

BOND GIRL BEGINS NEW MISSION ON 007'S SECRET SERVICE

By Brian Pendreigh,
September 18 2012

James Bond returned to his roots in Scotland yesterday for the start of a new mission to mark the golden jubilee of his reign in world cinemas.

Eunice Gayson, the first Bond girl, got "007 Days of Bond" under way at 10.07 when she set off the timer in a "top secret" golden briefcase at Eilean Donan, the picturesque castle in Wester Ross that served as MI6 headquarters in *The World is Not Enough*.

The briefcase – containing the new Blu-ray boxed set of all 22 "official" Bond movies – was then whisked off in an Aston Martin in classic Bond style.

A few hours later it was on a helicopter in Argyll for a recreation of a dramatic chase scene from the second Bond film *From Russia with Love*. The hills above Lochgilphead doubled for the Adriatic.

Some of the most iconic stars from the Bond series, including Roger Moore, Britt Ekland and Richard Kiel, who played the popular villain Jaws, are taking part in the mission to mark the anniversary and the release of the films on Blu-ray.

One notable absentee is Sean Connery, who is no longer making any public appearances, US Open tennis championship last week notwithstanding.

The briefcase will travel round some of Bond's most famous UK locations before arriving at HMV in London's Oxford Street at 10.07 next Monday.

The itinerary includes Stoke Park in Buckinghamshire, scene of the Goldfinger golf match, and Cornwall's Eden Project, which was the villain's diamond mine in *Die Another Day*.

Dr. No opened on October 5, 1962, the same day the first Beatles single 'Love Me Do' came out. It cost around $1 million, grossed $60 million and Bond went on to become one of the most successful film series ever.

Eunice Gayson played Sylvia Trench, who is losing at cards to Bond at the beginning of *Dr. No*. She asks her opponent's name. "I was lucky to have the iconic scene where he said to me 'Bond, James Bond', so I'm part of that," said Ms Gayson.

Sylvia was the first of many women to succumb to Bond's charms. Odd though it now seems, it was intended that she should be his regular girlfriend.

They share a picnic in *From Russia with Love*. "The gag was meant to be that he was always getting called away just as they are getting down to it," said Ms Gayson. "They were supposed to get married in the sixth film."

Ms Gayson, who is now 84, said she was disappointed not to have been involved in the Scottish leg of *From Russia with Love* and the regular girlfriend idea was dropped after that.

She spent several years in Edinburgh and Glasgow as a child, was delighted to be back in Scotland yesterday and thought it was "lovely" that so many people had turned out. "Scotland is my second home," she said.

From Russia with Love was shot largely on location in Turkey, but bad weather and other problems forced them to relocate to Scotland and shoot the climactic helicopter and motorboat chases in Argyllshire.

Only recently the exact location was confirmed as Barrachuile Hill, an open stretch of boggy hillside and exposed rocks. It is only a few miles outside Lochgilphead by helicopter, but a tortuous half-hour drive up a track overland.

Almost half a century after the scene was shot, a helicopter yesterday swept once more over the very same rocks where Bond took cover from the pursuing aircraft.

In the film a Spectre agent pulled the pin out of a grenade. Before he could drop it, Bond shot him and his helicopter exploded. Locals can remember finding debris on the hillside for years afterwards.

The Bond team's latest visit to Argyllshire went a little more smoothly yesterday than it did in 1963, despite yesterday's rain and a delay for poor visibility. In 1963 one of the helicopters had to ditch in water and director Terence Young had to swim to safety.

Initially author Ian Fleming was horrified by the choice of Sean Connery as Bond. He changed his view when he saw the grosses and created a Scottish background for Bond in one of the later books, including a Fettes education.

Bond will be back in Scotland again in the next film *Skyfall*, which is out in October. The producers shot at Glen Etive and it is understood Bond visits his ancestral castle, which comes under aerial attack by enemy agents.

Casino Royale

Review by Wendy Ide,
November 16 2006

The stakes are high in *Casino Royale*. And it's not only a poker-playing Bond who is risking hundreds of millions in this, his 21st official outing. The producers have decided that the time is right for their own personal gamble – a "reboot" of a franchise which, despite being dismissed by fans and critics alike as utter bilge for the past few outings, has consistently raked in generous box-office returns. The initial question from Bond fans – why fix what wasn't, financially speaking, broken in the first place? – was rapidly superseded by another: Daniel Craig as Bond – what are they thinking?

The immensely enjoyable *Casino Royale* answers its critics with an insouciant sneer and a self-confident swagger. The Craig naysayers are suddenly far less vocal as it becomes clear that the controversial casting is the best thing that's happened to the franchise in years. Craig brings a brutally efficient physicality to the role and a thrilling undercurrent of sadistic cruelty – his is a Bond you feel gains real job satisfaction from his licence to kill.

In this back-to-basics episode of the Bond story, that licence has only recently been earned – we witness the two official hits necessary for 00 status in a grainy black-and-white pre-title sequence. The contemporary setting is explained by the term "reboot" rather than "remake" or "prequel", although this is a selective reboot as it turns out.

4 August 2000. Daniel Craig.
(Richard Cannon)

Casino Royale retains Judi Dench as M – her crisp, no-nonsense head-girl take on the role would have been a sad loss. And the director, Martin Campbell, has previous *Bond* experience as the man behind *GoldenEye*, the film that introduced Pierce Brosnan as Bond.

What's new here, apart from the first Bond since Connery who looks as if he could do some serious damage, is the fact that this episode lets that damage show. Bond is battered and bruised. He makes catastrophic errors of judgement. His anger flares and he loses his cool – which ironically makes him cooler still. Crucially for the success of the story, Craig's Bond is prepared to show his weakness in his dealings with a glamorous Treasury official, Vesper Lynd (a spirited Eva Green), who is bankrolling his efforts in a high-stakes poker match to bankrupt a terrorist financier. His unexpected tenderness with Vesper is disarming, his pugnacious prize-fighter's face is suddenly naked in its vulnerability. We have Craig and, I suspect, Paul Haggis, the co-screenwriter, to thank for the most satisfying element of the film – the fact that Bond actually gets to develop as a person. He is older and wiser at the end of the film. For better or worse, he's a changed man.

PERSONAL CHOICE

by David Walliams,
October 15 2015

1. On Her Majesty's Secret Service

The best story (and incidentally the most faithful to Fleming's book), the best direction (former *Bond* editor Peter Hunt brings new energy to the series), the best Blofeld (a mesmerising Telly Savalas), the best Bond girl (a troubled Diana Rigg), the best score (John Barry's explosive theme, and Louis Armstrong singing 'We Have All the Time in the World') and the best ending (leaving you deeply upset). The film is perfect and, despite what some might say, George Lazenby is excellent. I had dinner with him in LA and he said: "I screwed it up." I replied: "No, you didn't and you made the greatest Bond film of all." He signed my first edition of *OHMSS*, writing: "We have all the time in the world."

2. Goldfinger

The film effortlessly sets up what the series was to become. The humour, the car, the henchman and most notably that the Bond world is larger than life and not quite our own. Sean Connery is on magnificent form. It is a faultless film. For me, *OHMSS* just beats it for having an emotional journey for Bond.

3. Skyfall

Sam Mendes managed to bring together all the elements you want to see in a Bond film, and yet tell a story that is totally new, especially visiting Bond's family home and killing off M. The dialogue sparkles. An instant classic.

4. The Spy Who Loved Me

The perfect 1970s Bond film. My first and probably my favourite, if not quite the best. Roger Moore is now totally at ease in the role, there is Jaws, Ken Adam's sets, that song, and the most beautiful Bond girl of them all, my first love Barbara Bach.

CINEMA HISTORY

HOLLYWOOD HAS SINKING FEELING OVER $200M EPIC

From Giles Whittell in Los Angeles, April 29 1997

In the spring of 1912 the *Titanic* sank in a disaster matched only by the ship's epic scale and frightening cost. Eighty-five years on, a film attempting to re-create that fateful night is months behind schedule, up to $90 million (£55 million) over budget and battling to avoid a similar fate. With a budget now put at $200 million, *Titanic*, starring Kate Winslet, the British actress, as a Philadelphia heiress, is the most expensive film in history and is taking so long to complete that its original release date is expected to be pushed back from July 4 until late summer. The film, jointly financed by Paramount Pictures and 20th Century Fox, was shot mainly on a 775ft replica of the doomed liner on the Pacific coast in northern Mexico, and was conceived by its backers as an action blockbuster on the scale of last year's *Independence Day*. Instead James Cameron, the director, has reportedly set his heart on a sweeping love story in the tradition of *Doctor Zhivago*, raising the stakes on a tense project and fuelling rumours that the postponement of its release may have been deliberate. The two studios were expecting an out-and-out thriller, one industry source told *Daily Variety*, "What they got was a romancer."

23 March 1998. Kate Winslet attends the 1998 Oscars Vanity Fair party in Los Angeles. (Peter Nicholls)

Sebastian Silva, the film's first assistant director, said of a production apparently driven by Mr Cameron's perfectionism and short temper, "The fault of the movie was its sheer size. Sometimes I'd find some of the 1,000 extras sleeping under the ship."

Ms Winslet, who endured the most punishing hours of the entire cast, admitted to the *Los Angeles Times*: "It was hard to concentrate when [Mr Cameron] was losing it and shouting and screaming." She added: "You'd have to pay me a lot of money to work with Jim again." She later apologised for the remark. *Titanic* will have to break most box office records to be considered a success.

TRAGEDY REPLAYED AS EPIC SPECTACLE

Titanic has the power to 'shake us and touch the soul', writes Geoff Brown

Review published January 22 1998

Kate Winslet and Leonardo DiCaprio are smooching up deck and down on a large ocean liner, the *Titanic* by name, as it glides across the Atlantic. She is Rose DeWitt Bukater, an upper-class Philadelphia girl journeying back with her mother to a financially advantageous marriage. He is Jack Dawson, a hobo with an artistic gift, a ready smile and no thought to tomorrow, travelling in steerage.

They stand at the prow before the setting sun; they run full tilt through the engine room; they make love in a plush car stowed in the hold, and raise the ire of ship society, especially Rose's attendant fiancé (Billy Zane). Rose and Jack are young and attractive, but their billing and cooing does take some time. "Come on, iceberg," you feel like saying. "Hurry up!"

When the iceberg arrives, after 100 minutes, it looks peculiarly insubstantial, almost made of cardboard. Yet that is the only major visual shortcoming in *Titanic*, a film that otherwise sets new standards in special effects and Hollywood spectacle. No model ship bobbing in a tank was going to satisfy James Cameron, the exacting director of *Terminator 2* and *True Lies*. So, 30 miles south of San Diego on the Mexican coast, he built a staggeringly detailed, 775ft replica of the White Star

Line's pride and joy, only to break it in two, as history demanded, and sink it.

Such extravagance comes with a price tag, in this case $200 million – bigger than any attached to a movie before. It took two big studios, Twentieth Century Fox and Paramount Pictures, to foot the bill and meet the payroll: the end credits of cast and crew list over 1,100 names.

Given enough time, money and skills, *Titanic* was always going to look impressive. And so it does, dwarfing that honourable British account, *A Night to Remember*, which did well by the standards of 1958. But after the fuss has abated, such films live or die through their characters and the emotions stirred. On board the *Titanic* on that fateful voyage in April 1912 were 2,200 passengers. We get stuck, mostly, with two: fictional creatures of limited interest.

No young American actor today is more equipped than Leonardo DiCaprio for standing at the ship's prow, arms outstretched, gleefully yelling "I'm the king of the world!" But there is only so much cocksure grinning one movie can stand, especially if there is nothing much in the script to back up the dental display.

Winslet's character is more substantial: she has a mother (Frances Fisher) to rebuke, a fiancé to joust with, inner fires to ignite. Yet as the waters invade and the ship slides down, you beg the film to find someone other than this Edwardian Romeo and Juliet.

Too often, the camera's response is to turn towards Billy Zane and his henchman valet David Warner, so obsessed with the status quo that they aim pistols at DiCaprio's interloper even when water laps around their ears. Zane's character, in fact, behaves like a villain in a 19th-century melodrama. But then Cameron's entire script delights in broad strokes. The upper decks are unfeeling stuffed shirts, holding icy conversations at dinner; for real human life, the film insists, you must go down below and join the knees-up in steerage.

The English officers who man the *Titanic* are also part of the film's class war. They snap out their orders – "Put that down!"; "You can't do this!" – as the horde struggle to break free from the bowels of the ship and join the lifeboats' glitterati. Class distinction was rife aboard the *Titanic*, but Cameron certainly milks it.

Yet for all the sluggish script and the enormous weight of the special effects, this movie behemoth still has the power to shake us rigid and touch the soul. Our hearts are stirred especially by the Hollywood veteran Gloria Stuart, cast as Rose in extreme old age, who is summoned to tell her story to the aquatic fortune hunters, met at the start, prowling the *Titanic's* remains for missing diamonds.

Stuart, erstwhile star of *The Invisible Man*, *Gold Diggers of 1935* and others, has not acted in films since 1946, but her skills have matured wonderfully: she vaults over the unlikelihood of a 102-year-old *Titanic* survivor being so spry, and draws us right into the overwhelming tragedy, the pain and loss, at the heart of the *Titanic* story. If you care at all for Rose and Jack, it is because of Gloria Stuart, not Winslet

or DiCaprio.

The spectacle itself is at times undeniably moving. The ship splitting in two; the passengers, helplessly tumbling down the decks as it plunges vertically into the depths; those in the ferocious cold water, clinging to anything floating, with nothing to do but wait for death: these are sights never staged before with such realism, and power. When it works, *Titanic* works magnificently; when it doesn't, you try to be patient and bide your time. Full steam ahead now for the Oscars.

◇◇◇◇◇◇◇◇◇◇◇◇◇◇◇◇◇◇◇◇◇◇◇◇◇◇◇◇◇◇◇◇◇◇◇◇

Editor's note: *Titanic* went on to become the highest-grossing film of all time, a record it held until the release of the same director's *Avatar* 12 years later, and it equalled *Ben-Hur's* record of 11 Oscars, including Best Picture.

◇◇◇◇◇◇◇◇◇◇◇◇◇◇◇◇◇◇◇◇◇◇◇◇◇◇◇◇◇◇◇◇◇◇◇◇

CLASSIC CINEMA

<><><><><><><><><><><><><><><><><><><><><><>

Editor's note: Hailed as a masterpiece by critics from its appearance, *Citizen Kane* would regularly top polls on the greatest film of all time, though it lost out in the vote for Best Picture Oscar to *How Green Was My Valley*.

<><><><><><><><><><><><><><><><><><><><><><>

MACABRE SATIRE

Citizen Kane

Unbylined review (Albert Cookman), October 13 1941

This modern morality may well startle an unsuspecting audience accustomed to having a good deal of jam with its satirical powder. The satire here is as savage as Swift's, and in its unrelenting light the victim becomes positively nauseous; yet the treatment is brilliant and continuously pleases the aesthetic sense. Citizen Kane is the owner of a chain of American newspapers, and through the Kane Press he can give unedited expression to the grandiose workings of an essentially trivial mind. The film fastens in the end on the magnate's attempt to create a satellite wife worthy of his millions. She is a hopelessly incompetent singer, but he buys opera houses, critics, orchestras, and singing masters in the almost maniacal resolve to make her famous in opera. The wretched woman, who knows she cannot sing, is forced to continue her fantastic career until exposure to ridicule produces a nervous breakdown. All the horror of her ordeal is conveyed with extreme economy of means and unsparing cruelty. Their home is a palace which even Mussolini would think a little too palatial and they are surrounded with costly works of art which have meaning only for others. When she shouts across vasts of marble flooring the wish to go on a picnic a dozen limousines are driven to a private beach. When she leaves her husband she walks away along an interminable corridor, slamming innumerable doors, and he is left with his loneliness reflected in a hundred ornate mirrors. Then he gives way to an orgy of destruction, and he dies, and the apparatus of happiness which money has bought is sold to the dealers and great bonfires burn. These last scenes are masterly in their fierce, cruel ridicule of a rich man who, do what he will, cannot buy happiness and has absolutely no other idea of how it might be procured. There is not much acting: there is no need for it: the rare distinction of having made a film entitled to rank as a work of art belongs almost exclusively to the director, Mr Orson Welles.

CLASSIC FILM

Citizen Kane

Orson Welles's tale of media magnate Charles Foster Kane's will to power, excess and hubris has deep resonances today

Review by Kate Muir,
April 29 2016

Orson Welles created the media magnate Charles Foster Kane 75 years ago, but the tale of will to power, excess and hubris has deep resonances today, not least in the form of that other millionaire-turned-politician, Donald Trump. "He spoke for millions of Americans, and was hated by many more," says the opening voiceover.

Welles was only 25 when he starred in and directed his debut, which was voted the greatest American movie in a BBC poll. What's striking now is how utterly modern it is in structure, with its faux-documentary newsreel style zipping into sudden intimacy or conflict, and the gorgeous black-and-white cinematography, which pioneered deep-focus.

The movie begins with the funeral of Kane aged 70 at Xanadu, an estate that looks very much like the magnate William Randolph Hearst's real castle, and ends with the explanation of that totemic last word, "Rosebud". In between, Kane is sent to boarding school, builds a newspaper empire, aspires to the US presidency and finds – what's new? – that celebrity is a punishable offence: "Kane caught in love nest with 'singer'" is one of the many headlines shown.

TOP 100 COUNTDOWN

THE TOP 100 FILMS OF ALL TIME

By James Christopher, Wendy Ide, Kevin Maher, Nigel Kendall, Ed Potton and Tim Teeman, Special supplement, April 26 2008

Arts reporter Ben Hoyle introduced the list in an article in the main paper: While *Citizen Kane*, *The Searchers* and *Lawrence of Arabia* don't make the cut, *Point Break*, an action thriller with preposterous stunts, a threadbare plot and Patrick Swayze as a philosopher-surfer-bank robber, does. The list, compiled by *The Times*'s film critics, is an attempt to re-evaluate the sacred cows of cinema and determine whether they still justify their traditional lofty status.

100 – *JURASSIC PARK* (Steven Spielberg, 1993)

Michael Crichton's novel theory that DNA specialists could clone a Tyrannosaurus rex from a mosquito trapped in amber inspired the greatest theme-park movie ever made. Doctors Sam Neill, Laura Dern and Jeff Goldblum test-drive a dinosaur park on a tropical island before Richard Attenborough's bumbling billionaire opens it to the public. The awe at the first sight of grazing Brachiosaurs and a galloping herd of Gallimimus was not confined to the cast. No one had seen computer-generated miracles on this scale before. Spielberg's touch of genius was to make his meat-eating predators far more intelligent, indeed "human", than the sloppy scientists who cloned them.

James Christopher

27 January 2003. Steven Spielberg arriving at the premiere of *Catch Me If You Can* at The Empire, Leicester Square. (Alan Weller)

99 – *LA BELLE ET LA BÊTE* (Jean Cocteau, 1946)

Few directors are as skilled at enchantment as Jean Cocteau, as this dreamlike version of the fairy-tale Beauty and the Beast demonstrates. *La Belle et la Bête* must be among the most achingly beautiful films yet made. The black and white photography adds a sensual mystery to the story. Surreal visual enigmas captivate the viewer and the design of the beast's magical domain, by Christian Berard, is exquisite. Jean Marais spent five hours every day in make up for the role of the Beast. His interpretation is skilfully nuanced, despite the layers of fur: this beast is fearsome, dignified and tragic.

Wendy Ide

98 – *MY FAIR LADY* (George Cukor, 1964)

Audrey Hepburn as a grubby urchin was always going to be a bit of a stretch, even for the most credulous audiences. But her repartee with co-star Rex Harrison (on magnificently irascible form) and the delicious design of the film by Cecil Beaton ensure that any minor quibbles about her Cockney authenticity are soon forgotten. This screen adaptation of Lerner and Loewe's musical take on *Pygmalion* embraces its theatrical roots: it is archly stagey and the stylised design heightens the artificiality of the story and some of the performances. But it's a glorious confection blessed with some of the catchiest songs and most memorable dance routines in Hollywood musical

history. And Hepburn's poise is positively regal. The film won an impressive eight Oscars in 1965.

Wendy Ide

97 – *POINT BREAK* (Kathryn Bigelow, 1992)

The surprise in *Point Break* is not that it redefined the macho action flick, but that it was done by a woman. From within a derivative tale about a rookie undercover FBI agent, Keanu Reeves, who infiltrates a gang of, yes, bank-robbing surfers led by Patrick Swayze, director Bigelow magnified the homoerotic tension between agent Reeves and surfer Swayze (parodied recently in *Hot Fuzz*). She made an action star out of the epicene Reeves and turned the movie's "100% Pure Adrenaline" mantra into a shooting style – the effects of which are still felt today (the Bourne movies are an elaboration of the Reeves–Swayze chase in *Point Break*). The surfing scenes aren't too shabby either.

Wendy Ide

96 – *LOST IN TRANSLATION* (Sofia Coppola, 2003)

This brief encounter between Bill Murray and Scarlett Johansson in a five-star hotel in Tokyo is a remarkable follow-up to *The Virgin Suicides*. Murray plays a washed-up Hollywood star who fronts adverts for cheap whiskey. He hasn't been so mordantly funny since *Groundhog Day*. Johansson is the frustrated wife of a photographer forever on shoot. The magic of their hotel romance is how little needs to be said. The melancholic humour is deliciously taboo. The platonic loners visit karaoke bars, watch *La Dolce Vita* at 3 am, and sizzle politely in hotel lifts. The ending is one of life's great mysteries.

James Christopher

95 - *GRAND HOTEL* (Edmund Goulding, 1932)

One of Hollywood's first ultra-glamorous A-list ensembles, *Grand Hotel* and its legendary producer Irving Thalberg boasted the genius idea of sticking a slew of headlining stars such as Joan Crawford, Greta Garbo and John Barrymore in a Berlin hotel for 48 hours, and simply watching the drama unfold. The resulting movie is famous for a typically steely turn from Crawford, a clever criss-crossing narrative, and a scene-stealing performance from Garbo as a suicidal Russian dancer who rebuffs Barrymore with the iconic line: "But I want to be alone!"

Kevin Maher

94 - *THE TOWERING INFERNO* (John Guillermin, Irwin Allen, 1974)

Trash this good cannot be ignored, this is the granddaddy of disaster flicks. There's a brand-new hotel, all the guests have some extra layer of drama attached to them, and there's a raging fire. Steve McQueen and Paul Newman play the heroes. There are brilliant scenes set in a rooftop ballroom, kiddies in peril, baddies you

want to burn and an overused dangling rope ladder. OJ Simpson plays a security guard. Elements have become so parodied in films like *Airplane!* you may find yourself laughing at inappropriate moments.

Tim Teeman

93 - *COOL HAND LUKE* (Stuart Rosenberg, 1967)

Eight years before Jack Nicholson took on the system in *One Flew Over the Cuckoo's Nest*, Paul Newman's prisoner strained against the chains of a Florida work camp in Rosenberg's sweat-soaked allegory. Blue-eyed Newman was set up as a Christ figure, earning hero status via prodigious egg-eating and frequent escape attempts before being disowned by his fellow inmates, broken by the guards and gloriously resurrected. Luke's prison number, 37, is a biblical reference to Luke 1:37: "For with God nothing shall be impossible."

Ed Potton

92 - *A BOUT DE SOUFFLE* (Jean-Luc Godard, 1960)

The movie that launched the French New Wave, Godard's *A bout de souffle* is often mistakenly perceived as a formal experiment in film-making and an intellectual event. Whereas in fact, this story of a chain-smoking petty criminal (Jean-Paul Belmondo) and his impressionable American girlfriend (Jean Seberg) is a testament to the power of propulsive film-making (the title in English, *Breathless*, is a hint). Everyone here is running, fleeing or marching around Paris (Belmondo in particular is evading *les flics* after an opening-reel murder). The camera too, wielded by the legendary Raoul Coutard, rarely stops moving. Even a quiet bedroom scene between the two star-crossed leads is spliced to giddy shreds by Godard's then infamous jump-cuts. The results are anything but dull.

Ed Potton

91 – *SHORT CUTS* (Robert Altman, 1993)

The ensemble promise of Altman's *Nashville* and *The Player* are fully realised in this breathtakingly confident homage to Los Angeles and to the poetry of alienation it engenders in its residents. Actors as disparate as Robert Downey Jr, Jack Lemmon and Julianne Moore, working from a Raymond Carver adaptation, play struggling Los Angelinos with emotional wounds and fractured relationships. Best is Jennifer Jason Leigh's phone-sexpert, whose explicit hotline conversations eventually drive frustrated husband Chris Penn to a random act of violence. The film, ultimately, is beautiful but without hope. Which, of course, is very LA.

Kevin Maher

CINEMA HISTORY

FILM CENSORSHIP

Mr T.P. O'Connor's reply to critics

Unbylined new report,
January 29 1923

We have received from Mr T. P. O'Connor MP, president of the British Board of Film Censors, a statement in which he defends the existing film censorship, and replies to the recent criticism of the Board's action in deleting certain scenes from the film version of *Oliver Twist*.

He states that it is perhaps not generally realized that on every working day throughout the year, with the exception of short vacations taken in turn, the four examiners spend from five to six hours in the inspection of films. Two of the examiners have been engaged in that work since the inception of the Board, and there is a lady examiner.

Referring to the Board's decision in the case of *Oliver Twist*, Mr O'Connor states: "We have been accused of silly presumption, of a wanton slur on the purity of one of the most moral, and one of the greatest, men of genius English literature has ever produced, and of spoiling a good story told by a good film.

"The deletion we made was very small. It was in a part of the scene in which Oliver Twist is instructed by Fagin in the art of pocket-picking; and even this is not entirely eliminated; it is shown, but not elaborated. I hold that we had no other course which would be in accord with the principles and precedents we have laid down during our existence.

"What did I find when I took up the censorship some six years ago? That there was not a day's paper which did not contain the suggestion, either from the Bench or from the pulpit, that the cinema was increasing, even to an alarming extent, the amount of juvenile crime in the country. This, the first serious problem I had to confront, compelled me, after consideration, to take a strong stand, and to announce this stand to the trade. In the circular I issued I laid it down emphatically that no film would be passed showing the actual method of crime."

After quoting Dickens's description of the murder of Nancy by Bill Sikes, Mr O'Connor asks: "Will anybody in his senses maintain that I should allow on the screen a realistic representation of the ghastly murder of Nancy, or the awful scene of the death of Bill Sikes? Of course not. What, then, becomes of this extravagant theory that because a thing is in Dickens it must be accepted for the film, without even the change of a word or a scene?"

VIDEO CASE ANGERS WHITEHOUSE

By Frances Gibb,
Legal Affairs Correspondent,
September 25 1982

Mrs Mary Whitehouse, the anti-pornography campaigner, yesterday accused the Director of Public Prosecutions of failing to take tougher action against "video nasties" after a firm of video distributors had been ordered by magistrates to forfeit 34 obscene tapes, depicting 'quite unnecessary violence'.

After the hearing, at Croydon Magistrates' Court, Mrs Whitehouse, president of the National Viewers' and Listeners' Association, described the proceedings as a public scandal.

The DPP had failed to bring charges under section two of the Obscene Publications Act, which would have made the distributors liable to up to two years' imprisonment, or a fine if found guilty, she said. Instead the DPP brought charges under section three, which involved only forfeiture and destruction of tapes under a magistrate's warrant.

The prosecution over the video, entitled *Spit on your Grave* [*sic*], described by Mr George Mitchell, presiding magistrate, as depicting scenes of "quite unnecessary violence" likely to deprave, was brought after a raid by police on the offices of Astra Video Ltd, of Commerce Way, Croydon.

26 May 1977. Mary Whitehouse, President and founder of the National Viewers' and Listeners' Association with her newly published book *Whatever Happened to Sex?* (Peter Trievnor)

A spokesman for the DPP said yesterday that a decision to prosecute under section three had been taken with this film, and four others seized about the same time. They were the first prosecutions of this kind of film under the Act, and the DPP was anxious to establish a ruling.

At the end of August Willesden magistrates, London, had ordered the forfeiture and destruction of two other video nasties, *The Driller Killer* and *Death Trap*.

VIDEO NASTIES

Unbylined sidebar, accompanying an article on concern over violent video games, November 11 2009

The early days of video in the 1980s brought with it a panic over "video nasties". Mary Whitehouse, of the National Viewers' and Listeners' Association – who is credited with dubbing the phrase "video nasty" – led a high-profile campaign, with the backing of the tabloid press, against certain video releases in 1982 and 1983.

In retrospect, it is apparent that most videos banned by the Video Recording Act (1984) were low-budget imported films that were really quite tame and often downright ridiculous. Melodramatic advertising for films such as *The Driller Killer* and *Cannibal Holocaust* were arguably more to blame for their "video nasty" status than anything that they actually contained.

As with so many panics, in reality most of those who proclaimed themselves to be outraged by video nasties had never watched one. Today only a tiny handful of the films that were banned remain unavailable: most have been released uncut in the past ten years and, to the disappointment of pro-censorship campaigners, have failed to cause the breakdown of society.

DVD REVIEWS

Unbylined final paragraph, September 17 2005

Also out… *Box of the Banned* (18)

A collection of video nasties, including *Last House on the Left*, *The Driller Killer* and *I Spit on Your Grave*.

ANIMATION: PART TWO

LAUGH, CRY, BUY THE DOLL

The stars of *Toy Story* may come from a computer, says Geoff Brown, but the emotions are definitely human

Toy Story

Review by Geoff Brown,
March 21 1996

Looked at from one angle, *Toy Story* could be taken as the ultimate expression of dehumanised cinema. This is an animated film, but nobody picked up a pencil or brush to create the images seen on screen: instead they sat pressing keys or pushing a mouse. It was all done by computer. And, with its cast of toys, the film, produced for the Disney empire, is a merchandiser's dream. What child would not crave their very own Woody, the endearing cowboy marionette voiced by Tom Hanks, or the bumptious space ranger Buzz Lightyear, with his folding wings and push button-operated laser beams?

Toy Story is a slick commercial package, but it is not soulless. John Lasseter's Pixar Animation Studios, practised in shorts such as the Oscar-winning *Tin Toy*, uses its first feature for something beyond technical stunts. It has a story to tell – a parable, almost, about belonging and friendship – and it crams the drama with comedy, chases, thrills, spills and recognisable human emotions.

It also [has] to keep every age group entertained. When we hear that the toys hold "plastic erosion awareness" meetings, adults will probably laugh. The more cynical kids, meanwhile, may appreciate Sid, the delinquent child across the street, who cannibalises toys to create bizarre mutants. Simpler souls may enjoy Hamm, the know-all piggybank, Slinky the dog or the platoon of Green Army Men, ready for deployment at any emergency. The film begins with Andy, a six-year-old boy, playing with his toys, especially Woody, an old-fashioned cowboy whose voice box contains a few choice phrases, such as "You're my favourite deputy" and "Somebody's poisoned the waterhole". But the story begins once Andy leaves and the toys come to life to argue, frolic and express their big fear: the fear of being replaced by a new toy. Andy's birthday brings Buzz Lightyear, who immediately becomes his favourite. To add to Woody's irritation, bumptious Buzz (voiced by Tim Allen) believes he is a real space ranger, not a toy, a notion knocked from his noddle during adventures in the dangerous world outside Andy's room.

The film's look is amazing. The camera darts and swoops over settings with the sleek, sharp contours of super-realist paintings or Charles Sheeler's industrial landscapes. Detail is pared down, but precise: note the scuffs and scratches on the skirting board around Andy's room. Some of the toys remain one-joke objects, but Woody and Buzz grow in stature, and their progress from enmity to friendship is entirely convincing. Hanks and Allen's voices play a key part in the humanising process; but the pair would not come to life as they do without the range of expressions on their three-dimensional faces. Although the credits list the names of five dogs used for "live action dog reference", no mention is made of the veteran actors who must, in part, have inspired Buzz and Woody: Buzz resembles a chunky Kirk Douglas, while Woody's gosh-darn lanky face suggests the young James Stewart.

The credits also list a "digital massage therapist". The mind boggles. But whatever unfathomable technology brought *Toy Story* into being, the completed film is delightfully user-friendly.

PERSONAL CHOICE

ANIMATED FILMS, CHOSEN BY JOHN LASSETER

July 16 2011

〈〈〈

Editor's note: John Lasseter is one of the key figures in Pixar and directed *Toy Story***.**

〈〈〈

Animation and cartoons have always been the most important thing in my life. Ever since I was a kid I would look forward to every release of a Disney animated film; I'd race home from school in the afternoon to see the *Bugs Bunny* cartoons when they were on.

I just love what they did. They made me laugh. I loved the artistry.

My mother was an art teacher and I drew all of the time. I did my own cartoons. And when I found out that people actually made cartoons for a living, that's all I ever wanted to do. If you do animation right, it can deeply entertain audiences of all ages. And that's what we strive for.

I just love the times when I'm out and about and I'll see a family and a little boy or a girl and they have either a shirt or a toy or something that's from one of our characters.

It just makes me so happy, not because of the toy or the product, but because it indicates what our character means to them. They want to be with that character.

When I was making *Toy Story*, Steve Jobs said to me: "You know, John, the computers I make at Apple have a life span of maybe three years or five years at the max, then they become doorstops. But if you do your job right, these films can last for ever.

"Look at the films of Walt Disney. They will entertain your nine-month-old grandchildren the same as they entertained audiences when they first came out." Great animation is timeless.

Dumbo (1941)

It has one of the most emotional sections in any animated film, when Dumbo goes to see his mother. They can't see each other. They can only communicate by touching each other's trunks.

My Neighbor Totoro (1988)

This is such a magical story about mythical creatures that can be seen only by children. It's not a crazy fast-paced movie, it's kind of peaceful.

The Iron Giant (1999)

It's a boy's adventure: a boy, a dog and a gigantic robot. When he discovers that the robot can fly, the little boy in me comes out. It's so beautifully made. I get choked up at the end.

Pinocchio (1940)

It's Walt Disney at his peak. Every single frame is as detailed and as beautiful as they possibly could have made it. The artistry is unbelievable.

Bambi (1942)

It was a real step for the artists at the Walt Disney studios, moving away from the cartoon world and studying anatomy. It's one of those films that is truly timeless.

Coraline (2009)

It was the first stop-motion animation film in which I really felt that I was 100 per cent engaged with the characters. And it is one of the finest animated films in 3-D. I also love Henry Selick's unique outlook. What's so special about it is that it's such a personal work of art that is also universal and entertaining for all audiences.

CINEMA HISTORY

PROGRESS OF
THE CINEMA

The Birth of a Nation

Unbylined review (Arthur Holyoak, who was actually one of the paper's Parliamentary reporters), September 28 1915

Mr D.W. Griffith's spectacle *The Birth of a Nation*, which was given at the Scala Theatre last night on the re-opening of the house, is an ambitious attempt to present by means of the cinematograph a historical drama founded on Thomas Dixon's story *The Clansman*. Some of the leading incidents of the American Civil War are represented in the first act, and the second part treats of the troubled times in the Southern States, when, after the war, the coloured race obtained a temporary dominance, and the white people were driven to form a secret organization for their own protection.

The sarcastic suggestion made by Sir Alfred Mond in the House of Commons last week when, in opposing the Chancellor of the Exchequer's proposed duty on imported cinematograph films, he asked whether a committee of the Cabinet was to assess the comparative values of last night's Scala production and of a Charlie Chaplin film, caused some merriment in the House, but it will be of interest to the film industry to note the degree of popularity which may be obtained

by a serious work, such as this of Mr Griffith's, unrelieved by anything lighter than a love interest. The producer has shown notable artistic ability in his arrangement of scenes such as the assassination of Abraham Lincoln, the riotous assemblies of negroes from the Southern plantations, and the movement of large forces of mounted white clansmen in fantastic attire. The whole of the proceeds of last night's production will be devoted to the Serbian Relief Fund.

GREAT FILM DRAMA AT DRURY LANE – *THE BIRTH OF A NATION*

Unbylined review (Harold Child, assistant dramatic critic), March 23 1916

This is not the first time that the Cinematograph has invaded the "legitimate" theatre. *The Miracle* was given for a time at Covent Garden; the adventures of a baby, a perambulator and some robbers formed part of the diverse charms of *Rosy Rapture* at the Duke of York's; and there have been other cases. But the production of an American film, *The Birth of a Nation*, at Drury Lane, which is still, after all, in a sense the National Theatre, is an event of considerable theatrical interest and significance.

For the moment, however, that is less important than the fact that *The Birth of a Nation* is an extraordinarily fine entertainment, instructive, thrilling, amusing, pathetic. It has grandeur. It makes one realise more than any film before – more than *The Miracle*, more than *Cabiria* – the amazing things that this machine, with an ambitious and skilled producer, can achieve. At one moment it shows you the face of a baby in tears; at the next a vast battle-field – miles of country covered with charging soldiers, smoke, flame, wheeling cavalry, manoeuvring troops. Now you see a squirrel up a tree, cracking nuts; and then a town on fire, or a street filled with a mob of rioting, pillaging negroes.

There are 18,000 people, says the programme, and 5,000 horses. Had it said 80,000 and 20,000 it would have been equally credible, or incredible. For the final impression is that you have seen the real thing; and in the real thing numbers mean very little. Somebody, moreover – perhaps Mr DW Griffith, the producer, perhaps Sir Thomas Dixon, author of *The Clansman*, the novel on which the show is founded – has managed to weave great and small into a whole. You see war; you see riots; you see men in the mass; you see, indeed, the birth of a nation. But you see also a girl in tears, another in terror of her life, a soldier returning to his waste and desolate home, a noble old man looking woefully forward into a future of shame and humiliation.

The story, as many people know, is the story of the birth of the American nation through the Civil War, and through the union of feeling between North and South which the extreme champions of the negroes forced upon the whites after the war was over. The political and historical story is linked with the private affairs of two families – the Stonemans of the North and the Camerons of the South – the boys being friends, and love coming in to unite boys and girls in closer bonds. Then the war – the war reconstructed in detail, impeccably convincing; the trials of the Confederates, and their final defeat.

Probably, however, to most people the most interesting and informative part, historically considered, will be the exhibition of the events that happened after the war was over; the incredible sufferings of the whites at the hands of the liberated and deluded blacks, and the formation of that strange, romantic, somehow intensely American affair, the Ku Klux Klan, whose members, disguised in strange medieval garments – something of the Knights Templar, something of the brother of the Miserere, and something of the ordinary ghost – rode to and fro about the country on the new crusade of rescuing the oppressed whites from their horrible tyrants. The sufferings of our particular friends, the Camerons, are almost unbearably dramatic and moving, but the Stonemans are not exempt; and when at last peace descends, and the once more united families – or what is left of them – can start afresh to pick up and mend their broken lives, the relief one feels is the measure of the interest and excitement that have been aroused.

PEOPLE

STEVEN SPIELBERG: 'ROALD DAHL WOULD SAY THINGS JUST TO GET PEOPLE TO REACT'

The legendary film director was unaware of Dahl's antisemitism before he made *The BFG*. If he had known, he'd have filmed it anyway

By Ed Potton, July 22 2016

Never work with children and animals: one of many maxims that Steven Spielberg has ignored in a career of almost half a century. It's a sweltering Saturday afternoon in a central London hotel and the world's most successful director – who defined the blockbuster with *Jaws* and *ET*, before moving with stubborn, Oscar-winning versatility to war (*Saving Private Ryan*), the Holocaust (*Schindler's List*) and politics (*Lincoln*), and whose movies have grossed more than $9 billion – is promoting his latest film, *The BFG*.

It's a delightful adaptation of Roald Dahl's book about a giant, played by Mark Rylance, who blows dreams into kids' heads while they sleep. Spielberg has agreed to be interviewed on the proviso that he is joined by Ruby Barnhill, the 12-year-old from Knutsford in Cheshire who beat 800 others to the part of Sophie, the girl who befriends the BFG. This is surely a PR trick, a way of softening the questions, but it does give an insight into how one of the great children's storytellers is around real kids.

Very good, it turns out: warm, encouraging, but never patronising. He has had lots of practice, being a father of seven and grandfather of three who has worked with child actors from Drew Barrymore in *ET* to Christian Bale in *Empire of the Sun*.

Spielberg, a grey but energetic 69, is dressed in the uniform of a billionaire slacker: blazer, suit and tie on the top half, jeans and garish trainers on the bottom. He is worth an estimated $3.6 billion, with homes including a farmhouse in New England and an estate in Pacific Palisades, Los Angeles, where Cary Grant once lived. When he learns that this is a print interview, he sighs with relief: "It's not on camera, so I can just get schleppy and open my shirt."

There's steel with the informality, though. "I'm not going to answer any questions about present-day current politics," he says firmly.

Melissa Mathison, the screenwriter of *The BFG* and *ET* – and the ex-wife of Harrison Ford – died of cancer before *The BFG* was finished. She was close to Spielberg, who has said that he hasn't had time to mourn her properly, such has been his furious schedule.

Her death, and that of Rylance's step-daughter, Nataasha, in 2012 from a brain haemorrhage, added a bittersweet air to the shoot. That may actually have worked to its advantage because, like *ET*, it's about "isolation and loneliness", the friendship between two outsiders – Sophie the orphan and the BFG, who is bullied by larger, man-eating giants. Both films are also, Spielberg says, "a celebration of diversity, very consciously".

Dahl's stories often celebrate difference, which is a big reason why Spielberg insists he is not overly disturbed by allegations that the author was anti-Semitic. The allegations centre on a comment Dahl made about Jewish people to the *New Statesman* in 1983: "Even a stinker like Hitler didn't just pick on them for no reason."

Spielberg says he wasn't aware of that comment when he started the project and has pointed out that several of Dahl's inner circle were Jewish and that the writer enjoyed winding people up. "I think he liked to pull people's chain and to see what kind of a rise he could get," he says.

Still, it must be uncomfortable for him, especially having been the victim of antisemitism as a child. Spielberg grew up in Phoenix, Arizona, the son of an electrical engineer father and a concert pianist mother; they were the only Jewish family in their neighbourhood. Local kids would run past their house shouting: "The Spielbergs are dirty Jews!" Young Steven retaliated by smearing peanut butter on their windows.

Would he have hesitated about *The BFG* had he known about Dahl's comments? "No, I would not have." He is certainly a fan of Dahl's, having read his books to Max, his son by his first wife, the actress Amy Irving, and to his other children (he and Kate Capshaw have five together and Capshaw a daughter from a previous marriage). "I enjoyed playing the BFG. I would do the voice," he says.

He still radiates the zeal of the film-school nerd, the childhood outsider who directed home-made films as a way of being accepted.

SPIELBERG: THREE HITS AND THREE MISSES

Hits

Schindler's List (1994) Having had his faith renewed after his wife, Kate Capshaw, converted to Judaism, Spielberg — several of whose family died in the Holocaust — embarked on his most personal and risky project. His adaptation of Thomas Keneally's novel about a Nazi Party member who saves 1,200 Jews was a gut-wrenching masterpiece, winning him his first Oscar.

ET (1982) The weepy to end all weepies. The tale of a boy and a stranded alien is, like *The BFG*, about "isolation and loneliness", Spielberg says, and also "a celebration of diversity, very consciously".

Jaws (1975) The original blockbuster, a triumph of suspense and, like the airport thriller on which it was based, full of post-Watergate cynicism about authority figures. The true villain of the piece is not the Great White but the unscrupulous mayor, played by Murray Hamilton.

Misses

Always (1989) Starring Richard Dreyfuss as the ghost of a dead pilot and Audrey Hepburn, in her final screen role, as a supernatural hairdresser, this romantic drama was arguably Spielberg's silliest moment.

Hook (1991) The director was on autopilot for this flat reboot of *Peter Pan*, with Dustin Hoffman as the titular pirate and Robin Williams as the Boy Who Never Grew Up. "It made a lot of money and it's actually been very successful with young audiences but it never worked for me," Spielberg says.

Indiana Jones and the Kingdom of the Crystal Skull (2008) After a hiatus of almost two decades, Spielberg revived his most beloved franchise, unwisely plonking Harrison Ford's creaking archaeologist into a Fifties world of B-movie flying saucers and atomic bomb tests. No. Just no.

CLASSIC CINEMA – FIRST IMPRESSIONS

THE SHARK HAS PRETTY TEETH

Jaws

Review by David Robinson, December 24 1975

Perhaps the most fascinating aspect of the success of *Jaws* – it is already the all-time box office record breaker – is that the producers and distributors had no doubt that it was a winner even before it was released in the United States in the summer. This confidence in itself could be one of the reasons: so long as the right enthusiasm and push bring in the first few hundred thousand, curiosity to see what the noise is all about will ensure that the millions follow them.

In a situation where not more than half a dozen films a year ever make it

big, how could they have been so sure that they had the formula right? First of all, it was based on a proven best-seller by Peter Benchley; and with intelligent ruthlessness the writers pared away all the inessentials of sub-plot and reflection. The script, which is now admirably spare and precise, was subject to the sort of laborious working-over that has almost become obsolete since the great Hollywood days: Howard Sackler, the playwright of *The Great White Hope*, and John Milius, who wrote *The Wind and the Lion*, worked on it as well as the credited writers, Benchley and Carl Gottlieb.

The story accords very happily with demonstrable current box-office tastes: a revived yearning for traditional action adventure (*The Wind and the Lion*, *The Man Who Would Be King*), and the odd phenomenon that in a period of acute anxiety and disorientation audiences apparently yearn for vicarious experiences of fictional disaster, such as *Earthquake*, *The Towering Inferno* and *Airport 75* have profitably provided. The shark, a survivor of the primeval whose habits are ultimately as little known as those of the Loch Ness Monster, has, moreover, an eerie mystery about it in its way comparable with *The Exorcist*.

There are, too, hints of parable about our ecological concerns. The story (should anyone still need reminding) simply tells how a polite and thriving sea resort (the film was shot at Martha's Vineyard) opens its season inauspiciously with a couple of sudden deaths and the discovery that a Great White shark is marauding the coast.

The mayor wants to hush it up as bad for business; but the local police chief (Roy Scheider), together with a new killing, force the authorities to hire a latter-day Captain Ahab (Robert Shaw), a roaring old salt with a leaky boat, a wealth of wily lore about sharks and a phobia about the monsters, acquired when he was adrift after his ship (the one that had delivered the Hiroshima bomb) was sunk 30 years ago.

Even if the special attractions of the subject can be identified, *Jaws* could hardly have been the hit it is if it weren't an exemplary bit of film-craft and story-telling. It speeds along, without allowing you time to look too closely at the mechanisms of the special effects or for refinements of character and conflict.

It imposes on its high seas adventure a Hitchcockian feeling for suspense and shock. The director, Steven Spielberg, Hollywood's boy wonder (now a mere 27, his previous cinema feature was *Sugarland Express*) and his editor Verna Fields cunningly pace their film to give maximum effect to their surprises: the first face-to-face encounter with the great jaws, or the livid corpse face that leers startlingly out of a hole in a wrecked boat.

Spielberg has his own special style in terror. Here, as in his remarkable debut work *Duel*, a television film-of-the-week which later had a restricted screening in cinemas, he is dealing with a menace that remains most of the time elusive and faceless. In *Duel* a man quietly driving along the highway finds himself lethally threatened by a great, dirty juggernaut whose driver he never even sees.

The juggernaut of *Duel* is most terrifying at those moments when it has temporarily vanished from sight and relief is edgily tempered by apprehension that it may roar back upon us round the next corner. *Jaws*, too, is most frightening when the sea lies calm, sparkling and untroubled under the nervous gaze of the holidaymakers and the desperate civic officials. The special effects work to produce the shark is brilliant (and it is hard to suppress a sneaking affection for its great silly yawning face, and to feel more pang when it meets its explosive end than when it busily gobbles up the screaming Robert Shaw). But its appearances are far less alarming than the briefly glimpsed shadows on the ocean, or the scudding barrels which the hunters have pinned to it with harpoons, and which, unseen itself, it angrily whips about above the waves.

As a thriller of exactly calculated effect, and a brisk old-fashioned efficiency that is almost forgotten now, *Jaws* deserves the rewards that come from giving sheer value for money.

CINEMA HISTORY

AND THE AWARD FOR BEST FIASCO GOES TO ...

Academy 'deeply regrets' best picture mix-up

By Ben Hoyle, February 28 2017

It was a single envelope passed in error to Warren Beatty. Yet the mistake – made by accountants at the most hallowed moment in the Hollywood calendar – ensured that this year's Oscars will go down as one of the biggest fiascos on live television.

With 23 of 24 Oscars handed out, the 89th Academy Awards were on course to be remembered for such moments as the crowning of the youngest best director (*La La Land*'s Damien Chazelle, 32) – if they were remembered at all.

Observers noted a more diverse cast of acting honours while the audience was treated to a cavalcade of jokes about President Trump.

When it came to the final, coveted award for best picture, however, it all fell apart. Beatty, 79, and Faye Dunaway, 76, the veteran actors, mistakenly presented the prize to the wrong film and chaos ensued. The team behind *La La Land* flocked on stage and began their acceptance speeches only for euphoria to give way to disappointment. It became clear that *Moonlight* – a tiny $1.5 million-budget film about growing up gay in 1980s Miami, shot in 25 days – had in fact triumphed.

PWC, the professional services firm that has handled the Oscar ballot for 83 years, took responsibility for the mistake yesterday. The Academy said it deeply regretted the error and would "determine what actions are appropriate going forward".

Martha Ruiz and Brian Cullinan, the accountants in charge on the night, had gone to ground, however.

Barry Jenkins, *Moonlight*'s director, said that the error had "made a very special feeling even more special but not in a way I expected".

La La Land was not short of awards, even though it missed the biggest. "Is that the craziest Oscar moment of all time?" asked its star, Emma Stone, who won best actress. "Cool," she said, unconvincingly. "We made history."

Mr Trump blamed the organisers' obsession with politics for the blunder. "I think they were focused so hard on politics that they didn't get the act together at the end," he told the *Breitbart News* website.

WHAT I OVERHEARD AT THE OSCARS AFTER-PARTY AT 1AM

There was only one conversation at the annual *Vanity Fair* bash. Ben Hoyle went inside to get the gossip in the year the ceremony turned to farce

By Ben Hoyle, February 28 2017

It's half past midnight at the fabled *Vanity Fair* Oscar party and still all anyone seems to be talking about is the disastrous gaffe they witnessed almost four hours earlier.

Outside under the palm trees and the patio heaters Chris Evans – Captain America in the Marvel films – is half-shouting to the group he's with: "I just want to know how it happened!" How on earth had Faye Dunaway and Warren Beatty, Hollywood titans with two Oscars and 17 nominations between them, ended up announcing the wrong best picture winner?

I happen to know the answer – or some of it at least – because I have just that minute picked up an emailed statement from PricewaterhouseCoopers (PwC), the accountancy firm that counts the votes and hands out the winners' envelopes backstage. Immediately before the final award, "the presenters had mistakenly been given the wrong category envelope," PwC states.

I interviewed one of the two unfortunate PwC partners in charge last week and he is, after Dunaway and Beatty, probably the person I most want to find right now. Brian Cullinan looks strikingly like a sturdier version of Matt Damon and a little earlier I thought I had spotted him. He was telling his friends he needed a beer. I had to stare at him for rather longer than was really polite before I realised that, irritatingly, it actually was Matt Damon. That can happen at the *Vanity Fair* party.

Anyway, I wouldn't normally just plunge into conversation with a bunch of very famous people but this best picture mix-up is so obviously an instantly minted piece of Hollywood legend that

it feels like we've all shared something profound together, like survivors of a natural disaster in which everybody felt a shiver of mortality but miraculously did not actually get hurt.

So I lean in and start explaining what the statement says. "Yes," says the comedian Sarah Silverman excitedly. "It was the wrong card," she adds loudly and then she freezes.

An unmistakable blonde figure in a clingy white dress has emerged from the press of expensively primped people behind me and is gliding towards the table. There is silence until Faye Dunaway speaks.

"You are so wonderful," she says to Silverman. "You're so funny." Dunaway is radiant and gracious, as if she has not a care in the world. It's hard to tell if this is a feat of invincible Hollywood face-saving or a woman who doesn't quite understand that people all over the planet are laughing at her. Either way it's a fabulous glimpse of old-school stardom from a woman who could already lay claim to the greatest morning-after Oscar photo, slouching in silk dressing gown and high heels with her best actress trophy by the pool of the Beverly Hills Hotel 40 years ago.

Dunaway blinks, smiles regally and sails off. I give chase.

A few minutes later I manage to briefly prise her away from another conversation, explain that I'm a reporter from *The Times* and ask about the incident where she named the wrong film as the best picture in front of a global audience of tens of millions.

"It was the wrong card," she says simply, still beaming. I thought you handled it very, er, gracefully. Dunaway pulls a mildly amused face as if conversing with a talking frog. "How so?" I start telling her about my interview with the man from PwC and a light goes on somewhere. "What business did you say you were in?" she says, bending in. I work for a British newspaper. "Oh, I see," she says, her face tightening. "Nice to talk to you."

The best picture fiasco has been ricocheting around the party all night. I've already heard Jeff Bezos, the Amazon founder, on the subject ("nobody comes out of this a winner"); discussed it with the British late-night host and *Carpool Karaoke* sensation James Corden ("incredible, astonishing"); watched the eyes widen on Andrew Garfield, Emma Stone's former boyfriend, as he tried to imagine what it must have been like for the *La La Land* crew; and heard innumerable versions of the same conversation from people I couldn't place. Rachel from *Vanity Fair* had explained that everybody was "a bit glazed" when it happened and most of them don't seem keen to recover.

The magazine has thrown its party every year but one since 1994 and even if it's no longer quite the most exclusive Oscar-night knees-up in town it's probably the most fun and certainly the most brilliantly marketed.

You get a flavour of what's in store before you arrive. Tickets are hand-delivered a day or two earlier – the courier who brought mine had come straight from dropping Maria Sharapova's off.

On the night you see the searchlights raking the sky above the venue first, then the long line of backed-up black SUVs with tinted windows, then the rings of security guards.

The party takes place in what are essentially a series of temporary sheds thrown together at the back of an arts centre, next to a petrol station. You pass the mariachi band at the front door, try not to step on Charlize Theron's dress as she shimmies in ahead of you and pause briefly to admire the hedge sculpted in the shape of a human-sized Oscar. Then, while various improbably elongated women in elaborate dresses whom you do not recognise twirl slowly in front of a giant bank of barking photographers, you scurry past and into the scrum.

Inside there is no roped-off area – the whole party is a VIP section. It's like stepping through the wardrobe into Celebrity Narnia. The designer and film director Tom Ford is standing by the first sofa you come to. Elton John, who holds his own charity bash every Oscar night and auctioned two tickets to this party for $100,000, will soon appear at the next sofa along.

A little farther and you get Judd Apatow, the comedian and film director, chatting to Miles Teller, the star of the *La La Land* team's previous film, *Whiplash*. Outside, the fashion designer Ozwald Boateng is cracking jokes with Jason Statham, Seth Rogen is bellowing slow guffaws nearby and Salman Rushdie is heading back inside.

The longer you stay the more things become a bit of a blur. A leggy woman in a sparkly thigh-slit dress getting her friend to take pictures of her doing saucy poses back near the bar is almost certainly Katy Perry. A heavily bearded man in a large red coat and a giant woolly hat who looks like a lost bohemian salmon fisherman definitely is Jared Leto. And yes, Helena Christensen, with a huge burgundy flower in her hair, is munching a doughnut.

By now the *Moonlight* team have arrived and set up camp on one side of the room, with well-wishers swarming around them. I can't see anyone from *La La Land*.

CAITLIN MORAN'S CELEBRITY WATCH

March 3 2017

1 UP THE OSCARS

And so, inevitably, to the screw-up at the Oscars, an event that generated much heat primarily because it's the first OH MY GOD! DID YOU HEAR? story since late 2015 in which neither a much-loved public figure died prematurely nor a painstakingly constructed bulwark of peace and progress was exploded by some preening millionaire white dude with no f★★★s to give because he has some millionaire bunker to retreat to if it all goes tits up for the rest of us.

This is why the Wrong Oscar was thrilling. Because – everyone survived! Satan was not served! It was all OK, but it still felt like the biggest drama in the world! O sweet, innocent, absolutely inconsequential Oscars night screw-up! You are like balm to burnt souls!

Hollywood being Hollywood, CW is sure there are already three treatments

in the works for The Wrong Envelope – one of which already has Andy Serkis attached to play the envelope – but before this story gets a makeover, a two-hour backstory and a soundtrack by Sting, let us remember what we loved about it, as it happened:

The "They're back! They're gone again!" unfortunateness of *Bonnie and Clyde* finally being resurrected – after 50 YEARS, goddamnit – only for them to immediately die again in an international hail of "ZOMG YOU IDIOTS!" tweets.

Warren Beatty promptly launching into his very long, very sloooooow explanation of why it wasn't his fault – "I want to tell you what happened. I opened the envelope and it said 'Emma Stone, *La La Land* …'" – sounding like the Grampa Simpson monologue that ends, "So I tied an onion to my belt, which was the style at the time … They didn't have white onions because of the war. The only thing you could get was those big yellow ones."

La La Land's producer Fred Berger – who by this point knew that *La La Land* hadn't won after all – still stepping up to the mike and giving his "thank you" speech because, well, he's there, and he might as well.

La La Land's other producer, Jordan Horowitz, correctly assessing that no one on stage had the faintest idea what to do, taking charge and announcing that there had been a mistake and that *Moonlight* had won: "This is not a joke." In doing this, Horowitz achieved a piece of characterisation it would be almost impossible to get from an actor: he came across as simultaneously incredibly commanding and alpha but also looooooving the draaaaamaaaaa. When he snatched the right card from Beatty's hands and held it up? He practically says "GASP! REVEAL!" as he does so. The whole thing is as camp as a penguin. But a very masterful penguin. Accordingly, CW has made a note of this exact vibe for all future business meetings/unexpected events.

The joy of this event is that it works by way of a veritable arc of memes – the evening had hundreds and hundreds of separate, breedable incidents, all of which are now replicating across the Earth at a ferocious pace. The "The Rock's Shocked Face" meme. The "What's on the dramatically held-up card?" meme. The idea of *Moonlight* gazumping *La La Land* – a joke so universally known that at the Rio cinema in Dalston last Tuesday they began their 8pm viewing of *Moonlight* by showing the first five minutes of *La La Land* just to make a room full of people eating popcorn laugh.

Laughing! Laughing at a silly thing! CW had forgotten how good it feels. When we are all finally hunkered down in the bunker eating the last three-eyed rat, we will remember this week and smile. If we still have faces.

TOP 100 COUNTDOWN

90 – *TRAINSPOTTING*
(Danny Boyle, 1996)

You need both hands to count the number of careers this heroin-laced black comedy helped to launch. On screen, there's Ewan McGregor, Ewen Bremner, Jonny Lee Miller, Robert Carlyle, Kelly Macdonald and Shirley Henderson, and off it the author Irvine Welsh, the director Danny Boyle, and the photographer Lorenzo Agius, whose publicity shots for the film still adorn a million student bedsits. The film was shot in just eight weeks. For its first hour, Boyle's frenetic editing style produces a rush that perfectly matches his subject matter.

Nigel Kendall

89 – *TOUCH OF EVIL*
(Orson Welles, 1958)

Touch of Evil may not have the dazzling virtuosity of Welles's debut, *Citizen Kane*. But it has far uglier, darker and truer things to say. The agile opening tracking shot, which follows a car across the US-Mexican border, is legendary. Atmosphere and words conspire as Charlton Heston's self-righteous Mexican narcotics agent goes toe-to-toe with Welles's monumentally

8 February 2008. Danny Boyle arrives at the British Academy Film Awards at the Royal Opera House, London. (Ben Gurr)

sleazy detective, Hank Quinlan, over the motives behind a fatal bombing. The moral corruption is as ripe as Welles's enormous gut. His relationship with Marlene Dietrich's gypsy brothel keeper is an unconsummated mystery.

James Christopher

88 – *WILD STRAWBERRIES* (Ingmar Bergman, 1957)

This beautiful film gives the lie to Bergman's reputation as difficult to watch. An ageing professor, as dusty as the tomes on his study wall, makes the trip across Sweden to collect a prestigious award, and memories of his youthful, playful self flood back. An elegy to lost youth and the regretted compromises of adult life, the film is notable for its spectacular camera work, and for the performance of Swedish film pioneer Victor Sjöström in the lead role. Sjöström, who directed Lillian Gish in the silent classic *The Wind* (1928), died three years after *Wild Strawberries* was released.

Nigel Kendall

87 – *THE SILENCE OF THE LAMBS* (Jonathan Demme, 1991)

A stunning movie that introduced the greatest monster of them all. Brian Cox had already played Hannibal "Lecktor" in Michael Mann's adaptation of Thomas Harris's novel *Red Dragon*, but it was Anthony Hopkins who turned the erudite, Chianti-loving cannibal into an unforgettable icon. The brilliance of the film is that it excels on every level: as a nerve-shredding whodunnit, horror film, chase movie, and vertiginous psycho-drama. The inspired idea of using a psychopath to catch a serial killer reinvigorated a genre that had been flat-lining since *Dirty Harry*. The mental chess between Jodie Foster's

Agent Starling and Anthony Hopkins's perfectly still, perfectly precise Lecter will forever send shivers down the spine.

James Christopher

86 – *NOSFERATU* (FW Murnau, 1922)

As the disturbing flipside to the patrician Draculas of Bela Lugosi and Christopher Lee, the vermin-like bloodsucker in Murnau's silent masterpiece is a creature not from Hollywood, but from the id itself. The film, which brazenly pilfers Bram Stoker's *Dracula* (the German production company was later sued into bankruptcy by Stoker's widow), follows the misfortunes of real-estate agent Thomas Hutter (Gustav von Wangenheim) who is summoned to the Carpathian hideout of bald-headed, crooked-framed, kohl-eyed, bat-eared, rat-toothed Count Orlock (Max Schreck). Much neck-biting ensues, Orlock moves to Hutter's home town, and the film produces some seminal horror images, including Orlock's final agonising fade in the morning light.

Kevin Maher

85 – *DOG DAY AFTERNOON* (Sidney Lumet, 1975)

A real-life botched Brooklyn bank robbery is the subject of this fascinating portrait of a charismatic criminal caught in the glare of the media spotlight. Al Pacino gives the wildcard performance of his career (he was beaten by Jack Nicholson's *Cuckoo's Nest* turn at that year's Oscars) as

Sonny, the skittish bisexual Vietnam veteran who's robbing the bank to fund his gay lover's sex-change operation. His incendiary relationship with the gathering crowds, the police and the rapacious news media quickly becomes the real focus of the film. Director Lumet's depiction of the flimsy and treacherous nature of instant celebrity seems eerily prescient.

Kevin Maher

84 – *FESTEN*
(Thomas Vinterberg, 1999)

This incredibly savage comedy about a Danish family reunion was a genuine breath of fresh air. It is the first, and finest, of the Dogme films whose collective ambition was to rescue cinema's credibility as an art form by stripping it to the bone. Vinterberg duly ditched every prop except his camera, and the result has influenced a generation of guerrilla film-makers. The splintered story about grown-up siblings who fail to bury their differences at their father's 60th birthday party has a documentary intensity that is cleverly aggravated by an almost alarming lack of editorial control. The oldest son (Ulrich Thomsen) is manhandled out of the dining room before the main course for toasting his father's sexual abuse of himself and his twin sister. The way the guests plough politely on is horribly real. An extraordinary piece of story-telling: chaotic, spontaneous, and refreshingly unpredictable.

James Christopher

83 – *SPARTACUS*
(Stanley Kubrick, 1960)

The making of Kubrick's epic tale of slave rebellion under Roman rule would make an epic in itself. Kubrick was summoned by the film's star and producer Kirk Douglas, who was at daggers drawn with the original director, Anthony Mann. Douglas also insisted that the script be written by the blacklisted Dalton Trumbo, and the finished film therefore emphasises the power of mass uprising against a tyrannical state. Kubrick found the experience so draining that he returned to the UK, never to work in Hollywood again. The original director Mann's work is uncredited, as it had been on the earlier epic *Quo Vadis*. The veteran western director finally got back into the epic saddle with *El Cid* and *The Fall of the Roman Empire*.

Nigel Kendall

82 – *CHUNGKING EXPRESS*
(Wong Kar-wai, 1994)

Wong Kar-wai's parallel stories of lovelorn Hong Kong cops is an impressionistic feast of vivid neon and jewel-like colour. With its trademark slow motion and artful blurring, this was one of the films to launch the career of the maverick cinematographer Christopher Doyle. The two stories are slight, as disposable as the fast food and pop culture that form the movie's backdrop. But there's something seductive about the half-realised love affairs. Story one has a femme fatale and a lost soul looking for meaning in the sell-by dates of cans of pineapple; story two stars Faye Wong as a fast-food waitress obsessed with a cop in a half-hearted relationship with an air hostess.

Wendy Ide

81 – *NORTH BY NORTHWEST* (Alfred Hitchcock, 1959)

Hitchcock's classic contains many elements familiar to viewers of his films, notably the theme of mistaken identity, the "MacGuffin" (a term coined by Hitchcock to denote an object that the cast is chasing, in this case a microfilm), a beautiful blonde, and a monumental climax, here on Mount Rushmore. But the film also leavens its thriller components with humour. The makers of the *Bond* films, three years later, would use this formula, MacGuffin and all, to create the most successful franchise in cinema history. Serious critics, notably the French, point out that every single character in the film is playing a part and that even Cary Grant's hero, the executive mistaken for a government agent, works in advertising: his profession is deception. The crop-dusting chase scene is rightly fêted.

Nigel Kendall

FIRST FILMS

ELVIS PRESLEY

Love Me Tender

MR ELVIS PRESLEY'S FIRST FILM

Unbylined review (Dudley Carew), December 11 1956

Mr Elvis Presley, who stands in the eyes of many for a new and revolutionary fashion in song and entertainment, steals gently on the scene in *Love Me Tender*. *Love Me Tender* is, indeed, more original in being a black-and-white film in Cinemascope than anything else, and the story is a conventional, if complicated, one of a band of brothers, literal and metaphorical, in the days immediately following the Civil War.

But Mr Presley sings – certainly he sings, but not, it would seem, authentic Rock 'n' Roll. He has a small mouth, which can fall easily into a pout of sulkiness, but for that pout the character of Clint, the youngest of the brothers, must bear the blame. He sings with a kind of outsize mandolin, with jerks that suggest a species of St Vitus's dance and a breathlessness natural to the end of a cross-country race. There is some attempt to keep his style tied down to the 1860s, but it has a way of escaping, and certainly the ecstatic moans set up by the muslin-dressed maidens at the country fair whenever he waggles his knees indicate that time has somehow slipped forward a matter of 90 years or so. There are some pleasant scenes of train hold-ups and robberies, and others sharing the burden of a somewhat muddled and confusing Western are Mr Richard Egan, Miss Debra Paget, and Mr Robert Middleton.

MR. ELVIS PRESLEY'S FIRST FILM

"LOVE ME TENDER"

Mr. Elvis Presley, who stands in the eyes of many for a new and revolutionary fashion in song and entertainment, steals gently on the scene in *Love Me Tender*, which goes to the Rialto Cinema on Thursday. *Love Me Tender* is, indeed, more original in being a black-and-white film in Cinemascope than anything else, and the story is a conventional, if complicated, one of a band of brothers, literal and metaphorical, in the days immediately following the Civil War.

But Mr. Presley sings—certainly he sings, but not, it would seem, authentic Rock 'n Roll. He has a small mouth which can fall easily into a pout of sulkiness, but for that pout the character of Clint, the youngest of the brothers, must bear the blame. He sings with a kind of outsize mandolin, with jerks that suggest a species of St. Vitus's dance and a breathlessness natural to the end of a cross-country race. There is some attempt to keep his style tied down to the 1860s, but it has a way of escaping, and certainly the ecstatic moans set up by the muslin-dressed maidens at the country fair whenever he waggles his knees indicate that time has somehow slipped forward a matter of 90 years or so. There are some pleasant scenes of train hold-ups and robberies, and others sharing the burden of a somewhat muddled and confusing "Western" are Mr. Richard Egan, Miss Debra Paget, and Mr. Robert Middleton.

CINEMA HISTORY

Carry On Sergeant

Review by Our Film Critic
(Dudley Carew),
September 22 1958

Editor's note: *Carry On Sergeant* **was the first in a series of 31 feature films over 34 years, making it undoubtedly one of the most successful film series in British cinema history. They were famously cheap – the original reportedly cost only £73,000 – and there was little indication at the outset that this was the beginning of anything special.** *The Times* **reviewed the film in a single paragraph, tucked beneath crits for** *The Defiant Ones,* *The Proud Rebel* **and** *Rockets Galore!,* **the sequel to** *Whisky Galore!.*

Mr R.F. Delderfield, from whose *The Bull Boys, Carry On Sergeant* is adapted, has shown a shrewd sense of what the public wants. What audiences on both sides of the Atlantic seem to revel in are films which perform their farcical manoeuvres on the barrack square, and *Carry On Sergeant* explains its simple ideas by its title. The awkward squad bashes away with any amount of good will and every now and again a line or a situation is genuinely funny.

5 January 1971. Kenneth Williams and Ingrid Bergman at a press conference in London. (Horace Tonge)

13 August 1971. Barbara Windsor and Charles Hawtrey at a press reception after a showing of *Carry on Henry* at the Odeon, Marble Arch. (Peter Trievnor)

Carry On Nurse

Review by Our Film Critic
(Dudley Carew), March 9 1959

This British farcical-comedy, directed by Mr Gerald Thomas, is a series of broad music-hall jokes set in a hospital, and anything less edifying it is difficult to imagine. Once or twice, out of the blue, in more than one sense of the phrase, there emerges a moment of shrewd observation, and perhaps the ward inhabited by Mr Kenneth Connor, Mr Kenneth Williams, Mr Charles Hawtrey and Mr Bill Owen, among others is not so fantastic a place as the film in general is determined to make it out to be. Miss Shirley Eaton, Miss Susan Stephen, and Miss Joan Sims add up to a decorative trio of nurses, while Miss Hattie Jacques, as Matron, steam-rolls her way through script and ward with majestic authority. Mr Wilfrid Hyde-White, as the "guest star," is a patient with a private room – and probably he felt the need of it.

Carry On Up the Khyber

Review by John Russell Taylor,
November 28 1968

Another never-never land, though a rather rowdier one: this time the old team are following The Drum with a lot of dirty doings on the North-West Frontier. The whole plot is based on that favourite subject of speculation for seaside postcards: what exactly does the Scotsman wear under his kilt? The answer, it appears, is far too much: flowered camiknickers, after all, are hardly calculated to strike terror into the heart of the average plotting native. But when the chips (or rather the knickers) are down, the British come up trumps, and the series reaches a new height of happy delirium in the dramatic sequence, a terribly stiff upper-lip formal dinner at the Residency while the tribesmen demolish the place about its inhabitants' ears. Carry Ons have had their ups and downs; this is decidedly an up.

CARRY ON UP THE CRITICS

The Carry On films have achieved respectability, but do they need a season, Clive Davis asks

August 7 1995

High culture and the belly laugh ethos of the Carry On films have encountered each other, briefly, once before. In the late 1950s, soon after the premiere of the first instalment in the long-running comedy series, the revellers at the Last Night of the Proms greeted the venerable Sir Malcolm Sargent with banners proclaiming – what else? – "Carry On Sargent". Nearly 40 years later, those very same Promenaders may be less amused to hear that one of Britain's leading arts institutions, the Barbican Centre, is about to devote an entire season to the seaside-postcard romps starring Sid James, Kenneth Williams, Joan Sims, Barbara Windsor and the rest of the team. All 31 of the comedies are to be shown in a retrospective which opens on Friday and continues until the end of the month.

We seem to be in the middle of a miniature *Carry On* revival. Admirers of Sid James have been able to read of his on and off-screen exploits in a recently published biography by Cliff Goodwin, who will be making an appearance at the Barbican. Academics gain a foothold in the season as well, contributing to a debate on The *Carry On* Legacy. As if that were not enough, the faces of Kenneth Williams and his co-stars can be seen on a poster campaign for KP Nuts, alongside suitably louche slogans.

Though Gerald Thomas, the films' director, died in 1993, his partner, the producer Peter Rogers, is still working in an office at Pinewood Studios. He will be feted on Sunday at the screening of *Up the Khyber*, a North-west Frontier parody considered by some to be the wittiest of all.

When the two men put the very first film into production, the idea of a marathon series was far from their minds. The script they were working on was loosely based on an R.F. Delderfield play about national service, entitled *The Bull Boys*. Rewritten as a broad comedy, it portrayed the misadventures of three hapless recruits – Kenneth Williams, Kenneth Connor and Charles Hawtrey – who find themselves at the mercy of a hectoring sergeant-major played by William Hartneil.

An unexpected box-office success, *Sergeant* was followed the next year by *Carry On Nurse*, a farce which established the soon-to-be-familiar pattern of lavatory jokes, forceful matrons and timid but lustful males. Rogers and Thomas were embarked on a highly profitable path. Budgets were trimmed to the minimum – according to Cliff Goodwin, *Sergeant* was made for a mere £74,000, while even the relatively lavish cod costume epic *Carry On Henry*, released in 1970, cost only about £250,000. All the films, with the exception of the dismal "comeback" of 1992, *Carry On Columbus*, made a profit.

Connoisseurs have their own favourites. Rogers chooses *Up the Khyber*, others prefer *Carry On Cleo*, an energetic send-up of the Burton-Taylor epic which, as every schoolboy knows, contains the most frequently quoted line of all: Kenneth Williams's lament as his assassins close in on the Ides of March – "Infamy! Infamy! They've all got it in for me!"

By the early 1970s, the nudge-nudge formula was already showing signs of fatigue. Rogers always said that "the star is the *Carry On*, actors are expendable". But the quality of the finished product suggested otherwise. He was cajoled into returning to the fray in 1992 in *Carry On Columbus* – which featured Alexei Sayle and Julian Clary – but by then the patient was long since brain-dead.

FILM DIRECTORS

SHOOTING STARS

Actors are shouting "Action" in order to get a piece of it. Three of the most interesting films of 1988 are directed by actors: Robert Redford's *The Milagro Beanfield War,* Clint Eastwood's *Bird* and Sam Shepard's *The Far North.* It is, David Thomson writes, a reminder that those handsome guys can think too

August 13 1988

When Jack Nicholson was about to direct his first film, he rang Clint Eastwood for advice. "Get a lot of sleep," came the laconic reply. Eastwood may have made the transition from actor to director look easy. Behind the scenes, it can be hell.

Someone has to act as if in charge on a film set. The picture won't get made without that show of management: the script has problems; the re-writes are worse; the actors playing the lovers don't get on; the cameraman believes he should be the director; the Teamsters have asked for more; today's scene calls for three actors, a crew of 27 and lights that create a temperature of 108°F in a room hardly big enough for two.

In such turmoil, directors have been elected because they were tall and commanding. Some say those assets helped DW Griffith to creative power and glory, and that he strove for further authority by wearing hats on the set.

Other directors sported riding boots, cracked whips and gave way to theatrical fury if crossed. They acted like directors, for they understood two principles of the business – that any decision brings reassurance in a crisis; and that everything has to do with the business of show. Griffith, Erich von Stroheim and Ernst Lubitsch had all been actors before they played the part of director.

In the robust, early days of picture-making, it was easier to go from one side of the camera to another. Not many people believed in directors then. Movies required action and a camera. A cameraman, it was assumed, knew where to put the camera and how to expose the film. Actors could do the rest perhaps with the aid of "story" merchants who shouted out some inspired action seconds before the actors improvised it.

It was in the making of comedies that the comedians saw how some jokes worked, or played better, depending on the way they were filmed. Those clowns truly "made" their films, in the way that it is now apparent Fred Astaire "directed" many of his numbers. (Astaire insisted on a certain camera style: the whole figure must be in the frame; no close-ups of feet or face; each dance filmed in real time, in one shot when possible. Astaire deserves much more than a dancer's credit.)

In the language of film criticism, those clowns were responsible for the *mise en scène* – the precise way in which action is visualized. From Charlie Chaplin to Jacques Tati to Jerry Lewis, comedian-directors explored the double helix of action and camera.

Chaplin took over every task; he even became the company that made the pictures. But Buster Keaton gradually lost credit and control, and made only a fraction of the money that Chaplin made. Chaplin was a genius of a clown and a domineering producer. Buster was only a genius and a forlorn businessman.

In our own time, there are superstars who have directed – to try it, and to avoid being exploited: Jack Nicholson with *Drive, He Said* and *Goin' South*; Warren Beatty with *Heaven Can Wait* and *Reds*; Robert Redford with *Ordinary People* and *The Milagro Beanfield War*. Not one of those films is bad, and two won Oscars for Best Direction. But the one with the most pronounced personal style was the greatest flop – Nicholson's *Drive, He Said*. If you want real flair, style or beauty from a modern actor-director, I recommend *Yentl*, by Barbra Streisand.

"Making a movie" has always meant so many things. On the one hand, it is dreaming up a project and a way to film it, then realizing that dream on film with all the arts and crafts involved – but doing it for someone else. That's how Marlon Brando made *One-Eyed Jacks*. But when he delivered a film so long, and so obscure, he was told he hadn't known what he was doing. The picture was taken out of his hands – because it had never been in his control.

Orson Welles was in a similar position with *Citizen Kane*. He was given a remarkable "carte blanche" contract by RKO in the late 1930s. He was to be responsible for the script, direction and production of a film. And act in it. Welles could not have won that liberty if RKO hadn't felt he was known as an actor, as well as a producer/director. Nor would *Citizen Kane* be as moving as it is (that's why it endures) if Welles was not acting in it, pretending to be Charlie Kane, but doing what he always liked best, flirting with the image of himself.

But Welles had no "participation" in the film. He was not "in charge" in the way that now seems essential to Beatty, Redford or Eastwood – as it did 70 years ago to Chaplin. Welles was paid for what he did, for the job. But if *Kane* had made a profit, Welles would have seen none of it.

When today's actors propose to direct, they may have Welles's love of the medium, if not his prowess or the passion, but not one of them goes to work without a percentage of the profits, and priority with it – in other words, something from the first dollars earned, not just when accountancy declares a profit.

Such actors are producers before they are directors. And producers are most celebrated and treasured for reason, prudence, clarity, efficiency, toughness, compromise and talking big – virtues not always compatible with passion, daring, originality and film style. *Ordinary People* seems to me like a film made by a sound textbook – whereas *Drive, He Said* is the reverie of an intense nut, and *Yentl* the outpouring of a headlong, lyrical egotist. Next to *Yentl*, the very intelligent *Reds* seems like a plan for an epic, a way of putting John Reed, the subject of the film, and Beatty together on the cover of *Time*.

Of course, if actors have the wit and clout to get a major piece of the action it may seem naive not to take it. In the history of film-making, actors have had ample opportunity to believe they could do things better. Many of the famed directors of film's golden age confined their advice to actors to "Action" and "Cut". They did not know how to talk to actors, or consider that it was necessary. Hence the impact in the 1940s and 1950s of a director like Elia Kazan; who loved nothing better than prolonged intimate colloquy with actors – and actresses – about their motivation.

From early days, actors thought they had been in enough films to know how to direct. The experiment seldom lasted. Lillian Gish directed her sister in one picture. Lionel Barrymore did several movies. In the 1950s and 1960s, when actors were taking charge of their careers, Burt Lancaster, Dick Powell, Karl Malden, Ida Lupino and John Wayne directed a few. Cornel Wilde went from being a dull actor to an authentic primitive as a director.

One actor who had slipped from stardom into difficulty directed a masterpiece: Charles Laughton with *The Night of the Hunter*. He was not tempted to act in the film; in any case, the studio wanted a star like Robert Mitchum. But Laughton seems to have recognized the task and beauty of directing: he studied movies in museums before he began, and he hired Stanley Cortez, the cameraman on Welles's *Magnificent Ambersons*. He understood what direction could be, and thereby, outshone most of the directors for whom he had acted.

There have also been occasions when essentially non-acting directors have elected to go in front of the camera. I am not thinking of Alfred Hitchcock's copyright walk-ons, deft turns that help us see how all the actors are his toys. Rather, I mean cameos where, a director signs a film or finds a very telling entrance to it, a way to help us in – like Michael Powell in *Peeping Tom*, the cruel father who raises his son in cinema; Roman Polanski electing to be the one to slit Nicholson's nose in *Chinatown*; the woeful figure of Nicholas Ray, arriving too late at the planetarium at the end of *Rebel Without a Cause*, Martin Scorsese as the neatly dressed raging cuckold in the back of the cab in *Taxi Driver*; Sam Peckinpah, the coffin-maker at the end of *Pat Garrett* and *Billy the Kid*, dryly commending his Garrett for seeing where the story has led him.

Such directors' performances have their model and peak: it is Jean Renoir's Octave in *La Regie du Jeu*, the director playing a man who has to help his friends' arrangements, and who causes tragedy when he tries to find a role for himself. The alertness Renoir gives Octave, the encouraging gestures with which he urges his actors on, are the clearest signs of a director who has felt compelled to cross over the line and join his own work. I would guess that being with Renoir in that film was like being with Welles in *Kane* or with John Cassavetes in his films – it was to be better, more alive. For there are movies in which acting and life are indistinguishable.

PUTTING THE MA IN CINEMA

In the infancy of the film industry, it was women who rocked the cradle, Stephanie Billen discovers

October 23 1996

Before 1920 there were more women working in the film industry, often in exalted positions, than in any subsequent period, yet many of them died in obscurity, and reference books have reduced them to footnotes. How, one wonders, did they ever achieve such power in the first place? "Because it was a new technology, it was a free-for-all," says Louise Anderson, a lecturer in media theory at the University of Northumbria. "As soon as it was realised that it would be a massively popular form of entertainment, the production targets were enormous, so they needed as many people as possible. Gender didn't come into it."

In 1895, Alice Guy-Blache was Leon Gaumont's secretary in Paris. She asked to film her own stories and was granted permission "as long as it did not interfere with her secretarial duties". She wrote, directed and starred in her first film, *The Cabbage Fairy*, in 1896 and amazingly went on to become head of production while still a secretary. "I think the fact that she could be doing both jobs gives you an idea of the kind of regard film-making was given initially," Anderson says.

Guy-Blache's stories may not have been earth-shattering but her style was influential. She put up signs for the actors saying "Be Natural" – rare advice in those days – and moved in for close-ups years before DW Griffith made them fashionable. Her use of special effects was also startling. Disliking models, she once blew up a real boat in the name of art – her husband was injured in the process. She even experimented with synchronised sound and colour tinting. On moving to Hollywood with Herbert Blache, her husband and cameraman, in 1910, she founded her own production company, but it ran into financial problems and she returned to France in 1922, husbandless and bankrupt.

Women directors had an extraordinary freedom. "It was a new industry and censorship was not as rigorous as it became in the 1920s," Anderson says. Thus, in 1916, Lois Weber, then the highest paid director in Hollywood, was able to make a film about abortion called *Where Are My Children?* and have it shown in most states of America, despite the fact that it caused great controversy and was dismissed by the chief censor in Pennsylvania as "unspeakably vile".

If women wielded surprising power behind the camera, they were goddesses in front of it. "Female stars had a huge following of female fans writing in for their beauty tips and so on," Anderson says. "It was big business, and women such as Mary Pickford or Mabel Normand were also able to set up their own production companies or direct. It was possible to move between different areas quite easily." The target audience was women. "Cinemagoing came from a tradition of nickelodeons and seedy arcades," Anderson explains. "When the money-making potential of film was realised, there was a drive to make it respectable, and the way to do that was to encourage women and children to go to the cinema. These days the desired audience is probably young men." Ironically, as the middle-class housewife was successfully courted, the standardisation of film production in the 1920s and the resulting unions and hierarchies led to the decline of opportunities for women behind the camera, although they remained important as stars and writers.

The fact that female pioneers have been largely forgotten has had an unfortunate knock-on effect, Anderson says. "Women making films now can feel unusual, as if there has been no precedent. That's clearly not the case."

CLASSIC CINEMA – FIRST IMPRESSIONS

◇◇◇◇◇◇◇◇◇◇◇◇◇◇◇◇◇◇◇◇◇◇◇◇◇◇◇◇◇◇◇◇

While *Citizen Kane* and *Vertigo* may come top of critics' polls to determine the greatest movies of all time, *The Shawshank Redemption* has long been rated best by the public on the Internet Movie Database website. As with many other films, its elevation to classic status was gradual. It lost money on its initial cinema release, but video release and television screenings took it to new and more appreciative audiences. Critics did not have years and the luxury of repeat viewings before sharing their views with the public. In *The Times* it was not considered the most important film in its week of release, with the review slotted in after assessments of the Indian film *Bandit Queen* and the latest version of *The Jungle Book*.

◇◇◇◇◇◇◇◇◇◇◇◇◇◇◇◇◇◇◇◇◇◇◇◇◇◇◇◇◇◇◇◇

LONG, BUT ENGROSSING PRISON MOVIE

The Shawshank Redemption

Review by Geoff Brown,
February 16 1995

In its early stages, *The Shawshank Redemption* tries to please with the manly delights of old prison movies. You know the line-up: gruelling brutality from guards and inmates. A cold-blooded warden ever-ready to quote the Bible. Grey bricks, grey uniforms. Women? Non-existent, except in posters stuck on walls: the hero, Tim Robbins, starts with Rita Hayworth decorating his cell, then replaces her with Marilyn Monroe and Raquel Welch.

A convicted murderer, although he bears himself like a model citizen and always proclaims his innocence, Robbins is in for the long haul. So are audiences: Frank Darabont's Oscar-nominated film, adapted from one of Stephen King's non-horror stories, lasts more than two hours. Luckily, changes of mood, a regard for character and excellent performances keep the fidgeting at bay.

At first a punchbag for others' anger, Robbins, a banker by trade, is warmed by friendship with another life prisoner. Morgan Freeman. He then improves his lot further by advising on the warden's crooked finances. However, when justice demands Robbins's parole the warden cannot afford to release him: he knows too much. A writer turned director, Darabont treats his own screenplay with reverence. This is understandable, especially when the dialogue is good, alive to quirks and ironies. But time is wasted on peripheral characters; the number of swings between grim violence and comedy relief also becomes a problem. You emerge from your incarceration in Shawshank Prison exhausted, incredulous at some of the plot twists, but still cheered by Robbins and Freeman's performances.

PERSONAL CHOICE

PRISONERS, CHOSEN BY ROBERT PESTON

April 29 2017

◇◇◇◇◇◇◇◇◇◇◇◇◇◇◇◇◇◇◇◇◇◇◇◇◇◇◇◇◇◇◇◇

Editor's note: Robert Peston is political editor of ITV News.

◇◇◇◇◇◇◇◇◇◇◇◇◇◇◇◇◇◇◇◇◇◇◇◇◇◇◇◇◇◇◇◇

Primo Levi's *If This Is a Man* is probably the most powerful and upsetting book that I've read. Because it's not just about the physical horrors that Nazis inflicted on the Jews. A lot of it is obviously about the murder, the exterminations and the gassings, but the book is primarily about the way in which the Nazis dehumanised the people in these camps, and about how civilised people became so brutalised that all they could think about was personal survival. In the words of Levi's poem: "Consider if this is a man/ Who works in the mud/ Who does not know peace/ Who fights for a scrap of bread/ Who dies because of a yes or a no…"

Levi's work is so profoundly upsetting that almost any other work of art doesn't seem to me to come close to it.

Therefore in picking pieces about prisoners, I've decided instead to go for escapist movies. So many films have prison scenes in them, partly because they are self-contained worlds that lend themselves to both comedy and tragedy. I've decided to go for comedy, as I normally do in life.

The Blues Brothers (1980)

Two petty crooks, total recidivists, who have been brutalised by being educated by strict nuns, are redeemed by the best soul music soundtrack ever.

Jailhouse Rock (1957)

The film that showed how Elvis had been sanitised by Hollywood. But I love Elvis's performance of the eponymous song – so camp and electric. Three minutes of pure joy: the most beautiful, stylish man in history with the sexiest hips. What more could you possibly want?

Blazing Saddles (1974)

This is the opposite of grim, gritty realism. I love our first encounter with the sorely missed Gene Wilder as the Waco Kid – who retired as a gunman and took to the bottle after a six-year-old told him to "reach for it". Wilder says: "I just threw my guns down and walked away. Little bastard shot me in the ass."

The Italian Job (1969)

Everyone thinks *The Italian Job* is about that race through Turin in Minis. It isn't. It's all about Noël Coward in a grim British jail as a suave gangland leader planning the daring heist – and celebrating it as a great British victory.

Goodfellas (1990)

One of Scorsese's best. Probably my favourite scene is the Mafiosi banged up and cooking the most delicious marinara sauce – using razor blades to slice the garlic into microscopically thin slivers, because that is the way you have to do it, wherever you happen to be living!

Guardians of the Galaxy (2014)

My favourite action adventure movie of the past few years, much wittier than the new *Star Wars* films, and with a stunning 1970s disco soundtrack. At the heart of the film our antiheroes bust out of a prison spacecraft – a *Great Escape* for our comic-book age, with a talking tree played by Vin Diesel in the Steve McQueen role.

24 July 2014. Vin Diesel and fans at the *Guardians of the Galaxy* film premiere in Leicester Square. (Andrew Sims)

TOP 100 COUNTDOWN

80 – *TOKYO STORY*
(Yasujiro Ozu, 1953)

The spare wonder of Ozu's masterpiece is that his characters and plot are as plain and honest as old shoes. The film is a portrait of middle-class siblings who put on their Sunday best when their elderly bumpkin parents travel to meet them in Tokyo. The excitement of the genial old couple is salted by a gradual and unspeakable awareness that their children regard them as an expensive, time-consuming inconvenience. The humble grace with which the elderly parents accept the drift between themselves and their impatient children would make stones weep. The original release was totally unmatched by anything happening in Western cinema, and made Hollywood look thoroughly superficial. Ozu would rather die than use a studio sleight of hand. His camera barely moves from the sitting position adopted by his elderly stars. The tension is exquisite. The result is profoundly moving.

James Christopher

79 – *DELIVERANCE*
(John Boorman, 1972)

The original hillbilly thriller, and the scariest of them all. Boorman's sour and violent classic loomed over the early 1970s like a Darwinian nightmare about the condescending rich and the feral poor. Four Atlanta businessmen (including two of the biggest names in Hollywood, Jon Voight and Burt Reynolds) are on a canoe trip in Georgia when they find themselves stalked by remorseless inbred woodsmen. A romantic alpha-male camping trip turns into a squalid fight to stay alive. The bleak message of the film – that there's absolutely nothing civilised about survival – shook audiences to the core.

James Christopher

78 – *THE LADY EVE*
(Preston Sturges, 1941)

Charles Pike (Henry Fonda) has been studying snakes in the Amazon for two years, and hasn't seen a woman for the duration. He was always going to fall hard for the first resourceful young woman to cross his path – literally in this case. Cruise ship con-artist Jean (Barbara Stanwyck) trips him up and reels him in. But when Charles gets wise to his lady friend's dubious line of work, he breaks off their relationship. Sturges's film now kicks the comedy up a notch as Jean reinvents herself as a British aristocrat, the eponymous Lady Eve. Fonda and Stanwyck have a sexual chemistry that all but melts the screen.

Wendy Ide

77 - *THE APU TRILOGY* (Satyajit Ray, 1956–1959)

Former ad man Ray here turns heads and preconceptions away from the idea that Indian cinema is synonymous with all-singing, all-dancing, multicoloured camp. Instead, this tri-part celebration of lived reality is defined by a quasi-documentary style, light, observational camera work and convincing non-professional acting. *Pather Panchali* focuses on the hardships of Apu (Subir Bannerjee, one of the three actors to play the protagonist through the series), growing up in an impoverished rural idyll. In *Aparajito*, his father dies, he trains to become a priest, but eventually abandons the vocation for a place at Calcutta University. While *Apu Sansar* details our hero's impulsive marriage, his wife's death in childbirth and his attempts to reconcile with his estranged son. It's epic stuff, but on a quiet, intimate scale.

Kevin Maher

76 - *BLAZING SADDLES* (Mel Brooks, 1974)

The first and the best of the "spoof" movies (*Airplane!* would follow five years later), Brooks's comedy satire took a genre that was sacrosanct to American cinema and culture – the Western – and simply eviscerated it. A deliciously wild-eyed Gene Wilder was perfect as the alcoholic gunslinger, the Waco Kid, who joins forces with black sheriff Cleavon Little (a stinging barb at the inherent racism of the genre) to fight the expansionist plans of corrupt businessman Hedley Lamarr (Harvey Korman). Mostly, however, it's just an excuse for a roll-call of anarchic gags, including the most famous flatulence scene in cinema history.

Kevin Maher

75 - *THE GOOD, THE BAD AND THE UGLY* (Sergio Leone, 1966)

Ponderously slow, but never less than gripping, the third of Leone's spaghetti westerns with Clint Eastwood is rightly the most celebrated. The Spanish army supplied the hundreds of extras needed, and agreed to build the bridge that is destroyed by explosives, on condition that a Spanish army captain got to press the button. He blew up the bridge when the cameras weren't turning, so his army colleagues rebuilt it, and they blew it up again. The $200,000 in gold that our unlikely alliance is hunting would be worth around $8,960,000 at today's prices.

Nigel Kendall

74 – ROSEMARY'S BABY
(Roman Polanski, 1968)

Inspired by Ira Levin's novel, Polanski returned to the themes of urban alienation and the descent into madness explored in his earlier *Repulsion*, but this time with a genuinely horrific twist. Mia Farrow took the role against the wishes of her then husband Frank Sinatra, who threatened her with divorce if she disobeyed. In a curious echo of the film, in which Rosemary's husband endangers his mortal soul for an acting career, she took the part and lost Frank.

Nigel Kendall

73 – GREAT EXPECTATIONS
(David Lean, 1946)

David Lean's finest two hours, and still the best big-screen version of a Dickens novel yet made. The director's master stroke was to open it like a ghost story and film it like a ripping yarn. Guy Green's magnificently broody photography was an Oscar-winning ingredient. So too the gothic sets. There is so much to admire: the crisp pace, the crackling atmosphere, and John Mills as the arrogant hero whose expectations are built on delusions. But it is Martita Hunt's matchless Miss Haversham that most of us will take to the grave.

Wendy Ide

72 – DAYS OF HEAVEN
(Terrence Malick, 1978)

Malick's follow-up to his extraordinary *Badlands* is one of the great art films of the 1970s. A young Richard Gere stars as Bill, a hot-tempered labourer who is forced to flee the industrial blight of Chicago with his lover Abby (Brooke Adams) and his sister Linda (Linda Manz). They seek sanctuary in the rural heartlands, and find it on a farm owned by the ailing Sam Shepard. *Days of Heaven is* celebrated for the eerie half-light of the cinematography – Malick insisted that the film was shot at the "magic hour", first thing in the morning and late at night.

Wendy Ide

71 – THIS IS SPINAL TAP
(Rob Reiner, 1984)

Starting life as a stunt, this faux documentary about a British heavy metal band on a disastrous tour of the United States is cinema's most legendary spoof. Shot with deadpan candour, the film charts the squabbles, the gaffes, and the cock-ups as Nigel Tufnel (Christopher Guest), David St Hubbins (Michael McKean) and Harry Shearer (Derek Smalls) threaten to implode after 17 years on the road. It's a terrific fly-on-the-wall comedy. Some scenes will forever be cherished: the band totally lost back stage before a concert; the drummer getting trapped in a stage pod; Derek Smalls setting off an airport metal detector because of a large foil-wrapped gherkin in his underpants; and Stonehenge.

James Christopher

PEOPLE

DEBT THE CINEMA OWES TO LEAN

Director was a master of both suburban love stories and wide-screen drama.

David Lean, who died yesterday, was a leading figure in British films for 50 years. The doyenne of film critics, Dilys Powell, assesses his career

April 17 1991

The great names in British cinema vanish one by one; David Lean was among them. He was one of the three who won an international reputation for British cinema in the Thirties and at the beginning of the war.

He first came to prominence with *In Which We Serve* which he directed in co-operation with Noël Coward; it still stands as possibly the best of this country's war films beautifully played by John Mills, Bernard Miles and Celia Johnson and Coward himself. It responded to the emotions felt by the British public in 1942.

Not that Lean was to be a director of war films except indirectly. His next work was again on a Noël Coward script but the characters were civilians at war; it was the emotions of the characters behind the war which were concerned. And for some years David Lean moved from theme to theme but usually concentrating

12 February 1985. Sir David Lean, film director. (Frank Herrmann)

on the affections and the quarrels of middle-class figures.

A little after the war something else showed itself; his feeling for those not so much engaged in fighting but troubled by responsibility for them. One remembers *The Sound Barrier* for the first experiments on flying faster than sound and the sacrifices and the triumphs.

But it was when American finance entered that David Lean came into his own. He used in his latter days to complain of the timidity of the people who backed his work; but he was fortunate when he found a theme which could appeal to both British and American taste. *The Bridge on the River Kwai* had the dramatic quality which British cinema often lacked; the story of a party of prisoners of war in Japanese hands involved in an ironic act of heroism had the true international feeling.

Lean was the director who understood the contradictory movements of action; and he was the perfect director for Alec Guinness. He had opened the way to a valuable British-American co-operation; another large-scale piece, still with a British centre and British stars, was to follow, and *Lawrence of Arabia* established the right of the British cinema to be everywhere honoured.

Somehow the record seems to be getting round to the success of a war director. But perhaps Lean's value was larger than that; it was the emotion behind war in a period governed by the sense of war which the cinema owes him. He once asked me about a German war film; I admitted that I didn't like it. He was disapproving but when I confessed to nationalist feelings he softened: That, he said, is honest, anyway.

I don't think he had strong nationalist feelings; I think he gave his feelings to themes which served courage and self-respect. And he tackles a great variety of tales: the story of human relationships in *The Passionate Friends*, the problem of the woman trapped in an approach she is not experienced enough to resist (*Summer Madness*, with the wonderful Katharine Hepburn); then serious comedy in *Hobson's Choice*, fantasy comedy in *Blithe Spirit*, and an early success with a Dickens' story, *Great Expectations*.

He was an unwilling subject of criticism; it was said that the reception of his *Ryan's Daughter* stood in the way of his devotion to cinema. But devotion was there – and literary taste; he liked the work of Joseph Conrad and was recently working on a Conrad novel. As a person he could seem remote; there was none of the warm excitement which Michael Powell expressed, or Carol Reed, the two British directors who with him fought for the success of British cinema. Perhaps warmth went into his work, though his screen was never emotional in the accepted sense. But we owe him a great debt; he gave the British cinema a great reputation.

Really what should be said is simple: he made good films. He began making them when something powerful, something startling and capable of standing on its own, was needed.

CLASSIC CINEMA

BEYOND THE PLOT BARRIER

2001: A Space Odyssey

Review by John Russell Taylor, September 7 1968

There are times in the cinema these days when I begin to feel that perhaps I have a faint inkling of how the mammoth felt when the ice began to melt. It struck me with peculiar force this week when I took a friend to see *2001: A Space Odyssey*.

On second viewing my pleasures, and my reservations, came in precisely the same places. I enjoyed, and was held, by the plotty bits, particularly the whole middle section in which the human inhabitants of the space-ship find themselves locked in deathly combat with a rogue robot which has gone mad and is bent on destroying them. I found the beginning as long drawn out, and the end as wilfully obscure, as before. (I notice, by the way, that in the more recently published novel-of-the-film both of these sections are much clarified: it is made explicit, for instance, that the black basalt slab the apes encounter is a teaching machine from outer space, and that the Claridges-rococo room at the end is a tool of the astronaut's imagination, abandoned when he has no further use for it.) I admired the elaboration of the technical scenes showing the arrival of the space-ship at the space-station and so on, but still tended to feel that they were over-long in relation to the film as a whole, as though Stanley Kubrick had had so much fun devising them that he failed, when editing the film, to appreciate that they would be considerably less interesting to an audience than they were to him.

Ah, but that was where I was wrong. In the audience when I saw the film again there were lots of children, especially boys, under 15, generally with fathers and sometimes with mothers in tow. A characteristic group sat just behind me: father and mother in their mid-thirties, boy of about 11. And their reactions were fascinating. The mother was clearly a trifle restive. Like me, she was most held by the plot; otherwise, she kept asking her husband, sotto voce, what this meant, what was happening there, did he think a space-craft would really be like that, and so on. To which he gave answers more hopeful than confident, I thought. But evidently what interested him above all was the purely mechanical side, the sort of thing which should appeal at once to Meccano addicts; the plot for him seemed to be pretty incidental, like the plot in a musical, something which was there as the bread in the sandwich of really attractive items.

The boy, on the other hand, obviously loved it all. He shushed his parents whenever their dialogue became too insistent, and in the interval kept bubbling "Isn't it good? Do you like it? Don't you understand it? What's there difficult to understand?" Maybe, of course, he was just an infant genius, but I doubt it. He seemed an ordinary enough child. But clearly his attention was not functioning in the same sort of way that his parents' was, and that mine was. He was, that is to say, not in the slightest worried by a nagging need to make connections, or to understand how one moment, one spectacular effort, fitted in with, led up to or led on from another. He was accepting it like, dare one say, an LSD trip, in which a succession of thrilling impressions are flashed on to a brain free of the trammels of rational thought. Nor can one put this down to his age and education: it is not, after all, a particularly childish way of seeing things. As any teacher will tell you, children tend on the whole, especially at that age, to be the most stuffily rationalistic of all, constantly demanding believable hows and whys.

No, it seems to me that what we have here, in a rather extreme form is a whole new way of assimilating narrative. It is not only children who exemplify it: many young and some not-so-young adults seem to accept things in the same way. What they want, or at least what they accept without demur, is not an articulated plot, but a succession of vivid moments. They are, one might say, the audience envisaged by Artaud in his proposed theatre of cruelty, ready conditioned, perfectly prepared to abandon ratiocination and take drama straight in the solar plexus. Naturally, I have a theory to account for this, and it is hardly a new one. But it seems to me that, despite Marshall McLuhan and the sense he occasionally talks among a lot of provocative nonsense, very little practical attention has yet been paid to the way that a life with television is affecting our mode of perception. In television, for all sorts of reasons — not least the manifold distractions of life at home as against the narrowly directed attention to stage or screen required of us in a darkened theatre — attention is always liable to drift away, and in a matter of seconds rather than minutes. What is needed, therefore, is not so much something which will keep one glued to the small screen every instant of a programme — that would be too exhausting — but something which will keep bringing back the wandering attention with a new titbit at regular intervals. How the transition from one titbit to another is achieved remains fairly immaterial.

Hence, plot in particular does not matter greatly, and neither does an overall sense of form. Provided the attention-grabbers are spectacular enough in themselves, no one is going to question the rationale behind them too closely. And once this habit of mind is established, it is bound to affect other fields of activity, notably the screen and the stage. I find myself worried quite frequently by evident weak points in plot — there are, for example, quite blatant inconsistencies and violent ruptures of tone in both the new films about police methods and ethics, the British *Strange Affair* and the American *Detective* — but they seem, I find, to bother ordinary paying members of the audience not at all. To me it would seem a mark against the possible popularity of *Yellow Submarine* that it has no coherent plot at all, but simply makes up its feature length out of varied bits and pieces. Not at all though: where it has been shown it seems to have gone down very well with audiences, and not necessarily highbrow audiences either, on its power to excite and enliven moment by moment.

I have, little by little, acclimatized myself to the Frank Tashlin/Jerry Lewis type of comedy, careless as it is of overall form, and dedicated to the elaboration of a succession of isolated gags. But evidently audiences habituated to television and the strip cartoon were there way ahead of me. I suppose I shall adjust eventually to incoherent plotting in drama, to films that are all flash and outbreak, with little sense beyond the sound and the fury. But meanwhile it really is rather worrying to think of current cinema as an unknown territory into which, perhaps, only a little child can confidently lead me.

CLASSIC FILM OF THE WEEK

2001: A Space Odyssey

Review by Kate Muir,
November 28 2014

Stanley Kubrick's work of mad, transcendent genius seems all the smarter when viewed in the recent context of the laboured and expensive Interstellar. Kubrick's spaceships are perhaps little more than Airfix models, but he makes them majestic, even awesome in the proper sense of the word, with those opening bars from Richard Strauss's 'Thus Spake Zarathustra', and utterly weightless to the waltz of 'The Blue Danube'.

Co-written by Arthur C Clarke, Kubrick's film was a mind-busting experience back in 1968 and it still leaves the viewer wrestling with philosophical issues that arise with the ascent of man in the early ape scenes, when a smooth-as-basalt black monolith appears on Earth, until the final psychedelic interstellar ride through a wormhole and the sight of the embryonic Star Child.

The movie features William Sylvester as Dr Heywood Floyd, who discovers another black monolith on the Moon, and the alien signal is later investigated by astronauts David Bowman (Keir Dullea) and Frank Poole (Gary Lockwood). But the real star of the space-show is HAL, that polite, manipulative computer voiced by Douglas Rain. Looking back, the design is particularly glorious: the multicoloured liquid-food TV meals, the pastel Swinging Sixties' costumes by Hardy Amies, the space-helmets with frog-like eyes – and, of course, the "zero-gravity toilet". Often as funny as it is monumental, the new digital transfer of *A Space Odyssey* is showing as part of the BFI's UK-wide celebration Sci-Fi: Days of Fear and Wonder.

PEOPLE

Editor's note: *The Prime of Miss Jean Brodie* **was the first film set I ever visited, when I was still at primary school. Decades later I had the pleasure of visiting its director Ronald Neame at his home in Beverly Hills. He started off in silent movies, worked regularly as David Lean's partner and made more money as director of** *The Poseidon Adventure* **than all his other films put together. He was a fascinating man, a natural raconteur – the** *Times* **obituary mentions his house being damaged by earthquake, but Neame brought the story to life by pointing out that he was asleep in the building at the time and awoke to discover his home was on the move, heading down through Beverly Hills. "Much more frightening than the Blitz," he recalled. Not only did he direct Judy Garland's final movie, as mentioned in the obit, but he also served as a sort of personal therapist – she was battling addiction and personal demons and twice tried to commit suicide during filming.**

Ronald Neame

Obituary (Peter Waymark),
June 19 2010

Ronald Neame made a distinguished contribution to the British film industry over five decades, as a cameraman, as producer on the early films of David Lean and finally as a director of craftsmanlike pictures notable for the strong performances he drew from his actors, from Alec Guinness, Edith Evans and Judy Garland to Maggie Smith.

Neame came from a tradition of film-making that saw the director's role as being as unobtrusive as possible and he was in any case too self-effacing to impose his own personality on his work. He was scornful of young directors trying to make a name for themselves by putting their egos on the screen, and insisted that it was the actors who mattered.

In an interview in 1970, he said: "So long as I am able to make films, actors and actresses who work with me will get good reviews in the press because I dedicate myself to them. I will never make a film that overlooks the actors and gets all the praise for me as the director."

Born in London in 1911, he was the son of Elwin Neame, a leading society photographer and later film director, and Ivy Close, a theatrical beauty and a star of the silent cinema. He was educated at University College School and Hurstpierpoint College but was forced to leave school at 14 after his father's death in a road accident.

After brief spells as a clerk and in his father's profession of photography, he entered the film industry, starting as a teaboy at British International Studios at Elstree. In 1929, still in his teens, he was an assistant cameraman on Alfred Hitchcock's *Blackmail*, the first British talkie. By 1934 he had risen to director of photography, one of the youngest in the industry.

From the cheaply produced "quota quickies" he moved to Ealing, where he photographed a number of George Formby comedies, encountering the star's legendary meanness and formidable wife. By the late 1930s he was one of the British film industry's premier cameramen, working on the Shaw adaptations *Pygmalion* and *Major Barbara* and the Powell-Pressburger *One of Our Aircraft Is Missing*.

In 1942 he photographed Noël Coward's tribute to the Royal Navy at war, *In Which We Serve*. The co-director was David Lean, whom Neame had met while Lean was editing *Major Barbara*. Neame joined Lean and Anthony Havelock-Allan in forming the production company, Cineguild, which, working within the Rank Organisation but enjoying a large measure of autonomy, became a significant force in the British cinema.

With Neame as cameraman and then producer and screenwriter, and Lean directing, Cineguild was responsible for some of the most polished films of the 1940s. They included Coward's *This Happy Breed*, *Blithe Spirit* and *Brief Encounter*, as well as the brilliant Dickens adaptations, *Great Expectations* and *Oliver Twist*. *Great Expectations* won two Oscars and Neame was nominated, along with Lean and others, for the screenplay.

His association with Cineguild ended unhappily over an adaptation of the H.G. Wells novel, *The Passionate Friends*. Neame, who had turned director in 1947 with a crisp little thriller, *Take My Life*, had set up the project with the writer Eric Ambler, intending to direct. He and Ambler completed the screenplay and did the main casting. But colleagues in Cineguild, including Lean, took strong objection to the script and Neame was effectively sidelined.

His directing career took off in 1952 with *The Card*, sympathetically adapted from Arnold Bennett's novel and with Alec Guinness as the social climber Denry Machin. It was the sort of project that suited Neame best, a solid, middlebrow literary pedigree and the opportunity for quality acting.

A similar enterprise was *The Horse's Mouth*, with Guinness (who also wrote the script) playing Joyce Cary's rascally painter, Gulley Jimson. Other films of the fifties included *The Million Pound Note*, an enjoyable adaptation of the Mark Twain story starring Gregory Peck, and a fact-based Second World War drama, *The Man Who Never Was*.

Neame's favourite film, and arguably his best, was *Tunes of Glory* (1960), in which Guinness donned a red wig to play a hard-drinking Scottish army officer in conflict with John Mills. In 1963 Neame directed Judy Garland in what turned out to be her last film, *I Could Go On Singing*. She was difficult and unreliable and likely to disappear from the set for days. It needed all of Neame's tact and patience to hold the picture together and capture Garland's unique style.

In 1968 he guided Maggie Smith to an Oscar-winning performance as the unorthodox Edinburgh schoolmistress in Muriel Spark's *The Prime of Miss Jean Brodie*. He made the musical, *Scrooge*, with Albert Finney and in 1972 went to Hollywood for *The Poseidon Adventure*, in which an all-star cast has to escape from a capsized liner. One of the first of the cycle of 1970s disaster movies, it was a huge box-office success. Although it made Neame, who had a percentage, a rich man he tended to dismiss it as a routine chore. In 1974 he filmed Frederick Forsyth's serpentine thriller *The Odessa File*.

During the 1970s Neame settled in California and most of his later pictures were made in Hollywood. They included *Meteor*, another much inferior disaster movie and two middling comedies, *Hopscotch*, a spy caper with Walter Matthau and Glenda Jackson, and *First Monday in October*, with Matthau and Jill Clayburgh as the Supreme Court's first woman judge. In 1974 his Beverly Hills house was badly damaged in the Los Angeles earthquake and took more than two years to rebuild.

Neame married Beryl Heanly in 1933 and they had a son, Christopher, who became a producer at Hammer films and for television. The marriage was dissolved after nearly 40 years when Neame fell in love with a younger woman. She died in her thirties and in 1993 he married an American, Donna Friedberg. He was appointed CBE in 1996 and in the same year was given a Lifetime Fellowship Award by Bafta.

Ronald Neame, CBE, film cameraman, producer, writer and director, was born on April 23, 1911. He died on June 16, 2010, aged 99.

SCANDAL

ARBUCKLE CHARGED WITH MURDER

Reuters news report,
September 13 1921

"Fatty" Arbuckle, the cinema actor, has been arrested on a charge of murder in connection with the death of Virginia Rappe, a film actress, who died after a party at Arbuckle's apartment at an hotel here last Monday evening. The District Attorney states that Arbuckle is charged under the section of the Criminal Code providing that life taken in rape or attempted rape shall be considered as murder.

CLEANSING THE FILM WORLD

AMERICAN PROTESTS

News report, from Our
Correspondent, September 16 1921

The demand that the film industry in America shall forthwith "clean its house" is today spreading over the entire country. The "orgy" which resulted in the indictment of "Fatty" Arbuckle for man-slaughter is but one of a long series in which film "stars" and producers have recently figured in various parts of the United States. Yet it is only just to the many reputable film performers to emphasize, as the secretary of the Los Angeles Morals and Efficiency Association does this morning, that "the great body of actors in filmdom are not involved" by the investigation he has just completed.

The results of this investigation he has placed in the hands of the Public Prosecutor. They disclose an appalling state of licentiousness among a coterie of grotesquely overpaid actors and actresses, who have come to be known as "the live one hundred" of Los Angeles and Hollywood, a suburb where many film actors and actresses have their homes. The police have long had their eye on this particular coterie, from which the best-known artists of Hollywood keep rigorously aloof.

Stories of the unbridled licence of these people, who seem to command unlimited wealth, fill the newspapers. Their character is indicated by the description of a party recently given in a palatial residence in Hollywood. In the "Grotto of Good Fellows" the "live one hundred" were assembled. At a signal from the host a maid, pushing before her a tea wagon, entered the spacious grotto, but on the tea wagon there were no teacups, but an assortment of hypodermic needles and narcotic drugs. The neatly clad maid passed before each of the gorgeously clad guests, who selected the favourite drug or potion.

It is stated to-day that the authorities have already identified an officer and a petty officer of a Navy tug from which the "one hundred" drew their liberal supplies of smuggled liquor, which was paid for at the rate of £8 a quart. Pending further investigation of these charges, however, public interest is concentrated on the immediate fate of "Fatty" Arbuckle, who is frantically seeking to be released on bail.

Bail apparently cannot be refused if the charge remains one only of manslaughter, but the Public Prosecutor is urging the grand jury to make the charge that of murder. He is supported in this demand by a committee of club women in Los Angeles, who have adopted a resolution calling for Arbuckle's trial for murder. Meanwhile the coroner's jury has addressed an urgent appeal to the Public Prosecutor, the police, and the prohibition agents promptly to concert measures for the prevention of any repetition of the drinking parties which culminated in the death of Virginia Rappe.

ARBUCKLE'S ACQUITTAL

A NEW FILM

News report, from Our
Correspondent, April 15 1922

The end of the third trial of Roscoe ("Fatty") Arbuckle, the film comedian, on a charge of having caused the death of Miss Virginia Rappe, a young film actress, came last night, when the jury returned a verdict of Not Guilty after less than five minutes deliberation. On two previous occasions the jury had been unable to agree.

The third trial has lasted five weeks, and over 70 witnesses have been examined. After the Court rose a number of jurymen issued a statement to the effect that mere acquittal was "not enough," and added the opinion that there was

"not the slightest proof adduced to connect Arbuckle with the commission of the crime." The three trials have cost Arbuckle over £25,000, including a fee of £12,500 for his leading counsel, Mr Gavin McNab.

Mr Adolf Zukor, president of the Famous Lasky Players Corporation, states today that a new Arbuckle film will be released immediately. "On the manner in which this film is received by the public," he adds, "will depend whether the company makes a further contract with Arbuckle."

ARBUCKLE FILMS BARRED

News report, from Our
Correspondent, April 20 1922

"Fatty" Arbuckle's acquittal on the charge of having caused the death of a young film actress at a drinking party will not be followed by his reappearance on the screen. It is announced today that at the request of Mr W.H. Hays, who recently resigned the office of United States Postmaster-General to become director-general of the reorganized film industry, persons and firms handling Arbuckle's films have cancelled all contracts for their exhibition and have agreed to suspend further releases and bookings pending an inquiry into the whole question of Arbuckle's future in the industry.

The cancellation of the contracts involves a sacrifice on the part of exhibitors and distributors of over £500,000. Mr Hays's announcement as to Arbuckle is the first action he has taken publicly since he was appointed to his present position with a mandate to "restore the prestige" of the cinema industry.

few seconds for air and then resume where they left off in a scene that lasts over two minutes. The code continued in effect into the 1960s.

DEATH OF "FATTY" ARBUCKLE

Unbylined news report,
June 30 1933

The film comedian Roscoe ("Fatty") Arbuckle died suddenly yesterday in New York at the age of 52. He had been in poor health, but he started work as an actor in a new film on Wednesday. From vaudeville he went on the films in 1908, and made a great success in "slapstick" comedy. In 1921 he was charged with the manslaughter of a young film actress at a Hollywood party, and though he was acquitted his films were everywhere withdrawn owing to the action of the women's clubs in America. Later he began a new career as a film director under the name of William Goodrich.

Editor's note: Arbuckle was one of the biggest Hollywood stars of his era. WH Hays went on to produce the Motion Picture Production Code. Known in the industry simply as the Hays Code, it banned nudity, with a few exceptions, profanity, miscegenation, having clergy as comic characters or villains and "excessive kissing", which seemingly meant anything over three seconds. Alfred Hitchcock got around this in Notorious by having Cary Grant and Ingrid Bergman break off every

SCANDAL

HOLLYWOOD NEEDS A REFORMATION AFTER WEINSTEIN SCANDAL

Opinion piece by James Eglinton, Meldrum lecturer in reformed theology at the Edinburgh University

October 31 2017

The exposure of Harvey Weinstein's abuse of power and treatment of women has offered a reminder that Hollywood's vast influence is riddled with corruption. Media commentators and increasing numbers of actors are coming forward to condemn Weinstein – all the while admitting that Hollywood has many more like him.

Can such a decadent industry – abundantly mighty and amoral – be reformed? Paul Haggis, Weinstein's fellow Oscar winner, has argued that the pursuit of money has brought Hollywood to the point of artistic and ethical bankruptcy. Is Haggis right in seeing Hollywood as beyond redemption?

Among the greatest examples of a vast, corrupt, power-hungry institution being challenged and changed was the

16th-century Protestant reformation. Like Hollywood in 2017, the Catholic church – then a far more influential institution than Hollywood now – struggled to deal with its corrupt elements: nepotistic cardinals, financial corruption and rogue clergy who sold forgiveness for profit.

Martin Luther, the German monk, risked his life by challenging the church to change. His efforts were remarkably successful. His protest prompted the Catholic church, via the counter-reformation, to face up to its corruption and abuses. A better Catholicism would emerge and Protestant Christianity, growing out of this attempt to reform the church, would change the course of history.

What can the reformation teach Hollywood? It succeeded because it posed a piercing existential question of the church: why does the church exist, if not for the consolidation of wealth and individual power? This was a dangerous question for a whistle-blower like Luther who was declared an outlaw and forced into hiding. His reimagining of the church's purpose as an institution focused on its gospel message and the empowerment that message offers ordinary people proved persuasive and spread rapidly thanks to the printing press, the new media of his day.

Hollywood's challenge is to ask its own existential questions: does it exist for what its films do for someone like Harvey Weinstein, or rather, because of the power of cinema in the lives of ordinary people? Hollywood needs its own reformation.

SCANDAL

STEVEN SEAGAL, LOUIS C.K., ED WESTWICK: FALLEN STARS LITTER STUDIO FLOOR AS LURID SCANDAL GROWS

Actors and comedians are seeing projects cancelled as one claim after another rocks Hollywood

News report by Josh Glancy, New York, November 12 2017

While Westminster tears itself apart over the alleged peccadilloes of misbehaving MPs, the town that triggered the world-wide calling to account of sexual bullies – Hollywood – is convulsed by ever more shocking revelations about the behaviour of some of its most famous names.

Sexual assault allegations – some going back two decades or more – continue to spool out every day in the aftermath of the Harvey Weinstein scandal. The Emmy award-winning actor and comedian Louis C.K., best known for his hugely popular Netflix specials, has admitted that accusations of sexual misconduct by five women are true.

The action star and director Steven Seagal is also among those caught up in the blizzard of allegations. The actress Jenny McCarthy claims that Seagal harassed her during an audition for *Under Siege 2* in 1995. She claims he said: "You know, this part has nudity in it, and I can't really tell what your body looks like in that dress you're wearing."

He then allegedly asked her to lower her dress so he could see her breasts.

The British actor Ed Westwick was also the subject of serious allegations last week. The heart-throb star of teen TV drama *Gossip Girl* was accused by the actress Kristina Cohen of raping her at his home in 2014. A second actress, Aurelie Wynn, also accused him of raping her in the same year. Westwick denies the allegations. "I do not know this woman," he tweeted. "I have never forced myself in any manner, on any woman. I certainly have never committed rape."

Last night the film star Richard Dreyfuss denied claims by a writer, Jessica Teich, that he had exposed himself to her in the 1980s but acknowledged he had acted in other ways he now realised were inappropriate. Another Hollywood titan, the *Mad Men* creator Matthew Weiner, was also under fire after his former assistant, Kater Gordon, accused him of making a lewd request while she was working for him. Gordon, who won an Emmy for co-writing an episode of the hit series about the world of advertising with Weiner, alleges that he told her that she owed it to him to let him see her naked. A representative for Weiner said that "he does not remember saying this comment nor does it reflect a comment he would say to any colleague". Three women have also come forward to accuse *Entourage* star Jeremy Piven of sexual assault, something that he categorically denies.

In fact so many stars had their reputations tarnished last week that late night comedy host Trevor Noah joked: "At this point, we're going to need a new Oscar category this year: best actor whose movies we can't watch anymore."

CLASSIC CINEMA

FINE LINES FROM THE HIGH PRIEST OF HATE COUTURE

Pulp Fiction

Review by Geoff Brown, October 20 1994

Two dictionary definitions of the word "pulp" launch *Pulp Fiction*, Quentin Tarantino's rollercoaster ride through the Los Angeles underworld of hit-men, molls, boxers and Mr Bigs. "A soft, moist, shapeless mass of matter" is the first. This is not Tarantino's pulp, unless it refers to the bloodied state his characters reach after a violent confrontation. He is, after all, the director of *Reservoir Dogs*, and he does not believe in pinpricks.

The second definition is: "A magazine or book containing lurid subject matter and being characteristically printed on rough, unfinished paper." Lurid? Certainly: the script's three main stories, meshed together with diabolical ingenuity, involve drug overdoses, botched shootings, sadomasochistic doings in pawn shops, death in a lavatory, all wrapped in the kind of dialogue that stings the ears.

But where is the rough, unfinished paper? For the abiding impression of this flamboyant homage to the cheap crime fiction of the 1930s and 1940s is of plush settings and vast expense. With *Reservoir Dogs* and a bankroll from the Miramax company behind him, Tarantino called upon the services of Bruce Willis, John Travolta, Uma Thurman, Samuel L Jackson, Rosanna Arquette and Christopher Walken, among others.

He also spent pots of money building a themed restaurant called Jack Rabbit Slim's: an incredible temple to 1950s pop culture, where diners sit in converted convertibles and the waiter resembles Buddy Holly. Granted control over the final editing, Tarantino let many sequences run on well past their bedtime, and eventually produced a fat film two-and-a-half hours long.

But if there is too much swagger to *Pulp Fiction*, at least Tarantino has something to boast about. His ear for dialogue is extraordinary; and he gives his characters so many quirks that you never know what they will prattle about next – television pilots, quotations from Ezekiel, women's pot bellies, or the French names for hamburgers. The script is published by Faber & Faber at £7.99, so you can savour such details at your leisure.

Performances match the script's exuberance. Rescued from trash like *Look Who's Talking*, Travolta reveals hidden

7 December 2012. Director Quentin Tarantino. (Jon Bond)

strengths as the hitman Vincent (long hair, one earring), whose uneasy night out with his boss's wife climaxes in a drug overdose. In the middle stretch; Willis, hair shaved to stubble, plays the double-crossing boxer with a short fuse, trying to escape with his French girlfriend before retribution comes.

No one character, however, can claim supremacy. Tarantino constantly throws in monkey wrenches, yanking the stories back on themselves, and injecting amusements such as Harvey Keitel's Mr Wolf, summoned to help Travolta and Jackson hide a headless corpse and clean up a blood-spattered Chevy.

Throughout *Pulp Fiction* dark comedy and hard violence run neck and neck. Tarantino does not paint a pretty picture of mankind. But the film's very gusto keeps total nihilism at bay; and while the over-indulgence may be regrettable, you have to admire the spectacle of a film-maker grabbing his talent and running hard.

CLASSIC FILM OF THE WEEK

Pulp Fiction

★★★★★

Review by Kate Muir,
January 8 2016

Pulp Fiction will always be a cinematic adrenaline shot, and it is back on the big screen as part of a massive Quentin Tarantino retrospective at BFI Southbank in London throughout January. It's full of perfect Tarantino moments, with meta references, B-movie sleaze and a sheer sense of fun.

As Uma Thurman takes John Travolta up on to the stage and forces him to dance, she says: "I do believe Marsellus Wallace, my husband, your boss, told you to take me out and do whatever I wanted." Travolta, his moves etched on our retinas from *Grease* and *Saturday Night Fever*, makes a play, at first, of being reluctant to boogie to 'You Never Can Tell' by Chuck Berry. Perfection.

The film also stars Bruce Willis, Tim Roth, Ving Rhames and Rosanna Arquette, as well as some enjoyably graphic violence. *Pulp Fiction* plays with narrative structure, unfurling three stories at once, with Tarantino's dialogue polished to its circuitous but sharp peak.

Travolta plays the hitman Vincent, alongside his partner Jules (Samuel L Jackson), and their conversation about the Royale burger – the name for a quarter-pounder with cheese in Paris – as they head in for the kill is a teasing scream. The film brought a daring, lurid jolt of irony into the Nineties, and cinema was never quite the same again.

TOP 100 COUNTDOWN

70 – *THE CONVERSATION* (Francis Ford Coppola, 1974)

This was the sorbet that Coppola made to cleanse his palate in between the first two *Godfather* films. But it's anything but purifying, as Gene Hackman's anorak-swaddled surveillance geek pulls out what remains of his hair trying to figure out whether the couple on whom he is eavesdropping are about to be murdered. Set against a claustrophobic backdrop of post-Watergate paranoia, Coppola's favourite of his films hinges on the intonation of a single word, much as Antonioni's *Blow-Up* had revolved around a single detail in a photograph. Except with much less fashionable threads.

Ed Potton

69 – *HIDDEN* (Michael Haneke, 2005)

With the recent release of his terrifying remake of *Funny Games*, Haneke has justified his reputation as the most unnerving auteur in Europe. *Cache* (*Hidden*) is his masterpiece: a magnificently understated thriller about guilt and race that begins, innocuously enough, when a popular television personality and cultural commentator, Georges (Daniel Auteuil), keeps finding surveillance tapes on his doorstep with footage of his family. The menace is terrific. Failure to find a culprit, a camera, or a reason, acts like poison on Georges's relationship with his wife (Juliette Binoche), and ultimately his sanity. His desire to pin the guilt on Maurice Benichou's luckless immigrant, Majid, exposes an ugly, long-buried secret. Haneke brilliantly needles fears and prejudices that the educated middle-classes would be horrified to admit. Political cinema at its intimate best.

James Christopher

68 – *THE MALTESE FALCON* (John Huston, 1941)

Was there ever a greater MacGuffin in the movies than the fabled black statue sought by Humphrey Bogart, Sydney Greenstreet and Peter Lorre? The great director John Huston keeps the action rolling along at such a cracking pace that it papers over the cracks in the plot, but it is Bogey, before this a bit-part player, who gives the defining performance of his career.

Nigel Kendall

67 – *THE PIANO*
(Jane Campion, 1993)

Campion's third film, a period melodrama set in 1850s New Zealand, redefined the concept of the Art House Blockbuster. The movie described an erotic love triangle between priggish landowner Stewart (Sam Neill), the earthy and slightly simian Baines (Harvey Keitel) and the mysterious, piano-playing protagonist Ada (Holly Hunter).

Kevin Maher

66 – *TOY STORY*
(John Lasseter, 1995)

It was with this deliriously entertaining feature film that the Pixar Animation Studio burst on to the scene, rejuvenating an animation industry that had sunk into a creatively moribund routine of fairy tales and prissy princesses. *Toy Story* reminded audiences that family entertainment didn't necessarily have to exclude adults, and proved digital animation didn't have to be ugly and sinister to behold. At the heart of the story is Woody (voiced by Tom Hanks), a toy cowboy who is profoundly jealous of a shiny new spaceman action figure called Buzz Lightyear, which has usurped his position as favourite toy of Andy. When Buzz accidentally falls out of the window, Woody is blamed. He must prove his innocence by rescuing Buzz from the toy-destroying terror next door …

Wendy Ide

65 – *THE THIN BLUE LINE*
(Errol Morris, 1988)

Errol Morris's unconventional documentary employed a series of stylised dramatic reconstructions of a crime that resulted in the death of a Dallas policeman in 1976, a murder for which a drifter called Randall Adams was convicted and sentenced to death. The event is replayed several times, incorporating new evidence and fresh perspectives each time. The resulting movie puts a persuasive case for a miscarriage of justice and poses fundamental questions about the nature of truth. As a result of its allegations, the case was reopened and Adams was eventually released.

Wendy Ide

64 – *DO THE RIGHT THING*
(Spike Lee, 1989)

It marked the feature debut of Martin Lawrence, but don't hold that against Spike Lee's sweltering tale of racial tension in Brooklyn. It had an ensemble cast that also featured actors as charismatic as Samuel L. Jackson, Rosie Perez, Danny Aiello and Lee himself, and a killer script in which grievances slowly bubble to the surface between blacks, whites and Asians on the hottest day of the year. The presidential race has demonstrated that race remains a hot potato in America, but no film in the intervening two decades has addressed it with as much honesty, nuance – and style – as this one.

Ed Potton

15 November 1995. Spike Lee at a press conference at the Odeon, West End. (Denzil McNeelance)

63 – *ON THE WATERFRONT* (Elia Kazan, 1954)

Two years after he had identified a list of alleged communists to the House Un-American Activities Committee and been ostracised by much of Hollywood, Elia Kazan set about proving to the world that there could be honour in being "a man who named names". Inspired by a Pulitzer Prize-winning series of exposes by journalist Malcolm Johnson, he cast Marlon Brando as a guilt-ridden dock worker who risks becoming a pariah among his colleagues by testifying against the local gang boss (memorably snarled by Lee J. Cobb). Brando, who was excused from set early every day to see his therapist, walked out of a test screening because he was so depressed about his performance. Posterity, and the Academy, disagreed.

Ed Potton

62 – *TAXI DRIVER* (Martin Scorsese, 1976)

"You talking to me?" is the repeated line but, as several observers have pointed out, the next one is the more telling. "I'm the only one here," mumbles cock-eyed cabbie Travis Bickle into his mirror, and *Taxi Driver* has proved as powerful an essay as any on the pain, frustration and mania of isolation. There was also an uncomfortable connection with assassination attempts: Bickle was partly based on Arthur Bremer, the would-be killer of the presidential candidate George Wallace, and in turn inspired John Hinckley Jr to make his attempt on Ronald Reagan's life.

Ed Potton

61 – *RASHOMON* (Akira Kurosawa, 1950)

Kurosawa's influential film has become a reference point for countless later pictures: it was remade as *The Outrage*, and was cited as an inspiration for *The Usual Suspects*, *Basic* and most recently *Vantage Point*. Set in feudal Japan, the story explores a single event – an ambush, rape and murder in a forest – from the conflicting points of view of four different characters: a bandit (played with gusto by Toshiru Mifune); a nobleman; his wife; and the simple woodcutter who witnessed the tragedy. As a portrait of human weakness and mendacity, it is damning. The subjective nature of each character's account leads to the conclusion that everyone lies. It's visually arresting: the black and white compositions are as elegant and bold as ink calligraphy. The score is magnificent, but it's Kurosawa's decision to let the final account play out without musical accompaniment that confirms his genius.

Wendy Ide

FIRST FILMS

CHRISTIAN BALE

Empire of the Sun

David Robinson discovers Spielberg dwelling over-long on the tribulations of a British boy caught up in the fall of Shanghai

Review by David Robinson, March 24 1988

In *Empire of the Sun*, two masters of science-fiction revert to historical reality. Steven Spielberg (whose craving to be serious was first embarrassingly manifested in *The Color Purple*) brings to the screen JG Ballard's autobiographical novel about boyhood during the occupation of Shanghai and in a Japanese prison camp.

Eleven-year-old Jim Graham is suddenly snatched from his privileged life among the top people in the British community when he is separated from his parents in the chaos of the evacuation. In Soochow Creek camp he is befriended by a scavenging American merchant seaman (John Malkovich) who teaches him to hustle, and an upright British doctor (Nigel Havers) who teaches him Latin. In four years the polite little schoolboy grows into the camp wheeler-dealer.

Jim is a finely rounded characterization, and Christian Bale's performance renews amazement at the integrity of which the best child actors are capable. While he toughens and hardens and has

his first brushes with death and sexuality, he still retains a residue of boyishness – fascination with new words and phrases (he pompously calls the camp his "University of Life"); romantic dreams of flight and flyers (without prejudice he admiringly salutes the kamikaze pilots taking off from the adjoining airfield).

Perhaps the success of Spielberg and scriptwriter Tom Stoppard in entering Jim's mind is at the same time a handicap, for the grown-ups appear as if through the child's limited vision. Malkovich's American shyster, Havers's kindly doctor, Miranda Richardson as a sickly fellow-inmate, Emily Richard and Rupert Frazer as Jim's parents, seem always on the verge of becoming fully-fledged characters, yet stay to the end unrealized and two-dimensional. This lands the weight of the film on

Christian Bale's small shoulders: and the strain is too great: there are some wearisome passages in the long 153 minutes.

Spielberg is above all a creator of spectacle and visions, and these provide the best parts of the film: the vast chaos of the evacuation of Shanghai (shot in a city today largely unchanged); the romantic back-lighting of the Japanese flyers, recalling *ET*; the stadium surreally filled with the booty of war; the bombardment of the camp. There is the poignant sense of a world destroyed as the starving inmates listen over the camp radio to the voice of Elisabeth Welch singing "A nightingale sang in Berkeley Square".

PEOPLE

DAVID LYNCH ON *TWIN PEAKS*, MAKING MUSIC AND WHY HE HATES GOING OUT

From his concrete complex in LA, Hollywood's last real eccentric reveals why going out to dinner is a 'nightmare'

By Ben Machell, June 22 2013

The perception of David Lynch as one of cinema's great outsiders has existed for more than three decades. But visit his home in LA and you realise that, if only in terms of real estate, he ghosted in among the showbiz establishment some time ago. To find him you drive up into the leafy exclusivity of the Hollywood Hills; past Orlando Bloom's house, past the place where Gary Oldman used to live, just around the corner from where the Academy Award-winning director Ron Howard is having work done on a mansion overlooking Mulholland Drive. Lynch's work may have a reputation for dark, sometimes nightmarish surreality – from *Eraserhead* to *Twin Peaks* to *Lost Highway* – but day to day he inhabits a world of eucalyptus-scented sweetness and light.

Still, his home has a touch of brutalism about it, a modernist concrete complex built into the side of a hill. A back door leads you to a recording studio where Lynch sits, surrounded by guitars, amplifiers and mixing equipment. He is about to release an album, *The Big Dream*. It's his second LP in three years – its predecessor, *Crazy Clown Time*, received positive reviews – and it involves the 67-year-old performing his own swampy, atmospheric rock'n'roll numbers, delivering them in his distinctively reedy singing voice.

Lynch possesses a peculiar charisma. His hair still looks fantastic, swept up and set in a messy white quiff. He wears a shirt buttoned to the top, a crumpled jacket and a pair of grubby trousers ("I do things where I get very dirty," he says, speaking about the art studio and workshop he has within the grounds of his home, "so I don't like to dress up"). He looks as though he could have stepped out of a Norman Rockwell painting, some cheerful mechanic or carpenter from a 1950s Midwestern town. It's a vibe that's carried through into his manner, which is affable, but also politely distant.

21 May 2013. David Lynch photographed at his home in the Hollywood Hills (Steve Schofield)

He says that people often seem surprised by his otherwise sunny disposition. This is a writer-director, remember, whose 1977 debut, *Eraserhead*, included the film's protagonist attacking his freakish, mutant baby with a pair of scissors, who featured sadomasochistic rape in his Oscar-nominated *Blue Velvet*, and for whom psychosis, alienation and a sense of gnomic mystery are recurrent themes. The idea of him as a cheerful guy doesn't always compute.

"But actually, when you meet people who have made dark things, a lot of the time you'll see a kind of happiness in them," he says. "It's not all brooding and suffering. If you're suffering all the time, you can't really get much work done."

As well as his forthcoming album this year he's had a book of his photography published, while last year he held his first solo exhibition of paintings in New York. There's other stuff, too. He has his own brand of coffee – the David Lynch Signature Cup – which you can buy online (a coffee obsessive, he drinks more than a dozen cups a day), while not long ago he was asked to design a nightclub in Paris (the French love him). He recently shot a Duran Duran concert movie. He keeps busy, basically.

What he hasn't done since 2006 and *Inland Empire*, though, is actually direct a feature film. On one hand, his inactivity could be seen as an industry issue. Lynch concedes that, in the current economic climate, there is no guarantee he'd be able to get a project off the ground.

"The industry is totally different than it was when I made my last movie," he says. "Film is still a pretty expensive medium, even in the digital world. There's certain things that they've found that make money and get people in the theatres," he says. The implication is that he is not necessarily one of them.

But on the other hand, Lynch says that it is also a simple question of inspiration. He genuinely hasn't come up with a movie he'd want to make. "You can't just push a button and get a cinema idea. They come along when they come along. I love cinema. I love it. But until the ideas come, you do other things."

In September, Lynch and his wife, the actress Emily Stofle, announced the birth of their daughter, Lula. "You should see her! She's so beautiful." He already has three adult children from three previous marriages. His eldest is the director Jennifer Lynch, now 45, who found notoriety in the early Nineties with the film *Boxing Helena*, about a surgeon who amputates the limbs of the woman with whom he is obsessed. She has since worked on a string of thriller and horror releases. "It's funny when people say, 'Oh! You're weird like your dad'," she told me last year. "But I don't think he is weird. He's just a storyteller who, thankfully, looks at things very differently."

Lynch's own childhood was nomadic, his family criss-crossing the United States as a result of his father's job as a research scientist with the Department of Agriculture. It was growing up in the small towns of Middle America – places like Spokane, Washington;

Boise, Idaho; Alexandria, Virginia – that helped nurture a fixation with not just the picket-fence perfection of his country's postwar baby boom, but with the unspoken corruption beneath the veneer. He describes walking through one of these towns as a boy.

"There would be things going on that were hidden," he says. "But you could feel it in the air. If you were sensitive, you could feel certain things were wrong: something in that house isn't good. That person is in some kind of trouble. Something is not right here," he explains, pretending to point out these incongruities with an index finger and thoughtful frown. "But at the same time, you just felt you were surrounded by some kind of fantastic beauty. Like you were in a dream. The smell of the grass and the way the light would play. It was just unreal."

PERSONAL CHOICE

SIMON CALLOW CHOOSES

Six of the best ... films about musicians

May 7 2016

For some reason, films about musicians have a tendency to tip over into the absurd. Most films about virtuoso performers have to be cheated; few convince. Representing the act of composition is challenging: one thinks of *Night and Day*, the Cole Porter biopic, in which the sumptuously handsome, athletic Cary Grant – cast as the dwarfish, bug-eyed composer – improvises the title song by reference to what he sees around him: "Like the beat, beat, beat of the tom-tom, when the jungle shadows fall" (shot of tom-tom), "like the tick, tick, tock of the stately clock" (shot of clock tick, tick tocking), "like the drip, drip, drip of the raindrops when the summer shower is through" (shot of raindrops dripping). Deliciously ludicrous. The blood-spattered keyboard in Cornel Wilde's Chopin epic *A Song to Remember* invariably raises laughs in the cinema. *The Chronicle of Anna Magdalena Bach*, though, is on another plane, a very sober but entirely convincing dramatisation of Johann Sebastian's attempt to teach his wife how to play his music. Bach's life, however low on incident, is challenging to dramatise – the romantic composers offer more by way of emotional thrills and spills.

One always rather hopes that the film will reflect the richness and fullness of their music, but that way lies, well, Ken Russell. After a handful of extraordinary films on composers for BBC's *Monitor*, he rapidly veered off into self-parody with the lurid *Mahler* ("But Alma – don't you realise? The Andante of the Sixth Symphony – it's you") and *Lisztomania*, whose title speaks for itself. Tony Palmer has made a remarkable series of dramatised films about composers, of which *Testimony*, about Shostakovich, is perhaps the greatest, though the most ambitious is the eight-hour *Wagner*, with an oddly phlegmatic Richard Burton in the title role.

Amadeus
(Milos Forman, 1984)

The film that made Mozart a bestseller. I may perhaps be pardoned for having a sneaking preference for the play, but Peter Shaffer's great melodrama is served up in sumptuous style, dark and glittering, and continually illuminated by Shaffer's deep understanding of the music. Tom Hulce's death scene, composing the Requiem, is especially finely done.

Magic Fire
(William Dieterle, 1955)

This Hollywood take on Wagner is very much a Teutonic production. The director, screenwriter, cameraman and costume designer were all German or Austrian. The real reason to see the movie, though, is the extraordinary performance of the mercurial English actor Alan Badel, a dead ringer for the composer, who makes you believe that he wrote every bar of the music.

Tales of Manhattan
(Julien Duvivier, 1942)

A film in several episodes that describes the adventures of a tailcoat. In the best sequence, the coat comes to the down-at-heel composer and conductor Charles Smith (Charles Laughton), who gets a lucky break conducting his music at the Carnegie Hall for which he has to be properly attired: the coat falls apart as he steps on to the podium. Laughton gives a superlative display of comic brilliance, at the same time convincing you of the composer's passion for his music.

Dangerous Moonlight
(Brian Desmond Hurst, 1941)

Anton Walbrook plays a wartime pilot with a case of amnesia, who remembers at the climax that he once composed a piece called Warsaw Concerto. Walbrook delivers a performance of high romantic splendour as he bashes out the wonderfully hammy sub-Rachmaninov piece by Richard Addinsell.

Deception
(Irving Rapper, 1946)

Erich Wolfgang Korngold, the great Viennese composer who spent ten years of exile in Hollywood writing some of the best scores composed for film, provides a superb cello concerto, whose first performance forms the weepy climax for this Bette Davis vehicle, about a demonic composer and his attempt to destroy the cellist for whom he has written a concerto.

Sid and Nancy
(Alex Cox, 1986)

A savage, searing account of a musician who seemed determined to destroy himself – but rock musicians scarcely have a monopoly on that syndrome. In the film, Gary Oldman lives as dangerously as Sid Vicious did, with astonishing intensity on stage and off.

PERSONAL CHOICE

MUSICALS ON FILM CHOSEN BY DIRECTOR ROB MARSHALL

May 9 2015

◇◇◇◇◇◇◇◇◇◇◇◇◇◇◇◇◇◇◇◇◇◇◇◇◇◇◇◇◇◇◇◇◇◇◇◇◇◇

Editor's note: Rob Marshall directed the film version of *Chicago*.

◇◇◇◇◇◇◇◇◇◇◇◇◇◇◇◇◇◇◇◇◇◇◇◇◇◇◇◇◇◇◇◇◇◇◇◇◇◇

The famous philosophy about musicals is: when words aren't enough you sing and when movement isn't enough you dance. When you go to the theatre, you're in a false place, a highly stylised world and so an audience will accept more readily that people break into song. But film is a much more realistic medium than stage, so if a character opens their mouth to sing and the song doesn't feel earned, it feels very awkward. In *The Sound of Music*, the fact Maria loves to sing makes the singing feel organic. In *Cabaret*, all the numbers take place on a cabaret stage. In *Chicago*, which I directed, all the numbers are fantasies. There is no one singing in a living room for no reason.

In the late 1960s and early 1970s it was very difficult to make musicals work. As a form, they seemed bloated and there was a wave of realism in film. But in harder times, people want to escape into fantasy: all the Fred Astaire and Ginger Rogers films came out of the Depression. When I did *Chicago*, they were out of fashion. There is a resurgence now – I would count films like *Frozen* in this. I think people looking for joy, escapism, something to lift their lives. Musicals have made a return.

Singin' in the Rain, 1952

It's perfect in every way. The dancing is brilliant, the story is brilliant, the performances are brilliant. And I don't think you get better than 'Moses Supposes'.

Cabaret, 1972

It was incredibly smart conceptually. Bob Fosse reimagined the stage version completely and he places all the musical numbers on stage so you could readily accept the singing.

Meet Me in St Louis, 1944

The beautiful thing about it is the simplicity of it: it's about a family who plan to move to New York. It's funny, warm and it's a beautiful innocent time. There's something incredibly heart-warming about it.

Funny Girl, 1968

The central performance by Barbra Streisand is brilliant, it drives the whole piece. It was reimagined from the stage version to get rid of most of the ensemble numbers and brought a great deal of depth to the story.

The Sound of Music, 1965

I don't like it when people do the parodies of it because it's a beautifully structured film. It has that central amazing performance of Julie Andrews, and Rodgers and Hammerstein are the greatest composers. One of the smartest things it does is make Austria its main character. It's thrilling.

Funny Face, 1957

It's about the modelling world and it stars Audrey Hepburn. The photographer Richard Avedon does all these wonderful, stylised images from the Fifties throughout – and it also benefits from Paris as a backdrop.

PERSONAL CHOICE

FILM SOUNDTRACKS CHOSEN BY MARK KERMODE

June 29 2013

◇◇◇◇◇◇◇◇◇◇◇◇◇◇◇◇◇◇◇◇◇◇◇◇◇◇◇◇◇◇◇◇

Editor's note: Mark Kermode is co-presenter of Radio 5 Live's Kermode and Mayo's Film Review.

◇◇◇◇◇◇◇◇◇◇◇◇◇◇◇◇◇◇◇◇◇◇◇◇◇◇◇◇◇◇◇◇

When I was growing up films changed over at the cinema every week. You couldn't rewatch your favourites on videos or DVD (the idea of owning prints of films that you could screen was like *Thunderbirds* to me), but what you could take home was the music.

Back then the films were in our heads and on our record shelves. The first soundtrack I bought was for *Silent Running* (1972). I remember listening to the music and looking at the sleeve, which had stills printed on it. The film came to life in my mind. I had the soundtrack album for *Rollerball* (1975) too – I'm not even sure that I was old enough to see the film. When video came about, I remember being a bit bothered that there were people talking all over the piece of music I loved. Now soundtracks are marketing tools. The album for Baz Luhrmann's *The Great Gatsby* was a huge hit in its own right, and you can download the music as ringtones.

When directors are fighting for their vision, it often comes down to a fight about the score. Just because a score doesn't work away from a film doesn't mean it isn't good. Peter Maxwell Davies's music for *The Devils* (1971) is extraordinary: unsettling and jarring, strange and demonic. But would you really want that on while you're driving the car?

Mary Poppins (1964)

A lot of our love of cinema is tied up with what we saw at a young age. This was one of the first films I went to. As soon as I hear the overture, I see Mary Poppins and I remember what it felt like to be swept away by the film.

Twin Peaks: Fire Walk with Me (1992)

I drove around America listening to this soundtrack. The film was received badly by critics. Had it been a hit, this would have been everyone's favourite album.

Planet of the Apes (1968)

You hear Jerry Goldsmith's soundtrack and (particularly if you are of a certain age) you know immediately where you are: it's an alien world, but it's a familiar one too.

Local Hero (1983)

When you hear Mark Knopfler's riffs and motifs, you're there, on that beach. The music seems to come out of the rocks, the waves, the village. It's a perfect blend of music and moving image.

Blackmail (1929)

In 2008 Neil Brand wrote a score for the restored silent version. It is, as far as I know, the first full orchestral score written for a British silent dramatic feature since the dawn of sound. He manages to bring out the complexity of the drama without overshadowing it.

Taxi Driver (1976)

Bernard Hermann's last film score before his death in 1975 is an extraordinary accomplishment. You can almost hear the sound of the steam coming up from the street; you envisage the taxi driving through the fog and Robert De Niro's voice.

CULT MOVIES

SCARY BUNNIES AND SUPER GEEKS

A stunning addition to the horror genre is a real treat

Donnie Darko

Review by James Christopher,
October 24 2002

Films rarely offer much cause for celebration. But occasionally the form book is ripped up by a film that makes its own strange rules look disturbingly plausible. Richard Kelly's debut feature, *Donnie Darko*, has that kind of goosebump ambition. It's a tragicomedy about growing up and realising that the adult world is predicated on some deeply rusty truths.

Jake Gyllenhaal plays a troubled misfit plagued by disturbing visions. His psychiatrist thinks he's a paranoid schizophrenic. His parents can't cope. And the school wants to expel him. You can appreciate their reasoning. At night Donnie sleepwalks through town under the spell of a six-foot talking rabbit called Frank.

According to Frank, the world will end in 28 days, six hours, 42 minutes and 12 seconds. A prediction that starts looking slightly less preposterous when Donnie returns from a nocturnal jaunt to discover a jet engine has scored a direct hit on his bedroom. Is he mad, hallucinating or possessed? Most locals

think he's insane. Under the spell of the satanic bunny, Donnie floods buildings, puts an axe through the head of a solid-bronze bust and burns down the mansion of a TV self-help guru.

Yes, it's impossible to describe this film without making it sound utterly ghastly. But Gyllenhaal's performance as a small-town existential anti-hero is simply terrific. Like *Hamlet* his Me is one giant anxiety attack. But he is far more curious than he is tortured by his waking nightmares. He is that strange thing in a teen-centric film: a cool nerd; a witty rebel; an adult thinker in a teenage head. He sticks up for the quirky irregulars when they are poked by rednecks and slackers. He rails at the sheer inadequacy of the school's prevailing "social philosophy" (marvellous grating turns by Beth Grant and Patrick Swayze). He even starts a touching, gawky romance with a new girl, Gretchen (Jena Malone). Yet there's a demonic side to Donnie that triggers one of the creepiest personality changes this side of *Jekyll and Hyde*. I haven't seen such icy malevolence in a smile since Malcolm McDowell in *A Clockwork Orange*.

Like *Clockwork*, *Donnie Darko* has "cult" stamped all over it But it also comes with the thematic muddle that "cult" invariably entails. The plot is a haystack of coincidences. The characters are eccentric to the point of surreal. And the script is a stomach-churning mix of science fiction, teen horror, bald satire and suburban smuggery. You could spend months ticking off Eighties film references and procrastinating about what it all means.

During one trippy afternoon, Donnie watches watery spears of liquid sprouting out of the midriffs of his family:

huge transparent follicles that wiggle around the house like giant glass worms. Whether you have the time or inclination to deconstruct this decidedly odd universe is a moot point. But the bravura of Kelly's camerawork speaks for itself. Particularly the way he caricatures the town. Several majestic tracking shots, filmed in rippling slow motion with backing tracks by Echo and the Bunnymen and Tears for Fears, are worth the price of entry alone.

In these sweeping panoramas, women commune like Stepford Wives and middle-aged men tend perfectly manicured gardens. Through Kelly's disconcerting prism, the Eighties look as old-fashioned, eerie, and faintly ridiculous as the Fifties once did to Generation X. It's a stunning piece of cinema by a 27-year-old first-time director.

Ultimately, his film poses far more questions than it dares answer. Perhaps it is too cryptic for its own good. What keeps it fresh is that it never settles long enough to feel derivative of anything except its own barmy puzzles.

CLASSIC FILM OF THE WEEK

Donnie Darko

Review by Kate Muir, December 9 2016

An almost baby-faced Jake Gyllenhaal stars in this surreal cult movie alongside his sister Maggie, and of course that giant, grinning, rabbit-eared demon-creature called Frank. No one knew quite what to make of *Donnie Darko* when it came out, just after 9/11, with an unfortunate plot point involving an aircraft engine falling from the sky into Donnie's bedroom. Fortunately, Donnie was out that night, sleepwalking with Frank and feeling the pain of puberty.

Now, a whole body of work is dedicated to interpretations of the story, which include theories of parallel universes and time travel. This was an accomplished first film from the director Richard Kelly, with a terrific soundtrack of 1980s classics from Echo and the Bunnymen (was that a clue?), Tears for Fears and Duran Duran. The supporting actors include Patrick Swayze and Drew Barrymore, as the hot high-school teacher Ms Pomeroy, who tells new student Jena Malone to "sit next to the boy you think is cutest". Donnie scores.

However, his main relationship is with Frank, his "imaginary friend", who tells Donnie that the world will end in 28 days, 6 hours, 42 minutes and 12 seconds. The space-time continuum opens up like a huge jellied eel sliding through suburbia, and the young Gyllenhaal is up to the task of making it all seem weirdly convincing.

TOP 100 COUNTDOWN

60 – *THE CRYING GAME*
(Neil Jordan, 1992)

The daddy of all "twist" movies, Jordan's thriller puts the revelations in films such as *The Usual Suspects* and *The Sixth Sense* into what lead protagonist Fergus might call "The ha'penny place" (i.e. not very good). However, the key to the movie, which details the botched kidnapping of British squaddie Jody (Forest Whitaker) and the subsequent romance between kidnapper Fergus (Stephen Rea) and Jody's partner Dil (Jaye Davidson) is that the twist itself is subservient to the drama. The deftly written relationships between Fergus, Jody and Dil gave the movie its unexpectedly soft heart, and ultimately earned Jordan a Best Original Screenplay Oscar.

Kevin Maher

59 – *PULP FICTION*
(Quentin Tarantino, 1994)

Tarantino might have settled into a rut of semi-autistic genre pastiches, but there was a time when his films got your pulse racing. He originally intended the intersecting crime stories in his and Roger Avary's Oscar-winning script – tales of a wife, a watch and a corpse – to be handled by different directors.

Thankfully, he ended up doing all three himself, shuffling them into a non-linear sequence which contrasted with the vivid naturalism of the dialogue. Laughs and thrills were never in short supply: one viewer had a seizure after watching John Travolta stab a syringe into Uma Thurman's chest. Tarantino's response? "This movie f***ing works!"

Ed Potton

58 – *DOCTOR ZHIVAGO*
(David Lean, 1965)

Reunited with Robert Bolt, the screenwriter of his earlier *Lawrence of Arabia*, Lean produced another sprawling masterpiece. *Lawrence* veteran Omar Sharif was surprised to be cast in a lead role that Lean had reserved for Peter O'Toole. O'Toole, however, had other ideas after the difficult shoot for *Lawrence*. *Zhivago* was critically panned on its release in 1965, but went on to make more money at the box office than all of Lean's other films put together. The shoot, in Spain, dragged on for 12 months.

Nigel Kendall

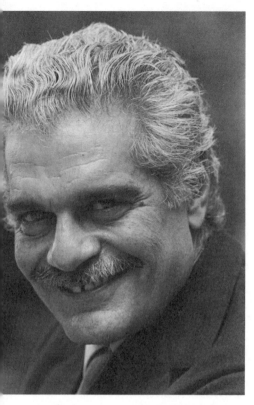

6 July 1983. Omar Sharif in rehearsal for *The Sleeping Prince* at Chichester Festival. (Harry Kerr)

57 - *RAGING BULL* (Martin Scorsese, 1980)

Despite years of barracking from his leading man Robert De Niro, Scorsese was reluctant to bring the turbulent life of granite-jawed middleweight Jake LaMotta to the screen. It was only when he found himself at death's door, bleeding internally after a decade of success and excess, that the director began to empathise with a man who maimed himself as much as his opponents. Convinced it would be his final film, he pulled out all the stops, shooting the fight scenes, innovatively, from inside the ring and filming throughout in apocalyptic monochrome. LaMotta was played by De Niro as a quasi-biblical figure, who paid for his director's sins in an inferno of blood, bile and, ultimately, flab.

Ed Potton

56 - *WHISKY GALORE!* (Alexander Mackendrick, 1949)

For a magical period of ten years from the end of the Second World War, Ealing Studios produced a run of gently satirical comedies which still command affection. *Whisky Galore!* by Ealing regular Alexander Mackendrick is perhaps the archetypal Ealing comedy, celebrating the eccentricity of its characters and applauding their ingenuity when it comes to bending the law and outsmarting those who would uphold it. A cast of Ealing regulars give larger-than-life performances as the inhabitants of a tiny Scottish island cursed by a wartime shortage of whisky. When a cargo ship filled with 50,000 cases of the stuff is wrecked just off the coast, the islanders plunder as much as their boats will carry. Which is quite a lot, as it turns out.

Wendy Ide

55 - *THE MATRIX* (Andy and Larry Wachowski, 1999)

Arriving on the cusp of the new millennium, *The Matrix* was so zeitgeisty it was almost painful. The idea of a computer hacker called Neo (Keanu Reeves) who lives in a fake alternate reality, wears a leather trench-coat and saves mankind through kung-fu and interballistic mayhem spoke to the paranoia and alienation of an entire pre-9/11 generation. It helped too that the coolly aloof Reeves was born to play Neo, that the pacing was almost relentless and that the Wachowski brothers seemed intent on ripping up the blockbuster rule book even as they reinvented it. Every action movie since then (including its own sequels) has been derivative. The genre is still recovering from the shock.

Kevin Maher

∞∞∞∞∞∞∞∞∞∞∞∞∞∞∞∞∞∞∞∞∞∞∞

(Editor's note: The sibling co-directors both subsequently came out as transgender and are now called Lilly and Lana Wachowski.)

∞∞∞∞∞∞∞∞∞∞∞∞∞∞∞∞∞∞∞∞∞∞∞

54 – *L.A. CONFIDENTIAL* (Curtis Hanson, 1997)

Hanson's labyrinthine noir homage is a tour de force police procedural and an evocative glimpse of the seedier side of 1950s Hollywood. It's a magnificently corrupt town that feeds upon itself, discarding the weak and attacking the strong in the pernicious gossip rags. The film launched the careers of two Australian actors – Guy Pearce, who played ambitious golden boy cop Det Lt Ed Exley, and Russell Crowe, who played the hot-tempered Officer Bud White. Even Kim Basinger acquits herself admirably as the film's femme fatale, Lynn Bracken. Ambitious and multi-layered, this is an elegant piece

of film-making that lives up to anything produced in Hollywood during the richly creative period in which the story is set.

Wendy Ide

53 – *MILDRED PIERCE* (Michael Curtiz, 1945)

Joan Crawford suffers and then some in this archetypal women's weepie in which she plays a middle-class mother who strives tirelessly for her ungrateful, vile daughter, Veda (Ann Blyth). Mildred is so withstanding that when she snaps and slaps Veda you can only cheer. How horribly it goes, and Crawford – playing the prototypical soap matriarch who really will do anything for her child – provides a lavish, huge performance. Later she said: "I harness that intensity and I hold it till it's ready to go for the camera." When she had to slap Blyth, Crawford – who won the Best Actress Oscar for the role in 1946 – remembered: "I put my arms around her and said, 'Darling, did I hurt you?'"

Tim Teeman

52 – *LA DOLCE VITA* (Federico Fellini, 1960)

Fellini's prescient film (it coined the term "paparazzi") is both a celebration of hedonism and a cynical satire of a celebrity-obsessed culture. Marcello Mastroianni stars as a tabloid journalist and man about town torn between the shallow pleasures of Rome's decadent cafe society and the domesticity offered by his girlfriend; the allure of chasing titbits of gossip from the glamorous set and the urge to become a serious writer. Some of the most iconic images of Italian cinema came from this film: the statue of Christ suspended over Rome by a helicopter, and Anita Ekberg, fully clothed, wallowing in the Trevi Fountain.

Wendy Ide

51 – *CABARET*
(Bob Fosse, 1972)

The role of cabaret star Sally Bowles earned Liza Minnelli an iconic status to rival her mother's: the bowler hat and black stockings became inextricably linked to her identity, as did the catchphrase "Divine decadence darling!" There's a forced gaiety and a desperate hedonism in the world she inhabits. Under the glitter and the greasepaint is something dissolute and decaying. The musical numbers are magnificent. The beer garden scene, where an angelic Nazi sings 'Tomorrow Belongs To Me', remains one of cinema's most chilling moments.

Wendy Ide

PEOPLE

∞∞∞∞∞∞∞∞∞∞∞∞∞∞∞∞∞∞∞∞∞∞∞∞∞∞∞∞∞

Editor's note: I met Kay Mander for lunch in 2010, at a hotel in the little town of Castle Douglas in Kirkcudbrightshire, where she lived in a local authority bungalow. With her grey hair and walking stick, there was little in her outward appearance to distinguish her from thousands of other pensioners in dozens of towns across Scotland. But what a fascinating interviewee she turned out to be. A few years later I wrote her obituary for *The Times* and quoted from the interview.

∞∞∞∞∞∞∞∞∞∞∞∞∞∞∞∞∞∞∞∞∞∞∞∞∞∞∞∞∞

Kay Mander

Pioneering wartime film-maker who enjoyed a brief grand passion for the actor Kirk Douglas

Obituary (Brian Pendreigh),
January 4 2014

Kay Mander was one of Britain's first women film directors who got her break writing and directing documentaries during the Second World War. She graduated to work on Hollywood blockbusters, rubbed shoulders with David Niven and Sean Connery and had a passionate fling with Kirk Douglas.

It is only recently that film critics and historians have acknowledged her importance, both as a pioneering director and an innovative documentary maker.

Given the task of making a film about a pilot social health scheme in the Hebrides, Mander recruited actors and turned it into a drama-documentary, *Highland Doctor* (1943). A member of the Communist Party, she was politically committed, and artistically daring, always looking for new ways to tackle her subjects.

She persuaded working-class women to speak directly and bluntly to camera about the need for decent housing. When she made a film about malaria, she shot a mosquito biting her and used "microphotography" to film it filling with her blood in close-up.

She found it tough winning commissions after the Second World War when experienced male directors returned to the industry. She took work as a "continuity girl", the person charged with making sure, for instance, cigarettes get shorter rather than longer over the course of a scene.

Mander was in charge of continuity on dozens of films from the 1950s to the 1980s, working into her seventies. They included the second James Bond film, *From Russia with Love* (1963), François Truffaut's adaptation of Ray Bradbury's dystopian story *Fahrenheit 451* (1966), Ken Russell's treatment of The Who's rock opera *Tommy* (1974) and in the midst of these the Second World War adventure *The Heroes of Telemark* (1965) when she got to know Kirk Douglas. Both were married and in their late forties at the time.

"He had this awful reputation," she said in an interview many years later when living quietly in retirement in Kirkcudbrightshire in Scotland. "He flew his ladies in first-class, kept them there for a long weekend, and sent them back tourist."

But Mander thought him "wonderful" and took the initiative in their relationship. "I made approaches to Kirk that I wouldn't have done to another actor … Kirk Douglas was my passion."

Mander was less impressed with his son, who was in charge of the lavatories. "It was Michael's first nominal job," she said, "but he didn't know what a job was in those days. He was put in charge of the loo caravans and he always managed to get them in the wrong place. They were always at the top of the hill when the crew was at the bottom and vice versa."

Michael Douglas later won an Oscar as a film producer as well as an actor.

Her only regret about the affair was the hurt that the relationship caused her husband, the film-maker Rod Neilson Baxter, whom she married in 1940. "I never wanted to get involved with anybody except my husband," she said. They remained married until his death in 1978.

Although her own films tended to be about serious and worthy subjects, and her politics were left-wing, Mander enjoyed working on big-budget Hollywood films and mixing with the stars. With the exception of Charles Bronson, she said she found them to be charming and interesting people. As for Bronson, she considered him to be "a really nasty piece of work", adding: "Charlie Bronson's life enjoyment was to point out everybody else's mistakes".

An only child, she was born Kathleen Mander in Hull in 1915, but she grew up partly in France and Germany. She had hoped to go to Oxford, but her father, who worked for a company that made radiators, lost his job and she was forced to look for work.

Mander's first experience of the film industry came in 1935 while she was living in Berlin, which was about to host an international film festival. She worked as a translator and receptionist and made important contacts. A year later, back in England, she worked as a translator on the Laurence Olivier film *Conquest of the Air* (1936), which was filmed by a German cameraman.

In those days women were largely restricted to a few posts such as publicity, continuity, wardrobe and make-up and Mander wound up with a job as a publicist with Alexander Korda's London Films. The upheaval of the Second World War provided her with the opportunity to direct.

Her first film was a seven-minute short instructing apprentices how to file metal. Other early films included shorts about the fire service and civil defence.

After the war, she and her husband lived and worked in Asia for a while. She subsequently wrote and directed one feature, *The Kid from Canada* (1957), for the Children's Film Foundation, but she found her post-war career thwarted by sexual prejudice.

She moved to Scotland shortly after her husband's death to work on a film about barnacle geese. The film was never made, but she stayed on, latterly living in a council house and then a nursing home in Castle Douglas. She had no children. Mander was the subject of a documentary, *One Continuous Take* (2001) and a boxed set of her films was released in 2010.

Kay Mander, documentary filmmaker, was born on September 28, 1915. She died of pneumonia on December 29, 2013, aged 98.

WESTERNS: PART TWO

A FILM FROM JAPAN

Seven Samurai

Unbylined review (Dudley Carew),
February 21 1955

When *Rashomon* was seen in England three or four years ago it started an enthusiasm for Japanese films which had its parallel in the craze for Japanese pictures and porcelain in the 1860s and 1890s, when *Whistler* was the high priest. Both the present enthusiasm and the Victorian fashion had something more than the attractions of novelty behind them, and *Gates of Hell*, with its colour harmonies typical of the painting of the country that made it, proved the loveliest film the cinema has ever produced. *Seven Samurai* is not in colour, but it is further evidence of the quality of the Japanese cinema which, however, seems to incline overmuch, as here, towards bloodthirstiness, sadism and cruelty.

Though not in colour, there are a number of shots, a wood at dawn, a close-up of a human face pressed to the earth, framed with flowers, which are not only lovely in themselves but which perfectly convey the mood and emotion of the sequence. *Seven Samurai* is set in the sixteenth century and the medievalism seems, at least in western eyes, right and fitting – this is not Japan in fancy dress as our own historical films show us in fancy dress; this is Japan as she was the day before yesterday, as perhaps she is – the thought will not be denied – today. The conditions roughly resemble our own at the time of the Wars of the Roses, when life was cheap and violence everywhere. A poor village is raided every year by bandits and, to protect themselves, the villagers hire seven Samurai, professional warriors who sell their swords where they can.

The chief of them is Kambei, and the impression of strength, of violence, and of danger Takashi Shimura manages to pack into the broad figure with the shaven head is astonishing. But then Japanese films have a strange power of drawing the audience into the circle of their action. The film is long – indeed it runs for 150 minutes – but, as real danger heightens the concentration and stimulates the senses, so does its shadow on the screen hold the attention so that time ceases to have significance.

There is nothing particularly new about the general pattern of the events, but when, for instance, the bandits ride up to the outskirts of the village on a reconnaissance and are watched in silence by the defenders crouching behind their barricades, it is as though the tension and the sense of violence to come had escaped from the screen and got loose in the auditorium. The lyrical, as distinct from the aggressive, side of the film is graced by the acting of Keiko Tsushima as a peasant girl who falls in love with the youngest of the Samurai (Ko Kimura). But it is the tragic figure of Kambei which dominates the film, bestriding it like a Colossus – and the magic of the director, Akira Kurosawa, must not be forgotten.

JAPANESE THEME IN A MEXICAN SETTING

The Magnificent Seven

Unbylined review (Dudley Carew), April 12 1961

Let it be granted that there may be good reasons for taking a work of art to pieces, altering its clime and colour – and here literature provides some illustrious examples – and then reassembling the bits to conform, although in another age and in different circumstances, to the original outlines of the pattern. The experiment with *Carmen*, for instance, which became *Carmen Jones* and saw the opera brought up to date with the bull-ring giving way to its boxing counterpart, was a success, yet it is difficult not to think that the disadvantages of the process tend to outweigh any benefits that may derive from it.

Kurosawa's *Seven Samurai* was a work of art, a Japanese film with its roots in Japanese traditions, and now Mr John Sturges has transplanted it to Mexico and turned it into a full-scale, sophisticated Western. This is not a question of putting a play into modern dress, as *Hamlet* has been put into modern dress, but of striking at the heart of the work as it was originally conceived. Indeed, it is best to forget all about *Seven Samurai* when contemplating *The Magnificent Seven*. The Samurai are transformed into gunmen, agreeing, for a suspiciously small fee, to undertake the defence of a poor Mexican village which is being harried by bandits.

Regarded as a Western, and with no thoughts of Japan in mind, *The Magnificent Seven* has much to commend it: the Mexican landscape is impressively photographed – the Mexican villagers themselves, however, look a little too clean and picturesque for their parts and, as Chris, the leader of the band of mercenaries determined that the particular bit of sky over the village shall stay suspended, Mr Yul Brynner is, as usual, in perfect control of himself and the situation. The odds may be against him and he, as Chris, may feel that he and his kind are, in a world that is progressing too fast for them, going the way of the dinosaur, but the authority is there. It works well with Mr Sturges's eye for the visually dramatic effect. Mr Eli Wallach,

Mr Steve McQueen and Mr Horst Buchholz play supporting parts as they should be played.

THIS RELOAD OF THE CLASSIC WESTERN HAS TOO MANY BANGS FOR YOUR BUCK

The Magnificent Seven (2016 version)

Review by Kate Muir,
September 23 2016

★★★

This new iteration of *The Magnificent Seven* is more middling than magnificent. Set just after the American Civil War, it's certainly fun, and a spectacle to behold in IMAX, but if you're going to remake the 1960 classic, which starred Yul Brynner and Steve McQueen, you need to make a cinematic cavalry charge into the territory of modern sensibilities. Unfortunately, Quentin Tarantino has made that charge twice, with the deeply ironic *Django Unchained* and *The Hateful Eight*.

So the director Antoine Fuqua (*Training Day*, *King Arthur*) had to think of something novel for his reboot and came up with a multi-racial scenario, with Denzel Washington in the lead role as the bounty hunter and warrant officer Sam Chisolm, Lee Byung Hun as a Korean knife-spinning assassin, Manuel

Garcia-Rulfo as a Mexican outlaw and Martin Sensmeier as a Comanche warrior. The always-hilarious Chris Pratt (of *Guardians of the Galaxy*), Vincent D'Onofrio and Ethan Hawke complete the shoot-out's septuplets.

Great casting, and Washington has real quick-draw, spur-clanking, lanky-legged cool in his black stetson up there on the giant screen, but the film is ultimately forgettable. It's five minutes longer than the original, at 2 hours and 13 minutes, and sometimes it tends to drag. Let's pause, though, and look at the movie from the perspective of

11 September 1978. Yul Brynner at a London Palladium press conference. (Harry Kerr)

those who didn't watch the original on telly in the rainy days of childhood, or gallop along to the theme tune, or see Akira Kurosawa's *Seven Samurai* (1954), which inspired the first film. My 19-year-old son came to the new version fresh, and loved its big skies and ballsy splatter fest.

The story opens in Rose Creek, a gold-mining town under the capitalist cosh of Bartholomew Bogue, a bogeyman who is dialled up to 11 by Peter Sarsgaard. Bogue is intent on buying everyone's land for a paltry $20, and when the local farmers stand up to him, his thugs leave main street littered with corpses and burn down the church for good measure. While the men look a tad upset, Emma Cullen (Haley Bennett), who has just lost her husband, gets mighty ornery and goes to find some mercenaries to defend the town.

Chisolm is her first pick, particularly after he does what a sharp-shooter must do in a saloon filled with less-than-friendly white locals. The only man in town who seems unflustered by the bounty hunter's presence – and his self-parking horse – is Josh Faraday (Pratt), a gambler in all senses. Pratt brings his usual relaxed amusement to all that he surveys, especially extreme danger. Faraday and Chisolm join forces and the recruitment drive of badass nutters with nothing to lose begins; basically, it's *Suicide Squad* on horseback.

The early part of the movie is entertaining, with actual character conflict and development, but somehow that gets put aside by the time the seven settle into booby-trapping Rose Creek with explosives, digging trenches and awaiting the return of Bogue's hired army of thugs. Fuqua tries to make a feisty female gunslinger out of Cullen, giving her lines such as, "I seek righteousness, but I'll take revenge," but then her character fades into the background behind the men. Shame, because a Calamity Jane figure might have given the film more oomph.

Of course there is plenty of oomph in terms of ballistics and explosives, and the final firefight lasts roughly an hour. Fuqua is a competent action director and there is enough detail amid the smoke and shouting to give some sense of what's happening. Fuqua did, after all, trash the White House in *Olympus Has Fallen*, but there are just too many bangs for your buck in *The Magnificent Seven* and eventually I was just willing everyone to die, quickly. By contrast, my son didn't want the film to end.

CINEMA HISTORY

GHOST WRITER CREDITED AT LAST FOR MOVIE THAT MADE HEPBURN

By Will Pavia, December 21 2011

Decades after his death, the Hollywood screenwriter Dalton Trumbo is to be officially recognised for his work on the Oscar-winning film *Roman Holiday*, a script he wrote secretly from exile in Mexico after falling victim to a government investigation of suspected communist influences in Hollywood. The Writers Guild of America West (WGAW) has restored Trumbo's screenwriting credit for the film, which launched the career of Audrey Hepburn, while acknowledging that it could not "erase the mistakes or the suffering of the past".

Trumbo had been blacklisted by the House of Un-American Activities in 1947 for refusing to give evidence against colleagues or offer testimony about communist influence in the film industry. He became part of the so-called Hollywood Ten, the list of workers who were summarily dismissed by studio executives. After eleven months in a federal prison, he left with his family for Mexico. His friend, the British writer Ian McLellan Hunter, who would later also be blacklisted, offered to help by serving as his "front writer" in Hollywood. Trumbo would write from Mexico, Hunter would take credit for the scripts and forward him the fees. In this manner Trumbo helped to produce a script for *Roman Holiday*, alongside Hunter and John Dighton. "I believe Dalton Trumbo did write the first draft," Hunter's son, Tim, wrote in a letter to John Wells, then President of the WGAW, which has now been published by the guild's magazine. His father had been "very English, very close-mouthed about the whole thing and never spoke of it. I don't believe he regretted fronting for Trumbo but he didn't enjoy the ongoing experience either, in any way".

Trumbo, who was one of the first blacklisted writers to break through the ban by putting his real name on the screenplay for *Spartacus* in 1960, had told his friend's son during a trip to New York that he was the author of *Roman Holiday*. "He took me, 13, out one afternoon and told me he had written *Roman Holiday*," Hunter's son wrote. The sons of Trumbo and Hunter would also be long-time friends. Earlier this year, when Trumbo's son, Chris, was close to death, Hunter's son promised he would attempt to ensure his father finally gained a posthumous credit for *Roman Holiday*. The WGAW has now fulfilled the pledge. "We can make amends, we can pledge not to fall prey again to the dangerous power of fear or to the impulse to censor. And, in the end, we can give credit where credit is due," Chris Keyser, the guild's president said. "The WGAW has not undone the hurt, but it has, at last and at least, told the truth. That fact is a tribute to the friendship of two fathers and then two sons and to a thing we can hold on to, which is that the friendship was stronger than and outlived the hate."

∞∞∞∞∞∞∞∞∞∞∞∞∞∞∞∞∞∞∞∞∞∞∞∞∞∞∞∞

Editor's note: The Hollywood blacklist was one of the most controversial and arguably shameful episodes in Hollywood history. *Roman Holiday* won the Oscar for best story and it was presented to Ian McLellan Hunter at the time. In 1992 the Academy of Motion Picture Arts and Sciences actually got in ahead of the Writers Guild in acknowledging Trumbo's authorship and retrospectively assigned the award to him. It was one of two Trumbo scripts to win Oscars. The other, for the 1956 film *The Brave One*, was written under the alias Robert Rich. It was presented to Trumbo in 1975, the year before his death. Perhaps the most farcical Oscar screenplay award was the one that went to *The Bridge on the River Kwai*. The two writers, Michael Wilson and Carl Foreman, were both blacklisted and so the script was credited to Pierre Boulle, who wrote the original novel, in French. In fact he could not speak English, let alone write an Oscar-worthy screenplay in the language, and did not attend the Oscars. The Academy eventually acknowledged Wilson and Foreman after their deaths.

∞∞∞∞∞∞∞∞∞∞∞∞∞∞∞∞∞∞∞∞∞∞∞∞∞∞∞∞∞∞

TOP 100 COUNTDOWN

50 – *BLADE RUNNER* (Ridley Scott, 1982)

Scott's ravishingly dark vision of Los Angeles in 2019 is the ultimate old-fashioned movie dystopia: a fabulous hell of skyscrapers and monolithic factories. The sky is cluttered with fuming aircraft and floating neon adverts. It never stops raining on the cramped and seedy streets, and everyone, apart from Harrison Ford's blade runner, smokes like a chimney. What does it mean to be human in such a diseased world? This is the thrust of Scott's film noir, which charts Ford's quest to terminate four genetically engineered replicants who want to exact revenge on the humans who invented them. The director has never ceased to tinker with the movie. The final cut is a slightly colder and lonelier place.

James Christopher

49 – *HIGH SOCIETY* (Charles Walters, 1956)

A sore point for fans of *The Philadelphia Story*, the original 1940 comedy upon which this is based, *High Society* is a musical that's smart enough to refocus attention on the Cole Porter standards and the louche milieu. Frank Sinatra and Bing Crosby provide the cocktail drinking insouciance as, respectively, a *Life* magazine journalist and an ex-husband of soon-to-be-remarried Rhode Island socialite Grace Kelly. The tunes include 'Who Wants to be a Millionaire?' and 'True Love'. But the highlight is Sinatra, glugging champagne, and slurring through a duet of 'Did You Ever?' with a typically mellow Crosby.

Kevin Maher

48 – *SHOAH* (Claude Lanzmann, 1985)

A nine-hour documentary about the Holocaust may sound like a difficult sell, but Lanzmann's movie is unrelentingly gripping. Eschewing traditional historical documentary methods (there is no archive footage) Lanzmann instead puts human faces on camera and lets them talk. He divides his subjects into three categories – Jewish witnesses, Polish bystanders and German Nazis. With deft judgement he intercuts their testimonies with peaceful and benign footage of contemporary life in Poland. The effect, both in time and in intensity, can be dizzying and profound.

Kevin Maher

47 – *FARGO* (Joel Coen, Ethan Coen, 1996)

A pitch-black comedy set against a white winter in Minnesota and North Dakota: all the better to contrast with the liberal amounts of blood splattered by the film's close. Eccentric characterisation is one of the trademarks of the Coen brothers' films. But in *Fargo* they outdid themselves. William H Macy has the look of a desperate man trying to claw his way out from under his own stupidity – he plays car salesman Jerry Lundegaard, cinema's most inept would-be criminal. Steve Buscemi and Peter Stormare are, respectively, a garrulous rodent and a stoic psychopath hired by Lundegaard to kidnap his wife to claim a ransom from her father. And heavily pregnant detective Marge Gunderson (Frances McDormand) is a movie heroine to be reckoned with.

Wendy Ide

46 – *ALL ABOUT EVE* (Joseph L. Mankiewicz, 1960)

It's the role that Bette Davis credited with resurrecting her career. But chain-smoking drama queen Margo Channing was almost played by another movie icon, Claudette Colbert, who had to pull out from the film after suffering an injury. Davis was going through an acrimonious divorce during the shoot, her distinctively raspy line-delivery was apparently the result of all the screaming rows with her soon-to-be ex-husband William Sherry. A peerless backstage drama, spiked with the kind of acidic wit that Davis could spit with joyous savagery, the film pits Davis's Channing, a stage actress at the top of her game with everything to lose, against hungry newcomer Eve Harrington (Anne Baxter). Baxter's Eve is terrifyingly driven, but it is Davis's tough-cookie vulnerability that steals the film.

Wendy Ide

45 – *THE LIFE AND DEATH OF COLONEL BLIMP* (Michael Powell, Emeric Pressburger, 1943)

The Powell and Pressburger stable produced some of the great cinema of the 1940s. This glorious film introduces the central character, British officer Clive Candy (played superbly by Roger Livesey), in a Turkish bath in 1943. He's a blustering old duffer wearing a walrus moustache and a towel. He seems little more than a relic. But then the film rewinds to the Boer War and we get to know him as a hero, a romantic and a thoroughly decent chap – a relic only in that his unwavering belief in good sportsmanship is sadly out of step with modern warfare.

Wendy Ide

44 – *A STREETCAR NAMED DESIRE* (Ella Kazan, 1951)

Tennessee Williams's most famous play will always be identified with Marlon Brando. No actor had displayed such raw machismo on screen before. His mesmerising performance as Stanley

Kowalski – a blue-collar brute who is forced by his pregnant wife to put up her neurotic and delusional sister, Blanche (Vivien Leigh) – is also his best. What's often overlooked is that the film features some of the finest ensemble acting ever committed to screen. It is one of the very few productions in our Top 100 that succeeded in making that perilous leap from Broadway to Hollywood.

James Christopher

43 - *TERMINATOR 2: JUDGMENT DAY* (James Cameron, 1991)

It's a decade since Sarah Connor destroyed the Terminator, an emissary from a machine-ruled future world. Its mission was to kill her, thus preventing her unborn son from leading a human uprising that threatens the dominance of the computers. In *Terminator 2*, Arnie is back, accessorised with a pair of Ray-Bans and just the hint of a sense of humour. The mission this time is to protect the young John Connor (Edward Furlong) from a newer, deadlier Terminator. Cameron's sequel works on the principle that bigger is better. The whole film is pitched at the high-octane level that most action films reserve for their big climax. This is muscular, macho, ballsy film-making – and it's tremendous fun.

Wendy Ide

42 - *BLUE VELVET* (David Lynch, 1986)

From *Twin Peaks* to *Mulholland Drive*, David Lynch has long been obsessed by the gruesome monsters lurking behind the white picket fences of the American Dream. But this maelstrom of kinky torture, voyeurism and sadomasochistic sex remains the classic crystallisation of his preoccupation. In Kyle MacLachlan, Lynch had a leading man whose matinee looks concealed a more ambivalent psyche, while Dennis Hopper's ether-inhaling Frank Booth was one of the most disturbing villains to stalk the screen. Steven Berkoff was among the actors who balked at the latter role; no such qualms for Hopper, who, legend has it, said, "I've got to play Frank. Because I am Frank!"

Ed Potton

41 - *A STAR IS BORN* (George Cukor, 1954)

Cukor's remake of the 1937 musical is now the one most people remember, thanks to a central performance of real class from Judy Garland, and James Mason's memorable, tragic drunk. In the years since being fired by MGM in 1950, Garland had toured Europe to great acclaim, but the mental problems that had resulted in at least two suicide attempts were to resurface before the end of this long shoot as she became increasingly unreliable. She and Mason were both nominated for Oscars, just as Janet Gaynor and Fredric March had been 17 years before, the first time that actors playing the same roles had been nominated.

Nigel Kendall

CULT MOVIES

MEN OF TWO WORLDS

Performance

Review by John Russell Taylor,
January 1 1971

Performance, like all good films, starts from an idea which is also an image – or an image which is also an idea. The image-idea is the meeting of two worlds, equally bizarre, equally remote from the everyday world we all know, unthinkably remote from each other. One world, that represented in the film by James Fox, is the ruthless, casually and sometimes manically savage underworld of the Kray brothers and their kind; the other, represented by Mick Jagger, is the turned-on, freaked-out world of pop music, drugs and the hallucination generation. Neither understands the other, each, in his own way, is deeply disapproving of everything the other stands for. No moral position is adopted beyond the statement of these two, unmistakably biased views; and yet the film is deeply moral, achieving to an extraordinary degree an understanding of both ways of life without implying approval of either.

The confrontation is brought about in what one can only call, despite the film's intricate and ornate style, a reassuringly old-fashioned, plotty way. In the opening sequences we see James Fox (giving the performance of his career, incidentally) at work as a strong-arm man for a gang which specializes in protection and enforced "mergers" with small but potentially profitable enterprises. His advantage, his employer observes, is that he enjoys his work; his disadvantage is that he enjoys it too much. When personal passions are engaged as well (a childhood friend whom he now, for rather neurotic-sounding reasons, hates and despises) he oversteps the mark. The victim oversteps it still farther and gets killed for his pains. Chas is on the run not only from the law but from his own people, who now find him an embarrassment.

At this point he walks, by an elaborate coincidence, into what seems the ideal hideout: the home of Turner, a once big pop star who has retired and gone funny in a mouldering Notting Hill Square. Chas is quite puritanical, and of course disapproves intensely of the sexual laxity, the indiscipline, the general untidiness of his only half-willing hosts (he himself is obsessively neat, tidy, self-consciously male). They (Turner has a German girlfriend and an androgynous French girl who looks like a refugee from Satyricon in attendance) disapprove of Chas's violence, his stiffness, his squareness: but maybe, they reason, a snack of hallucinogenic mushroom may do the trick – or at any rate make him much easier to live with. At the start of their relationship neither knows even how to speak to the other: by its bloody end they are at least beginning to communicate.

The idea of *Performance* is superb. But it is the sort which could all too easily be fumbled in the execution. Especially since it seems to require an intricate structure of cross-references, a highly-wrought photographic and editing style. There are times in the first 10 minutes or so when one fears the worst: the cross-cutting between Chas's beatings-up and a trial arising out of some dubious financial transaction is too long and too explicit in the way it pushes the relationship of violent crime to bourgeois morality. But in spite of occasional irritations of the kind, the film grips, the style works. Both sides of the film, though weird, are completely, sometimes horribly believable. And the fidgety editing, the visual pyrotechnics all fall into place as the necessarily complex way of saying a complex thing, rather than so much swinging top-dressing.

The success of the film is all the more surprising when you consider that it is codirected by its writer, Donald Cammell (who wrote *Duffy*) and its photographer, Nicolas Roeg (who photographed *Petula*), and that it is a first essay in direction for both of them. For all that it is extraordinarily consistent in style, remarkably controlled: the points are made equally by words and visuals, the writer and the photographer as equal partners being, as it were, subsumed into the joint direction. It is not at all an easy film to like: it is not meant to be. But it is one of those rare films which, once you have seen them, send you out wanting to see them again as soon as possible.

CLASSIC FILM OF THE WEEK

Performance

Review by Kate Muir,
July 24 2015

With a pleasurably peculiar cast of James Fox, Mick Jagger and Anita Pallenberg, *Performance* is one of the weirdest slices of Seventies London around, combining gangster violence and ritual humiliation with decaying rock-star glamour.

Directed by Nicolas Roeg with the writer Donald Cammell, the decadent tale begins as it will continue, cutting between a sleek Rolls-Royce and a rough sex scene. Emerging from the bed is Fox, playing the obsessively tidy psycho-bully Chas, who "feels like a bit of a cavort" and goes round intimidating small shopkeepers and pouring acid on vintage cars to please an organized crime boss. However, when the besuited Chas finds himself the victim, he hides out as a lodger in the house of Mr Turner (Jagger) and his entourage and the film takes a surreal turn.

The young Jagger is electrifying, as Roeg (also the cinematographer) lets the camera linger on his rouged lips. Although it is hard to tell how much acting is involved as Jagger lolls around his vast, blood-red lacquered London pile with a mostly naked Pallenberg and a French girl. In a *ménage-à-trois* bath scene Jagger asks: "Do I need to wash my hair?" and his girlfriend sniffs to check.

Under the influence of magic mushrooms and heroin, Fox and Jagger's identities melt and reform, and the denouement comes with a bullet tunnelling into the brain.

PEOPLE

Donald Cammell

Obituary (Paul Mayersberg),
May 1 1996

Donald Cammell will be best remembered as the writer and co-director (with Nicolas Roeg) of the 1970 film, *Performance*, which starred Mick Jagger, James Fox, Anita Pallenberg and Michele Breton. The film, a surreal melodrama of gangsterism, drug-taking and general decadence gained much from its featuring as stars one Rolling Stone and the then girlfriend of another. Greeted with some perplexity by mainstream film critics, it was defiantly modernist, utterly provocative and hence totally in tune with the chaotic popular art mores of its time.

Donald Seton Cammell was the elder son of the writer and poet Charles Richard Cammell and of Iona Macdonald. He began to paint at the age of three and was judged an art prodigy. He went to Westminster School but left at the age of 16 to attend the Byam Shaw Art School. From there he gained a scholarship to the Royal Academy School of Art and became a student of Annigoni in Florence.

A literate and charming man, Cammell was the centre of a salon life when he returned to London to set up his own studio in Flood Street, Chelsea. Among the many beautiful women who gravitated there, he met the Greek actress Maria Andipa, whom he married. She played prominent roles in *High Wind in Jamaica* and *From Russia with Love*. Their marriage was perhaps his first contact with the cinema which was to become the centre of his life.

In the early 1950s Cammell was a full-time portrait painter. His picture of Sheridan, the Marquis of Dufferin and Ava, who was a page boy at the Coronation of the Queen, was seen as the society portrait of the year. But he was dissatisfied. He moved to Paris in 1961 to start a new life as a painter. But he failed to find a style that satisfied him. Abstract art did not particularly interest him. He wanted intensity and movement. Models fascinated him. He lived for several years with the American model Deborah Dixon. Artist and model, role-play and identity, and the interchange of personalities emerged as subjects in his most celebrated, yet in conventional quarters most denigrated film, *Performance*.

Cammell's first screenplay *Duffy* was produced in England in 1968. It starred James Fox with whom he became friends. Fox, after his success in *The Servant*, was seen as the weak English schoolboy. In *Performance* he was transformed astonishingly into an East End thug who breaks into the world of a reclusive aesthete rock star, Mick Jagger. Cammell felt the need to direct his own work. The film was photographed and co-directed by Nicolas Roeg and produced by Sandy Lieberson, with Donald's younger brother David as associate. Here, in the artist and the gangster, sexual male-female ambiguity and role reversal, Cammell achieved the fullest expression of his preoccupations.

Paradoxically, Roeg's subsequent success as a director had the effect of obscuring Cammell's original contribution to *Performance*. The co-directors, as friends, always refused to discuss who did what. In retrospect, this merging of roles was to haunt Cammell's career. His first Hollywood film was *The Demon Seed* (1977) in which a woman is impregnated by a computer. In it, he exacted an extraordinary performance from Julie Christie.

For the next 25 years Cammell spent most of his time in Los Angeles, where he attracted a circle of talented friends outside the purely commercial world. He wrote a film called *Jericho* with Marlon Brando. It was never made. Another project with Brando, *Fan-Tan*, about a woman pirate, remained on the page. It was to be a film and a book but the latter has yet to be published. Through Brando, Cammell met and married China Kong, with whom he collaborated on all his subsequent screenplays.

He wrote a screenplay *Ishtar*, to star Mick Jagger, in which Norman Mailer was to play a role. But it, too, was never made. There were, however, brighter spots. Cammell directed *White of the Eye* (1988), an extraordinary story of a woman who unknowingly lives with a serial killer, set in the Arizona desert.

Donald Cammell's last film *The Wild Side*, with Christopher Walken and Joan Chen, completed in 1995 was, to his chagrin, recut by the producers, and has yet to be seen. It tells of a business-woman who loses her money, meets the wife of the man who ruined her, and together they plot to ruin him. He is survived by his second wife China Kong and the son of his first marriage.

Donald Cammell, painter, film director and writer, died on April 24 aged 62. He was born on January 17, 1934.

◇◇◇◇◇◇◇◇◇◇◇◇◇◇◇◇◇◇◇◇◇◇◇◇◇◇◇◇◇◇◇◇

Editor's note: The film *Wild Side* was re-edited after Cammell's death in line with his vision and the novel *Fan-Tan* was published posthumously, with Cammell and Brando listed as joint authors. Cammell was a hugely fascinating man. To the details in the obituary, it might be added that he was part of the Cammell Laird shipbuilding dynasty, that he was born in the Outlook Tower, at the opposite end of the Esplanade from Edinburgh Castle, and that he committed suicide by shooting himself.

◇◇◇◇◇◇◇◇◇◇◇◇◇◇◇◇◇◇◇◇◇◇◇◇◇◇◇◇◇◇◇◇

SUPERHEROES

THE DARK KNIGHT MARKS NEW CHAPTER IN BATMAN'S SEVEN DECADE SCREEN CAREER

From a low-budget start in the 1940s, Batman's film persona has evolved into today's complex loner

By Dominic Wells,
July 12 2008

When the new Batman film, *The Dark Knight*, opens on July 24, Hollywood pundits expect it to break all box-office records – as well as attracting more female viewers. It arrives in a blaze of publicity of the most unfortunate kind, thanks to the untimely death of Heath Ledger in January. The star was chosen to play the super-villain the Joker after the director Christopher Nolan admired his "lack of vanity" in *Brokeback Mountain*, and his total absorption into the role of the gay cowboy. Some speculated, after Ledger's accidental overdose on prescription pills, that the absorption went too far.

This Joker is, in Ledger's words, a "psychopathic, mass murdering, schizophrenic clown with zero empathy", far removed from Jack Nicholson's Cheshire Cat portrayal in the 1989 blockbuster. To achieve the necessary mental dislocation, Ledger spent a month alone in a hotel room, working on his character, his voice, and an unhinged cackle that sends a shiver up the spine. His inspirations included *A Clockwork Orange* and Pete Doherty, and his slowly decaying make-up, with a livid red lipstick slash and heavily blacked-out eyes, make him look like some doomed indie-Gothic junkie-poet.

Michael Caine, who again plays Batman's butler Alfred, said Ledger's performance was so frightening he sometimes forgot his lines. Christian Bale, who plays Batman, found a kindred spirit – another actor prepared to undergo an extreme mental and physical transformation for his roles.

It's all a long way from the Biffs and Pows of the 1960s TV series, so fondly recalled by those of a certain generation that an Italian newspaper referred to "the three Bs of the Sixties: Beatles, Bond and Batman". Yet Nolan's vision reflects the Batman that has become one of the most flawed and fascinating icons in the comic-book pantheon. This Batman is a morally ambiguous loner, consumed with violent hatred for the criminals who shot his parents. He has no superpowers, and so is vulnerable and able to feel pain. However, he is rich enough to invent fantastic gadgets, and disciplined enough to train his body to tremendous feats.

Will the real Batman please stand up? Here, then, is a behind-the-scenes guide to the Five Ages of Batman. Like the Sixties series, it comes complete with shadowy corporate villains, seemingly fatal cliff-hangers and, in the shape of the imminent Dark Knight movie, a happy ending – for everyone but the troubled actor playing Batman's nemesis.

THOSE FOOLISH FORTIES

Batman (1943) and Batman and Robin (1949)

These two 15-episode serials, made for the big screen, are so bad as to be hilarious. The costumes don't fit; special effects are non-existent; Batman and Robin drive around not in any kind of supercar, but in an ordinary black Cadillac (1943) and a Mercury convertible (1949). All in glorious monochrome. Yet a lot of key Batman elements began here: Commissioner Gordon; Alfred the butler; the Batcave; and most importantly, a gigantic jaw, good for jutting out forcefully from under a cowl. The 1943 series is the racier, a piece of wartime propaganda in which the chief villain is a Japanese agent called Daka. The 1949 series introduces the Batsignal, and the concept of a hooded supervillain ("The Wizard").

WHOLLY CAMP, BATMAN!

The TV series (1966–68)

It's hard to believe that anyone could ever again think it wise to film a man and his teenage sidekick in panto costumes. And yet the 1960s TV serial owes its existence directly to those 1940s movies: an ABC executive attended some riotous late-night screenings at the original Playboy Club in Chicago, and deduced that a remake could attract a following.

Cashing in on Pop Art's obsession with comic-book stylings, the series was hip and knowing for grown-ups – and unbearably exciting for young kids glued to the cliff-hanger endings: "Tune in tomorrow, same Bat-time, same Bat-channel."

Biff! Pow! To the batcave, Robin! Holy Halloween, Batman! The show that launched a thousand catchphrases actually had very high production values. When ABC cancelled the series after 120 episodes, NBC tried to buy the rights, but pulled out when it discovered the set had been destroyed. It would have cost $800,000 to rebuild it.

This was also the dawn of colour television and the show's garish costumes and backdrops were made for it. Finally, there was some top-notch hamming from the villains, notably Cesar Romero as the Joker, Burgess Meredith as the Penguin, and Eartha Kitt (who replaced Julie Newmar in series three) as the purringest Catwoman ever.

Batman (Adam West) and Robin (Burt Ward) also starred in a still entertaining big-screen spin-off filmed on an even bigger budget. Added to the Batmobile, which was a converted 1955 Lincoln Futura, was a Batcycle, Batboat and Batcopter. The Penguin got his own submarine, and Batman unleashed the most surreal of all the suspiciously convenient Batgadgets in his "utility belt": a can of Shark Repellent Batspray.

GOING FOR A BURTON

Batman (1989) and *Batman Returns* (1992)

The *Batman* TV series made $80 million in merchandising in a single year – much more than even James Bond. Obviously execs were desperate to bring Batman back. But the 1960 series was still fresh in the mind: too camp, too hokey. Who could take the Caped Crusader seriously? One man changed all that. Frank Miller, now better known as the creator of *300* and *Sin City*, banished all thoughts of camp with his 1986 graphic novel *Batman: The Dark Knight Returns*. It posited an older and embittered Batman, bordering on the psychotic, engaged in a life-or-death struggle with the Joker.

The book was a critical and commercial smash, and plans were laid for a film. Adam West, now 58, lobbied to reprise the role, which would have suited the *Dark Knight Returns* storyline. I met him in 1988, when Britain was again gripped by Batmania (TV-am's ratings leapt 25 per cent after screening the Sixties episodes), and he sounded as though he'd given it considerable thought: "In the final scenes of the film, if it's bizarre and mysterious, you can still have Alfred the butler driving the old Batmobile to the rescue. We'd have been using all hi-tech, wonderful slick new stuff, and at the critical moment, there's Alfred, driving the old Batmobile. People would stand up and cheer."

But no. The maverick director Tim Burton had other ideas, casting the indifferently chinned comedian Michael Keaton as the dark avenger, a decision that attracted 50,000 protest letters. It didn't matter. The film was the runaway blockbuster of 1989, and merchandise revenues alone topped $750 million. It had songs by Prince, then the hippest musician on the planet; extraordinary sets by the troubled Anton Furst, who two years later would leap eight floors to his death; and Jack Nicholson's famous grin.

Even so, it's not particularly good. There are strange holes in the plot where the producer Jon Peters and Tim Burton didn't see eye to eye, and Kim Basinger, then the producer's real-life girlfriend, is a waste of space.

Burton's sequel, *Batman Returns* (1992), is infinitely more watchable. Danny DeVito delivers a terrific performance as the Penguin. As for Michelle Pfeiffer, dressed in skin-tight rubber, licking Batman's face, and kick-boxing on a sloping roof … we'll let one of the enthusiastic audience members at the first American preview sum it up. "She's hot! She's really hot!" came an over-refreshed cry from the front row, startling the convocation of European journalists. "Aooooow! Man, that chick is hot!"

Meanwhile, the men in suits made licensing deals with 130 companies, while conveniently merchandisable additions to the Batarsenal included computerised Batarangs, a Batglider and a Batboat.

SNOWED UNDER IN BASE CAMP

Batman Forever (1995) and Batman and Robin (1997)

Oh dear. Oh dear oh dear. This is when the toy manufacturers and bean counters took over completely. The darker, more adult stylings of Burton's *Batman* gave way to a campy, colourful aesthetic, chasing a younger demographic. Batman's youthful ward, Robin, whom Burton had successfully fought against including, makes his first appearance. Jim Carrey is let loose to do his crazy Carrey shtick as the Riddler. And of course the Batsuits, Batmobile and Batcave had to be completely redesigned: how else could they sell new lines of toys, sorry, allow the new director, Joel Schumacher, to express his artistic vision?

For critics, this is the moment the Batman franchise went tits-up – literally. Schumacher, who had worked as a costume designer before becoming a director, added noticeable nipples to the new Batsuits as well as giant codpieces. But viewers lapped it up and the movie made even more cash than *Batman Returns*.

In fairness, Carrey is never less than watchable. Val Kilmer, replacing Keaton as Batman, was adequate, though famously difficult to work with. But Tommy Lee Jones never quite convinced as the coin-flipping villain Two-Face, and the film was further dumbed down by a late decision by the studio to cut half an hour of Batman character development from the film.

As for *Batman and Robin* (1997), not even the Great American Public could stomach this witless and pointlessly gadget-laden farrago. It did so badly at the box office that a projected fifth movie was summarily cancelled. Arnold Schwarzenegger, whose box-office muscle was already flagging, played the not-quite-evil villain Mr Freeze, complete with atrocious Austrian-accented puns: "You're not sending me to the cooler"; or "The Iceman Cometh". As if you could believe he was a Eugene O'Neill devotee.

Uma Thurman looked uncomfortable to be just playing sexy as Poison Ivy, delivering innuendo-laden lines about her "honey-pot". George Clooney, too, was unusually uncharismatic as the man in the sweaty rubber suit. He has since enjoyed referring to himself wryly as the man who killed the Batman franchise.

BAT TO BASICS

Batman Begins (2005) and The Dark Knight (2008)

In the end, you can't keep a good multi-billion-dollar franchise down. Strangely enough, before the men in suits changed his mind, Schumacher had wanted to make a Batman origin story based on Frank Miller's graphic novel *Batman: Year Zero*. This now helped to inspire a complete "reboot" helmed by Christopher Nolan.

Memento, a film told backwards about a hero with acute memory problems, made Nolan one of the most respected directors around. And Christian Bale, who signed up soon after, had long

21 July 2008. The 'batmobile' arrives for the European premiere of *The Dark Knight* in Leicester Square. (Ben Gurr)

been a fan favourite to play Batman. Having starved himself to a skeleton for *The Machinist*, this extraordinarily versatile and dedicated actor now piled on 100lb of muscle in two months. Technological developments also permitted a Batsuit you could move and act in (previous suits had been stiff and weighed 90lb). The omens were good but could this talented team jump-start Batman's nearly lifeless body?

The resulting film, *Batman Begins* (2005), is close to a triumph. It takes the trouble to show Batman's origin in some detail: his hatred of crime after seeing his parents gunned down before him; his initial fear of, and eventual fascination for, bats; his apprenticeship in martial arts. For the first time you can really buy into what is otherwise, let's face it, a ludicrous premise for a film: that a millionaire playboy would dress as a bat by night and fight crime.

And now we can hardly wait for *The Dark Knight*, though Ledger's death has produced a buzz around the film that nobody wanted.

Katie Holmes, whose vapid non-performance as Bruce Wayne's love interest was a weak link in *Batman Begins*, is replaced by the feisty indie actress Maggie Gyllenhaal, and Christian Bale has more freedom thanks to further refinements in that hated Batsuit. And though Nolan is keeping the tone as dark as the title would suggest, even the men from Mattel are happy: there are many nifty new gadgets, including a new-look Batcycle called the Batpod.

The director and comics aficionado Kevin Smith has called *The Dark Knight* "The *Godfather II* of comic-book movies"; every early review has been positive. So it's official. Nearly 70 years on, the bat is back. And this time, it really is forever.

PEOPLE

Editor's note: As in any industry, the film industry has its share of fascinating characters and people whose company may become a little tiresome after the briefest of encounters. The latter category includes many big-name stars, who have been persuaded by reckless publicists that their every utterance stands comparison with Oscar Wilde. The former category often includes less familiar names, whose life experience is not restricted to the industry itself. One such individual was John Chambers, a pioneering figure in film make-up. I met him in 2001, just months before his death. He was living quietly in the film industry hospital in Woodland Hills, California. He was a big man, a modest man, but a great talker. He talked freely about his work on *Planet of the Apes* and Star Trek, but also pioneering work with disfigured servicemen. What he did not talk about was the top secret work he had done for the CIA, producing disguises for overseas agents and, more interestingly, his involvement in a plot to rescue American embassy personnel during the Iran hostage crisis, by setting up a fake film project and persuading the new Iranian authorities that six embassy staff who had escaped capture during the seizure of the US embassy, and who had been hiding out in the Canadian embassy, were really part of the crew for a new sci-fi film. It all came out a decade after Chambers's death in the Oscar-winning film *Argo*, with John Goodman playing Chambers.

John Chambers

Make-up artist who created the masks for *Planet of the Apes* – and Mr Spock's ears

Obituary (Brian Pendreigh),
September 1 2001

Not only did the Academy of Motion Picture Arts and Sciences create a special Oscar for John Chambers, they hired a chimpanzee, in a tuxedo, to hand it over. The presentation in 1968 seemed entirely appropriate in recognition of the ground-breaking work Chambers had done designing the make-up for the original *Planet of the Apes*.

The film had been turned down by every studio in Hollywood for fear audiences would not take talking apes seriously. Chambers successfully transformed actors of the calibre of Roddy McDowall into simian versions of themselves and the end result was one of the biggest hits of 1968, a classic that more than holds its own against the current remake.

Chambers is a cult figure in *Star Trek* circles too, for being the man who designed and created Mr Spock's famous pointy ears – ears only rivalled by Mickey Mouse's as the most recognisable in 20th-century popular culture. Chambers is regarded by many as the father of modern cinema make-up. He inspired a generation to take up the craft and helped to persuade the Academy that make-up artists should have their own Oscar.

But movies were not his first career. He was lured by the promise of

Hollywood escapism only after years of pioneering, and sometimes heart-breaking, work with disfigured war veterans, producing artificial ears, noses and even whole faces.

Chambers was a big, straight-talking, happy-go-lucky man, born in Chicago, and fiercely proud of his family's Irish roots. He trained as a commercial artist, designed jewellery and exhibited as a sculptor before the Second World War, in which he served as a medical technician. Cosmetic surgery was in its infancy; Chambers helped to develop new rubber compounds and prosthetics, and established a reputation as a miracle worker.

But the work took a huge emotional toll and he felt too much was expected of him. He was able to use his artistic gifts to recreate faces, but there was no technology at the time to animate the features, and he was deeply affected by the hopes and despair of victims and relatives.

He thought his work with prosthetics might open doors in Hollywood and in 1953 he secured a post with NBC television. He worked on such enduring TV series as *Lost in Space*, *The Munsters*, *The Outer Limits* and *Star Trek*.

There was a Hollywood tradition of actors in ape costumes and masks, but usually these were comedies or B-movies, and they were not normally required to speak. But *Planet of the Apes* was set in a world where evolution had been turned upside down, humans were dumb and chimps, gorillas and orang-utans were the superior species. Chambers had to devise a new type of make-up in which the ape lips would seem to form words.

When it came to the ability of the subject to express emotion, Chambers knew, from his experience as a medical technician, the difference between a mask that covered the whole face and individual false features. He and his team worked round the clock to perfect designs, using plaster likenesses of the actors' faces as the starting point. Make-up was glued, piece by piece, to the actor's skin. Part of the face was painted, but otherwise left exposed, enabling actors to wrinkle their faces and express emotion. In the course of his work he developed new adhesives, raw non-cracking paint and a new type of foam rubber, which allowed heat and sweat to pass through.

Initially the make-up process took five or six hours, and it never came down below three or four. Actors had to turn up in the middle of the night so they would be ready to shoot in the morning, and often slept as make-up was applied.

Latterly he was confined to a wheelchair by a stroke and paralysed on one side. He remained a great talker and storyteller, and an Irish tricolour brightened up his room at the motion picture industry hospital in Woodland Hills, California, not far from the Fox ranch, where he worked on *Planet of the Apes*. He is survived by his wife Joan.

John Chambers, make-up artist, was born in Chicago on September 12, 1922. He died in Woodland Hills, California, on August 25, 2001, aged 78.

IT MAY BE ABOUT TEARING IT UP IN TEHRAN, BUT THERE'S MORE TO BEN AFFLECK'S FINE FILM THAN JUST SAVING DIPLOMATS

Argo

Review by Kate Muir,
November 12 2009

Ben Affleck has delivered a knuckle-muncher of a thriller and a satire on Hollywood, both in one unlikely package. Based on the true story of the rescue of six American diplomats after the Iranian revolution in 1979, *Argo* actually refers to the title of the fake sci-fi movie created as cover by the CIA to make the Iranians think the diplomats were merely a Canadian film crew. "It's the theatre of the absurd," sighs one CIA honcho when he hears of the plan.

Affleck directs and also plays Tony Mendez, the lead CIA agent with a talent for "exfiltration" – getting Americans out of sticky situations – and he handles the absurd with aplomb. The Americans escaped by a back door as the American Embassy in Tehran was stormed and its staff taken hostage by the Revolutionary Guards. The Americans were then hidden by the Canadians in their ambassador's residence.

Argo begins with an unpromising piece of pedagogy, as graphics explain the history of British and American interference in Iran, but then the film gets into its stride with burning US flags and hysterical crowds storming the embassy. Affleck brilliantly conveys the panic, incomprehension and terror of the staff as the streets outside vibrate with anger.

Meanwhile, back in the States, Mendez is plotting his fake movie (only marginally better than his superiors' plan to send in six bicycles). He heads to Hollywood to find an old crony and movie prosthetics expert, John Chambers, played by John Goodman, who waddles wearily but cheerily into shot like a baby elephant. Chambers recruits wizened producer Lester Siegel (Alan Arkin) and the Little and Large comedy begins.

Worries that the diplomats will be unable to behave like film-makers are scotched: "You can teach a rhesus monkey to direct in a day," they tell Mendez. Deals are cut over the script, a sort of *Star Wars* rip-off. Sci-fi language is understood everywhere, even in deepest Iran, which will provide a moonscape-style background. Hollywood's power, it seems, transcends revolutions.

In Iran, the six Americans are less than delighted when Mendez turns up with his ridiculous plan. They do, however, sport marvellous Seventies fashions in mustard and orange with wide shirt collars and pussycat bows, as well as facial hair that is surely a tribute to the release month of "Movember". In particular, Scoot McNairy and his moustache give a fine performance.

Aside from the introduction, the Iranians in the film are mostly portrayed as crazed nutters. A few officials are given subtitles, but the screaming soldiers are left untranslated, delivering an unexplained barrage of abuse. Elsewhere, Affleck shows great attention to detail, particularly the film's retro look and colour palette, like old, faded Kodak snaps. Affleck plays his own part cryptically, and all we know is that Mendez eats a lot of fast food and drinks heavily since his estrangement from his wife and son. He seems more at ease behind the camera and, after the brilliantly tense ride of *Argo*, he should have no trouble finding offers to direct.

40 – *THE LIFE OF BRIAN* (Terry Jones, 1979)

Despite an interlude in which its put-upon hero is abducted by aliens, this savage deconstruction of the Christian story is by far the most coherent of the Python movies. Presented with a proper budget, fancy North African locations and sets borrowed from Franco Zeffirelli's *Jesus of Nazareth*, Jones and his team combined public-school humour, religious satire, surrealism and timeless daftness, sidestepping accusations of blasphemy by having Graham Chapman's messiah born on the same day as Jesus, but in the next stable.

Ed Potton

39 – *THE GRADUATE* (Mike Nichols, 1967)

There have been few more memorable depictions of the transition from education to adulthood – or, indeed, of the complex charms of the older woman – than Nichols's adaptation of the novel by Charles Webb, which Webb wrote shortly after graduating from Williams College, Massachusetts. Dustin Hoffman beat a far-too-assured Robert Redford to the role of Ben Braddock while Anne Bancroft, in reality only six years Hoffman's senior, was a purringly predatory Mrs Robinson (we never learn her first name). Her stockinged leg in the promotional poster actually belonged to Linda "Sue Ellen" Gray, who went on to play the role on the West End stage four decades later.

Ed Potton

38 – *REAR WINDOW* (Alfred Hitchcock, 1954)

Like *Rope* and *Lifeboat*, *Rear Window* was one of Hitchcock's exercises in cinematic economy: virtually every shot originates from the apartment of James Stewart's photographer, holed up with a broken leg during a Manhattan heatwave. He becomes fascinated by the shady deeds of his neighbours, specifically Lars Thorvald, played by Raymond Burr, whose resemblance to Hitchcock's interfering producer David O Selznick has been noted. The result was one of Hitch's most gripping and cheekily symbolic films. Freudian analysts had a field day with Stewart's immobile (read impotent) state, and his subsequent resort to larger and larger spying apparatus: binoculars, telephoto lenses.

Ed Potton

37 - *BEAU TRAVAIL* (Claire Denis, 1999)

Loosely based on Herman Melville's *Billy Budd*, Denis's stunning film is powered by wordless physical tensions and the repetitive rhythms of sculpted bodies training under the desert sun. Denis Lavant, his face weathered into a bitter history, plays Galoup, an ex-soldier who recalls his time as a Sergeant Major in the Foreign Legion. Stationed in Djibouti, Galoup is second-in-command to a commandant he idolises. When Sentain (Gregoire Colin), a new soldier, arrives at the camp, Galoup immediately sees him as a threat; a rival for the approval of the commandant. Galoup's jealousy is the kind that drives a man to desperation. None of this is explicitly spelt out – Denis instead creates an increasingly oppressive mood. She films the soldiers' exercises like a piece of gymnastic ballet; meanwhile gnome-like Galoup is tortured by the beauty around him.

Wendy Ide

36 - *JAWS* (Steven Spielberg, 1975)

The blockbuster was born thanks in part to the efforts of a tuba player called Tommy Johnson and a lump of fibreglass named Bruce. Johnson played the famous "daa-da" motif on John Williams's ominous soundtrack; Bruce was a mechanical shark, named after the lawyer of the film's sophomore director, Spielberg. In the summer of 1976, 67 million Americans flocked to hear one, see the other and develop lifelong fears of the ocean.

Curiously, though, tourist figures trebled at Martha's Vineyard, the Massachusetts resort where the film was shot.

Ed Potton

35 - *WITHNAIL AND I* (Bruce Robinson, 1987)

For students of the late 1980s, this bohemian comedy is as iconic as the Clash. Robinson's scabrous account of two unemployed actors with no money – but an insatiable appetite for drugs, lighter fuel and alcohol – captures that fearful crunch when a young man's dream hits the steel buffers of reality. Richard E. Grant is perfectly cast as Withnail, the self-appointed scourge of mediocrity, who uses his naive flatmate, Marwood (Paul McGann), to stoke his ego and fund the booze. The genius is in the gaseous mix. Withnail's fruity blasts of indignation, and Marwood's shrieking panic, create the combustible atmosphere of hysteria. Ralph Brown's deadpan drug-dealer, Danny, inventor of the Camberwell Carrot, strikes the match.

James Christopher

34 - *THE MAN WHO SHOT LIBERTY VALANCE* (John Ford, 1962)

Forever hidden in the shadow of the bloated and overrated *The Searchers*, the subsequent John Ford/John Wayne collaboration is in fact their greatest movie, and one of the smartest Westerns ever made. Wayne plays rugged frontiersman Tom Doniphon, a two-fisted hero who is gradually ostracised by the increasingly civilised West, as

embodied by lawyer and idealistic smoothie Ransom Stoddard (James Stewart). And though Doniphon rids the town of the titular menace Valance (Lee Marvin), he is declared obsolete by a movie that laments the rise of a vulnerable American democracy and includes the knockout line "When the legend becomes fact, print the legend!"

Kevin Maher

33 – ONE FLEW OVER THE CUCKOO'S NEST (Milos Forman, 1975)

Passed the rights to Ken Kesey's asylum novel by his father Kirk – who had played its central character, Randall McMurphy, in a stage version – producer Michael Douglas binned the old man in favour of Jack Nicholson, and the rest is history. With Nicholson on riveting form, Louise Fletcher chilling as Nurse Ratched and a supporting cast full of frazzled humanity, it became only the second film after Frank Capra's *It Happened One Night* to win all five major Oscars: actor, actress, director, picture and screenplay.

Ed Potton

9 March 1979. Mark Hamill and Carrie Fisher filming *Star Wars: The Empire Strikes Back* on location in Norway. (Stephen Markeson)

32 – THE EMPIRE STRIKES BACK (Irvin Kershner, 1980)

The only one of George Lucas's six multi-billion-dollar blockbusting space operas with an emotional kick, *The Empire Strikes Back* surrounded the usual pyrotechnics with narrative twists and morbid themes, transforming the further adventures of Luke Skywalker (Mark Hamill) with dream sequences, Oedipal revelations ("I am your father!"), torture scenes and a gob-smackingly downbeat ending (Solo frozen and kidnapped, everyone else a bit tired).

Kevin Maher

31 – HIS GIRL FRIDAY (Howard Hawks, 1940)

The fizzing, crackling dialogue and the careless way that Cary Grant and Rosalind Russell chuck their lines at each other like lit fireworks makes this one of the great screwball comedies of all time. Grant is delicious as Walter Burns, a newspaper editor and an incorrigible cad; Russell plays Hildy Johnson, his star reporter and sometime wife who is about to give up the newspaper game for a quiet married life in suburbia with Bruce (Ralph Bellamy). Meanwhile Hildy can't resist the thrill of one final big scoop for *The Morning Post*. The wisecracks come so thick and fast that you barely dare breathe in case you miss one.

Wendy Ide

PEOPLE

Dennis Hopper – wild man of Hollywood

Psychopath roles are good news for the reformed *Easy Rider* star. Julia Llewellyn Smith reports

Published September 28 1994

When Dennis Hopper turns up on screen, audiences titter unhappily. Those ice-blue eyes, that hacking laugh signal only one thing: some innocent is about to be horribly tortured or spectacularly killed.

In *Speed*, Hopper's latest extravaganza, it's a poor security guard who gets it through the ear with a screwdriver because he politely attempted to stop Mr Hopper (aka Howard Payne) from inserting a bomb in a lift shaft. "Nothing personal," says Payne, before going on to massacre a few cops and booby trap a Los Angeles bus so that it will explode once its speed drops below 50 mph.

At the age of 58, Hopper has an assured status as Hollywood's number one nutter. Since his comeback in 1986 as the deliciously demented Frank Booth in *Blue Velvet*, he has been on a psychotic treadmill. He was a snarling southern bigot in *Paris Trout*, a deranged hitman in *Red Rock West* and next year he will play – surprise – a crack-brained pirate in *Waterworld*, a Kevin Costner film billed as the most expensive movie ever.

He has come a long way from the days when he breakfasted on beer, had half a gallon of rum for lunch and ended the day with a "speed-ball", heroin and cocaine shot straight into a vein. No studio then would touch him, but he has been clean now for 12 years. Sitting opposite me in a Knightsbridge hotel suite, he is a dream interviewee; courteous, funny and unlikely to go berserk with a pickaxe; despite the bald head, which he assures me has been shaved for thespian purposes. He sits for photographs like a puppy and only occasionally sears you with his intense gaze. Hopper knows that he has had a lucky escape from his past.

"It shows that if you just live long enough you can see anything happen," he muses in a Californian drawl. "It's certainly ironic that I'm in the most expensive movie ever made, which is being produced by Universal, the people who turned down *The Last Movie*." *The Last Movie* was Hopper's directorial folly, a huge project launched after his success with *Easy Rider*, the plot was about a movie company making a western in a remote Peruvian village. It took Hopper two booze-fuelled years to edit it and although it won the Venice Film Festival, Universal never distributed it. Hopper was blacklisted and retreated to his home in Taos, New Mexico and consoled himself with more chemicals.

"Yeah, some of them were very good drugs," he says. "They work for the moment. I hear even some extroverts like them. All my heroes are drug addicts, so it was very easy for me. Saying 'I'm an artist' is a great device when you are in total denial. You say let's talk about Baudelaire, Henry Miller, WC Fields, John Barrymore, blah, blah, blah. But all

16 August 1994. Dennis Hopper at the Hyde Park Hotel. (Chris Harris)

these people ended up rather tragically. Drugs work for a while and then they don't work anymore."

It was a lost decade and one that Hopper fervently regrets. Remind the boy from Kansas that he has worked with some of the movie greats, from James Dean (in *Rebel Without a Cause* and *Giant*), to Elizabeth Taylor, John Wayne and Jodie Foster, and he merely sighs.

"I'm not terribly excited about my career," he says bluntly. "My most productive period was lost in being an *enfant terrible*. My body of work was a mixed bag. Vincent Price used to say that I would make a great heavy. I thought that was ridiculous; I was going to be a leading man. I always thought some day I'd play King Lear, that somewhere inside me there was a Gandhi."

Hollywood took Hopper back on sufferance and he will do its bidding. "I play psychos because they're offered to me. I'm just not offered anything else. I have a little son (Henry Lee) who's four. He saw *Super Mario Brothers* where I play Cooper, the evil lizard. He said: 'I saw you play the evil lizard. Why did you do that? he muses in a Californian drawl.' 'To buy you shoes.' He said: 'I don't need shoes that badly'."

He has nothing to be ashamed of with *Speed*, which, despite barely scratching Hopper's abilities, has one of the slickest and scariest scripts of the year. The star billing, however, does not go to Hopper, but to a bristle-headed, pectorally perfect LA cop played by Keanu Reeves. "I worked with Keanu before on *River's Edge*. He was a very dedicated young actor then, a very introverted, shy person. He doesn't participate in the social life of Hollywood; he never stops working. Women love this film because he's all beefed up and looking like a bulldog. They think it's wonderfully romantic."

In the movie, Hopper plays the disgruntled former cop who was cheated by the force, while Reeves is the pretty-boy face of the Establishment. It's easy to make parallels with real life, especially when Howard Payne lectures his fresh-faced enemy: "You can't understand the commitment I made." How does the original easy rider feel when surfer dudes like Keanu describe him as a role model? "Oh pretty good," says Hopper, looking wary. After all, these days he works out, goes to bed early and, after four marriages, he has settled for happy cohabitation with Victoria Duffy, a 20-something actress who can hardly have been toddling when he wrote, directed and starred in *Easy Rider* 25 years ago. "Yeah, *Easy Rider*. It was an experience," he says with characteristic understatement. "It made a lot of change, however temporary. There were no independent movies at that time. Unfortunately, that has died recently."

Editor's note: *Speed* **was a major hit, grossing more than $350 million worldwide.** *Waterworld,* **however, failed to recoup its budget on its cinema release, although it went on to do well on video and television, reportedly pushing it into profit.**

CLASSIC CINEMA

The Third Man

Unbylined review (Dudley Carew), September 1 1949

For three-quarters of its length this film is pure enchantment. The end, with its scene in the fairground and the long. echoing chase through the sewers of Vienna, has the air of being a deliberate attempt to do better what has often, in the more recherche films, been done before, but nothing can dim the existing excellence of all that has gone before.

The story by Mr Graham Greene, has its setting in present-day Vienna and sets Holly Martins, an agreeable American, the task of finding out exactly how his friend Harry met with a death officially labelled accidental. Since Harry is played by Mr Orson Welles the cunning will guess that the coffin which is supposed to contain Harry's corpse does in fact do nothing of the kind, and although the suspense is most admirably sustained, the fact of that suspense becomes, paradoxically, a source of grievance. The truth is that Mr Carol Reed, as a director, has in common with Dickens a rare appreciation of incidental types and characters. Indeed his own humour, and his understanding of the absurd and grotesque in life combine to make the author's characters so entrancing that any interruption in their introduction to us is to be resented. Harry may have been a particularly loathsome racketeer or he may not, and it does not greatly matter so long as Mr Reed is conducting his tour of the kind of people who were interested in him. The dialogue is a triumph of casual naturalness and the acting of Mr Joseph Cotton as the perplexed Holly, of Valli as the girl who loved Harry, and of Mr Trevor Howard as the head of the British military police, is in itself a tribute to the power and persuasion of Mr Reed's art. Since Mr Greene is responsible for the plot, it has a significance by no means exhausted in its surface manoeuvrings. The musical accompaniment consists of an invisible zither played with immense skill and effectiveness.

CLASSIC FILM OF THE WEEK

The Third Man

Review by Wendy Ide,
June 26 2015

★ ★ ★ ★ ★

Few films more effectively capture the crumbling infrastructure and opportunistic lawlessness of postwar Europe. And none better translate the snaking treachery of Graham Greene's stories and his worlds of cynical expats and casual betrayal. *The Third Man*, which has been treated to a 4K restoration and returns to our cinemas this week, is a masterpiece of postwar noir and is arguably one of the greatest British films yet made.

Joseph Cotten stars as Holly Martins, a down-on-his-luck writer of dime store fiction. He's a two-bit hack who recycles tales of Wild West outlaws, detectives, liquor and dames. He arrives in a bomb-scarred Vienna, populated with the kind of characters that throng his novels. There is a promise of work from his old friend Harry Lime (Orson Welles), but he discovers that his friend is dead. He's just in time for the sparsely attended and suspiciously unsentimental funeral.

The international police are keen to see the back of any friend of Harry Lime, but bullish Holly is determined to unearth the truth about his death. In doing so, he befriends Harry's heartbroken former lover, Anna Schmidt (Alida Valli) and encounters two of the three men who helped to carry his body away from the scene of the accident.

Carol Reed crafts a masterfully suspenseful thriller; his Vienna is a city torn apart and stalked by huge monstrous shadows that seem to loom, independent of the scuttling men who cast them. The final chase, in the city's labyrinthine sewer system, is a brilliantly executed onslaught of echoes and threats.

BLOCKBUSTERS

ONE MAN'S CREATIVE S-F FANTASY

Star Wars

Review by David Robinson,
December 16 1977

If anyone could ever really explain, even post facto, what makes a wild, runaway box-office success like *Star Wars*, the film business would be a very different game and our lives would not be littered with spin-offs and sequels and counterfeits and daughters of *Emmanuelle*.

Two factors, though, have clearly played a part in the *Star Wars* miracle. One is that this is a film not made by 'a committee' of accountants trying to devise a chemical formula out of the incalculables of box-office attractions but a single person's creative fantasy, which by grace of 'luck' and a moment of bravery at 20th Century-Fox, he has been able to realize. George Lucas, the writer-director, belongs to the group and generation (thirtyish) of Francis Ford Coppola, Martin Scorsese and Steven Spielberg.

Lucas says that even before *American Graffiti* (1973) he had the idea of doing a space fiction movie on the classic, elemental lines of *Flash Gordon*. Since the rights to *Flash Gordon* were tied up, he was obliged to research the whole archaeology of science fiction and come up with his own story.

The story – and this is a second major factor in the *Star Wars* phenomenon –

synthesizes a whole body of the most potent myths on which we have all been reared. Lucas's uncomplicated, essential characters – heroes, villains, beautiful princess and venerable seer – with their odd dialogue, at once formal, stilted, and comically colloquial, are the very stuff of strip cartoon. But there are much broader references. The golden robot, the hooded midgets in the desert, the great, fearsome, whimpering simian who is navigator of the spacecraft, are none other than reincarnations of the Tin Man, the Munchkins and the Cowardly Lion from *The Wizard of Oz*. When the prim gold robot is in company with his miniature partner, Artoo Detoo, with its expressive range of electronic chirps and grumbles, they are transformed, again, to Stan and Ollie (and John Williams's witty score even sneaks in a phrase of "The Dance of the Cuckoos" to underline the point).

The old seer (Alec Guinness) is Merlin; and it is he who hands over to Luke Skywalker (note the link of Luke/Lucas) the Excalibur which his dead father had left behind ... but then the story evokes the lore of the West, with Luke's return to the smouldering homestead which determine his course of action; and the lone gunfighter (called significantly, Solo) who makes the traditional transformation from reluctant mercenary to committed champion of the dispossessed heiress, who here happens to be a Princess of romance.

The storm-troopers in the streets, the gun battles on the space ship, the masked warriors (wearing the Samurai armour that gave us nightmares after childhood visits to the museum), the climactic dog-fights in the galactic sky dredge up lost memories of a lifetime of movie-house experience. John Williams's score meanwhile runs the gamut from biblical epic to *Lawrence of Arabia*, and finally brings us home to Ruritania, as the Musketeers stride side by side through the parted ranks in the courtroom where their restored Princess is enthroned.

It is an anthology not so much of actual scenes as of almost subconsciously recalled sensations and sentiments of the film-goer's memory. Maybe it is this more than anything that inspires such fierce loyalty in audiences. People who have already seen the film get snappishly defensive if you have the temerity to say things like "It's very silly, of course"; and retort "But it's such fun".

And, indeed, it is. *Star Wars* unashamedly restores all those qualities which film-makers and audiences have almost forgotten in their chase after illusory sophistication – brightly defined characters; a story that hurtles along at such a pace that it leaves no time for questions; a world of fantasy so confidently portrayed (in *Star Wars* special effects achieve new heights of technical expertise) that there is no thought of disbelief; a genuine escapism that obliges you to make no connexions at all with real worlds.

Not least, *Star Wars*, for all its own technological accomplishment, heartens the strong current sentiment of mistrust of technology, which has found its most notable expression in the proliferation of films of the occult. In this future world, the technological marvels (already showing signs of wear; the heroes' spacecraft is getting pretty crocky) exist alongside the dreadful mutants and zombies, preserving all the worst of human qualities, who appear in one of the film's most marvellous fantasy scenes, set in a galactic waterfront barroom.

In the outcome victory goes not to technology, but to the mystical and religious. Alec Guinness represents the old, suppressed religion, "The Force", and having warned the renegade Darth Vader that he will be much more powerful dead than alive, returns in spirit to guide Luke Skywalker with the advice that he will triumph not by thinking, but by feeling. It's a reflection worth considering in the historical view; and it certainly explains something of the triumph of *Star Wars*.

CLASSIC CINEMA

EXPENSIVE TOYS FOR GROWN-UP INFANTS

Ghostbusters

Review by David Robinson, December 7 1984

In less than half a year, *Ghostbusters* and *Gremlins* have together earned something between three and a half and four hundred million dollars in America alone that may be no more than a tiny percentage of the gross national expenditure or even the defence budget; but it is money on a scale that few of us can begin to comprehend.

14 October 2009. Bill Murray, who plays Peter Venkman in *Ghostbusters*. (Chris McAndrew)

What makes the phenomenon interesting is that the films in question, far from being extraordinary, innovatory or in any way elevating to the imagination, are banal, foolish and mechanical. They are costly and calculated industrial products; garish plastic toys for the grown-up infants who (to judge only from this box-office success) constitute the main population of our English-speaking world.

Their conception and characters are those of comic strip. Their subjects are elemental notions of alien invaders from other worlds. Their scripts dispense 'with any conventional requirement of dramatic argument or logic. With hindsight, it is possible to attribute their huge success to two elements in the formula. Above all there is the reliance upon special effects. The effects specialists have today become the masters of Hollywood: on the titles of both these films, "Special Visual Effects Unit" credits outnumber the rest, and certainly account for a major proportion of the huge budgets.

Then there is the sly mixing of terror and comedy. Audiences are invited to partake of all 'the old infantile thrills of horror movies and at the same time to mock with laughter both the style and their own fears. The voluntary regression to a comic-strip stage of intellectual development is excused by the illusion of sophisticated, cynical detachment.

Ghostbusters is really a comic version of a solemn, silly horror film, *The Sentinel*, directed by Michael Winner: a New York apartment house turns out to be the gateway to an infernal world. The comedy is provided by the team of Bill Murray, who specializes in characters of impervious slobbishness, Dan Akroyd and Harold Ramis, who also wrote the string of shocking verbal quips that does for a script. Not unreasonably thrown off the university campus, these three set up as professional ghostbusters, and are called on to relieve New York of its supernatural visitations, which include some Disneyland ghosts and a giant Marshmallow Man who stalks the city like a sugar-puff King Kong.

THE CLASSIC FILM

Ghostbusters

Review by Kate Muir,
October 31 2014

This Hallowe'en week, *Ghostbusters* is being rereleased in cinemas on its 30th anniversary in an ultra-high-definition restoration – but wait. Part of the sheer joy of this movie – aside from the comic timing of Bill Murray – is the cartoonish crapness of its apparitions and their placid acceptance by the *Ghostbusters* team. Do we really need a digitally improved pink Stay Puft Marshmallow Man or a less blurred, green, frankfurter-munching ectoplasm? Perhaps not, but the question still remains: who ya gonna call to accompany you to this big-screen treat?

Ivan Reitman's much-loved 1984 film stars Murray, Dan Aykroyd and Harold Ramis as sacked university parapsychologists who set up a ghost-catching service as New York is increasingly plagued by paranormal activity. Murray plays Dr Peter Venkman, who is called to the apartment of Dana Barrett (Sigourney Weaver) when her eggs self-fry and her fridge is possessed by something calling itself Zuul.

Venkman's enthusiastic but hopeless pursuit of Dana perks up when she is possessed by the "Gatekeeper" and tries to entice him to passion. "Sounds like you got at least two people in there already. Three might get a little crowded," Venkman says drily.

Amid much sliming and splurting, the movie ramps up its screwball supernatural comedy, perfectly countered by the laconic and ironic reactions of the ghostbusters. It was never bettered by its sequel, but perhaps the new bustier *Ghostbusters* planned by Paul Feig with an all-female cast, will come up to scratch.

WHO YOU GONNA CALL? THE NEW *GHOSTBUSTERS* IS A ROLLICKING, FUNNY DELIGHT THAT STAYS TRUE TO THE SPIRIT OF THE ORIGINAL

Review by Kate Muir,
July 11 2016

The new, bigger, bustier *Ghostbusters* is a rollickingly funny delight, paying homage to the classic film but rebooting it with four female protagonists who have the same laconic, ironic wit as the original men. The supernatural exterminator franchise is in the safe hands of the director Paul Feig, who previously launched the comic combo of Melissa McCarthy and Kristen Wiig in *Bridesmaids*.

These two are joined in the unfortunate orange-is-the-new-grey overalls and proton backpacks by Kate McKinnon and Leslie Jones. Like Bill Murray, Dan Aykroyd and Harold Ramis from the 1984 original, the women set up as rogue parapsychologists out to prove that ghosts exist, and soon find that

New York is experiencing as many pop-up apparitions as it has pop-up designer restaurants. It's not long before Wiig, who plays the physicist Erin Gilbert, is covered in projectile-vomit green slime. She takes it like a woman: "Gets in every crack. Very hard to wash off."

McCarthy is Abby, a paranormal researcher who initially teams up with the engineer Jillian Holtzmann played by McKinnon, who is the best new big-screen find here. McKinnon hails from *Saturday Night Live* and has a funny bone in every part of her skeleton: she plays the goggle and bovver-boot wearing geek engineer – and might become rather a hot lesbian pin-up in this role. In a sliming scene, she just keeps messily eating Pringles: "Try saying no to salty parabolas," she says. The wit here is different, less boom-boom and more va-voom, and tailored by Katie Dippold (who wrote the McCarthy comedies *The Heat* and *Spy*) to each of her characters. Jones plays the transport worker Patty who joins the team, tackles a gruesome electrocuted prisoner apparition in a subway station, and when he splats off into the Queens-bound express she says knowingly: "He'll be the third scariest thing on that train."

Our imperturbable crew are joined by Chris Hemsworth, who plays Kevin, the traditional thick secretary role created by Annie Potts in the first movie (she also has a cameo here). As the bespectacled Kevin arrives for his interview, Erin takes one look at his pulchritude and says: "You're hired." The constant turning of the feminist tables is an instant franchise refresher.

The stars of the originals have come to pay homage: Murray appears in a cameo as Dr Martin Hess, a "famed paranormal debunker", and Aykroyd drives a taxi. Sigourney Weaver is in the credit sequence and there's also a cameo from Ozzy Osbourne at a demon-haunted death-metal concert. Occasionally the ectoplasmic fight sequences drag on, but every time ECTO-1, the souped-up hearse, takes to the roads to the rousing *Ghostbusters*' anthem, you want to shout: "You go, girls!"

TOP 100 COUNTDOWN

30 - *REBEL WITHOUT A CAUSE*
(Nicholas Ray, 1955)

The film that gave voice to the new phenomenon known as the generation gap also created one of the lasting film icons of the 20th century. James Dean's Jim Stark is a masterful portrayal of a directionless teen seeking guidance from parents who are preoccupied with problems of their own. The film has acquired a morbid reputation since all three of its leads, Dean, Natalie Wood and Sal Mineo died in tragic circumstances. Dean's death mirrored the car accident in the film, while Mineo was murdered in 1976 and Wood drowned in 1981.

Nigel Kendall

29 - *DUCK SOUP*
(Leo McCarey, 1933)

Groucho Marx, toying with the matronly Margaret Dumont in *Duck Soup*: "Where's your husband?" Dumont: "He's dead!" Marx: "I bet he's just using that as an excuse." Dumont: "I was with him at the very end." Marx: "No wonder he passed away." Dumont: "I held him in my arms and kissed him." Marx: "I see, it was murder?"

And on it goes, breathtaking rapid-fire badinage coupled with a fantastically provocative satire about the tin-pot dictatorship of Marx's Rufus T. Firefly (he runs the European nation of Freedonia) at a time when genuine European dictatorships were emerging.

Kevin Maher

28 - *GONE WITH THE WIND*
(Victor Fleming, 1939)

Well fiddle-deedee, "as God is my witness, I'll never go hungry again!" Screen's biggest love story, as Atlanta burns around it, is not (at 222 minutes) for those with short attention spans. But *Gone with the Wind*, which won eight Oscars, is more than Scarlett standing on the scorched earth of her home, or the famous staircase scene. The chemistry between Vivien Leigh (as Scarlett) and Clark Gable (as Rhett) is as colourful as the scenery of Fleming's epic. It is remembered for "Frankly, my dear, I don't give a damn", but the sparring throughout is classy.

Tim Teeman

27 - A CLOCKWORK ORANGE
(Stanley Kubrick, 1971)

Kubrick's most notorious film is a striking vision of a world terrorised by fashionable delinquents. Malcolm McDowell's bad-boy reputation was cemented by his performance as Alex, a gang leader who memorably murders a professor's wife with a giant phallus. The film became a cult the moment the British release was pulled by Kubrick himself after tabloid reports of copycat violence. The film's real target is the Orwellian "cure" embraced by the Establishment: notably the use of psychological torture to transform sick minds into model citizens.

James Christopher

26 - GOODFELLAS
(Martin Scorsese, 1990)

"I've been waiting for this book my entire life," Martin Scorsese told Nicholas Pileggi after reading the proofs of his Mafia memoir, *Wiseguy*. "I've been waiting for this phone call my entire life," came the delighted answer. Their collaboration was a match made in, if not heaven, then a captivating version of hell. Assuaging Scorsese's worries about returning to the gangster genre, its authenticity and unflinching violence proved a key influence on that other Mob masterpiece *The Sopranos*, whose creator David Chase described it as "my Koran" and cast a total of 27 *Goodfellas* alumni.

Ed Potton

25 - PICNIC AT HANGING ROCK
(Peter Weir, 1975)

A film that seeps creepiness and atmosphere, which – while shocking – doesn't overdo overt shock. It's crept into our heads as being based on fact but isn't. A group of Australian Victorian schoolgirls go into the countryside for a day trip. It is stiflingly hot and Weir hints at all kinds of hidden passions and desires simmering beneath the surface. Four of the girls disappear; one returns with no memory of what has happened. A trailblazing film, it launched the Aussie avant-garde and Weir went on to direct *Gallipoli* (1981), *Dead Poets Society* (1989) and *The Truman Show* (1998).

Tim Teeman

24 - THE PHILADELPHIA STORY
(George Cukor, 1940)

Katharine Hepburn plays a naughty heiress in this fizzily brilliant romantic comedy. Hepburn was "box-office poison" after a string of flops, but the spunkiest of the Golden Age actresses was determined to revive her reputation. Bought the rights to Philip Barry's play by her then boyfriend Howard Hughes, Hepburn secured a sympathetic director, Cukor, and set about finding a pair of debonair gentlemen to play her competing suitors. First choices Clark Gable and Spencer Tracy were unavailable, so the poor girl had to make do with Cary Grant and James Stewart.

Ed Potton

23 - *SOME LIKE IT HOT*
(Billy Wilder, 1959)

A brawny man in a dress is one of those failsafe devices that will always get a laugh. Add to that a wickedly sophisticated script, a gang of lantern-jawed gangsters and Marilyn Monroe, and you have one of the great American comedy films of all time. Jack Lemmon and Tony Curtis play a pair of itinerant musicians on the run after they inadvertently witness a gangland shoot-out. They take cover, in somewhat unconvincing drag, in an all-girl jazz band. But boys will be boys, and the arrival of Monroe's delectable Sugar Kane has them battling for her attention like smitten schoolboys. Meanwhile Lemmon's Daphne has her own persistent admirer in the wealthy ankle-fetishist Osgood Fielding III. And while, to quote Osgood, "Nobody's perfect", this film comes pretty close.

Wendy Ide

22 - *THE BREAKFAST CLUB*
(John Hughes, 1985)

We felt we couldn't have both this and *Ferris Bueller's Day Off* (written and directed by Hughes, 1986), but boy it was close. The mix of characters stuck in a ball-achingly boring detention swung it: Emilio Estevez as jock Andy, Anthony Michael Hall as the nerd, Judd Nelson as the slightly terrifying John Bender, Molly Ringwald as brittle prom queen Claire and Ally Sheedy as the goth. As with *Ferris Bueller*, Hughes wrote and directed a teen classic, a zesty mix of squabbling, soul-searching and scrapping.

Tim Teeman

21 - *BONNIE AND CLYDE*
(Arthur Penn, 1967)

Arthur Penn's folk legend tapped into the late 1960s zeitgeist of rebellion and counter-culture like almost no other film of its time. Violent, stylish and sexy, it had its audiences sympathising with the bad guys – the young, glamorous bank robbers Clyde Barrow (Warren Beatty) and Bonnie Parker (Faye Dunaway) – while the cops are portrayed as the antagonists. Against the backdrop of depression-era America, the photogenic outlaw couple seem impossibly thrilling. Audiences adopted the distinctive fashions: thousands of berets were sold after Dunaway wore one.

Wendy Ide

PEOPLE

Editor's note: Michael Winner certainly had his detractors. He was in some respects a classic bully, rude to waiters in restaurants, but he was utterly charming in his dealings with me, in the knowledge that I was going to be writing about our encounters. He worked with some of the biggest stars around and commanded a sense of loyalty from many famous friends. And while many were dismissive of his films, they made money in the UK and the US. There is no record of who wrote the obituary, fuelling the suspicion that it may have been a collective effort, with a suggested draft possibly coming from Winner himself. He kept meticulous files, including all his reviews, and sent out Christmas cards a month ahead of time, often featuring a picture of himself. In many ways he was one of the most complex and fascinating people I ever met.

Michael Winner

Irrepressible director of commercially successful films who had a notable second career as a writer, broadcaster and controversialist

Obituary, January 22 2013

Michael Winner was one of the best-known film directors of his generation, a larger-than-life presence in British entertainment and popular culture for half a century. This perhaps had as much to do with his undoubted genius for publicity (and controversy) as with the artistic merits of his films. A man of firm views, which he was rarely reluctant to express, he developed a notable second career as a writer and broadcaster, not least an exacting and idiosyncratic reviewer of restaurants for *The Sunday Times*. Like him or loathe him, Winner was impossible to overlook.

His work and his life were all of a piece, flamboyant, sometimes vulgar, often knowingly pushed to excess. Scorned by the critics, but a hit with audiences (more so perhaps in the US than in his native Britain), his films were unashamedly commercial productions, made with a slickly professional command of the popular genres, especially the thriller, within which Winner chose to work. They almost always achieved precisely what they set out to do, and they made him extremely rich (in 1999 his wealth was estimated at more than £20 million). Fond of big cars, big dinners and big cigars, he lived expansively in a Victorian mansion in West London with 46 rooms, 100 telephones and an impressive collection of paintings and drawings. "Money has no value unless it is spent," he typically declared.

Michael Robert Winner was born into a Jewish family in Hampstead, North London in 1935. His father, who was of Russian origin, became rich through property dealings, while his Polish mother was a compulsive gambler who died £8 million in debt. He spent 11 unproductive years at a Quaker boarding school in

Hertfordshire before leaving at 16 to take private tuition, which got him into Downing College, Cambridge.

Meanwhile he had been reviewing films and interviewing celebrities, such as James Stewart and Marlene Dietrich, for newspapers and magazines. At Cambridge he took a third in law and economics and edited the university newspaper. He entered the cinema in 1956, writing scripts, directing documentaries and making naturist films with titles such as *Some Like It Cool*.

He directed his first feature, *Play It Cool*, in 1962. A comedy built round an unsuccessful rock group, it starred one of the leading pop singers of the day, Billy Fury. It had more energy than substance, as did *The Cool Mikado* (1963), a curious updating of Gilbert and Sullivan with Frankie Howerd as an unlikely lead.

After *West 11* (1963), a belated entry into the kitchen-sink genre, Winner, still not yet 30 but already his own producer, made *The System* (1964), a cynical comedy about young men chasing girls, starring Oliver Reed. Its surprise success in the United States brought its precocious director to wider notice.

Reed became a favourite Winner actor, appearing in seven of his films. He starred again in *The Jokers* (1967), a caper from a Dick Clement–Ian La Frenais script in which he and Michael Crawford "borrow" the Crown Jewels, and *I'll Never Forget What's 'Isname* (1967), a comedy with a more bitter flavour set in advertising. Always looking for star names, Winner persuaded Orson Welles to play the second lead.

Reed appeared yet again in *Hannibal Brooks* (1969), as a prisoner of war escaping over the Alps on an elephant, while Crawford reappeared for *The Games* (1970), a multi-stranded drama built around the Olympic marathon. Thus far Winner had worked only

in Britain but in 1970 he made his Hollywood debut with *Lawman*, a western with Burt Lancaster.

After securing another big name, Marlon Brando, for *The Nightcomers* (1971), a spin-off from *The Turn of the Screw*, Winner directed Lancaster again in *Scorpio* (1973), a serpentine spy thriller. But a landmark film was *The Mechanic* (1972), a violent study of a professional assassin which saw the first of several collaborations with Charles Bronson.

Bronson went on to play a brutal Los Angeles detective in *The Stone Killer* (1973) and, the following year, the vigilante Paul Kersey in *Death Wish*, a New York architect who abandons his liberal principles to avenge the murder of his wife and the rape of his daughter.

Originally assigned to the director Sidney Lumet, who was committed to another project, the film was widely condemned for its sadistic violence but in New York City, then plagued by violent crime, cinema audiences responded with cheers and whoops. *Death Wish* proved so popular with audiences that there were four sequels, though Winner made only the first two. It remained the film with which Winner was most readily associated.

In a different vein Winner directed remakes of *The Big Sleep* (1978), with Robert Mitchum as Raymond Chandler's Philip Marlowe, and *The Wicked Lady* (1983), with Faye Dunaway. After the third *Death Wish* (1985) he turned to gentler fare with an Agatha Christie whodunnit, *Appointment With Death* (1988), and an Alan Ayckbourn play, *A Chorus of Disapproval* (1989).

Michael Caine and Roger Moore co-starred in the 1990 comedy *Bullseye!* but it was heavy-handed and even in Winner's estimation his worst film. He returned to the vigilante theme in *Dirty Weekend* (1993), though this time with a woman (Lia Williams) who takes violent retaliation against men who molest her.

After a rare acting appearance in Steven Berkoff's *Decadence* (1994) he returned to directing after a gap of five years with *Parting Shots* (1998), a tasteless black comedy about a man (played by the singer Chris Rea) told he has not long to live who decides to kill all those who have crossed him.

In 1993, with his films becoming fewer, he became a food critic for *The Sunday Times*, with a column called 'Winner's Dinners' where he was famously rude about restaurants he disliked. He claimed he took the job to get back at Terence Conran, after a bad experience at a Conran restaurant.

It became an unmissable feature of the paper, attracting a large postbag, some of which – by no means all complimentary – appeared alongside his review. A weekly Jewish joke featuring a "Hymie" character also became a regular element of the weekly column.

Winner's final column appeared on December 2, 2012. "So this is it: goodbye," he wrote. "I've been writing this column for nearly 20 years and I don't want a carriage clock or a gold watch. I am trying to get rid of stuff, not collect it." His last restaurant review, the previous week, had been of Shepherd's in Westminster. He described the treacle tart as, "the best I've ever eaten".

Winner was an enthusiastic gourmet and considered himself an authority on food, but he admitted that his appetite had caused him medical problems – he had to have a triple heart bypass – and in 2004 he confessed "I think if I had my life again I would not be so utterly self-satisfied."

He published an autobiography, *Winner Takes All*, in 2004 and further volumes of memoirs *Unbelievable!* (2010) and *Tales I Never Told* (2011). There was a collection of his columns and, improbably, a diet book. His last publication, *Michael Winner's Hymie Joke Book*, appeared in 2012.

As a columnist he also wrote on politics for the *News of the World* – he was a staunch supporter of Margaret Thatcher – and opinion pieces for the *Daily Mail*. Law and order was a regular topic. He established the Police Memorial Trust after WPC Yvonne Fletcher was murdered in London in 1984. More than 30 local memorials to police officers killed while on duty were subsequently established and the Queen unveiled the National Police Memorial in 2005. For his work for the Police Memorial Trust Winner was offered an OBE. He declined the honour, saying it was what you got for cleaning the lavatories at King's Cross Station.

Latterly Winner became something of a fixture on the small screen. He lent his unmistakable presence to a number of television advertisements, most notably those for the insurance company esure, which spawned the catchphrase, "Calm down, dear, it's only a commercial". In 2010 he hosted *Michael Winner's Dining Stars*, an ITV show in which amateur cooks made him dinner in the hope of winning stars for their efforts. He was often as disparaging about the results as he was in his restaurant column.

In 2008 he announced that he wanted to leave his West London home, a grade II★ listed property designed by the architect Norman Shaw, to the nation, together with his art collection, furniture and 96 teddy bears. But negotiations with Kensington and Chelsea Council came to nothing. Even with 46 rooms, lack of space forced him to sell off his extensive collection of Donald McGill's saucy postcards. Last year he also sold a collection of children's book illustrations which included early drawings of Winnie the Pooh by E.H. Shepard.

Cars were another enthusiasm. He had a five-car garage and once claimed: "You need different cars for different journeys." He admitted, though, that private jets were his greatest extravagance.

In 2007 he became seriously ill after picking up a rare bacterial infection after eating oysters in Barbados and spent four months recovering in the London Clinic. Among hundreds of get-well messages was one from the Prime Minister, Tony Blair. He was not alone among Thatcherite Conservatives in switching to New Labour at the 1997 general election.

In 2011 he was again very ill, having picked up E. coli from a steak tartare. He was in hospital eight times in seven months and he revealed that liver specialists had given him between 18 months and two years to live, though it would be his heart condition not his liver that would kill him. He decided to give up his restaurant column after becoming too ill to enjoy food.

For years one of Britain's best-known bachelors, Winner said he had been put off marriage by the spectre of alimony, while a low sperm count had ruled out children. But he enjoyed many relationships with attractive women, usually many years younger than himself.

Late in life he proposed to one of his oldest girlfriends, Geraldine Lynton-Edwards, a former actress and ballet dancer, but told her that since it had taken him 72 years to get engaged she was not to hold her breath for the marriage. They finally married in 2011. His wife survives him.

Michael Winner, film director and food critic, was born on October 30, 1935. He died on January 21, 2013, aged 77.

PEOPLE

Oliver Reed: Saddam's secret weapon

By Valentine Low, July 16 2016

Oliver Reed was one of the great hell-raisers, a boozer who could strike terror into the hearts of anyone who stood in the way of him and a drink.

Saddam Hussein was a brutal dictator who tortured and murdered at will.

So when, in one of the oddest movie projects ever made, the Iraqi despot hired the English actor to star in a homegrown blockbuster, it was a close call as to which of them would be the more terrifying figure.

The extraordinary story of the production has now emerged in a Channel 4 documentary, *Saddam Goes to Hollywood*. It reveals how the film – which was thought to have disappeared without trace – had been lying in a garage in Surrey for the past 35 years.

Saddam kept a close eye on the production, got his henchmen to issue threats when things went wrong and was a deeply unnerving background presence. "It was extremely intimidating," said the actress Virginia Denham.

In the end, however, it was no contest. Oliver Reed was much, much more frightening. As Denham noted: "Oliver Reed was a weapon of mass destruction."

His drinking was so heavy and his behaviour so appalling that the Iraqi authorities tried to get him sacked. But, as half the film had already been shot they had to ignore the fact that Reed was throwing hotel managers around and worse, and persevere regardless.

The film, *The Great Question*, also known as *Clash of Loyalties*, told the story of an Iraqi revolt against British colonial rule in 1920. The producer, Lateif Jorephani, told Saddam, who was funding it, that it would cost up to $30 million. "Saddam Hussein said, 'OK fine, carry on, whatever it takes. But don't let me down. Make a good movie'."

By the time filming started around Baghdad in 1981 the Iran-Iraq war had started. Iraqi actors would disappear because they had been conscripted. Roger McDonald, a camera assistant, said: "Three or four weeks later we would get a message saying that this poor actor had been killed."

The movie was chaotic, late and over-budget, and actors lived in fear of Iranian air attacks. When they were filming an attack on a train, they had to abandon the set because an Iraqi commander thought it was an Iranian invasion and was about to start shooting.

Whenever filming stopped, Reed would become restless. "Oliver Reed and boredom is not a good mix," said the actor, Stephan Chase. "Oliver managed somehow to be poolside at about eight in the morning with an enormous bowl of sangria."

Once, when food failed to arrive, he threw the manager of the restaurant across the room; on another occasion, he urinated into a bottle of wine and told the waiter to give it to the next table. No matter how drunk Reed was the night before, he always turned up on set on time and knew his lines. The actress Helen Ryan said: "Oliver was easy to survive as long as you were working with him. What was not so easy to survive was playing with him."

Somehow the film was finished, but the first cut, according to Mr Jorephani was terrible. It was recut and Saddam "liked it very much", he said. They never found a distributor and all that remains are the original rushes, sitting in rusty cans in Mr Jorephani's garage in Surrey.

Dictators and the movies

Before he became Supreme Leader in North Korea, Kim Jong Il, a huge film fan, kidnapped South Korea's leading director Shin Sang Ok in 1978 and used him to build the country's film industry, with works including the *Godzilla* knock-off *Pulgasari*.

Adolf Hitler persuaded Leni Riefenstahl to make *Triumph of the Will*, a propaganda film about the 1934 Nazi Party rally in Nuremberg.

Sepp Blatter may not have been a dictator in the full sense of the word but his vanity projects as president of FIFA were on a par with the worst of them. *United Passions*, a 2015 biopic starring Tim Roth as the president of world football's governing body, took just $918 at the US box office in its opening weekend.

FIRST FILMS

THE MARX BROTHERS

The Cocoanuts

Unbylined review (Alan Clutton-Brock), July 2 1929

The form of the musical comedy is here rather well adapted to the talking film. *The Cocoanuts* is certainly mechanical amusement, but at any rate the machine does work. The photography is good and both the conversation and Mr Irving Berlin's songs and music, which have a certain flavour of light opera and are in some measure expressive as well as excitatory, are well reproduced. The dancing is spirited enough and in the representation of this the technique of the stage has been well adapted to the more fragmentary manner of the films. But the chief merit of the comedy seems to be the clowning of Messrs Harpo and Chico Marx. They are clowns rather than comedians and, though they probably derive from the special clown of the silent film, they remind one at times of the circus.

Mr Groucho Marx is a comedian rather than a clown, and the difference is distinct. The comedian is silly, but he does not flout all causality so as to make one think one lives in a mad world. It is better to live in a mad than in a 'mechanical' world, and this clowning is refreshing enough, since it produces a fairy story atmosphere where, for example, everything is good to eat, even the telephones or the buttons of a page boy's suit. Messrs Harpo and Chico Marx are also conjurers and find an excuse to practise this art by picking pockets.

In fact, most of the amusing things in this musical comedy seem to need some excuse or other, and the excuses are very, transparent. For it is easy to fit anything into the conventional love story of the musical comedy, but here, as tends to happen more and more, the plot included crime and detection. The detective story is not yet as hackneyed as the love story, so that, without our noticing it, it may be diversified with any kind of irrelevant ornament.

BLOCKBUSTERS

Editor's note: Wendy Ide enthused about *Avatar*, doubting only that it could match the box-office receipts of James Cameron's previous film *Titanic*, which at that point was the highest-grossing film of all time. In fact it surpassed them to set a new all-time high.

SCIENCE FICTION GIVEN AN EXTRA DIMENSION BY THE TITANIC SCALE OF CAMERON'S GAMBLE

Avatar

Review by Wendy Ide,
December 11 2009

Movie events don't get bigger than this. James Cameron's long-awaited follow-up to *Titanic*, the most successful film to date, is immense in every way: from the ambition and scope of its vision, to the ground-breaking technological wizardry, to the staggering size of its budget.

Estimates of the production costs vary widely, but recent theories place *Avatar* alongside *Pirates of the Caribbean: At World's End* as one of the most expensive films made.

The success or failure of this high-stakes gamble of a movie will send seismic ripples throughout the film industry. If it tanks, *Avatar* could pose more of an immediate threat to the Hollywood infrastructure than the San Andreas Fault.

Film fans as well as business insiders have cause to root for *Avatar*'s success: the failure of such a high-profile original concept would mean that the industry will become even more risk-averse and reliant on the proven lure of sequels and remakes.

But on the strength of the film's well-received world premiere in the Odeon Leicester Square, in Central London, last night the movie industry players of Los Angeles should not be too worried about losing their houses just yet.

Avatar is an overwhelming, immersive spectacle. The state-of-the-art 3D technology draws us in, but it is the vivid weirdness of Cameron's luridly imagined tropical otherworld that keeps us fascinated.

It's a world that takes a little getting used to. Cameron's vision owes something to Hayao Miyazaki's meticulous fantasies and something to the 1992 Australian animation *FernGully: The Last Rainforest*. At times it verges on the tacky, like a futuristic air freshener advertisement with the colour contrast turned up to the max. The ethnically accented orchestral score certainly doesn't help matters. But mostly, it's a place of wonder full of exotically freakish animal composites – iridescent lizard birds, hammer-headed rhinos – and sentient vegetation.

Assuming correctly that the special effects would turn out to be the stars of this film, Cameron avoided the big name casting route, opting instead for the relatively unknown Australian actor Sam Worthington in the central role of paraplegic former marine, Jake Sully.

The wheelchair-bound war hero is selected to take part in a top-secret programme. He will travel to a lush extra-terrestrial moon called Pandora which is inhabited by a cobalt-skinned race of ten foot tall humanoid aliens known as the Na'vi.

Aware that the core audience for the film is likely to be teenaged boys, Cameron has equipped the female Na'vi with supermodel looks and curves in all the right places, as well as tails and pointy ears.

Sully finds himself a pawn, caught between two camps: the empathetic scientists led by Sigourney Weaver and the corporate guns for hire who want to aggressively plunder the mineral resources of Pandora.

Thanks to his blossoming relationship with Na'vi warrior princess Neytiri (a CGI motion-captured performance from Zoe Saldana), Sully begins to question the legitimacy of the mission.

With the use of such charged phrases as "shock and awe" and Sully's curt summation of the situation ("When people are sitting on stuff you want, you make them your enemy") Cameron adds a thought-provoking political dimension to the story.

Will the film match *Titanic*'s gigantic box office haul of $1.8 billion? Possibly not. The soppy, soggy doomed love story of Jack and Rose hit a particular chord with audiences. But I would be very surprised if James Cameron didn't have another sizable hit on his hands.

PERSONAL CHOICE

Editor's note: A while back I compiled a list of 20 less-well-known movies that might serve as alternative Christmas viewing in these days of online video on demand. It was a personal list of movies that had stuck with me over many years, but which I felt had not been as widely seen as they should have been. They are not all great, but all have something to commend them – a fresh take on a subject or genre, or some element that lingers in the memory, dialogue, a plot twist or maybe just a single scene, often a final scene that might leave a lump in your throat. I thought it might be interesting to see if *Times* reviewers shared my enthusiasm on their initial cinema release …

A Gunfight (1971)

Editor's note: Kirk Douglas v Johnny Cash, two great American icons face off in a western that boils the genre down to its essential set piece. A clip from *A Gunfight* appears briefly in Cash's famous video for the song 'Hurt', recorded shortly before his death.

Times review by John Russell Taylor, September 17 1971

A Gunfight is solid and well-meaning, but too schematic by half. As an idea, the plot is appealing. Two ageing gunmen meet in a one-horse town,

Kirk Douglas (Nick Rogers)

the Old West now hardly more than a memory, and everyone starts betting on which will win when they shoot it out. "But why should we?" asks one of them (Johnny Cash). "We don't stand to gain anything. Unless we sell tickets." At which the other (Kirk Douglas) comes up with just such a plan. They can sell tickets, shoot to kill and the winner take the money to start a new life.

Neat, you see: the honour of the Old West symbolically reduced to a sideshow: killing to make a Western holiday. The only trouble is that it is a sight too neat. The idea is excellent, but the more you explore it, the less there is in it. Or the less script writer Harold Jack Bloom and director Lamont Johnson seem to find in it.

Sands of the Kalahari (1965)

><><><><><><><><><><><><><><><><><><><><><><><

Editor's note: It begins with a plane crash and ends with another showdown to determine the alpha male. The twist here is that one of the contenders is a baboon.

><><><><><><><><><><><><><><><><><><><><><><><

Times review, by Our Film Critic (John Russell Taylor), December 2 1965

Another film which takes its pretensions to significance a trifle too seriously but works rather well for most of the way as a straightforward adventure story. A group of six disparate people, five men and one woman (young and attractive, of course) are landed in the middle of the Kalahari when their aircraft crashes, and the film then develops the various conflicts which arise among them while they are making a life in the wilderness and seeing what they can do about getting out of it. Occasional attempts to turn the struggle between the two principal men into one between humanism and fascism are rather heavy handed, but the desert locations are attractively used by the writer-director Cy Endfield. The humans, led by Stanley Baker, Stuart Whitman, and Susannah York do their best to fill the wide screen, and the animals, particularly a troop of baboons with whom they find themselves sharing a mountain and a water-hole are enchanting.

My Name is Nobody (1973)

><><><><><><><><><><><><><><><><><><><><><><><

Editor's note: Henry Fonda's ageing gunfighter shoots three would-be assassins. And this kid asks his dad if anyone is faster. "Faster than him?" says the father incredulously. "Nobody!" ... Cue Ennio Morricone's quirky music and cut to Terence Hill trying to catch fish by hitting them with a log. And the title *My Name is Nobody*. Has there ever been a better set-up?

><><><><><><><><><><><><><><><><><><><><><><><

Not reviewed.

DOA (1950)

><><><><><><><><><><><><><><><><><><><><>

Editor's note: "I want to report a murder." "Who was murdered?" "I was." A man is dying with slow-acting poison and must solve his own murder before time runs out.

><><><><><><><><><><><><><><><><><><><><>

Not reviewed.

Somewhere in Time (1980)

><><><><><><><><><><><><><><><><><><><><>

Editor's note: Christopher Reeve and Jane Seymour, two of the stiffest actors ever, star in a piece of romantic tosh. But it was written by Richard Matheson, who wrote *The Omega Man* and *Duel*. This was never going to be your regular romantic tosh.

><><><><><><><><><><><><><><><><><><><><>

Times review, by David Robinson, December 19 1980

An odd, unfashionable, gentle story of the supernatural, adapted by Richard Matheson from his novel *Bid Time Return*, it plays an elaborate Chinese puzzle game with time: the hero is impelled by lingering memories and associations to will himself back from 1979 to 1912, to relive a passionate, doomed, brief encounter. The director is Jeannot Szwarc, who made *Jaws II*, but here reveals a very different (and perhaps very French) style of romanticism. The atmosphere of the film is greatly enhanced by the location in which the entire action takes place – the Grand Hotel, Michigan, built in 1887, a wonderful fantasy of verandas, stairways, garden walks and grand salons, set on Mackinac Island. The principal players, Christopher Reeve (sometimes Superman) and Jane Seymour both have the charm, the belief and the lightness appropriate and necessary to the material.

Grace of My Heart (1996)

><><><><><><><><><><><><><><><><><><><><>

Editor's note: A fictional biopic of a female singer-songwriter, with echoes of Carole King. But as a professional biographer I know I could have made books more interesting if I could have made things up. There is no such constraint here. Great music, including Bacharach and Costello's 'God Give Me Strength' – "I'm only human … I want him to hurt!". A hugely powerful story of those who survived and those who didn't.

><><><><><><><><><><><><><><><><><><><><>

Times review by Geoff Brown, February 20 1997

Grace of My Heart takes us on a journey, through the late 1950s, 1960s and into the 1970s in the company of a woman singer-songwriter, played by Illeana Douglas. Her fictional name is Denise Waverly; for a real-life source, you could try Carole King. She starts out writing songs for others in the Brill Building in New York, home to many budding songsmiths who fuelled the new boom in teenage pop. Gradually she exerts her individuality in a male-dominated business. She goes through one marriage, one aborted pregnancy and one affair before becoming marooned in California with a Brian Wilson type (played by Matt Dillon) who lets the surf and drugs go to his head. She survives, and so do we. But it's a close call. In terms of pace and production values, Allison Anders, the writer and director, has taken a big step up from her previous movies, *Gas Food Lodging* and *Mi Vida Loca*. This time she has Martin Scorsese on board as executive producer, and Thelma Schoonmaker as supervising editor, to help to drive the images along; although even these two cannot stop the film grinding to a halt in California, or hide the pile-up of caricatures and shallow situations that come to surround Waverly's life. But if *Grace of My Heart* is trite, it accompanies the clichés with lively performances and a foot-tapping soundtrack with new songs styled in the old manner and supervised by Karyn Rachtman (she has also arranged Tarantino's soundtracks). Douglas may lack some of the weight needed to carry an entire film, and her singing voice is clearly not her own, but she has quirky vigour in plenty; while, as Denise's manager, John Turturro overcomes the year's strangest haircut (black thatch on top, a dribble of a beard perched on the chin) to find a warm human being under a hustler's exterior.

Frogs (1972)

Editor's note: Imagine Hitchcock's *The Birds*, but with frogs.

Times review by John Russell Taylor, June 9 1972

Frogs, a U certificate film if I ever saw one, though for some inscrutable reason granted the coveted X, is an elementary horror thriller masquerading as a contribution to the current ecology cycle. The trouble is that frogs are not in themselves inherently sinister, like birds, or susceptible to such usage, like the rats in Willard. They just sit there looking amiable while all the nasty things are done by spiders, crocodiles or a kind of ambulant moss, and occasionally permit themselves to be thrown on screen from the upper left-hand corner with a dull plop. In the circumstances it is hard to worry very much even when we leave Ray Milland waiting alone in the last reel, presumably about to be gummed to death.

Robin and Marian (1975)

Editor's note: It is tricky to revisit a legend, but Sean Connery manages it here, with a touching portrait of an ageing Robin Hood.

Times review by Philip French, May 28 1976

Richard Lester's *Robin and Marian* is a picture about being middle-aged in the Middle Ages, and a forceful demonstration of the old saying that you can't go home again, especially if your home was built of twigs in Sherwood Forest and you've spent

20 fruitless years slaughtering Saracens in the Holy Land. Sean Connery plays a grizzled, battle-scarred Robin and Nicol Williamson his disillusioned companion Little John, who team up with an ageing Friar Tuck and the crack-voiced balladeer Will Scarlett to take on the Sheriff of Nottingham once more. They're joined by Maid Marian, now a tough working abbess running a convent hospital. She's deliciously played by Audrey Hepburn, who looks more beautiful than ever when eventually she removes her wimple to shake her hair out and reveal again that swan-like neck. This time, however, the Merry Men don't win, and Marian administers poison to herself and her mortally wounded lover.

Robin and Marian is an elegiac tragi-comedy, sensitively performed, well photographed and all very modest. Unlike some other Lester pictures, the jokes arise naturally from the dramatic situations and are rarely ends in themselves, while the grimness of medieval life is part of the dramatic fabric, not a matter for special comment. Yet ultimately there is a sense of strain about this work, a contemporary self-consciousness that distances us from the action in a non-Brechtian way – which is to say that we are neither powerfully caught up in the events nor placed in an intelligently critical position in relation to them. I prefer it to Lester's other costume pieces, but cannot see it achieving the perennial popularity of the 1922 Douglas Fairbanks *Robin Hood* or the 1938 Errol Flynn version.

Two for the Road (1967)

◇◇◇◇◇◇◇◇◇◇◇◇◇◇◇◇◇◇◇◇◇◇◇◇◇◇◇◇◇◇◇◇◇◇

Editor's note: A second successive movie with Audrey Hepburn, a bitter-sweet tale portraying the ups and downs of a relationship over time.

◇◇◇◇◇◇◇◇◇◇◇◇◇◇◇◇◇◇◇◇◇◇◇◇◇◇◇◇◇◇◇◇◇◇

Times review by John Russell Taylor, August 31 1967

In his introduction to the published screenplay of *Two for the Road*, Frederic Raphael, its author, launches a spirited attack on the so-called "auteur" school of film criticism. It is, he suggests, mostly preciosity and perversity on the part of film critics to seek out the quirks and mannerisms of a number of very minor directors and to construct from them a "creative personality". What, wonders Mr Raphael, about the writer; who gives him a thought? But surely Mr Raphael need not have worried. Anyone can be an auteur, the dominant personality in a group of films may be the director (most often it is), but it may be the producer, the star (one Bette Davis film is likely to be more like any other than like anything else), the costume designer (how many MGM films of the 1930s are not effectively dominated by "Gowns by Adrian"?), or even, yes, the scriptwriter. Jacques Prevert is an auteur, Paddy Chayefsky is an auteur, and so, heaven help us, is Mr Raphael.

But there is one other thing he does not take into account: that being an auteur does not necessarily make everything grand and glorious. There are many perfectly estimable film-makers who are not auteurs, and some absolutely terrible ones, whose work one can pick out instantly. Mr Raphael's personality and mannerisms are obviously dominant in *The Best of Everything*, *Darling* and *Two for the Road*; they are recognizably from the same creator, whoever happened to direct them. But whether, having spotted the continuity, we are pleased by what we see is quite another matter.

One thing that is at once recognizable about all Mr Raphael's characters is their frantic smartness. The central couple in *Two for the Road* (Audrey Hepburn and Albert Finney), whose marriage we see through 12 years of sunshine and showers are Hush-Puppy sophisticates. They exchange, in winsome moments, strained bits of verbal humour suggestive of After-Eight munchers downing their gallons of black coffee on the terrace of that dream villa; they drive cars in a way known only to get-away people on National Benzole; and in their serious moments they fling at each other lines like "All you can do is take the salute at an endless march-past of yourself."

In other words, they come no closer to reality than figures from the glossier sort of television advertisement and Stanley Donen's direction, with its relentless pettiness and faintly deja-vu locations (wasn't that chapel in *Funny Face*? That villa in *The Champagne Murders*? That wood in *Pierrot le Fou*?), matches them in glamorous en-distancement from life.

Well, maybe it is meant to be "a holiday film", a picture of two lives seen only in moments off from the business of everyday living. But it is meant to be serious, and funny, and glittering, and deep. It is meant, in fact, to be very ambitious indeed. The structure, with its kaleidoscopic shifting backwards and forwards from journey to journey over a number of years, is not original in itself, but is original perhaps in its determination to slip the complications past us unnoticed. And here it generally succeeds – only very occasionally do we stop to wonder if we are still at the Triumph Herald stage or have come back to the flashier present. The changes in style of clothes and make-up for Miss Hepburn are very well managed, and Miss Hepburn herself gives one of her best performances. Mr Finney is rather charmless for a character meant to be a charming oddball, and no one else briefly glimpsed shows to much advantage. The saddest thing, though, is that Mr Donen has generally in the past shown himself a very likable auteur in his own right. It is a thousand pities that in this particular battle of the auteurs he is the one who has lost out.

In a Lonely Place (1950)

Editor's note: Sometimes love is not enough … Not that obscure, but not the first film that comes to mind when talking about Bogart. It is one of his most unsettling characters, a lot more complicated than the tough guy with the heart of gold in *Casablanca*. "I was born when she kissed me. I died when she left me. I lived a few weeks while she loved me."

Unbylined review (William
Lawrence), May 22 1950

The hero (Mr Humphrey Bogart) is not only a screen writer, not only in all probability the murderer of a harmless cloakroom girl, but is given to fits of wholly uncontrollable rage. There seems every reason why his neighbour (Miss Gloria Grahame) should be unwilling to marry him, and, indeed, there are times when she, as well as the audience, is unconvinced by the argument that these outbursts in a creative artist must be excused. What with one thing and another, such as being more and more strongly suspected by the police, becoming, it is to be presumed, increasingly creative, and eventually being suspected of murder by the girl herself, he becomes more and more violent, and it becomes more and more obvious that the marriage simply will not do. But there is a happy ending – they don't marry.

Monte Walsh (1970)

><><><><><><><><><><><><><><><><><><><><><><><><

Editor's note: A haunting elegy for the Old West with Lee Marvin and Jack Palance as ageing cowboys and a great seemingly optimistic, ultimately ironic theme song by John Barry, sung by Mama Cass.

><><><><><><><><><><><><><><><><><><><><><><><><

Times review by John Russell
Taylor, January 15 1971

Monte Walsh is one of those westerns which seem to be made boring mainly because interesting Westerns are not artistic enough. It features Lee Marvin as the last of the old-time cowboys and Jeanne Moreau as the last of the old-time western whores; it is all extremely self-conscious about exemplifying the inevitable decline of the Old West under the impact of the railway and enclosures. But too much to the point: everything in it is so calculated to reinforce the central thesis that it rapidly loses all feeling of life and unmanipulated reality, and instead we merely observe from a glum distance the falling into place of the pieces in a pre-arranged pattern. Perhaps a livelier director than William A Fraker could bring it off; but then it is doubtful if a livelier director would want to do it at all.

Scarlet Street (1945)

><><><><><><><><><><><><><><><><><><><><><><><><

Editor's note: Imagine the story of Paul Gaugin rewritten as American film noir, with Edward G Robinson.

><><><><><><><><><><><><><><><><><><><><><><><><

Unbylined review (Albert
Cookman), February 25 1946

There are several new films in London this week, including *Scarlet Street*, an American production directed by Mr Fritz Lang and based on a French novel and play called *La Chienne*, which M Jean Renoir also transferred to the screen. Mr Fritz Lang's direction of this tall story of a lonely little man in big trouble is so painstakingly slow and yet in its ponderous way so efficient that at last we grow tired of disbelieving and patiently believe. Mr Edward G

Robinson is the much respected cashier whose pathetic craving for affection leads him into illicit love, theft, murder and madness, and to this end there must apparently he a wholesale sacrifice of probabilities. But the probabilities are less to be regretted than the opportunities for satire which are thrown away. The little cashier is an amateur painter, and, while he is robbing his employers and his wife to keep a woman of the streets and her bully in luxury, the art critics of New York discover that his paintings, though they lack perspective, have power. It seems a pity that the critics are treated so respectfully; even in face of the pictures themselves we have to assume that they had made a genuine discovery. Miss Joan Bennett and Mr Dan Duryea are the glamorous slut and the smart rogue who make cruel sport of the elderly man's good-natured simplicity. All three major performances are technically brilliant.

The Rebel (1961)

Editor's note: Another film about one man's compulsion to create great art, with Tony Hancock treading his fine line between comedy and tragedy.

Unbylined review, March 2 1961

Mr Tony Hancock, after one insignificant trial run, has made the transition from small to large screen in *The Rebel* with gratifying success. Not that there is nothing wrong with the film (in particular, it could have been directed with a much firmer hand), but it is often very funny indeed, and as a film personality there is evidently nothing wrong with its star.

The main reason for this success, one imagines, is that Mr Hancock has had the good sense to wait until he could have the film made as he wanted it, with the writers who have worked consistently with him on his radio, and television series, Mr Alan Simpson and Mr Ray Galton. Consequently, instead of undergoing the usual cinematic fate of radio and television stars (relegation to a script originally intended for, say, Mr Norman Wisdom) he has been offered a part which is recognizably an extension of the Hancock personality, but at the same time demands a genuine performance, and takes its place in a coherent story.

The hero of *The Rebel* is a conventional clerk in a city office who suddenly decides to emulate Gauguin, liquidate all his assets and go off to Paris to paint and sculpt to his heart's content. Ah, but what happens if you do this without being a Gauguin, without indeed having any talent at all? Since this is a comedy nothing too awful does happen (the Hancock combination of pessimism – and sheer conceit keeps pathos safely at bay); after a personal success with the Avant Garde for his mad and muddled (but on the whole sincerely held) ideas about art he gets involved in a number of awkward situations when the highly-saleable works of a fellow-painter are attributed to him by accident and only with considerable difficulty do things right themselves at the end.

The Games (1970)

<><><><><><><><><><><><><><><><><><><><><>

Editor's note: Back in the day there were no mass-participation marathons: guys turned up at the Olympics, many never having run 26 miles before, no one knew much about them or who would win. This is an old-fashioned fictional story about four such men.

<><><><><><><><><><><><><><><><><><><><><>

Not reviewed.

Valdez is Coming (1971)

<><><><><><><><><><><><><><><><><><><><><>

Editor's note: Burt Lancaster is unlikely casting as a Mexican lawman who is tricked into killing a man and thinks those responsible should pay compensation to the widow. Instead they crucify him. He does not give up. The words "Valdez is Coming" echo through the film like a chorus. It is based on an Elmore Leonard novel, with all the moral complexities that brings.

<><><><><><><><><><><><><><><><><><><><><>

1 March 1976. Burt Lancaster at Cleopatra's Needle in London. (Harry Kerr)

Times review by John Russell Taylor, June 11 1971

Valdez is Coming is a perfectly respectable but rather pointless Western about a simple, idealistic constable (Burt Lancaster) who sacrifices everything for his fixed idea of getting 200 dollars compensation for an Indian squaw whose man has been shot down in error. It is decently directed by Edwin Sherin, and quite watchable, but most of the drama takes place below that threshold of minimum intelligence in the characters which prevents any real concern in the audience about whether they live or die.

The Two Jakes (1990)

<><><><><><><><><><><><><><><><><><><><><>

Editor's note: Strangely neglected sequel to *Chinatown*. "Does it ever go away?" "What's that?" "The past."

<><><><><><><><><><><><><><><><><><><><><>

Times review by Geoff Brown, November 21 1991

This is the long-planned sequel to *Chinatown*, which entranced in the mid-Seventies with its bizarre mix of murder, sex and duplicity in pre-war Los Angeles. Yet precise memories of even the best films fade, and many audiences will be struggling to link up the two stories. As Jack Nicholson wearily observes, reprising his character of private eye Jake Gittes, "It was a long time ago." Nicholson also directs: a job once slated for scriptwriter Robert Towne. There are some odd shots (who else has given us a camera's eye view from inside a golf-course hole?); but most of the director's energy seems taken with assembling mood and decor. As a thriller, *The Two Jakes* proves impossible to follow; as an exercise in retro style, it glows with sullen beauty. Forties suits, ties, two-tone shoes: everything is in place, bathed in hard-edged gloom. More to the point are the pylons, the oil derricks and the wire recorder used to catch incriminating evidence: we are almost given a documentary on its workings.

Harvey Keitel plays the other Jake, a real-estate developer caught in a *crime passionnel*, Madeleine Stowe is a suspiciously gleeful widow. The plot gets nowhere sensible, but there are three earthquake tremors, quirks galore and period songs. Something for everyone, except those expecting another *Chinatown*.

The Brothers (1947)

Editor's note: Melodrama set on a Scottish island where wrong-doers are sent bobbing out into the ocean, tied up with floats and a fish on their head, which will attract a seabird to dive down and pierce fish and skull together. It is pretty dark.

Not reviewed.

Max Manus (2008)

Editor's note: True story of a Norwegian resistance leader, whose men are killed, but he keeps living, **battling the Germans and his own demons, including a growing sense of "survival guilt".**

Times review by James Christopher, June 4 2009

The true-story shelf in the Second World War film library is not exactly bristling with tales of heroic Norwegian resistance. The country capitulated within two months of being invaded by the Nazis. So this overdue homage to *Max Manus: Man of War* – a handsome, red-haired resistance fighter who attached limpet mines to German supply ships in Oslo – is a powerful surprise.

Joachim Rønning and Espen Sandberg's raw epic has broken all sorts of local box-office records. There is no mystery as to why. The emotive punch of the film is perfectly tailored to the hazy facts. Manus is a national treasure. He defies the Gestapo by diving through the window of his fourth-floor flat when they discover a crate of dynamite under his bed.

"What kind of idiot hides explosives under his bed?" a Nazi officer asks. The better question surely is what kind of idiot dives off the top of an apartment block?

That Manus survives is a black existential joke. His early heroics unfold in flashbacks while he is lying comatose on a hospital bed. There is frightening footage of hand-to-hand combat with Soviet soldiers in snowy Finland where blood splashes across the camera lens.

The bleak magic of the film is Manus's uncanny luck, his ability to stay alive. His pipe-smoking chums from the *Chariots of Fire* school of guerrilla resistance are not so lucky. But the entire, fitfully interesting point of the film is watching Manus's mind splinter into bits and pieces. Aksel Hennie plays the conflicted hero as if possessed by the spirits of both Jekyll and Hyde. He is a wicked charmer on his boozy nights off and a guilty monster when it all goes wrong.

Without Limits (1998)

Editor's note: The story of Steve Prefontaine, who was Jimmy Dean for a generation of runners. "He gave it everything he had from start to finish," says Donald Sutherland. "He never ran any other way." A philosophy not just for running, but for life.

Times review by James
Christopher, June 3 1999

In *Without Limits*, Donald Sutherland re-emerges as a white-haired coach, Bill Bowerman, to nurse the 1970s American running legend, Steve Prefontaine, to one of the great track showdowns of the 1972 Munich Olympics. Robert Towne's sentimental period piece, the second such homage to Prefontaine, who died in a car crash at the age of 24, boils down to a battle of egos between Billy Crudup's insufferably arrogant track star and Sutherland's wily timekeeper. With his floppy David Beckham haircut, massive sideburns and aerodynamic collars, Crudup wafts through the film like an animated advert for Old Spice. Sutherland steals the podium with his coy smiles, icy eyes and little disgruntled twists of the neck. The slow-motion track sequences are psychological masterpieces, which is more than can be said for the rest of this slushy piece of showboating for the Good Old US of A.

The Last Sunset (1961)

Editor's note: Outlaw Kirk Douglas turns up on the doorstep of an old flame and discovers she now has a husband and grown-up daughter. This is nothing less than a full-blown Greek tragedy in a Wild West setting.

Unbylined review, July 28 1961

The sun has risen and set on a thousand Westerns no better and no worse than the specimen bearing the title *The Last Sunset*. Mr Kirk Douglas, lean and (almost) saturnine, is the lone rider with a past, and he dresses in black. Mr Rock Hudson, frank and fresh of face, is the man with a warrant for his arrest; he sports something lighter in the matter of shirts and scarves. The warrant, however, can only be served in Texas, and meanwhile there are cattle to be driven there from Mexico and much happens between the two men before the river, literal and metaphorical, is reached and crossed. Miss Dorothy Malone adds to the complications, and there is an entirely delightful performance on the part of Miss Carol Lynley as her daughter.

TOP 100 COUNTDOWN

20 – *THE WIZARD OF OZ*
(Victor Fleming, 1939)

The central scandal of *The Wizard of Oz*, the primal conceit, and the reason that it remains so resonant and so heartbreaking, is that the movie's beloved mantra, "There's no place like home", is revealed to be a lie. For Judy Garland's Dorothy leaves the grim grey drabness of Kansas for the musical multicoloured pleasure of Oz and there forges relationships, defeats her nemesis, and becomes a woman. Her return to Kansas in the film's finale may have us weeping with delight, but in it lies the sad recognition that this return to childhood and to the myth of home is perhaps the greatest fantasy of all.

Kevin Maher

19 – *THE EXORCIST*
(William Friedkin, 1973)

Friedkin's controversial masterpiece about the exorcism of a 13-year-old girl is the most toxic and disturbing horror movie yet made. Never mind the pea-soup vomit, Linda Blair's revolving head, or the famous refrigerated bedroom set. It is the sickening feeling of invasion, and the ceding of psychological control to a malevolent other, that freaked out an entire generation. There were ambulances outside cinemas in Dublin when the film opened, and spiritually there still are. Paul Schrader, the director who filmed *Dominion*, the prequel to *The Exorcist*, put it thus: "The metaphor is extraordinary: God and the Devil in the same room arguing over the body of a 13-year-old girl. It doesn't come much purer than that."

James Christopher

18 – *DON'T LOOK NOW*
(Nicolas Roeg, 1973)

It is impossible to pin down exactly why Roeg's masterpiece is so effective. Every viewing of this seminal ghost story, adapted from a Daphne du Maurier novella, yields some new and troubling thought. After their daughter drowns, John and Laura Baxter (Donald Sutherland and Julie Christie) take a working trip to Venice in an attempt to glue back their marriage. There's an extraordinary conflation of contrary images and emotions: the drab beauty of a wintry Venice; the inexplicable sense of loss; the intense and lonely sex; and the dribble of blood across a cracked photographic slide. One of the most haunting and enigmatic riddles in the history of cinema.

James Christopher

17 – *ANNIE HALL*
(Woody Allen, 1977)

Seven movies in, and Woody Allen finally hits his stride in a witty, intellectual and hugely cinematic comedy of near perfection. The multiple Oscar-winning *Annie Hall* revealed the tragic romantic in Allen, detailing the demise of his fictional relationship with the titular kooky soul-mate, played by Diane Keaton (then Allen's real-life partner). It also showed Allen the auteur at his most audacious, boldly intercutting the romantic action with direct addresses to camera, animated sequences, split screen, comedy subtitles and a game cameo from Marshall McLuhan, who helpfully silences a pontificating Fellini fan in a downtown cinema queue – Allen then turns to camera and shrugs, "Boy, if only life were like this!"

Kevin Maher

16 – *METROPOLIS*
(Fritz Lang, 1927)

For its scale and ambition alone, this silent film has earned its place on any list of classic movies. Lang's dystopian science-fiction picture employed more than 37,000 extras, took two years to shoot and nearly bankrupted its production company. The tragedy is that, despite meticulous restoration, modern audiences will never get to see the film as Lang intended as a quarter of it is lost forever. The design of the film is exceptional. The towering art deco skyscrapers – inspired, it is said, by Lang's first view of Manhattan – became the blueprint for futuristic cityscapes for decades to come.

Wendy Ide

15 – *APOCALYPSE NOW*
(Francis Ford Coppola, 1979)

The making of this astonishing movie – recorded in the documentary *Hearts of Darkness* – was almost as insane as the war itself. The result is the greatest war movie yet made. Martin Sheen's unlisted mission "to terminate with extreme prejudice" a mythic American colonel (Marlon Brando), who has turned psycho in Cambodia, owes as much to Dante and the Doors as it does to Joseph Conrad. The film is defined by its surreal set-pieces, most memorably the dawn helicopter attack on a Vietcong village so Robert Duvall's nutty Texan can go surfing. The terrific power of the scene lies in its absurd contradictions, and the fact that Sheen can barely believe what's happening in front of his eyes.

James Christopher

14 – *THE JUNGLE BOOK*
(Wolfgang Reitherman, 1967)

Disney's classic cartoon uses the character names, but otherwise bears little resemblance to the 1894 collection of Rudyard Kipling stories that inspired it. Kipling's widow was reportedly aghast at the pronunciation of Mowgli used in the film; her late husband had always pronounced it as Mau-glee. The star is undoubtedly Baloo the bear, voiced by Phil Harris, a big-band leader turned comedian whose voice would appear in Disney's later films *The Aristocats* and *Robin Hood*. The song

'The Bare Necessities' was nominated for an Oscar, but lost out to 'Talk to the Animals' from *Doctor Dolittle*.

Nigel Kendall

13 - *2001: A SPACE ODYSSEY* (Stanley Kubrick, 1968)

The greatest piece of quasi-mystical Art House sci-fi pop philosophy, *2001* is Kubrick's Promethean attempt to solve the riddle of man's place in the cosmos. Naturally, given the ambitious remit, this involves an epic, oblique journey from pre-Neanderthal crazy apes to a modern moon-base to the outer orbit of Jupiter and beyond, to a trippy multicoloured wormhole sequence that ends in a space-bedroom at the end of the universe. And all along the movie asks such questions as: "What is the nature of the black slab? Is man primarily destructive? Will technology set us free?" That Kubrick avoids answering these questions explicitly is part of the movie's provocative project and, ultimately, its genius.

Kevin Maher

12 - *ALIEN* (Ridley Scott, 1979)

It's impossible to exaggerate the influence Ridley Scott's movie has had on the science fiction genre. Dan O'Bannon's script, about an industrial mining ship that lands on a blasted planet, is the most spare and perfect tin-can horror ever written. The crew discover the ghostly skeletal shell of a spaceship, and a few weird pods, but think little of it until a screaming sausage erupts out of John Hurt's chest during supper. The downbeat pleasure of the film is the palpable lack of love or sophistication among this blue-collar crew. Their view of space travel is just another grubby means of getting paid.

James Christopher

11 - *THE SOUND OF MUSIC* (Robert Wise, 1965)

Despite the hipster cynicism that sees the film as extreme kitsch, this transparent tale of a guileless governess (Julie Andrews) who melts the heart of a martinet widower (Christopher Plummer), still commands a guttural draw. Whether it's Plummer's withdrawn Captain Von Trapp unexpectedly serenading his seven children with the title track, or his moist-eyed performance of Edelweiss in the finale, this is a film of simple yet big ideas – chiefly the need for forgiveness and the transformative power of, well, love.

Kevin Maher

PERSONAL CHOICE

SIX OF THE BEST

FILMS YOU WILL NEVER SEE

Film writer Simon Braund selects six of the greatest-sounding films that never ended up making it to the screen

November 30 2013

According to the proverb, man makes plans and God laughs. If that's true, he must piss himself whenever he casts an eye over the movie business. There are few film-makers who do not know the agony of embarking on a project, brimming with optimism and the thrill of creative endeavour, only to watch, with escalating frustration and dismay, as their baby sinks into the mire.

When you consider the multitude of elements that must fall into place before a film comes to fruition – scheduling cast and crew, finding locations, securing financing, striking distribution deals, ensuring adequate craft services and so on – it's a wonder that any make it to the screen at all. Many don't, of course, and it's not just the more vulnerable indie fare that falls by the wayside. Major studio movies can hit the buffers too, often after much money has been spent and many vast egos engaged. For proof of that, see Arnold Schwarzenegger's medieval epic *Crusade*, or Stanley Kubrick's monumental biopic of *Napoleon*. Actually you can't …

Nor can talent or prestige guarantee to keep the green light burning. The latter part of Orson Welles's career (i.e. the vast majority of it) consists almost entirely of grand schemes that stubbornly failed to get off the ground, chief among them his treasured adaptation of *Don Quixote*. Spielberg, Hitchcock, Coppola, even Fellini and Sergei Eisenstein have all seen potential masterpieces disappear into the gaping maw of Development Hell, never to be seen again.

Since the list of unmade movies grows ever longer, the six here are only the very tip of a prodigious iceberg. An iceberg made, not of ice, but of thwarted ambition, bloody-minded accountancy and a whole load of tantalizing what ifs.

Dune

Following the success of his bonkers Western *El Topo* (1970), the Chilean director Alejandro Jodorowsky dived into an adaptation of Frank Herbert's sci-fi classic. Pink Floyd were set to provide the score, H.R. Giger was on board as designer and the cast list included Salvador Dalí, Mick Jagger, Gloria Swanson and Orson Welles. Sadly, but somewhat inevitably, it sank under the weight of its own grandiose ambition.

Napoleon

Having amassed a mountain of Napoleonic artefacts and written a script the size of a carpet samples catalogue, Stanley Kubrick abandoned his sweeping Bonaparte biopic in the face of spiralling costs and the poor box-office performance of Sergey Bondarchuk's *Waterloo*.

Batman Year One

Darren Aronofsky's vision of the Caped Crusader as an adolescent street punk wielding an arsenal of jerry-built gadgets and driving a Batmobile fashioned from a beaten-up limo was certainly bold. Prohibitively so, as it turned out.

Crusade

Casting Muslims as the good guys and Christian knights as rampaging psychos, Paul Verhoeven and Arnold Schwarzenegger's hyper-violent historical epic could have been a sensation, especially at the time of the first Gulf War. A budget north of $125 million put the chain mail hat on it.

Gladiator 2

Rocker and screenwriter Nick Cave's audacious script resurrected Maximus as an eternal warrior, transported through time from Ancient Rome to the Western Front to the killing fields of Bosnia. Russell Crowe and Ridley Scott were keen; a timid Warner Bros gave it the thumbs down.

Giraffes on Horseback Salads

Salvador Dalí considered the Marx Brothers to be true surrealists. In 1934 he penned a script for them. It featured giraffes on fire sporting gasmasks, Harpo harvesting dwarves in a butterfly net and Chico playing piano in a diving suit. "It wouldn't play" was Groucho's succinct verdict.

The Greatest Movies You'll Never See, edited by Simon Braund, is published by Aurum, £20.

CLASSIC CINEMA

A HERITAGE AND ITS HISTORY

The Godfather

Review by John Russell Taylor,
August 22 1972

It is probably a misfortune that *The Godfather* is now certain to make more money than any other film in the history of the cinema (including *Gone with the Wind*). Not, of course, for the makers, who must be justifiably delighted, but for us, or those of us who are only getting to see it now, amid all the dazzling pre-publicity and faced with four major West End cinemas, where it is simultaneously showing, to choose from.

For how could any film quite live up to all that? Is it the greatest film ever made? No, of course it isn't, not by a long way. But it is very good, solid, entertaining – like *Airport*, I was going to say. As a matter of fact it is a lot better than *Airport*, but that should give you a rough idea. It is exactly the kind of holding, not too demanding entertainment you would love to drop into by chance and see at your local. And since there are so few these days it is no wonder that those that do come out make a mint.

It is no secret that the film is about the inner workings of the Mafia in New York. Not that anyone in the film actually uses the dread word, ever. But all the characters are Italian-American, all are involved one way or another in crime,

and the word "family" clearly has a far wider connotation than merely brothers and sisters and uncles and aunts. The central drama, though, is literally as well as metaphorically a family affair. The Corleone family are ruled over firmly but reasonably, by Don Vito (Marlon Brando), the father of three sons and one daughter, plus an adopted son who is actually German-Irish. And all of them are connected somehow with the family business, even the youngest, Michael (Al Pacino), who when we first see him is a fresh-faced young soldier who seems likely to make his escape, marry his crisp, WASP-ish girlfriend and perhaps become a respectable academic or something of the sort.

Of course, he doesn't. The film, like Mario Puzo's best-seller on which it is based, stays close enough to the familiar conventions of the gangster movie for us to be sure from the start that the mild innocent with vaguely idealistic instincts is bound to end up as the most ruthless of them all. In that respect the plot holds few surprises. But then, the plot is really only a framework for the real matter of the subject, which is a demonstration of how the Mafia works. The very opening scene gives some indication, and some indication, too, of the film's ambiguous attitude to its characters and situations. During his daughter's wedding reception Don Vito receives a petitioner, an undertaker whose daughter has been raped and brutalized, and then has seen the culprits let go free on a suspended sentence (unlikely, surely, in 1945?). He wants justice. And gets it – at the cost of promising a favour in return at some future date.

Already the implication is there that the "family" has its consoling aspect, almost a necessary corrective to the lapses of the official system. The next job too has this implication. An entertainer in the circle has been denied a role in a film which will put him back on top (no prizes for guessing the factual origins of this incident), and the family leans on the studio head to make sure he gets it. But again, everyone is agreed that he is ideal casting, and it is only personal spite which prevents him from being given the role at once. Again, a wrong is righted, if in a rather brutal fashion. Perhaps the key indication of attitude comes in a scene later on when Michael's girlfriend objects to the line of business he is in. He replies that really the family functions like the police and politics. She accuses him of being naive; after all, policemen and politicians don't have people killed. He replies, "Now who's being naive?"

Well, who says that gangster films ought to take a critical attitude to their subject, anyway? Just on a documentary level *The Godfather* is fascinating – cunningly constructed to lead us into the workings of the organization, show us exactly how it is put together. And then, once we have got the idea, comes the action half of the film, vividly illustrating just how the rival families cut one another down, how the business is modified and diversified in answer to the changing conditions of society (should the family dabble in drug distribution, for instance, and if it has to, can it stick to "clean" drugs for consenting adults?).

The film is long – almost three hours – and manages never to be boring. Though for those who loved *You're a Big Boy Now* and *Finian's Rainbow*, it is perhaps a little disappointing and square from director Francis Ford Coppola, it is a stunningly professional piece of work. Some of the 1940s period detail may give one pause – the hair is nearly always wrong, for instance – but otherwise it looks good, is confidently paced and excellently acted. Brando is perhaps a little too obviously giving a performance, but within those limits he is good. And the film is stolen by Al Pacino, who really has the central role (though it only gradually emerges that this is so) and gives a beautifully controlled picture of Michael's development from innocent to implacable godfather in place of his own father. It is a film everyone will want to see, and few find disappointing. But try to forget all the ballyhoo before you see it, just in case.

ALL IN THE FAMILY

The Godfather Part II

Review by Philip French,
May 16 1975

Few movie sequels are as good as the films they follow and even fewer have about them the air of necessity. Francis Ford Coppola's *The Godfather Part II* is among the rare exceptions. *The Godfather* traced the story of the Corleone family from just after the Second World War to the early 1950s when Michael (Al Pacino) reluctantly succeeded the founding father, Vito (Marlon Brando), as head of the criminal empire he had created. Part II, also carved by Coppola and Mario Puzo from the latter's novel, cuts back and forth between two parallel stories that simultaneously push the original story farther forward in time and dig deeper into its roots.

The first takes Vito from his orphaning in a Sicilian Mafia vendetta in 1901 at the age of nine, through his lone emigration to America, his gradual entry into a life of crime in New York's Italian ghetto, and concludes with him as a well-established gang boss and paterfamilias returning to Sicily to revenge the death of his mother, father and brother. The second strand of the narrative focuses upon his son Michael from 1958 into the early Sixties – the consolidation of his empire through shrewd business deals and murder, the threat of his wife to quit, the pressures from Senate investigatory committees, the constant fear of betrayal and exposure. At the end Michael is trapped, as his father was before him, by a web of obligations, and he looks back to the days after Pearl Harbour when he briefly thought he had a chance to break away and plan his own future.

Both are stories of corruption, fatalistically observed, in which the evil is concealed from its perpetrators and victims by a cloak of honour, benevolence and social ambition. We glimpse only rarely the sources of their tainted money – the brothels, the casinos, the illegal bookmaking joint, the heroin pushers and their adolescent victims, the petty crooks collecting protection money, the Mafia killers settling contracts. What we mostly see are the boardroom discussions, the whispered conversations in elegant, sepulchral interiors. A gently murmured "I'd be disappointed" can be a sentence of death, as menacing in context as that euphemistic *Godfather* phrase that has now entered the language: "I made him an offer he couldn't refuse." Only when the sanctity of the home and family is breached are angry voices raised. What really outrages Michael Corleone about an assassination attempt is less that the hail of bullets might have killed him than the fact that his wife and children were around him at the time.

As with the earlier film, Coppola has a marvellous capacity to animate a large crowded scene and keep it going while locating individual dramas within it. One thinks especially of Vito's arrival at Ellis Island; a religious festival in New York's "Little Italy" during which Vito stalks his first murder victim; a vast gathering for Michael's son's first communion at the family's fortified Nevada compound, with the "Sierra Boys Choir" in a bandstand beside Lake Tahoe serenading the philanthropic Mafia boss as "Mr Wonderful"; an opulent New Year's Eve ball in Batista's loathsome, Mafia-ridden Havana, where the Corleone mob represent "tourist and leisure interests" – it's 1958 and Coppola makes pretty clear that this is the last fling before Castro's cleansing fire. The acting of the large cast is uniformly excellent, with Robert De Niro confirming the immense promise of last year's *Mean Streets* with his splendid performance as the proud, lethally controlled Vito, subtly suggesting Brando's ageing godfather to come. As the Jewish racket-boss Hymie Roth, Lee Strasberg puts in a telling appearance, but his influence is also found throughout the picture in the Method style of acting from his Actors' Studio that most of the performers adopt.

The Godfather Part II is a very good film, too long perhaps at three hours and twenty minutes, though my attention rarely flagged. At its best the picture has the expansive quality of a novel, and Coppola uses his elbow room to probe and explore rather than to nudge. Ultimately the film is a kind of epic, an ironic one to be sure, mocking as it does the American Dream, and a dubious one perhaps, if we are seduced into accepting its central characters as tragic heroes.

MURDERING FOR MONEY IN THE CATHEDRAL

The Godfather Part III

Review by Geoff Brown,
March 7 1991

At a press conference with Francis Ford Coppola during the recent Berlin Film Festival, one journalist shattered the mood of intellectual reverence: "How much money will you be earning with *The Godfather Part III*?" "Many millions," the director replied; "enough to pay off my debts." Indeed, as Coppola's epic trundles waywardly over the screen, like a lavishly decorated Indian elephant

which has mislaid its procession, it is hard to resist the thought that financial, rather than artistic, necessity brought *The Godfather Part III* into being.

Yet there is one fierce bond between Coppola and the *Godfather* saga's main character, Michael Corleone (played, as before, by Al Pacino). They are both weighed down by their past. Michael is haunted by family skeletons soaked in blood – the Mafia killings he arranged or executed. Coppola carries the shackles of debts first incurred during his failed Las Vegas romance *One From the Heart*, ten years ago: thanks to interest charges and lawyers' machinations, a $3 million (£1.6 million) loan from a developer has swelled to three times that amount, and brought him near bankruptcy. The past looms large for Coppola in a different sense: aside from *Apocalypse Now*, none of his work since the first two *Godfather* films has achieved the same appeal and approbation. He has seemed a director without a rudder, lurching between journeyman assignments and personal projects, such as *Tucker*, that bemused rather than entertained.

In *The Godfather Part III*, largely filmed at the Cinecitta studios in Rome, Coppola tries desperately to get back on course, without quite succeeding. The story, devised with Mario Puzo, takes a 20-year leap from the concluding events of the first, brilliant, sequel. It is 1979: Michael continues to rule the Corleone dynasty, his brow furrowed with worry over his efforts to leave the next generation a legitimate business empire. There are three children: Vincent, illegitimate son of his late brother Sonny, ushered into Michael's employ; a daughter, Mary, who enjoys a secret love affair with Vincent; and the soft-hearted Anthony, who yearns for a career in opera.

Each person carries their parcel of plot, yet the film – two hours and 40 minutes in length – never seems in a hurry to unwrap them; indeed, some characters, like Bridget Fonda's photojournalist, are mysteriously dumped after a few scenes. Instead, Coppola lingers indulgently over clan gatherings, rich in Catholic clergy and Italian-American bonhomie, or brooding discussions about ethics and methods in dark-panelled rooms. Action is relegated to sudden lurches (Vincent biting a colleague's ear, a helicopter raid on a high-rise Mob meeting) or the grandiose finale, where four murders are fiendishly intercut with Anthony's debut in *Cavalleria rusticana*.

Working alongside *Godfather* veterans such as cameraman Gordon Willis and production designer Dean Tavoularis, Coppola ensures a high visual sheen: the opera finale, set in Sicily, shimmers with special audacity. Yet there is no fresh air by this point in the saga, the Corleones move in a hermetic landscape of sombre opulence with little meaning beyond the *Godfather* films themselves. Glimpses of the world outside enter when Michael deals with an affiliated partner of the Vatican Bank; but memories of the Banco Ambrosiano business and other pontifical mysteries are quickly dissipated. In the studied flamboyance of Coppola's style, the sharp prick of reality eludes this film entirely.

Al Pacino, released from the deep freeze that gripped Michael Corleone in *Part II*, moves through his scenes with haggard aplomb, though he scarcely seems like someone in his sixties. The make-up artistes are even kinder to Talia Shire (the family matriarch) and Diane Keaton (Michael's ex-wife) – two other troupers from the earlier films – but they convince through sheer force of acting. The one weak link in the cast's long chain is Coppola's own daughter Sofia, a late and ill-advised replacement for Winona Ryder in the part of the love-stricken Mary. From her looks and speech, she seems to have slotted in her scenes during a hard day on the California shopping malls; the entire love affair between Mary and Vincent (an agreeably smouldering Andy Garcia) is drained of resonance.

During shooting, Coppola predicted the film would be "the cathedral of *Godfather* movies". It can boast a cathedral's size, plus a scattering of gargoyles. But a cathedral's soul is missing – lost in the stampede to rekindle old magic and recapture Coppola's grand achievements of 20 years ago.

WORST FILMS

THE WORST OF HOLLYWOOD

Films on TV

By Peter Waymark,
October 22 1983

The premise behind Channel 4's "The Worst of Hollywood" season, which starts tonight, is that there are some films which are so bad that they thereby become enjoyable. Instead of being put off by wooden acting, dreadful dialogue and cheap sets, we can actually relish them.

Heading the parade of flops is a science fiction piece *Plan 9 from Outer Space*, which was directed by one Edward D Wood Junior in 1956. In the United States it has won the Golden Turkey Award as the "worst film of all time", while for this, and similar efforts, the hapless Wood has received the accolade of "worst director".

Plan 9 from Outer Space might never have been resurrected from well-deserved obscurity had not its star been one of the best-known Hollywood names, the Hungarian-born former stage actor who rose to fame as the sound film's first Dracula, Bela Lugosi.

By the 1950s, however, Lugosi's career was on the slide. In 1952 he came to Britain for an extraordinary picture called *Mother Riley Meets the Vampire*, and he first appeared for Wood in something called *Glen or Glenda?* with the director himself playing a transvestite.

In 1955 Wood and Lugosi were reunited for *Bride of the Monster* and in the following year they embarked upon what proved to be their final collaboration, *Plan 9 from Outer Space*. Hardly had shooting begun than, on August 6, 1956, Lugosi died. But Wood was not one to let so trivial a setback get in its way.

He carried on with the film, using an unemployed chiropractor to double for the dead star. Not only was the substitute taller, however, but he bore so little facial resemblance to Lugosi that he was obliged to keep a cloak over his face while on camera. Lugosi's contribution amounts to no more than two minutes of screen time, though he was still given top billing.

Apart from Lugosi the cast includes a 28-stone former professional wrestler called Tor Johnson, whose long career in low-budget shockers reached its apogee when he took the name part in *The Beast of Yucca Flats* in 1961.

The budget for *Plan 9* was apparently $800, which goes a long way towards explaining the frugality of the special effects. The flying saucers, for instance, are paper plates.

Whether all this is worth staying up into the small hours for will depend on whether we agree with the American fan magazine's assertion that the film "raises rank amateurism to the level of high comic art". If we do, we can look forward with keen anticipation to other such skeletons from the vaults as *Godzilla Versus the Smog Monster*, *They Saved Hitler's Brain* and *Santa Claus Conquers the Martians*.

LOSER – AND STILL CHAMPION

Geoff Brown on *Ed Wood*, the tale of a man who thought he was a great director, told by one who is

Review, May 25 1995

Perfect, print it! So beams film director Edward D Wood Jr as the 4001b Tor Johnson, a man once described as more living prop than actor, bangs into a door frame in a studio the size of a small garage. So another scene is popped in the can for *Bride of the Atom*, one of the Z-grade follies of the man anointed the world's worst director; and another delightful moment in Tim Burton's wonderful biography *Ed Wood*.

Wood's enraptured response to the business of making his movies serves as one of the film's running jokes. While bad actors struggle to spit out his clumsy dialogue, he mouths the lines reverently, as though they were Shakespeare. The joke is never cheap, never at Wood's expense: Burton and his lead actor Johnny Depp paint an immensely endearing picture of a sweet-natured man with an interesting taste for high heels and angora sweaters, blissfully ignorant of his lack of talent and determined to make his movies his way.

Undoubtedly this is a romantic conception of Wood, a director who toiled in deserved obscurity during the 1950s, declined into pornography and died in 1978, just too late to enjoy his slow ascent to cult status. Burton hides the more sordid facts. He prefers to view Wood as a cock-eyed visionary, a man who believes himself blood brother to Orson Welles, not a merchant of sleaze with a genius for ineptitude. Wood seems equally blood brother to Burton himself: you can feel the bizarre creator of *Edward Scissorhands* reaching out to caress this misfit from the industry's shadows.

Burton's homage is awesomely reverent and exact, and shot, of course, in authentic black-and-white. Here is the set from *Plan 9 from Outer Space* (the master's worst, or best, achievement): mist, wobbly gravestone and all. Here are the famous mismatched lighting and the goofy dialogue, flatly enunciated. But *Ed Wood* does more than tickle a film buff's fancy with fond re-creations and in-jokes. It also triggers unexpected, powerful emotions. The reason lies with the pride and glory of Wood's troupe, Bela Lugosi, magnificently incarnated by Martin Landau. Wood, ever star-struck, befriends the former Dracula, and shepherds him through morphine addiction, hospital treatment and the loss of his unemployment cheques. Visibly decrepit, and liable to froth at the slightest mention of Boris Karloff, Lugosi still clings to his dignity, as he clings, incongruously, to two pet chihuahuas.

TOP 100 COUNTDOWN

10 – *THE GODFATHER* (Francis Ford Coppola, 1972)

Nobody makes fully blown mobster movies like Francis Ford Coppola. They started with Brando and Pacino as Corleone father and son in the original *Godfather*, with the latter a revelation as the reluctant mobster enforcing the family tradition. In *The Godfather: Part II*, Pacino's Michael is still concerned with legitimacy, while Brando's Don is given a sprawling back story and a younger self in Robert De Niro. The film is longer than the first, and regarded as the best of the series. *The Godfather: Part III*, often derided, has another magnetic turn from Pacino, and, most importantly, reveals that the story is utterly incomplete without it.

Kevin Maher

9 – *ETERNAL SUNSHINE OF THE SPOTLESS MIND* (Michel Gondry, 2004)

It should never have been this good. The story of an introspective New Yorker, Joel (Jim Carrey), who erases his memories of a recent doomed romance with the irascible Clementine (Kate Winslet) emerged from a smart yet solipsistic school of tricksy movies that included *Being John Malkovich* and *Adaptation*. *Eternal Sunshine* took this same innovation, with non-linear narrative and berserker-style visual storytelling, and injected it with the agony and ecstasy of genuine human relationships. The result was a magnificent pairing in Winslet and Carrey, who transformed Clem and Joel's chemistry into a relationship as painfully touching as it was tragic.

Kevin Maher

10 May 2001. Francis Ford Coppola in Cannes. (Andre Camara)

8 - *SUNSET BOULEVARD* (Billy Wilder, 1950)

Wilder turns his razor-blade cynicism onto a subject close to home – Hollywood – and reveals it as a relentless machine that digests and discards its stars. It's a brilliantly cold-hearted piece of film-making, featuring several cruelly apposite pieces of casting. Forgotten silent star Norma Desmond was played by Gloria Swanson, whose career had stalled in the 1930s. Her butler was played by Eric von Stroheim, the silent-movie director who worked with Swanson on *Queen Kelly* in 1929. Screenwriter Joe Gillis is played by William Holden. The film's longevity is evident in Norma's endlessly quotable, magnificently deluded line: "I'm still big. It's the films that got small."

Wendy Ide

7 - *KES* (Ken Loach, 1969)

This beautifully judged adaptation of a novel by Barry Hines is never permitted to lapse into sentimentality or "it's grim oop North" clichés. Instead, the story of a lad from Barnsley who escapes the bullying of his older brother, the sardonic indifference of his teachers and the depressing inevitability of his future by training a kestrel is a clear-eyed portrait of a boy with few options and the bird that represents hope for him. The naturalistic performances are universally impressive but it's the teenaged David Bradley, who won the central role of Billy at an open audition, who dominates the film. He later said that he was more excited by the free food and drink at the audition than the role itself.

Wendy Ide

6 - *VERTIGO* (Alfred Hitchcock, 1958)

A disappointment on its original release, described as tedious and overlong, Hitchcock's *Vertigo* has grown in stature over time and has become, ironically, easily his best feature. It is, of course, a deeply creepy film, and the story of an obsessive relationship between a neurasthenic detective (James Stewart) and a suicidal blonde (Kim Novak) was hardly going to appeal to a contemporary audience expecting a cutesy *Catch a Thief* redux. Yet *Vertigo* gets more eerily modern as the years progress. When, for instance, Stewart's Scottie witnesses the "death" of his new lover, Novak's equally fragile Madeleine, he has a complete nervous breakdown. When he meets Judy (Novak again) her low-grade doppelganger (she has bad lipstick and hairy eyebrows), his bullying attempts to remake her in Madeleine's likeness cut to the heart of Hitchcock's project. Thus the film, it is said, is the director's most autobiographical, and speaks of his compulsive desire for, and brutish treatment of, icy blonde women. Yet it's also a testament to an image-obsessed culture that believes, like ours, in re-creating and re-moulding to create an archetype that doesn't exist – a culture, like Scottie, that has fallen completely for the allure of fantasy over reality.

Kevin Maher

5 - *THE SHINING*
(Stanley Kubrick, 1980)

The supernatural and the precarious nature of sanity are the themes explored in Stanley Kubrick's outstanding horror movie. Adapted from a novel by Stephen King, the film stars Jack Nicholson as former schoolteacher turned aspiring writer Jack Torrance and Shelley Duval as his wife Wendy. Jack has taken a job as a winter caretaker at the Overlook Hotel, where he and his family will be snowed in for several months. His son, Danny, senses that something is amiss at the hotel — a feeling confirmed by the hotel chef Dick Hallorann (Scatman Crothers), who shares Danny's telepathic gift. Danny's fears are well-founded. Before long his dad is conversing with the dead and pursuing his mother with an axe. Kubrick's perfectionism ensured that it wasn't the easiest film to make: he allegedly demanded 127 takes from Shelley Duvall in one scene, and reduced the 69-year-old Crothers to tears. But the film that resulted is one of the scariest yet made.

Wendy Ide

4 - *CHINATOWN*
(Roman Polanski, 1974)

This ultra-stylish thriller was the last film that its director Polanski made in the United States before his exile to Europe. By all accounts, *Chinatown* was not the easiest of shoots. Polanski apparently argued violently with both his leads. The movie truism that the more difficult the production, the better the film would seem to hold true. It is a masterful piece of work: superbly crafted and bleakly brilliant, it was one of the films that defined the golden era of Hollywood of the 1970s. Jack Nicholson plays small-time private detective Jake Gittes, Faye Dunaway plays Evelyn Mulwray, the mysterious blonde who hires him to investigate whether her husband is guilty of infidelity. The role of Evelyn was originally destined for Ali MacGraw, until she had the temerity to divorce the film's producer, Robert Evans, for Steve McQueen. It's evocatively set in the sun-baked Los Angeles of 1937, a city in the middle of a crippling drought where corruption is rife and nobody is trustworthy.

Wendy Ide

3 - *ET: The Extra Terrestrial*
(Steven Spielberg, 1982)

It happened, according to movie lore, at the first Cannes Film Festival screening of *E.T.* Hundreds of hardened critics and cynical industry watchers were gradually melted to mush, and eventually even stood up and cheered when the bikes took flight in the third-act chase scene. They did this because they were responding to a movie that speaks not to cinephiles, to sci-fi fans or to popcorn munchers (though, in truth, it gamely addresses all three), but to a film that goes deeper than that. For this, at its most chromosomal, is the story of two lost children who find each other. Elliott (Henry Thomas) is emotionally broken and abandoned by his parents' divorce, just as ET is literally abandoned by the spaceship that flees the menacing approach of Keys (Peter Coyote). The friendship of Elliot and ET is thus forged of necessity. Their adventures – ET's housebound antics, the Halloween escape, the bicycle flying – are exquisitely told by Spielberg from an exclusively childlike point of view (the camera even hovers at kiddie head height). Their bond is thus the promise of healing plenitude and total commitment that addresses the child, abandoned or not, in all of us.

Kevin Maher

2 – THERE WILL BE BLOOD
(Paul Thomas Anderson, 2007)

Few films in recent years have made such an instant and dramatic impact as Anderson's towering yarn about crude oil and God. Fewer still have put their finger on such a mortally topical concern, which is why this melodrama, inspired by an Upton Sinclair novel, has secured such a lofty berth on our list. It's a stormy thriller about how oil turns a frontier hero into a monster, and Daniel Day-Lewis takes possession of the role like a demonic force of nature. The year is 1898, and women have yet to be invented in Texas. After years of bitter nothing, Day-Lewis's rake-thin, hard-as-nails prospector uncorks his first gusher and starts building an empire. By 1911 Daniel Plainview is a fully fledged tycoon, mopping up land from dirt-poor pilgrims with neither the tools, nor the nous, to dig their

own fortunes. His ghastly ambition only becomes apparent when he clashes spectacularly with a young, evangelical minister, Eli Sunday (Paul Dano), whose tiny parish sits on top of the biggest untapped reservoir in America. What makes Anderson's film such a magnificent watch is the quality of the hypocrisy. The failure of these two emblematic characters to square religion and greed is quite sublime, and alarmingly relevant.

James Christopher

1 – CASABLANCA
(Michael Curtiz, 1942)

Casablanca is the greatest romantic thriller yet painted on screen. No one could accuse Curtiz of minting high art, but does that honestly matter? Casablanca is shameless entertainment. It's not, as many would have it, a noble melodrama about a grumpy nightclub owner with a broken heart. It is a terrific comedy of bad Vichy manners with genuine twists of repulsion and fear. The Second World War is still in its ghastly pomp, and loyalties are bought and sold in this Moroccan stew like black market favours. Humphrey Bogart's Rick Blaine is a bastard with a broken heart. How broken becomes apparent when the girl who broke his heart in Paris (Ingrid Bergman) walks through the door with her new husband, Resistance leader Victor Laszlo (Paul Henreid). Rick has the only two plane tickets out of Casablanca – a pair of precious transit papers. According to the screenwriter, Howard Koch, no one had a clue whose names would be on the boarding passes until the very end of the chaotic shoot. With no certainty about the ending, the actors went into scalding scenes with their hearts on their sleeves. The emotional shorthand between the two leads resonates more with every viewing. The dry-eyed lack of sentiment is, of course, exactly what you would expect from cinema's most hard-boiled romantic.

James Christopher

CLASSIC CINEMA

Casablanca – the original review

Film of intrigue and adventure

Unbylined review (Dudley Carew), January 13 1943

Casablanca in the days before the allied occupation had obvious possibilities as the background of a film of intrigue and adventure, and the film which goes into the Regal and Warner cinemas next Friday has taken at least a reasonable percentage of its opportunities.

The place is given an elaborate setting. Money is plentiful, time is meaningless, life is cheap. French, German, Italian, American, and native rub uneasy shoulders and no man is to be trusted. Meanwhile the cafe lights are brilliant, negroes strum at the pianos, and the camera, lingering over the decorative and the exotic, seems to be waiting for Miss Marlene Dietrich. Actually Miss Ingrid Bergman, a very different type, is the heroine of a story which seeks – at times successfully – to avoid the commonplace by the laconic manner of its expression. She is the wife of one of the leaders of the underground movement against the Nazis, but she has the misfortune to be in love with Mr Humphrey Bogart, who, as the owner of a night club, gives his usual deliberately flat performance of the sentimentalist masquerading as the cynic.

The incidentals of the film, however, are to be preferred to the main issue of visas, arrests, and escapes. Mr Claude Rains, self-described as "a poor, corrupt official," slightly overplays his hand as a French chief of police, but Mr Peter Lorre disappears all too soon from his scene, Mr Sydney Greenstreet, fat, jovial, and utterly unscrupulous, has too small a part, Mr Dooley Wilson's performance as a negro pianist is memorable, and at moments *Casablanca* seems genuinely to be trying to give expression to the emotions of those colonial French who were left bewildered by the fall of their country but did not lose their faith.

CRICKET

The Final Test

Mr Rattigan's film about cricket

Unbylined review (it seems fitting that the final review should be by Dudley Carew), April 13 1953

The ultimate feeling left by *The Final Test* is one of deep admiration for the consummate cleverness of Mr Terence Rattigan as a playwright – *The Final Test* is a film, but the word is apposite and must stand.

Cricket is a game for the contemplative, and, as its literature shows, for the poetic. It reveals character, certainly, but through the medium of action on the field; it is blessed with both emotion and humour, yet, here again, these qualities belong to the actual pitch and are not easily transferable to stage or screen. And yet Mr Rattigan, who is a good cricketer himself, has so contrived that in the 90 minutes the film takes to run, character, emotion, humour, and the essence of the game itself shall have their innings, and in this he has been greatly helped by the director, Mr Anthony Asquith.

His story is cunningly thought out and the film gets off the mark in the first scene. Mr Rattigan has decreed that Sam Palmer – a batsman of Sutcliffe-Leyland calibre – shall be playing his last match for England against Australia at the Oval. Sam has a son, Reggie (Mr Ray Jackson), who has, however, no intention of following in his father's footsteps. Reggie writes poetry and hero-worships not Hutton – who, incidentally, has a not so very small part in the film and acts it admirably – but an advanced poet, Alexander Whitehead. Reggie, on the morning he should be watching his father play his last innings for England, goes instead to visit Whitehead only to find, of course, that Whitehead has no thoughts for anything but the Test match and, on hearing that Reggie has a spare ticket, rushes him to the Oval. Add to this neat contrivance the fact that Sam is in love with Cora (Miss Brenda Bruce) who is a barmaid and who, through her calling, can introduce on to the screen the solemn Englishness of a public-house crowd listening to a Test match on the wireless, and it will be realized just how clever Mr Rattigan has been.

◇◇◇◇◇◇◇◇◇◇◇◇◇◇◇◇◇◇◇◇◇◇◇◇◇◇◇

Editor's note: SPOILER ALERT – Sam was out for a duck.

◇◇◇◇◇◇◇◇◇◇◇◇◇◇◇◇◇◇◇◇◇◇◇◇◇◇◇

PRINCIPAL FILM REVIEWERS FOR *THE TIMES*

Albert Cookman

He began with *The Times* in 1925 as a Parliamentary reporter, but just a few years later was to claim the distinction of reviewing *The Jazz Singer*, the film generally acknowledged as the first "talkie" – though Cookman was hardly likely to have thought his review would end up in an anthology 100 years later. It can be difficult for critics to offer instant judgements, but Cookman hailed *Citizen Kane* as a work of art long before it was voted the best of all time in various polls. He served as the paper's drama critic from the 1940s to early 1960s.

Alan Clutton-Brock

Clutton-Brock was a distinguished essayist and art critic, in which capacity he served at *The Times* from the 1930s until the mid-1950s, with a break for war service. He was a trustee of the National Gallery and Slade Professor of Fine Art at Cambridge, though earlier in his career he also reviewed films, including *Gone with the Wind* and the Marx Brothers's debut.

Dudley Carew

A close friend of Evelyn Waugh from school days, Carew was a poet, novelist and cricket aficionado as well as being the main film critic at *The Times* for 20 years from the 1940s to early 1960s. His work appeared anonymously in the days before every single-paragraph contribution had an author credit. He joined *The Times* in 1930 and wrote cricket and football reports and leaders, as well as theatre, book and film reviews. He was officially appointed as Film Critic in 1945 and offered initial assessments of everything from *It's a Wonderful Life* through to *Dr. No* – some of which do now seem a little out of step with the current critical consensus. He retired in 1963 and died in 1981.

John Russell Taylor

Taylor began writing for *The Times* in the 1950s, mainly on theatre and television. He was the paper's film critic for a decade from 1963 to 1972, beginning in the period when reviews were unbylined, before seeing his name alongside his words in the second half of his tenure. After stepping down as film critic, he continued to write on art and film for the paper for several years. His numerous books include an authorised biography of Alfred Hitchcock.

David Robinson

Well-known and respected through-out the film world, Robinson was the paper's principal film critic for 20 years from the 1970s to the early 1990s, was the director of Edinburgh International Film Festival at the end of the 1980s into the 1990s, and was the official biographer of Charlie Chaplin. Officially he served as the paper's film critic from 1973 to 1992, though he continued to write on film for many years after that. Before coming to *The Times*, he wrote reviews for *Sight & Sound* magazine, the *Monthly Film Bulletin* and the *Financial Times*.

Geoff Brown

Brown worked alongside Robinson from the early 1980s onwards. More recently he has written about classical music for the paper. He has also contributed to many other publications and has written several books on film-related subjects.

James Christopher

Christopher wrote theatre and film reviews for *The Times* in the 1990s and became the paper's official film critic in 2003, a post he held for six years.

Kate Muir, Wendy Ide and Kevin Maher

In recent years it has taken a team of reviewers to work their way through the tangle of film that descends upon the viewing public every week. Wendy Ide and Kevin Maher have been reviewing films for *The Times* since the early years of the 21st Century. They were joined by Kate Muir as Chief Film Critic in 2010. Muir had previously worked as a foreign correspondent for the paper. She has published several novels and left *The Times* in 2017 to pursue her career as a novelist and screenwriter. Ide has also moved on, becoming a film critic with *The Observer*.

The Times on Cinema Editor: Brian Pendreigh

Brian Pendreigh has written on cinema for numerous publications in the UK and abroad, including *The Times*, *Sunday Times* and *Guardian*. He was cinema editor of *The Scotsman* and associate editor of *Hotdog* magazine and has written several film-related books including *On Location: The Film Fan's Guide to Britain and Ireland*, *The Legend of the Planet of the Apes* and the novel *The Man in the Seventh Row*.

ACKNOWLEDGEMENTS

The original concept for the book came from Mark Beynon of The History Press and Richard Whitehead, formerly of *The Times* and editor of *The Times on the Ashes*. Richard worked hard to get the concept off the ground in the initial stages. Several others in various departments at *The Times* were involved in bringing the book to fruition, including Robin Ashton, Steve Baker, Martin Gibbs, Richard Hodson, Anne Jensen, Nick Mays and Trudy Zimmermann. Particular thanks is due to Andrew Sims, who was responsible for the huge job of researching and sourcing photographs, working from my list of possible subjects, and to Jessica Palmer and Jemma Cox at The History Press. Thanks also to the personal friends who responded to my query about what they might actually want to see in a book entitled *The Times on Cinema*. Several of those suggestions made it into the final volume.

INDEX

Note: illustrations are represented by *italicised* page numbers.

300 45, 269
2001: A Space Odyssey 88,
  99, 139, 218–21, 313

A bout de souffle 177–8
Adam, Ken 16–18, 19, 168
Affleck, Ben 274, 275
African Queen, The 27, 106,
  149
Airplane! 94, 95, 177
Alien 105, 142, 313
All About Eve 149, 261
Altered States 80
Always 189
Amadeus 241
And God Created Woman 83–4
Anderson, Louise 209–10
Andrews, Julie 135, 243
Annie Hall 312
Apocalypse Now 81–2, 139,
  312, 319
Apu Trilogy, The 215
Arbuckle, Roscoe "Fatty"
  224–6
Argo 6, 272, 274–5
Avatar 172, 298–9

Babette's Feast 129
Bacall, Lauren 106, 145,
  152–3
Badlands 76
Bale, Christian 46, 188,
  235–6, *235*, 267, 270–1
Bambi 185
Barbarella 86–7
Barry, John 18, 21, 168, 306
Batman films 46, 54, 116,
  267–71, *271*, 315

Beatty, Warren 115, 192,
  193, 195, 207, 291
Beau Travail 277
Beauty and the Beast 66
Bend It Like Beckham 33, 58
Bergman, Ingrid 148, *148*,
  202, 226, 326–7
BFG, The 188
Bicycle Thieves 138, 151–2
Birdman 54
Birds, The 6, 133, 134, 135
Birth of a Nation, The 186–7
Black Panther 51–3, *52*
Blackmail 222, 245
Blade 48
Blade Runner 28, 153–6, 260
Blazing Saddles 94, 95,
  212–13, 215
Blue Angel, The 82
Blue Velvet 238, 262, 280
Blues Brothers, The 84, 212
Bogart, Humphrey 28, 106,
  106, 152–3, 231, 305,
  306, 326–7
Bonnie and Clyde 108, 195,
  291
Boseman, Chadwick 51,
  52, 53
Boyle, Danny 197, *197*
Brando, Marlon 110, *110*,
  207, 234, 261–2, 266, 294,
  312, 316, 317–18, 323
Braveheart 41, 125
Breakfast Club, The 291
Bridge on the River Kwai
  106, 218, 259
Brief Encounter 7, 36–7, 222
Brosnan, Pierce *15*, 16, 20,

23, 25, *25*, 167
Brothers, The 309
Burke, Kathy 140
Burton, Richard *104*, 105,
  240
Burton, Tim 68, 116, 269,
  270, 322

Cabaret 242, 251
Cabinet of Dr Caligari, The 81
Caine, Michael 28, 77, 160,
  267, 294
Callow, Simon 240–1, *240*
Cameron, James 43, 170,
  171, 172, 262, 298–9
Cammell, Donald 264,
  265–6
Cape Fear 74
Carry On films 28, 201–5,
  202, *203*
Casablanca 28, 106, 148,
  153, 305, 326–8
Casino Royale 16, *17*, 24, 25,
  166–7
Cat People 84
Celine et Julie Vont en Bateau
  73–4
Chambers, John 6, 272–3, 274
Chaplin, Charlie 128, 186,
  206, 207, 330
Chariots of Fire 59
Chicago 242
Chinatown 107, 115, 116,
  208, 308, 309, 325
Chungking Express 199–200
Citizen Kane 6, 138, 139,
  159, 173–4, 175, 197,
  207, 208, 210, 329

Clockwork Orange, A 89, 97–101, 247, 267, 290
Cocoanuts, The 297–8
Coen brothers 141, 261
Colony, The 64, 65
Connery, Sean 5, *14*, 16–18, 19, 20, 21, 23, 25, 28, 162, 163, 164, 165, 168, 251, 303, 304
Constantine 47
Conversation, The 231
Cool Hand Luke 79, 177
Coppola, Francis Ford 77, 81, 82, 139, 231, 284, 312, 314, 317–20, 323, *323*
Coraline 185
Corman, Roger 43, 77, 85
Coward, Noël 36–7, 82, 213, 217, 222
Craig, Daniel *15*, 16, *17*, 19, *19*, 24, *24*, 166, *166*
Crawford, Joan 142, 149, 177, 250
Cruise, Tom 59
Crusade 315
Crying Game, The 248

Dahl, Roald 20, 188, 189
Dalton, Timothy 20, 21
Damned, The 76
Dance of the Vampires 74
Dangerous Moonlight 241
Daredevil 47
Dark Knight, The 46, 267, 269, 271, *271*
Dark Star 79
Davis, Bette 142, 149, 241, 261, 304
Days of Heaven 216
De Niro, Robert 59, 111–12, *111*, 148, 249, 318–19, 323
Dead of Night 68
Dean, James 87, 90, 281, 289
Deception 241
Delicatessen 129
Deliverance 214
Dench, Judi 19, *19*, 146, *146*, 167
Deneuve, Catherine 72, *144*, 145
Depp, Johnny 31, *31*, 32,

33, 128, 322
Diamonds Are Forever 21, 26
Die Another Day 16, 25, *25*, 165
Dietrich, Marlene 76–7, 82, 197, 293
Do the Right Thing 232
DOA 302
Doctor Zhivago 248
Dog Day Afternoon 198–9
Donnie Darko 246–7
Don't Look Now 90, 153, 311
Double Indemnity 73
Douglas, Kirk 6, 183, 199, 251, 252–3, 279, *300*, 310
Dr. No 5, 18, 28, 162–3, 165, 329
Dr. Strangelove 98
Drive, He Said 207
Duck Soup 289
Duel 191
Duffy 264, 265
Dumbo 184–5
Dunaway, Faye 86, 192, 193–4, 291, 294, 325
Dune 315

Eastwood, Clint 131, 206, 207, 215
Easy Rider 90, 107, 280, 282
Eat Drink Man Woman 129
Ed Wood 322
Edward Scissorhands 68
Ekland, Britt *14*, 21, *21*, 85, 161, 164
Empire of the Sun 188, 235–6
Empire Strikes Back, The 5, 279, *279*
Enter the Dragon 81
Eraserhead 87, 236, 238
ET: The Extra Terrestrial 188, 236, 325–6
Eternal Sunshine of the Spotless Mind 323
Evil Dead, The 76
Exorcist, The 136, 190, 311
Exterminating Angel, The 69–70

Fantastic Four 46
Fantastic Voyage 70
Fargo 141, 252

Faster, Pussycat! Kill! Kill! 88
Fellini, Federico 71, 250–1, 314
Festen 199
Fifty Shades of Grey 7, 38–9
Fight Club 5, 123–4
Final Test, The 328
Fitzcarraldo 70–1
For Your Eyes Only 23
Forbidden Planet 78
Ford, Harrison 115, 154, 155, 156, 188, 190, 260
Ford, John 86, 139, 277–9
Foster, Jodie 41, 148, 198, 281
Fox, James 91, 263, 264, 265
Freaks 90
Freeman, Morgan 102, 211
Friese-Greene, William 9
Fritz the Cat 78
Frogs 6, 303
From Russia with Love 6, 18, 162, 163–4, 165, 252, 265
Frozen 242
Funny Face 243
Funny Girl 243

Games, The 293, 308
Garbo, Greta 70, 141, 177
Garland, Judy 10, *10*, 12, 221, 222, 223, 262, 311
Gayson, Eunice 164, *164*, 165
Get Carter 77
Ghost Rider 47
Ghostbusters 142, 285–8
Gibson, Mel 40–2, *40*, 128
Gielgud, John 103, *103*
Giraffes on Horseback Salads 315
Gladiator 2 315
Glida 68
Godfather films 110, 111, 139, 316–20, 323
Gold Diggers of 1933 69
GoldenEye 20, 167
Goldfinger 16–18, 26, 27, 163, 165, 168
Gone with the Wind 6, 12, 28, 96–7, 289, 316, 329
Good, The Bad and the Ugly, The 69, 215
Goodfellas 213, 290
Grace of My Heart 6, 302–3

Graduate, The 276
Grand Hotel 177
Grant, Cary 102, 144, 188, 200, 226, 240, 279, 290
Great Expectations 216, 218, 222
Griffith, D.W. 186, 187, 206, 209
Guardians of the Galaxy 213–14, 256
Guinness, Alec 106, 106, 218, 222, 223, 284, 285
Gunfight, A 300–1
Guy-Blache, Alice 209

Hackman, Gene 108, 108, 125, 126, 131, 231
Hacksaw Ridge 41–2
Hamilton, Guy 26–8
Hancock, Tony 307
Harder They Come, The 78
Hardy, Robin 158–61, 159
Harold and Maude 78
Harry Potter 6, 60–4, 60, 64, 144
Head 85
Hellboy 49
Hellzapoppin' 68
Hepburn, Audrey 144, 144, 189, 243, 258, 290, 304, 305
Hepburn, Katharine 27, 142, 149–50, 150, 218
Hidden 231
High Society 260
Highlander 153, 156–7
His Girl Friday 279
Hitchcock, Alfred 6, 133–8, 148, 200, 208, 222, 226, 276, 314, 324, 330
Hook 189–90
Hopper, Dennis 90, 262, 280–2, 281
How I Won the War 73
Hulk, The 46–7
Hunger, The 72
Hustler, The 58

If… 88
In a Lonely Place 305–6
In Which We Serve 217, 222

Iñárritu, Alejandro González 54
Incredibles, The 44–5
Indiana Jones films 49, 190
Invasion of the Body Snatchers 75–6
Iron Giant, The 185
Iron Man 44, 50–1, 53
Italian Job, The 28, 213
It's a Wonderful Life 5, 7, 107, 130, 329

Jacob's Ladder 72
Jailhouse Rock 212
James Bond films 6, 14–25, 14, 15, 16, 17, 19, 20, 21, 22, 23, 24, 25, 26, 27, 146, 162–7, 164, 167, 252
Jaws 28, 188, 189, 190–1, 277
Jazz Singer, The 6, 33, 329
Jerry Maguire 58, 59
Johnny Guitar 83
Jubilee 73
Jungle Book, The 212, 312–13
Jurassic Park 175

Keitel, Harvey 86, 103, 230, 232, 309
Kendall, Nigel 197, 199, 215, 216, 231, 262, 289, 312–13
Killing of Sister George, The 80–1
Koyaanisqatsi 75
Kubrick, Stanley 19, 199, 219, 221, 290, 313, 314, 315, 325

La Belle et la Bête 70, 176
L.A. Confidential 250
La Dolce Vita 177, 250–1
La La Land 192, 194, 195, 196
Lady Eve, The 214–15
Lancaster, Burt 32, 208, 293–4, 308, 308
Lange, Jessica 147, 147
Lasseter, John 6, 182, 184–5
Last Sunset, The 310
Last Temptation of Christ, The 121–2

Last Wave, The 77
Lawrence of Arabia 175, 218, 248, 285
Lean, David 37, 216, 217–18, 217, 221, 222, 248
Lee, Christopher 21, 35, 85, 160, 198
Lee, Spike 232, 233
Licence to Kill 21
Life and Death of Colonel Blimp 261
Life of Brian 28, 276
Live and Let Die 20, 20, 21, 26, 27
Living Daylights, The 20
Local Hero 245
Lord of the Rings, The 33, 34–6, 34, 35
Lost in Translation 176–7
Lynch, David 236–9, 237, 262

M 78
Mad Max 41, 74, 128
Madchen in Uniform 79
Magic Box, The 9–10
Magic Fire 241
Magnificent Seven, The 254–5
Maltese Falcon, The 106, 231
Man Who Shot Liberty Valance 277–9
Man with the Golden Arm, The 73
Man with the Golden Gun, The 21, 26
Mander, Kay 6, 251–3, 252
Marx brothers 289, 297–8, 315, 329
Mary Poppins 244
Masque of the Red Death, The 77
Matrix, The 249–50
Max Manus 309–10
McDormand, Frances 141
McDowell, Malcolm 88, 89, 99, 246, 272, 290
Meet Me in St Louis 243
Melvin and Howard 70
Metropolis 153, 312
Mildred Pierce 79, 250
Miller, Frank 45, 269, 270

Mitchum, Robert 74, *75*, 103, 294
Mommie Dearest 86
Monroe, Marilyn 28–30, *29*, *30*, 291
Monte Walsh 306
Monty Python films 28, 117–21, *117*, 276
Moonlight 192, 195, 196
Moonraker 20, 23
Moore, Roger *14*, *15*, 19, 20, *20*, 21, *21*, *22*, 23–4, *23*, 26, 27, 164, 168, 294
Murray, Bill 176, 286, *286*, 287
My Fair Lady 144, 176
My Name is Nobody 301
My Neighbor Totoro 185
Mystery Men 49

Naked Gun, The 94–5
Nashville 71
Neame, Ronald 9, 221–3
Network 72
Never Say Never Again 16, 23, 25
Newman, Paul 58, 79, 115, 135, 147, 177
Nicholson, Jack 107, *107*, 114–16, 136, 198–9, 206, 207, 208, 267, 269, 279, 308–9, 325
Night of the Hunter, The 103, 208
Night of the Living Dead 86
Night Porter, The 75
Nightmare on Elm Street, A 31
Nolan, Christopher 267, 270, 271
North by Northwest 200
Nosferatu 83, 198

Octopussy *22*, 23
Oliver Twist 179
Olivier, Laurence 108–9, *109*, 253
On Her Majesty's Secret Service 18, 168
On the Waterfront 110, 234
Once Upon a Time in America 69

One Flew Over the Cuckoo's Nest 107, 115, 177, 279
One Million Years BC 75
Outlaw, The 77

Pacino, Al 28, 110, *110*, 198–9, 316, 317–18, 319, 320, 323
Pan's Labyrinth 129
Peeping Tom 79–80
Performance 91, 263–4, 265–6
Phantom, The 49
Philadelphia Story, The 102, 107, 149, 150, 260
Piano, The 103, 232
Picnic at Hanging Rock 74, 290
Pink Flamingos 91
Pinocchio 185
Pirates of the Caribbean films 32–3, 298
Plan 9 from Outer Space 321, 322
Planet of the Apes 6, 72, 245, 272, 273
Point Break 175, 176
Polanski, Roman 32, 74, 113, 208, 216, 325
Poseidon Adventure, The 221, 223
Powell, Michael 80, 208, 218, 261
Predator 153, 157, *158*
Presley, Elvis 201, 212
Prime of Miss Jean Brodie, The 221, 223
Psycho 135–6
Pulp Fiction 83, 101, 228–30, 248
Punisher, The 49

Quantum of Solace 24, *24*

Raging Bull 59, 111–12, 249
Rashomon 234, 254
Rattigan, Terence 328
Rear Window 107, 133, 135, 276
Rebel, The 307
Rebel Without a Cause 87–8, 281, 289

Redford, Robert 115, 131, 206, 207, 276
Reed, Carol 27, 109, 218, 282–3
Reed, Oliver 293, 296–7
Reeves, Keanu 47, 176, 249–50, 280, 281
Règle du Jeu, La 139, 208
Renoir, Jean 139, 208, 306
Repo Man 82
Reservoir Dogs 82, 103, 228, 229
Ricci, Christina 140, *140*
Robin and Marian 303–4
Rocky Horror Picture Show, The 91–2, 146
Roeg, Nicolas 77, 90, 264, 265, 266, 311
Roman Holiday 258, 259
Rosemary's Baby 216

Sands of the Kalahari 300–1
Satyricon 71
Scarface 28, 79, 110
Scarlet Street 306–7
Schindler's List 188, 189
Schwarzenegger, Arnold 43, 157, *158*, 270, 314, 315
Scorpio Rising 87
Scorsese, Martin *121*, 139, 208, 213, 234, 249, 284, 290, 303
Scott, Ridley 154, 155–6, 260, 313, 315
Scream 95
Seven Samurai 139, 254–5
Shaft 82
Sharp, Alan 124–7
Shaun of the Dead 94
Shawshank Redemption, The 102, 210–11
Shining, The 115, 136, 325
Shipman, Nell 6, 93
Shirley Valentine 72
Shoah 260
Short Cuts 178
Sid and Nancy 241
Silence of the Lambs, The 148, 198
Sinatra, Frank 8, 73, 216, 260
Singin' in the Rain 139, 242

Skyfall 19, *19*, 165, 168
Slover, Karl 12–13
Smith, Maggie 61, *143*, 144, 222, 223
Snow White 56–7
Solaris 80
Some Like It Hot 28, 105, 291
Somewhere in Time 302
Sound of Music, The 242, 243, 313
Spacey, Kevin 111, 112–14
Spartacus 199, 258
Spectre 16
Speed 280, 281, 282
Spider-Man 44, 46–7, 53
Spielberg, Steven 6, *175*, 188–91, 235, 277, 284, 314
Spy Who Loved Me, The 19, *19*, 20, 168
Star is Born, A 262
Star Trek films 6, 272, 273
Star Wars films *5*, 106, 132, 155, *278*, 279, 284–5
Stewart, James 107, 183, 276, 279, 290, 293, 324
Straw Dogs 71
Streep, Meryl 142, 150
Streetcar Named Desire, A 110, 261–2
Streisand, Barbra 207, 243
Sunset Boulevard 67–8, 95, 324
Superman films 27, 47, 108
Superstar: The Karen Carpenter Story 76
Sutherland, Donald 76, 90, 310, 311
Swamp Thing 50
Sweet Smell of Success 80

Tales of Manhattan 241
Tampopo 128
Tarantino, Quentin 82, 86, 139, 228–30, *229*, 248, 256, 303

Taxi Driver 86, 103, 112, 139, 148, 208, 234, 245
Taylor, Elizabeth *104*, 105, 147, 281
Teenage Mutant Ninja Turtles 48
Terminator, The 43, 262
Texas Chainsaw Massacre, The 90
There Will Be Blood 7, 326
Thin Blue Line, The 232
Third Man, The 109, 282–3
This is Spinal Tap 216
Thunderball 16, 19, 25
Thurman, Una 83, 229, 230, 248, 270
Titanic 170, 171–2, 299
To Have and Have Not 152–3
Tokyo Story 214
Tomorrow Never Dies 23
Touch of Evil, A 76–7, 197
Towering Inferno, The 177, 190
Toy Story 28, 182–3, 184, 232
Trainspotting 197
Trash 85
Travolta, John 229–30, 248
Trip, The 85
Trumbo, Dalton 258, 259
Twilight films 62
Twin Peaks 236, 245
Two for the Road 304–5
Two Jakes, The 308–9

Unbreakable 46
Up in Smoke 81

V for Vendetta 48, *48*
Valdez is Coming 308
Vertigo 69, 135, 137–8, 139, 210, 324
View to a Kill, A 23–4, *23*

Waitress 129
Warriors, The 82–3

Watson, Emma 61, 63, 64–6, *64*, *65*
Weaver, Sigourney 142, *142*, 287, 288, 299
Weir, Peter 41, 77, 290
Welles, Orson 109, *109*, 173, 174, 197, 207, 208, 282, 283, 293, 314, 315
West Side Story 67
What Ever Happened to Baby Jane? 84
When We Were Kings 59
Whisky Galore! 80, 202, 249
Whitehouse, Mary 180–1, *180*
Wicker Man, The 85, 153, 158–9, 160
Wild One, The 87
Wild Strawberries 198
Wilder, Billy 67–8, 73, 105, 144, 291, 324
Williams, John 277, 284, 285
Williams, Kenneth 28, *202*, 204, 205
Winder, Simon 18, 23, 24
Winner, Michael 286, 292–6, *293*
Withnail and I 28, 87, 277
Without Limits 310
Wizard of Oz, The 10, 11, 12, 51–3, 83, 284, 311
World is Not Enough, The 25, *25*, 164

X-Men 45–6, *45*

Yellow Submarine 74, 220
You Only Live Twice 20
Young Frankenstein 94, 95, 108

Zabriskie Point 83